TUDOR MUSIC

DAVID WULSTAN

Professor of Music, University
College of Wales, Aberystwyth

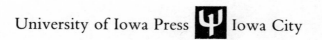

University of Iowa Press ❑ Iowa City

International Standard Book Number 0–87745–135–4
Library of Congress Catalog Card Number 85–51090
University of Iowa Press, Iowa City 52242
Copyright © 1986 by the University of Iowa

Printed in Great Britain by
Richard Clay plc, Bungay, Suffolk for
J. M. Dent & Sons Ltd
Aldine House, 33 Welbeck Street,
London W1M 8LX

Contents

Preface

The extension of the term 'Tudor' to embrace the period between 1485 and 1625 or so, is familiar from the title of the series *Tudor Church Music*, and is justified by several elements which give unity to the music of this era. In covering this vast topic, it would be fruitless to attempt to be encyclopaedic and try to mention every composer or instrument in passing, or to comment upon each development or genre, especially since there are many books and articles which have dealt at some length both with more familiar matters and with more specialist questions. Instead of vainly undertaking to distill the wisdom of other writers, I have sought instead to add a different, indeed personal, point of view, especially in such cases where I think the sources have been seriously misinterpreted. Above all, I have tried to emphasize the importance of the music itself and its recreation in modern performance; thus some matters have been discussed at length at the expense of others which in a larger work might have been more amply treated.

I have assumed that the reader requiring biographical and general bibliographical information concerning composers will turn to the *New Grove*; similarly, the reader is referred there for technical and bibliographical information concerning instruments and other specialist topics, eg. the article 'Sources': several of its articles, however, notably those on 'Performance practice', 'Pitch' and kindred matters, need to be treated with caution, as will be evident from these pages.

Series such as the *English Madrigal School, English Lutenist Songwriters*, or the facsimiles of *English lutesongs*, have not been specifically referred to in the text; works may readily be identified as necessary by reference to the original dates of publication given here. For keyboard and some other works, the volumes of *Musica Britannica* (abbreviated *MB*) have been used by way of reference. In addition, for church music, *Tudor Church Music* (*TCM*), *The Complete Works of William Byrd* or its successor *The Byrd Edition, Early English Church Music* (*EECM*) and *Corpus Mensurabilis Musicae* (*CMM*) may be consulted: except in special cases, individual editions have not been cited.

Musical illustrations are normally transcribed from the original sources, but are generally in modern format as to spelling and note-values (assuming a crotchet beat); church music is generally transposed up a minor third, or in conformity with the discussion in Chapter 8. In a few cases the sources have been rendered diplomatically for specific reasons, eg. in Chapter 6. Composers' names have been standardized to the most modern or most generally used form.

Texts directly quoted as literary passages are usually presented in their original spellings; otherwise, modern spelling is indicated. There are some obvious exceptions in these matters (especially in quotations from secondary sources, or where the orthography of Whythorne or Butler is necessarily modernized) but I have attempted to be reasonably consistent.

Full references given in the texts, or references to standard writers such as Shakespeare, are not normally given again at the end of the book. The citing of secondary literature is not to be taken as signifying general approval, nor is the absence of a reference to be taken as disapproval: works are cited for specific rather than general reasons. Similarly, references to modern editions for identification purposes are not to be taken as a guide to reliability.

Acknowledgements

First and foremost I should like to thank Miss Marion Lane and Miss Gill Parry for attempting to bring order out of chaos and furnishing typescript from hieroglyphs. Many scholars have been most generous with their time, notably David Evans, Desmond Hunter, David Mateer, John Milsom, Mary O'Neill, Nick Sandon and Ian Smaczny; their views, especially where they have conflicted with mine, have been invaluable. Sarah Cobbold, in addition to her painstaking copying of the music examples which grace these pages, has also made several important suggestions, many of which have been incorporated here.

Acknowledgement is made to the Trustees of the British Library for permission to reproduce photographs of materials in their possession (Figures 1, 4, 7, 8, 10, 12, 14, 32 and 34). Similarly, I am indebted to the Governing Body, Christ Church, Oxford, for Figures 3, 9, 24 and 30; to the Governing Body of King's College, Cambridge, for Figure 11 and to the Guildhall Library, London, for Figures 2 and 31. Figure 16 is reproduced by kind permission of St. Michael's College, Tenbury. Permission to reprint Figures 18, 19, 21(a) and 21(b) has been kindly granted, respectively, by the late Professor Cyril Darlington, Professor J. M. Tanner, Dover Publications Inc., New York, and The Syndics of Cambridge University Press.

Finally, and not least, I would like to thank my patient publishers in the persons of Malcolm Gerratt and Susan Mitchell. My move to Wales and initial duties there have encumbered the process of revision so severely as to delay the book's appearance several times. That the final revision will arrive on their desk after the book is printed must be blamed upon myself and the force of circumstances. In spite of the pressure of time I am glad that I was asked to write the book, and relieved that I was forced to finish it.

To Susan and Philip;
and to
Garret, Angela, Erik and Anna

CHAPTER 1

The Spirit of the Age

The phrase 'Tudor Music' was coined in the 1920s, and embraces what is more properly the span between the Henrician and Jacobean periods (1485–1625). Although there were many stylistic changes, there is sufficient homogeneity in the 'Tudor' age to justify using this avowedly inaccurate name to embrace the music of Richard Davy, who was writing in the reign of Henry VII, together with that of Orlando Gibbons, who died in 1625 as Charles I came to the throne. Indeed, 'Tudor' may justifiably be applied in this way to the music of Thomas Tomkins, who was active later, at the time of Cromwell's Commonwealth, yet was still essentially writing in the style of Byrd and Gibbons.

Few would question that this age nurtured a remarkable period of music, even if their sympathies were not overwhelmingly drawn to its style. It is here that a major difficulty arises; indeed a series of difficulties. The 'land without music', as England was described in the nineteenth century, could hardly be so described in Tudor times. Why then does greatness crown the art of one age, and elude that of another; and how can greatness be recognized? Is there a technical yardstick by which it may be measured, or is it merely some agreed standard of taste? These questions are important for any art; but for music there is the added difficulty that it must be recreated in performance. This leads to the question of how far a great work may be diminished — or even perish — in a bad performance, and whether an indifferent work might deceive the ear if performed surpassingly well.

It is generally agreed that a measure of authenticity is necessary for Tudor music, as for any music of earlier times, if it is to achieve its intended musical effect; so the importance of the question of performance can be taken for granted, and will indeed be discussed in due course. But the fragility of music — that a performance can at the very least make a great piece of music sound dull, or a trite piece sound fresh — reinforces the fundamental question concerning what it is in music that appeals to us, that allows some of us to call it great; and the problem of worth prompts the reiteration of the question why some ages appear to lack greatness, while others seem to have it in profusion.

Aristotle (*Met,* 6) distinguished between the *hulē* (matter) of an object which we see, and its reality, *schēma* (form), which we cannot. We can see part of a table, enough for us to know that it is a table, but we can never see all aspects of it simultaneously. A picture of a table has only two dimensions, but can hint at the perspective of a third and therefore can suggest enough to make it a plausible representation of a table. Similarly, a portrait, although it takes a fleeting glimpse of a face, endeavours to suggest a more prolonged gaze into the character of the subject; and a landscape painting, although it communicates nothing directly of the smells and sounds of the country, may nevertheless give something of this impression by indirect means. In either case enough is conveyed to enable us to recognize a certain reality in the picture, and to value it because something of the artist's view of his subject is communicated to us. But no work of art can do more than give a view of that subject: Gombrich (1960) and others have shown that even the 'realistic' landscapes of Constable are careful compositions in which the truth has been reordered to suit the artist's viewpoint. If we do not care for the viewpoint — the style — then our communication with the artist may be limited. Furthermore, if we also have little sympathy with the subject — for instance, if we dislike nudes or seascapes — our alienation from the artist increases. In this case, we can only judge the picture on a technical level: for brushwork, composition and so forth. However, since a 'great' work of art is usually acknowledged to have less definable, more sympathetic qualities than those which are normally called technique, the relationship between the artist and his public is crucial. If there is no sympathy between the two, the onlooker can only condemn the work, or acknowledge it as great merely on hearsay, relying on the judgement of someone else.

There is little difference in the case of music: lack of sympathy for the large-scale Tudor antiphon form or for the English virginalists' style cannot be overcome by pointing to mere technical features. After all, the way a piece is put together is not, and should not be, audible in all details: the beauty of Venus is not revealed by an anatomy lesson. Indeed, the very features which a critic may point out as especially noteworthy may be those which strike a listener as over-contrived; and the opposite may well be equally true. It is possible to regard a piece of music, or any art, as striving towards an unattainable perfection. As Aristotle says, what we hear and see — the *schēma* — can only represent the truth: it cannot *be* the truth. The viewpoint, or the style, represents the shortfall between perfection and what the artist is able to achieve. In some styles different imperfections are more tolerable than in others; and these differences explain why the shortcomings of some composers may pass unnoticed by their admirers, who would condemn the same deficiencies in other composers. There are many who forgive Elgar's formal ineptitudes and yet find Mahler intolerably rambling; no doubt equally many hold a somewhat contrary opinion. We sometimes admire others almost for, rather than in spite of their faults.

Unconsciously, the listener gives credit to the composer for surmounting technical difficulties in his journey towards the unattainable, just as he congratulates the performer for doing likewise. This is why mechanical performance and computer-generated music have rather less appeal than the human equivalent. This conative principle in music can be demonstrated in other arts: if an honest antique dealer tells us that a set of chairs includes one reproduction, and another which has been heavily restored, our regard for them is suddenly transformed. Although money may be no object, and the reproduction may be more perfect than the original, we prefer the genuine article. We look for the imperfection in the Persian rug; and in like manner the fact that Homer occasionally nods does not detract from his greatness but highlights it. A race is run according to various rules: it is not merely the winning but the manner of winning which is important. The element of fair play rules out a twentieth-century composer writing in the style of Byrd, just as running is ruled out of a walking race. Though he may do it better (and so he should, since he has all Byrd's efforts to build upon) the counterfeiter of Byrd's music is still judged harshly when he has been found out: van Meegheren's forgeries were looked at with interest when they were thought to be early works of Vermeer, but now they are forgotten. The imitator is at best a parodist, at worst a thief, since he reaps where another ploughed and sowed.

It is thus that historical perspective (specifically the history of musical culture) plays an important part in our conception of the language of music, since we need to know whether a work of art is genuine or a mere fake. We wish to be at one with the composer, or indeed performer, and to follow his struggle to overcome the technical limitations imposed upon him by the age in which he lives. This human sympathy can hardly extend to an imitation, whether by an animate forger or an inanimate electronic device. Admiration of either should not be equated with sympathy. This historical sense is as necessary for us as dimensional perspective is necessary if we are to understand a picture of a table: without it our understanding of the work will be two dimensional and foreshortened.

The need for a historical *mise en scène*, and indeed the whole question of taste, has recently been underlined, from a biological point of view, by Desmond Morris in his *Manwatching* (1977). The differing attitudes, both in regard to time and place, towards the human form and face, are a clear confirmation of the truth of the proverb that beauty is in the eye of the beholder. Added to this, there is the complication that 'attractive', 'pretty' and 'beautiful' are far from synonymous. The beautiful may be admirable and yet unattractive, while the less perfect may give a far more sensuous

3

impression. It is sometimes hard to resist the attraction of music which we know to be meretricious (say, a song which reminds us of a rosy youth) while equally, the perfect may leave the listener emotionally cold.

Morris suggests that the essence of beauty, taste, and our appreciation of art, is related to the human desire to collect and arrange. Whether it is beer mats or butterflies, old maps or old music, there does seem to be an underlying human passion for assembling and ordering a bewildering variety of the trivial and of the artistic. It is the urge to compare, says Morris, which informs our attitudes to art and beauty. This is why much modern architecture is so perversely mistaken in its aesthetic principles. A dwelling becomes a 'house' not according to the definition of an architect, but when people recognize it as a house within their own culture: a small variation in the pitch of a roof will be seen, in their home town, as a horrible travesty of domestic architecture, but as charmingly eccentric in another country.

The instinct for comparison is nascent. Many people will have observed a tiny child playing with an object, say a bottle, and his ecstatic delight when he finds *two* such objects. His gaze travels from the first to the second in wonderment, and as the bottles are compared, his face is wreathed with the expression of someone privileged to see for the first time a hitherto undiscovered masterpiece by his favourite painter. The baby, by comparing, is creating what Aristotle calls the *schēma*: indeed in his *Poetics* (IV) he remarks that the basis of our appreciation of art is that, like children, we delight in recognition.

This need for musical points of reference explains some of the contradictions concerning taste, style and so forth, alluded to in the previous pages. The need for an identity of time and place shows that the ethnomusiocologist's plea that we should treat all the various forms of world music as comparable or equals, is based on a false premise: it is unlikely that we can stray far beyond our own cultural milieu in a desire for equal satisfaction from all sorts and conditions of music — to us, some appear to be more equal than others. On the contrary, even within our own cultural purview we require canons of historical perspective by which to compare like with like. It is not very different, humiliating though it may appear to be, from the baby and the bottles.

This sense of history and of comparison has something to do with the 'spirit of the age'. Sir Kenneth Clark has observed (1969) how frequently composers seem to emerge from the slopes of Parnassus in pairs – Bach and Handel, Mozart and Haydn being the most obvious examples. Here there is, in my view, a serious point: the urge for comparison applies not only to the collector or audience, but to the factor and composer. A composer who has to compete, whether consciously or not, amicably or otherwise, is likely to be the better for it than one having a virtual contempt for his audience. As Paul Klee said in his Jena lecture, 'uns trägt kein Volk' — by which he meant that art cannot flourish without the participation of a critical public. The 'friendly aemulation' between Byrd and de Monte, as they composed their separate halves of the psalm 'Super flumina', the co-operative settings of 'In exitu' by Byrd, Mundy and Sheppard, or the masterly forty-part *Spem in alium* by Thomas Tallis, following on a rather dull forty-part piece by the elder Alessandro Striggio: these and countless other examples testify to the healthy effect of artistic rivalry. The spirit of the age enshrines the spirit of competition.

When the wits are not sharpened by such means, they may be dulled. It is commonly implied that the spirit of certain artists was broken by adverse criticism. It may be that one or two faint glimmers have been extinguished by a puff of animadversion, but it is hard to believe that greater embers were anything but fanned into full flame by criticism, misinformed or not. Indeed, there are several examples of composers, particularly in our own century, who thrived in spite of opposition, yet may be said to have relapsed into mediocrity when critical approbation was suddenly thrust upon them. Maybe in nineteenth-century Britain, 'das Land ohne Musik', there were many talented composers who might well have stood the test of time had they earlier been tested by a more critical contemporary public. That they came under the influence of Mendelssohn is indeed ironic, for he is a noteworthy example of the necessity for the interaction between an artist and a critical public. As a youthful prodigy, Mendelssohn acquired an immense reputation. Many of his works, however, seem to explore a more limited gamut than was promised by the technical assurance of his early compositions. Public adulation, notably by the English whose adoration for his oratorios was remarkable, seems often to have allowed him to fall into superficiality. It is understandable that uncritical approbation might dull the edge of a composer's technique; few artists have so sharp a sense of self-criticism that they can dispense with the whetstone of public criticism and competition.

Conditions in the sixteenth century were clearly conducive to that spirit of comparison and rivalry which encourages the highest standards. Even minor composers such as John Ward and Martin Peerson were swept along with the tide. Once the musical equivalent of the unattainable four-minute mile has indeed been attained, the race is on for the next goal. But if there is no sense of this continuing competition, musical standards may fall and history will take a sterner view. This is not to say, however, that a composer may not retire from the press, becoming musically eremitic like Schoenberg. Once he has proved himself in the world, he may cut himself off for a space: thus Purcell composed his *Fantazias* as a lonely act of faith. Using an outdated form, he poured forth some of his most inspired and complex music, doubtless knowing that he would not hear them performed. In his twilight years, and well after the Tudor sun had set, Tomkins composed quietly for himself in Worcestershire, while the tumult of Cromwell's Commonwealth raged about him. Earlier, his master Byrd had written a vast amount of music for the Roman Catholic liturgy, mostly, as Kerman (1981) has shown, as a personal affirmation of his faith, and for the decidedly limited public of the recusant chapels. But these were exceptions: in general, the most important element of the spirit of the age is a sense of excellence, of which the critical public is keenly aware, and for which artists are striving in healthy competition.

How far, nevertheless, can this spirit be a broader concept, a cultural movement, a united artistic brotherhood of musicians and poets, dramatists and painters? It is tempting to identify cultural movements, for they give comfort to such concepts as 'Renaissance man' and cohesion to the history of the arts. The fact that musical periods (Gothic, Renaissance, Baroque and so forth) are known by names taken from architecture or literature gives a symmetry to things, allowing 'collecting man' to marshal his achievements in an orderly fashion. In reality, the symmetry is illusory. The 'Renaissance' represented by Dante is separated from that of Tallis and Byrd by nearly three centuries. We gaze down the wrong end of the telescope of history and look upon things as contemporaneous which were in reality far apart; similarly, we see relationships, or causes and effects, which are but an illusion engendered by a foreshortened view. Equally, the bitter polemics of the past which appeared to concern issues hardly less grave than the meaning of life, now seem to us to have been storms in a teacup. The raging of the *nuove musiche* against polyphony — the conflict in the early seventeenth century between the modernist Claudio Monteverdi and the old-fashioned Giovanni Artusi — is irrelevant when we have heard the later seventeenth-century Bach, who was a considerably better polyphonist than Artusi.

Tempting though it is to see the Renaissance as a cultural whole — to envisage a 'Golden Age' which embraced music and drama, poetry and painting — in reality history is unhelpful, since the 'movements' in all of these arts seem to have taken place at wildly different times. Dante's *La Vita Nuova* was finished c. 1290, but St Peter's, Rome, was not started until 1506. However, if the renaissance of learning was marked by a renewed interest in classical scholarship, then it might be dated from the fall of Constantinople in 1453 when Byzantine monks fled to the West. Discounting the somewhat bizarre researches of Vicentino and others into intonations of the musical scale (which resulted from a study of Greek tunings) the most significant musical development purporting to be based on a classical model was that of opera at the beginning of the seventeenth century. But what have Dante and Bardi in common, and what do they have to do with Raphael and Leonardo? Classical learning proceeded by fits and starts: at the court of Charlemagne, and later when Greek texts began to be read in Latin translations by Spanish-Arab scholars, and finally when the Greek texts themselves were brought by the exiled Byzantine monks fleeing from the Turks. English music, meanwhile, is often regarded as being 'medieval' until well into the sixteenth century.

And if history is against the idea of cultural movements, the psychology of art also fails to provide any proof for the theory. Music is not expressive in the semantic way that words are. Indeed, it is surprisingly difficult to express joy and sadness (the association, respectively, of the major and minor keys with these emotions is quite recent, more or less dating from Baroque times), and whether a composer is in one mood or another has little or no bearing on his music; nor does it affect his music whether he is homosexual, reads Shakespeare or goes for long walks. He, or we, may *think* that these things are significant, but music, far from being an 'international language', means only what the listener takes it to mean, and that may be very different from what its composer had meant (see Wulstan, 1983).

Extrinsic factors, such as patronage or commercial pressure, may compel a composer to write one sort of music rather than another. Tallis and Sheppard wrote mostly for choral institutions and for their services, whereas the circumstances of Byrd and John Dowland, composing largely for private patrons and for the public press, were clearly very different. However, limitations are but a challenge to the good composer; only the indifferent hack merely succumbs to what he sees as pressure.

Incidental factors such as war, prosperity, and indeed the cultural milieu, may well have an effect on music; but on closer inspection this effect usually turns out to be of lesser import than is generally imagined. The advent of the printing press could be seen as a watershed in musical history; Petrucci's publications in the early years of the sixteenth century opened up the possibility of music being propagated outside the circle of the privileged few, and promised to accelerate musical developments by disseminating them with a speed hitherto unimaginable. But, centuries later, only a small proportion of Bach's music was printed in his lifetime; and several of Beethoven's and Bartók's works were printed only after their deaths. Byrd, since he had a printing monopoly granted to him by the crown, was the only Tudor composer to have a large amount of his music printed. To the extent that proportionately more of his music survives to this day, the printing press had an effect on musical history; but Byrd's influence on English or Continental music was no greater for this circumstance — his style had left nothing more to be said. The influence of the English virginalists, through Jan Sweelinck and others, had a much greater effect on the history of music: yet their music circulated entirely (with only a few exceptions) in manuscript. Strangely, the production of manuscript paper was far more profitable than the printing of music (see Price, 1980, p. 181); thus Byrd's publications did not halt the production of manuscript copies of his works, such was the prohibitive cost of printed music.

Music, in the last analysis, is influenced by other music, rather than by

Fig. 1 A printing shop (from *A Booke of Trades*, 1568)

outside influences. Such outside influences may produce innovation — for example, 'recitative' was due to a mistaken notion of the way Greek drama was originally performed — and such an innovation may be greatly influential. Far from proving the point, however, it more often paradoxically proves the reverse: for instance, the early operatic ventures of the *camerata* are largely forgotten, while more significant composers, who are not, borrowed the musical kernel rather than the philosophical husk from the earlier experimenters. Originality, which is internal to an art, often borrows from novelty, which may well arrive from external factors; yet originality transforms the experimental into the timeless. But outstandingly original composers, such as Bach or Byrd, usually have little to offer as far as the musical patrimony of influence is concerned: since they shunned novelty, they are inimitable. Their gold, refined and stamped with their likeness, can only be admired or counterfeited; the seam which they mined has been exhausted.

A striking feature of Tudor music is its lack of novelty, particularly in church music. New fashions on the Continent had a leisurely journey over the channel and were, more often than not, unable to penetrate the hinterland. And even when they were welcomed ashore (albeit long after they had set out upon their journey) the continental lines of these new fashions took on a more characteristically English cut. In the early sixteenth century, William Cornish and Robert Fayrfax were weaving their long arching phrases after the manner of extravagant Gothic tracery. Meanwhile, on the Continent, Josquin was writing in a close-knit imitative style of more 'Renaissance' proportion. When the latter style eventually became current in England — in the works of Tallis, Sheppard and others — it was the middle of the century; and by the early 1600s, when English polyphonic composition was still at its height, recitative and the operatic style had taken root in Italy.

This insular character, which served to make the nineteenth century a dismal period for English music, helped to make the sixteenth century a truly Golden Age. Perhaps it was because there was so little, or such gradual innovation that the originality of composers was severely tested. They vied with each other to approach more nearly the ideal of music, its Aristotelian 'form', by reaching out in their imagination to provide a mortal frame which, for some of us, comes as near to the immortal as may be comprehended. But because, in this striving for perfection, some vantage points have to be sought to the exclusion of others, certain technical features which seem admirable to one listener may well detract for another. It seems to me that there is no solution to this dilemma. The old idea, that all persons of taste will automatically discern greatness in exactly the same works and reject all others is hardly defensible, although not yet dead. Moreover, as I have tried to indicate, the general cultural background is not necessarily of particular relevance to composition, which is influenced by the more specific, musical, culture. Just as the only true criticism of a piece of music is another piece of music, the only true way to describe and comment on a musical composition is to perform it. For these reasons, a proportion of this book is devoted to the question of how to perform Tudor music. For the same reasons I have attempted to avoid the Scylla of analysis and the Charybdis of a 'life and works'. Neither approach is likely to convince the uninterested listener of the greatness of Tudor music (nor, as I have argued, should it be thought that it can). What follows may therefore be regarded largely as preaching to the converted. Yet, in eschewing the more commonly held notion of the 'spirit of the age', it is to be hoped that the narrower concept which has been arrived at in the preceding pages will help to set the stage for an understanding of the priceless legacy left by the Tudor composers.

CHAPTER 2

The Silver Swanne

Although the notion of a cohesive Renaissance, in which all the arts simultaneously took part, has little to commend it, the spirit of comparison and competition spoken of in the previous chapter can move between one art and another, and thus appears to give rise to a concurrent cultural movement. This seems particularly to be the case when the rise of humanism is considered: the focal point of the Renaissance world appeared to shift from the Deity to man himself, a change which affected all the arts. This renewed confidence in man to influence his own destiny and to challenge received dogma was to spark off the Reformation. But the Reformation cannot properly be viewed as the cause of musical change — neither in the use of the vernacular in the liturgy, nor in the less luxuriant style of word setting — but as part of the effect of the secularization of high art. For the first time secular music was beginning to make considerable inroads on the supremacy of church music as a vehicle for considerable composition. The trobadors and trouvères, Machaut, the trecento Italians and others had taken up the challenge of a vernacular art-music long before; but this time the shift in emphasis was to be permanent. Vernacular verse sung to straightforward chordal settings was popularized in the frottola at the court of Isabella d'Este. This fashion was to influence both the development of the madrigal and Franco-Flemish polyphony. The penetration of the vernacular into church, coupled with less elaborate music, can thus be recognized as being part of an artistic movement, rather than having been dictated solely by reformist tenets.

English vernacular poetry was at a low ebb at the end of the fifteenth century: Henry VII's preoccupation with restoring the country to post-war prosperity left little time for the encouragement of the arts. The style of John Lydgate and Thomas Hoccleve lay heavy, like musty trappings, upon the early Tudor Court; the arrival of the rebel John Skelton blew a sharp breath of fresh air upon the moribund poetic conventions. To the 'diffuse' high courtly style he added a touch of the low doggerel of the people, and affected a return to the forthright clarity of an earlier master:

> Chaucer that famous Clarke
> His tearmes were not darcke
> But pleasaunt easy, and playne
> No worde he wrote in vayne
> Also Jhon Lydgate
> Wrytteth after an hyer rate
> It is diffuse to fynde
> The sentence of his minde

('Philip Sparrow' in Skelton, 1568)

The courts of Henry VII and Henry VIII rang to this goliardic satire. Wolsey in particular was ridiculed in the rhythms of Skelton's jolting jibes. The abrasive tinder of this 'rude rayling rimer' failed, however, to strike much of a spark in Skelton's contemporaries; the flame had to be kindled anew by Sir Thomas Wyatt, bearing the torch of the Italian Renaissance. He, too, favoured irregular rhythms, the nature of which has frequently baffled critics. Some have laid these irregularities at the door of the prosody of his Italian models, which is a convincing explanation only in regard to the sonnets. Others have assumed that Wyatt misapprehended Chaucer's pronunciation and metric; thus, since 1557 (when Tottel's *Miscellany* was first issued) his metre has been heavily emended. But his manuscripts show that the irregularities were intentional; doubtless they stemmed from a desire for metrical variety, a desire which was subverted in the Tottel versions:

> This maketh me at home to hounte and to hawke (Wyatt)
> This maketh me at home to hunt and hauke (Tottel)

> By se, by land, of the delicates the moost (Wyatt)
> By sea, by land, of delicates the most (Tottel)

These examples (see Thomson, 1961) show that Wyatt is deliberately avoiding the 'minstrel's music', whose singsong iambic line was carefully reinstated in Tottel.

Although Wyatt's metrical experiments may have been misunderstood, his introduction of the Petrarchan sonnet into English eventually gave rise to a vogue which produced some of the finest poetry of the language. A particular feature of Wyatt's sonnet, generally avoided in Italian, was the closing rhyming couplet. It was used to great effect by many English sonneteers, including Shakespeare; indeed, it is tempting to trace the latter's penchant for a rhyming couplet at the end of a main–plot scene back to Wyatt.

The influence of Italian poetry on England, either at first hand or through French intermediaries, seems to emphasize the idea of a Renaissance spirit sweeping alike through music, poetry and painting. Yet, although the arts seem to have some affinity in this age of humanism, it is unwise to press the point too far. John Taverner's music is not a window upon his faith; his works neither support nor deny the possibility that he held strong reformist tenets. In the growth of instrumental music, or in the rise of the frottola, madrigal and other secular vocal forms, some parallels with humanism may be discerned; but the nearest music came to being directly influenced by another art (discounting opera, which is outside the scope of the book) was in the field of secular vocal music. Once again, interest was centred upon things classical, and sixteenth-century poetry self-consciously declared itself to belong to a new era. The intimate relationship between words and music, by which the ancients appear to set such store, was something which the New Poets sought earnestly to recreate.

Cardinal Bembo in Italy, and the Accademia della Nuova Poesia were followed in France by Pierre de Ronsard, Baïf and the Académie de Musique et de Poésie. This in turn, through Sir Philip Sidney, Gabriel Harvey and others, was to have some effect in England. Castiglione's *Il Libro del Corteggiano* of 1528 which records the work of Bembo and others of the Accademia, was read in England as *The Booke of the Courtier*, in a translation printed in 1561. As far as the Areopagites (as some of the English New Poets called themselves) were concerned, loftier content and greater technical variety were two of their main ideals, but contact between poets and musicians, so greatly emphasized by their Italian and French counterparts, was less marked in England until the time of Thomas Campion. Ironically, however, the strange result of this search for a truer marriage between music and poetry was to end in divorce. The silver swan of Jacob Arcadelt's madrigal 'Il bianco e dolce cigno' — echoed in Orlando Gibbons' setting of the text in translation — was to sing its sweetest song and sing no more:

> The silver Swanne who living had no Note,
> When death approacht unlockt her silent throat,
> Leaning her breast against the reedie shore,
> Thus sung her first and last, and sung no more,
> Farewell all ioyes, O death come close mine eyes,
> More Geese then Swannes now live, more fooles then wise
>
> (Gibbons 1612)

The reason was not far to seek. Gibbons' collection was published in 1612 as being 'apt for Viols and Voyces'. This phrase, as we know from other similar titles, means that viols may substitute for one, several or even all the voices; thus the madrigal can be played as an instrumental fantazia. Gibbons' collection includes so many fine texts that it is invidious to single out one above others, but Sir Walter Raleigh's poem is particularly striking:

What is our life? a play of passion,
Our mirth the musicke of division,
Our mothers wombes the tyring houses be,
Where we are drest for this short Comedy,
Heaven the Iudicious sharpe spectator is,
That sits and markes still who doth act amisse,
Our graves that hide us from the searching Sunne,
Are like drawne curtaynes when the play is done,
Thus march we playing, to our latest rest;
Onely we dye in earnest, that's no iest.

These evocative lines were set with consummate skill by Gibbons in such a way that not only does the music perfectly reflect the text (eg. in the musical equivalent of the 'drawn curtains' or the comical gait of 'Thus march we playing'), but it can indeed be played as a wordless instrumental piece in its own right. Here, the near impossibility of maintaining a stable union of two strong-minded partners — poetry of such imagery and virtuosity together with music of such character and technique — is readily apparent. Richard Barnfield (1599) wrote:

If Musique and sweet Poetrie agree,
As they must needes (the Sister and the Brother)
Then must the Love be great, twixt thee and mee,
Because thou lov'st the one, and I the other.

Dowland to thee is dear; whose heavenly touch
Upon the Lute doeth ravish humaine sense:
Spenser to mee; whose deepe Conceit is such,
As passing all Conceit, needs no defence.

Brothers and sisters are less likely to agree when they grow apart. Thus, verse and music, as they grew apart, would have to agree to differ; now one, now the other, would become dominant. If both were to be equal partners it had to be remembered, as George Wither said in *The Schollers Purgatory* (1625, p. 36) 'how many differences must be observed between Lyricke verse and that which is composed for reading only'. Some of these differences are to do with content, others are more technical. A simple example of the latter is enjambment, where the sense of a line requires to be completed in the next, by running over the line-end. In recited poetry this device greatly contributes to the forward movement of the verse. In sung lyric it is frequently lethal. In Wither's words: 'How harsh the musicke will be, if the chiefe Pauses be not carefully reduced unto the same lyne throughout the whole Hymne, which they have in the first Stanza' (loc. cit.).

This point is neatly illustrated in the first line of the hymn:

Jesus lives! No longer now

which (in this, the original version) resulted in a flat denial of the Easter message, because of the congregation's reasonable desire to take a breath before singing:

> Can thy terrors, death, appall us.

It is perfectly obvious that this hymn was not written to music; hymns written with a tune in mind avoid this type of irregularity and thus, their lines are normally end-stopped. Metrical dexterity in spoken verse is a different thing from the permissible variations which can be accommodated in music. Congregations which have struggled with Christina Rossetti's 'In the bleak mid winter' will know what this means. Since the poet had no tune in mind when she wrote the words, Holst, in attempting to fit a hymn tune to a rather wayward pattern of syllables and accents, set himself an impossible task. Although Wither was aware of the special technique of lyric, as opposed to recited verse, other critics did not admit to any knowledge of it. George Puttenham in his anonymously issued *The Arte of English Poesie* (1589) speaks of 'minstrels musicke' and the 'sharpe accent on the last sillable' which he finds in the lines: 'Now sucke childe and sleepe childe, thy mother's owne joy/Her only sweete comfort, to drowne all annoy'. This is a variant version (or perhaps a misquotation) of an anonymous song, sometimes ascribed to Byrd, beginning thus:

Ex. 1

(cf *MB* XXII no. 25)

It is hard to take offence at this song, but at the same time it is obvious that the words, if divorced from the tune, are not great poetry. The 'sharpe accent' (ie. the line ending on a stress) is one of the things from which the

New Poetry wished to depart, but the fact remains that trochaic endings are often a snare from the musical point of view, and English (whose grave-ending words are mostly participles, which become comical when over-used as rhyme words) does little to help the problem. So 'minstrels musicke' may have not been such a bad thing after all.

But the protests of Puttenham and others were heeded; indeed Shakespeare mercilessly ridiculed the choirboy plays from whence, no doubt, 'My little sweet darling' originally came. The 'death song' of Piramus in the last scene of *A Midsummer Night's Dream*, beginning at line 289, is a skit on those songs, heavy with alliteration and long drawn out death-throes, which were quite as inconsequential dramatically as their later equivalent in Grand Opera:

> . . . What dreadful dole is heere?
> Eyes do you see! How can it be!
> O dainty Ducke: O Deere!
> Thy mantle good; what staind with blood!
> Approach you Furies fell:
> O Fates! come come: Cut thred and thrum,
> Quaile, crush conclude and quell. . . .

> . . . Come teares, confound: Out sword, and wound
> The pap of *Piramus*:
> I that left pap, where heart doth hop;
> Thus dye I, thus, thus, thus.
> Now I am dead, now I am fled, my soule is in the sky,
> Tongue lose thy light, Moone take thy flight,
> Now dye, dye, dye, dye, dye.

Shakespeare, though the doggerel is exaggerated, could well be parodying the death-song of a lost play called *Guichardo*:

Ex. 2

Come tread the paths of pen-sive pangs with me, ye lov-ers true.

(cf *MB XXII* no.3)

The conclusion is as follows:

Ex. 3

Ah see, — I die, I die, I die, ah see, I die, I die, I die, ah, ah, ah, a-las, I die, I die, I die, I die

But although these songs may have tended to conform to the dictum 'that which is not worth saying is sung', the plain fact is they were show-stoppers — and no doubt the choirboys extracted every ounce of histrionics from their lines. Indeed, so popular was the set song that Shakespeare included several in his plays; some were more or less popular songs such as the 'Willow song' in *Othello*, others (eg. 'Under the greenwood tree' in *As You Like It*) were new words set to old tunes, and still others were parodies (eg. 'Farewell dear heart' in *Twelfth Night* — a skit on Robert Jones's 'Farewell dear love' from the *First Booke of Songes and Ayres, 1600*).

Shakespeare's attack was therefore directed against some of the conventions of the choirboy plays and the mannerisms of their particular songs, but not against songs in general. As his own lyrics show, he was not above the 'sharpe accent' of the 'minstrels musicke' so disliked by Puttenham. Ben Jonson, too, disliked tunes 'the fiddlers played': yet in the *Staple of Newes*

Fig. 2 Saint Paul's and the Globe Theatre (part of Vischer's panoramic View of London, 1616)

(IV,2) Madrigal sings a saraband beginning: 'She makes good cheare, she keepes full boards/She holds a Faire of Knights, and Lords'. The rhythm implied is roughly that of the ballet 'Sing we and chant it' by Thomas Morley (based on a model by the Italian Giovanni Gastoldi), though Morley avoids the 'sharpe accent' of his doggerel text by somewhat artificial means:

Ex. 4

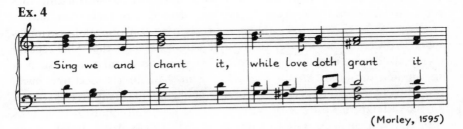

Sing we and chant it, while love doth grant it

(Morley, 1595)

Here, although somewhat disguised, there is both an up-beat beginning to the line and a grave line-end. This device is more obvious in Morley's famous 'Now is the month of maying', where the concatenation of up-beat and grave cadence (again, imitating an Italian, this time Orazio Vecchi) give a breathless effect:

Ex. 5

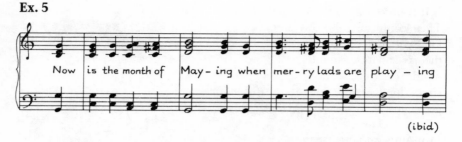

Now is the month of May-ing when mer-ry lads are play-ing

(ibid)

In spite of Jonson's jibe (elsewhere he speaks of the 'concupiscence of jigs and dances'), the saraband had a peculiar quality, which should have commended itself to the New Poets, to disguise the insistent up-beat felt in 'Now is the month' by using the equivocal three-beat pattern (where the second beat can take the stress in place of the first) employed in 'Sing we and chant it'. This rhythm was often used by Dowland: his songs to galliard tunes include 'Can she excuse my wrongs' and 'If my complaints' (Captain Piper's galliard):

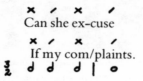

This device, to be sure, is old enough; it can be traced as far back as Adam de la Halle (who died before 1288) and further — to the tenth-century lyric 'Iam dulcis amica venito' found in the so-called *Cambridge Songs*.

Here then, is a good example of the way that the blend of music and verse in lyric has a different effect from pure poetry or pure music. It also illustrates a basic flaw in the way the New Poets philosophized about the Greek and Latin verse which they wished, in some measure, to imitate. It was their purpose to restore the intimate connection between music and verse, and to annex the great variety of metrical forms and the suaver prosody of the quantitative system for their own use. But they failed to appreciate that, of its nature, sung verse cannot be as complex as recited verse. If verse and music are to coexist with equanimity, rather than the one dominating the other, or both combining in their dullest elements, then enjambment and other licences natural to spoken verse must be exchanged for the different proprieties of lyric.

In addition to being blind to this reality, the proponents of classicism were also deaf to the true rhythm of quantitative verse in Latin or Greek. Quantitative verse (and this point is still misunderstood by classical metricians) had a beat, as well as lengths of syllables by which its rhythm was regulated. Furthermore, its quantities were more varied than the engagingly simple equation 1 long = 2 shorts.

18

It is necessary to bear in mind that beat and accent are not the same thing. Their confusion, and the failure to remember that there are several different kinds of accent, is the main reason for the unsatisfactory nature of metrical theory, and its terminology. The beat is a boundary which, although felt in the mind, is not necessarily physically perceptible. Many types of accent, notably stress (loudness), length and pitch, help to suggest the beat, or sometimes to go against it. If the beat is remorselessly emphasized, either in recitation:

The CURfew TOLLS the KNELL of PARTing DAY

or in musical performance — ONE two *three* four, ONE two *three* four — the result is inept. On the other hand, too many conflicts of accent can lead to metrical anarchy, so the disposition of accents, either in verse or music, is crucial. And when the two are united, the interplay of accents becomes correspondingly more complex. Even a simple phrase, such as 'Can she excuse my wrongs' with alternating stress accents in the verse, can be matched by what at first sight appears to be a conflicting rhythm in the music, and thus gives forth a surprisingly elaborate combinative metric.

It is clear that the usual prosodic jargon — whereby the 'foot' is the unit of movement — is wholly inadequate to deal with verse, let alone lyric verse since the supposed 'feet' of

The cur/few tolls / the knell / of part/ing day

correspond at no point with the boundaries dictated by the beat

The/ curfew / tolls the / knell of / parting / day.

What we have here is an alternating (disyllabic) rhythm; that it begins on an up-beat and ends on a down-beat is not particularly significant (to begin at 'curfew' or to end the line on the word 'day*light*' would not greatly alter the metre). So many of the common metrical distinctions — between 'iambic' and 'trochaic' for example — are beside the point. It is more important to describe the relationship of accent and beat. If Gray's 'Elegy' had been set by Dowland to a galliard, thus:

$$ | \; \breve{\text{♩}} \quad \text{♩} \quad \text{♩} \; | \; \text{♩} \quad \text{♩} \; | \; \text{♩} $$

/ The curfew / tolls the / knell

the first word, although on the beat, would be unstressed, as in Dowland's song 'Awake sweet love' (1597).

This is what Vladimir Nabokov (1964) describes as a 'scud'. The opposite, a reverse accent or anaclasis, occurs where a stressed syllable coincides with the off-beat, and 'level stress' describes something midway between a scud and a reversed accent, where two adjacent syllables could be regarded either as stressed or unstressed. These devices can be used in recited poetry to a considerable extent, but where music is involved, it is obvious that they can be employed only where the structure of the music permits. 'Ay me that love' by Philip Rosseter furnishes examples of various possible techniques: here most lines are the familiar alternating ten-syllable line with possible reversed accent opening, which goes back to Chaucer, and beyond him to the octosyllabics of St Ambrose, thus:

/ × × / × /
River or cloudy jet

The music, however, makes the metre far more varied:

Ex. 6

Ay me, that Love, that Love should na — ture's works ac-cuse

Where cru-el Lau-ra still__ her beau-ty views

Ri-ver or clou-dy jet, or crys-tal bright

Are all but ser — vants of her self de-light

(cf Rosseter, 1601)

Bars 4, 6, 8, 12 all begin with a 'scud' (ie. an unstressed syllable coinciding with the strong beat): this is the feature already noted, whereby triple time easily accommodates a stress transferred to the second beat. Bars 3–4 (cf. 11–12) are more of a special case, since *nature's* is set to a longer and higher note to its first syllable, thus attracting a length and pitch accent off- beat. The two $\frac{3}{4}$ units thus coalesce into a large $\frac{3}{2}$ unit — a device known as 'hemiola', a feature of galliard rhythm. Bars 14–17 are even more interesting, in which the iambic rhythm of the music, short-long, allows the verbal stresses to fall off-beat. This again is a device allowed by triple time, the main beat accommodating a scud, but the off-beats being accented by means of a length accent.

This example clearly demonstrates the techniques available to Elizabethan and Jacobean madrigalists and song-writers, who made full use of the possible counterpoints of musical and verbal accents. The Victorians, how-ever, who were unable to dissociate beat and accent, found these same composers guilty of poor word-setting.

It was a similar misapprehension which led the Renaissance poetasters to seek refuge in the quantitative system of Greek and Latin against what they believed to be the engulfing stress of English. In reality the danger was illusory: the haven proved to be no less rocky than the imagined peril. Some idea of the effect of quantitative verse in English may be gathered from a song by Campion in Sapphic metre. The Sapphic had been handed down through generations from classical times: Horace's 'Integer vitae scelerisque purus' had become a students' song in the Middle Ages, and many hymns (the most famous being 'Ut queant laxis') were composed in the same rhythm. Dowland himself employed this metre:

> Where Sinne sore wounding,
> daily doth oppresse me,
> There Grace abounding
> freely doth redresse mee:
> So that resounding
> still I shall confesse thee,
> Father of mercy.

(A Pilgrimes Solace, 1612)

But this form of the Sapphic had the so-called Roman caesura — a pronounced break between the fifth and sixth syllables — indeed here encouraging the formation of separate lines; what is more, Horace's lines, though quantitative, can be read accentually, no less than Dowland's:

Integer vitae scelerisque purus

But the Roman caesura and its accentual pattern were frowned upon by the New Learning, which affected to prefer the Greek caesura. Horace himself flirted with the latter device when he instructed the dancers to follow him in keeping to the Lesbian (Aeolic Greek) rhythms: 'Lesbium servate pedem meique pollicis ictum' (*Odes* IV, 6). Campion, therefore, chose the thorough-going 'Greek' Sapphic for his experiment:

Ex. 7

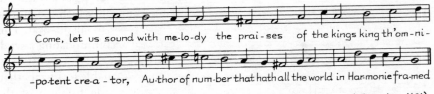

Come, let us sound with me-lo-dy the prai-ses of the kings king th'om-ni-
-po-tent cre-a - tor, Au-thor of num-ber that hath all the world in Har-monie fra-med

(cf Campion apud Rosseter, 1601)

The peculiar stilted gait of the lyric is due to the three main types of accent (stress, length and pitch) being forced into an equation within which they cannot naturally be made to fit.

Campion's espousal of the classical ideal fortunately had very little effect on his other songs, but it did prompt him to write a pamphlet entitled *Observations in the Art of English Poesie* (1602). Much of what he said there was sensible enough, and his imitation of 'Iambicks' was probably very much what a Latin iambic (as opposed to the 'iambic' of the prosodists, who would have us believe that Gray's 'Elegy' is in this metre) would have sounded like:

> Raving Warre, begot
> In the thirstye sands
> Of the *Lybian Iles*
> Wasts our emptye fields . . .

But amongst the truth there was much that was false, or at least open to misconstruction, mainly because much of this theory was grounded on the fallacies concerning classical prosody already discussed; so Samuel Daniel, in a reply called *A Defence of Ryme* (1603) was able easily to dismiss the case.

Campion's ill-fated attempt to win favour for classical rhythms was somewhat later than Edmund Spenser's, and a good deal less cautious; Sidney's imitations of the French school and Wyatt's and Surrey's of the Italian were also more sober. But on the musical side there are several fairly

Ex. 8

(Roy App 58 f 52ᵛ; cf Wulstan, 1968, no. 9)

extreme essays into *vers mesurés* in English, of which one of the most curious is the mid sixteenth-century lyric, 'This enders night', which in its original guise (modern versions are often bowdlerized) appears as Ex. 8.

This strange experiment, which must surely owe something to Baïf and his colleagues, goes so far as to assign different rhythms to each verse. Sidney's viewpoint was a good deal less extreme, confining his metrical experiments to imitations of the French psalm tunes:

Ex. 9

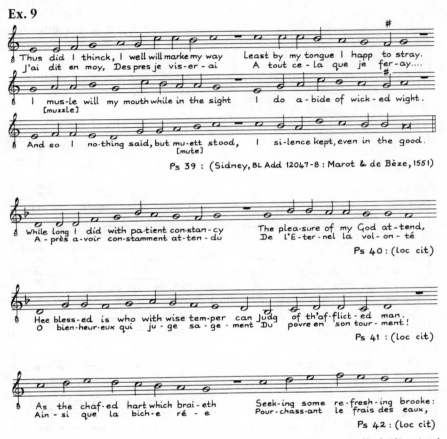

Thus did I thinck, I well will marke my way / Least by my tongue I happ to stray.
J'ai dit en moy, Des pres je vis-er-ai / A tout ce-la que je fer-ay....

I mus-le will my mouth while in the sight / I do a-bide of wick-ed wight.
[muzzle]

And so I no-thing said, but mu-ett stood, / I si-lence kept, even in the good.
[mute]

Ps 39 : (Sidney, BL Add 12047-8 : Marot & de Bèze, 1551)

While long I did with pa-tient con-stan-cy / The plea-sure of my God at-tend,
A-près a-voir con-stamment at-ten-du / De L'E-ter-nel la vol-on-té

Ps 40 : (loc cit)

Hee bless-ed is who with wise tem-per can Judg / of th'af-flict-ed man.
O bien-heur-eux qui ju-ge sa-ge-ment Du / povre en son tour-ment!

Ps 41 : (loc cit)

As the chaf-ed hart which brai-eth / Seek-ing some re-fresh-ing brooke:
Ain-si que la bich-e ré-e / Pour-chass-ant le frais dés eaux,

Ps 42 : (loc cit)

Sidney's habit of writing his words to pre-existing tunes, (called 'dittying' in contemporary parlance) guaranteed, as it would even in a poet a good deal less competent, that music and verse would fit hand in glove. Thus Sidney's verses were eminently singable, and by escaping from the 'chevy-chase' metre (8686) common in ballad-style lyrics of the period and turning to more varied metrical models (eg. unnamed French psalm tunes, together with Italian, English and Dutch tunes, which he did tend to name) he seemed to open the way for some of the principles of the New Poetry to be put into practice. By yet another irony, however, it was the psalm tunes which came to England on the tide of Calvinism that eventually established the supremacy of the 'chevy-chase' rhythms.

To begin with, the French Huguenot Psalters, followed by the Anglo-Genevan Psalter, displayed the varied rhythms encouraged by Baïf and Claude le Jeune: as the saraband and galliard had been used for secular tunes, so dance rhythms were pressed into service for the new French psalmody. The long-short-short pavan or strambotto rhythm (recognizable at the opening of countless French chansons and their Italian counterparts) is familiar in English and French psalm tunes alike (see the beginning of the previous example). This and the downbeat short-long-short rhythm is the staple of many tunes taken over in the English Psalters:

Ex. 10

(cf Day, 1563, Ps 100)

But the tunes of Sternhold and Hopkins' Psalter were a good deal less interesting, both melodically and metrically, than their French equivalents. The varied rhythms gradually became ironed out, due, no doubt to inertia; the psalms became slower and more straightforward as the years of the Reformation wore on. The Lutheran chorales were virtually all sung in slow, even, crotchets by Bach's time, when most of the English psalm tunes had also become stultified in a monotonous succession of minims. Moreover, the metres to become most firmly entrenched were the 'common metre' (8686 — the familiar 'chevy-chase') and its ballad relative of equal eight-syllabled lines, 'long metre' (8888); even the much despised 'Poulter's measure' was enshrined in the 'short metre' (6686).

This was unfortunate, for the original rhythms of the old psalm tunes brought metrical variety even within the somewhat hackneyed 'common' and 'long' metres. The long-short-short or short-long-short rhythms helped to solve the problem of the ubiquitous up-beat English line by allowing a reversed foot or level stress opening, in a manner analogous to the possibilities furnished by the triple time rhythms already discussed. William Kethe's famous paraphrase of the hundredth psalm (the tune, Ex. 10, being eventually known as the 'Old hundredth') is a good illustration of this technique. The basic line is the up-beat alternating pattern found in the doxology:

To Father Son and Ho-ly Ghost

The tedium of this movement is alleviated by the reversed and level stresses at the beginning of each line (and occasionally elsewhere):

´ ´ × × × ´ × ´
All people that on earth do dwell

´ × × ´ × ´ × ´
Sing to the Lord with cheerful voice

´ ´ × ´ × ´ ´ ´
Him serve with fear his praise forth tell

× × × ´ × ´ × ´
For it is seemly so to do

The rhythms of the tune allow this kaleidoscope of changing stress accents to be accommodated by the lengths and pitches of the notes, now emphasizing the beat, now allowing a 'scud'. If, as happened, the tune was ironed out into a tedious stream of minims (and sung lethargically at that) it is plain that subtle interaction of verse and tune would be traduced, as trite verse sung to a dull tune.

An amusing confirmation of the increasingly ponderous performance which led to the decay of the psalm tunes is found in the use of the term 'gathering note'. This epithet has applied to the long note which often began each line, and conjures up the bizarre image of a congregation confusedly mustering itself at vaguely agreed intervals. There would have been no time for singers to gather in this fashion when the tunes were sung at their original speed, often by solo voices as 'private music' in the home rather than the church; indeed, they could hardly have earned the name 'Genevan jigs' if these melodies sounded like doleful dumps. Thus the ideal partnership of music and verse envisaged by Sidney, Campion and others was not fulfilled. These two men had some modest reward however, since their names are those most frequently found as the authors of the verses set as lute-songs or as madrigals. But the doggerel returned, forming a verbal clothes-horse on which composers such as Purcell could hang their beautiful, fine-wrought melodies; or at the opposite extreme a poet like Milton could sound forth in sonorous declamation, and approve of any musical setting which did not assert itself above the level of modest re-citative. Thus, it came about that Milton wrote in praise of Henry Lawes (whose settings were often little more than successions of cadences strung together) the following lines:

> *Harry*, whose tunefull and well measur'd song
> First taught our English Music how to span
> Words with just note and accent, not to scan
> With *Midas* ears, committing short and long;
>
> (Sonnet XIII 1673)

What then, of the age of the silver swan? What did it achieve, and for how long?

It may seem an exaggeration to imply that this age was short-lived and, by implication, frenetic. But the printed collections of madrigals and lute-songs appeared in great numbers over only a comparatively short time: and although it would be unwise to take their appearance or disappearance as the beginning and end of the fashion, they were clearly intended to supply a demand. So 1588, the year of *Musica Transalpina*, which contained Italian madrigals provided with English texts, and also the year of Byrd's *Psalmes Sonets & Songs* (a hasty compilation of consort songs, anthems and so on, done up in madrigalian guise) is probably near the beginning of the fashion which lasted for a decade at full force and was all but done twenty years later. As for the lute-song, its reign was even shorter, from the close of the sixteenth century to 1612, the date of Dowland's *A Pilgrimes Solace* (Campion's 1617 collections, and Attey's of 1622, were autumn crocuses). Looking back to the concerted song, madrigal and lute-song, they all appear to be closely-related members of the family of Elizabethan and Jacobean music. The composers themselves would have expressed amusement, or even horror, at this notion. Very few of them wrote, or wished to write, in more than one genre. Byrd, for example, preferred the purely musical working-out of the concerted song.

The more familiar term 'consort song' was coined, I think, by Philip Brett (cf. Brett, 1962): since Warwick Edwards (1971) has shown that 'consort' denoted a specific kind of ensemble I have used the term 'concerted song' in its place. Although the partbooks in which these concerted songs are found do not specify any particular instruments, there is little doubt that viols were intended, since their use in the choirboy plays is well attested (see Woodfield, 1984, pp.213 ff): an ensemble consisting of a boy singer with viols is depicted in the left-hand panel of the Unton mural reproduced on the jacket of this book.

In marked contrast to the high standard evinced by Gibbons in his madrigalian collection, the texts of Byrd's concerted songs are often close to sheer doggerel. Furthermore, when he set a metrical psalm, he was often content to imitate the rhythm of its 'common tune'. Although it cannot be said that Byrd was indifferent to their texts, he generally approached his songs almost as though they were instrumental fantazias with added words. He rarely indulged in madrigalisms such as illustrative gestures or dramatic contrasts, nor did he work towards the intimate relationship of words and music which was the ideal of Dowland and Campion. His elegy on the death of his revered teacher, Tallis, displays as much in the way of madrigalism as he normally was wont to use (Ex. 11).

The opening, in strict imitation, is something of a musical pun on the technical expertise of the 'sacred muses' (compare Gibbons' 'O that the learned poets', 1612) while the long melisma on 'and Music dies' evokes the wonderfully tragic effect of a slowly falling teardrop. The text is set line by line, rather than in the madrigalian fashion, but 'bated with fuge', 'manie

Ex. 11

(cf *Byrd Edition* Vol. 15 no. 32)

rests' and 'a long Praeludium' to use the words of the disapproving Campion (apud Rosseter, 1601). But for the most part, Byrd's concerted songs reflect the words well, even if they do not treat them as though they were lyrics. The settings tend, indeed, towards the freely musical approach of Purcell, and are aeons away from Milton's ideal; yet they are some of the finest examples of song in any language. 'Come pretty babe' (apparently from a choirboy play) and the famous 'Lullaby, my sweet little baby', the elegies such as 'Ye sacred muses' and the sprightly 'Though Amaryllis dance in green', together with the carols 'O God that guides', 'From Virgin's womb' and 'An earthly tree' are some outstanding examples (printed in the *Byrd Edition*, Vols 13–16). They stand beside 'Pandolpho' (attributed alternatively to Robert Parsons or Richard Farrant), 'Come tread the paths' (Anon), and the vivacious 'In a merry May morn' (Richard Nicolson) and several others, as high points of the genre, printed in *Musica Britannica (MB)* XXII. Shakespeare, as we have seen, would hardly have approved of some of these choirboy-songs, but in most of them the supremacy of music over the words is not exaggerated.

In the madrigal proper, Byrd seems to have been less assured. His first efforts were not particularly successful. Kerman (1962) has described how the English music printing monopoly (though vested in Tallis and Byrd) was controlled by the exiled Huguenot, Vautrollier, who disapproved of secular music, thus acting virtually as a censor. Consequently, on Vautrollier's death in 1588 there was a scramble to get the new-fashioned madrigals into print. So Byrd pressed his concerted songs (such as 'Lullaby') into service by adding words to the accompanimental parts. The results were hardly convincing in their madrigalian versions, for the accompanimental parts were often clumsily underlaid and were frequently of too instrumental a character to be comfortably singable. But in his later collections (amongst the anthems and songs he was still mustering to make up numbers) Byrd managed to adopt a lighter tone, and wrote some convincing madrigals. In one, 'Come woeful Orpheus' he illustrates the words 'some strange chromatic notes' and 'sourest sharps and uncouth flats' with such an Italianate literalism that it seems for a moment that the quiet intellectual is making a determined effort to adopt a jocular tone. But Byrd's madrigalesque efforts cannot compete with his other styles, nor with the madrigals of Morley, Thomas Weelkes, John Wilbye and others.

The English madrigalists, particularly Morley, followed closely on Italian models. The *Triumphes of Oriana*, belatedly issued (1601) in honour of Queen Elizabeth, with items by most of the madrigalists of the day (though Byrd and the youthful Gibbons are notably excluded), was an imitation of *Il Trionfo di Dori* which appeared in 1592. Yet the striking element in the English madrigal is the degree to which the Italian madrigal is effectively naturalized. The French composers in their chansons wrote wholly French music, while the German madrigalists wrote in an Italian idiom betraying,

THE EXTRACT AND EFFECT OF THE QVENES

Maiesties letters patents to Thomas Tallis and VVilliam Birde,
for the printing of muficke.

ELIZABETH *by the grace of God Quene of Englande Fraunce and Irelande defender of the faith &c. To all printers bokefellers and other officers minifters and fubiects greting, Knowe ye, that we for the especiall affection and good wil that we haue and beare to the fcience of muficke and for the aduauncement thereof, by our letters patents dated the xx 11. of Ianuary in the xv1 1. yere of our raigne, haue graunted full priuiledge and licence vnto our welbeloued feruaunts Thomas Tallis and VVilliam Birde Gent. of our Chappell, and to the ouerlyuer of them, & to the affignes of them and of the furuiuer of them, for xx1.yeares next enfuing, to imprint any and fo many as they will of fet fonge or fonges in partes, either in Englifh, Latine, French, Italian, or other tongues that may ferue for muficke either in Churche or chamber, or otherwife to be either plaid or foonge, And that they may rule and caufe to be ruled by impreffion any paper to ferue for printing or pricking of any fonge or fonges, and may fell and vtter any printed bokes or papers of any fonge or fonges, or any bookes or quieres of fuch ruled paper imprinted, Alfo we ftraightly by the fame forbid all printers bookefellers fubiects & ftrangers, other then as is aforefaid, to do any the premiffes, or to bring or caufe to be brought out of any forren Realmes into any our dominions any fonge or fonges made and printed in any forren countrie, to fell or put to fale, vppon paine of our high difpleafure, And the offender in any of the premiffes for euery time to forfet to vs our heires and fucceffors fortie fhillings, and to the faid Thomas Tallis & VVilliam Birde or to their affignes & to the affignes of the furuiuer of the, all & euery the faid bokes papers fonge or fonges, VVe haue alfo by the fame willed & commaunded our printers, maifters & wardens of the mifterie of ftacioners, to affift the faid Thomas Tallis and VVilliam Birde & their affignes for the dewe executing of the premiffes.*

Fig. 3 Music Printing Monopoly granted to Tallis and Byrd (from their *Cantiones Sacrae*, 1575)

so to speak, hardly a trace of an accent; but in the English madrigals the extravagant gestures (chromaticism, word painting, literary dilletantism, abrupt changes of musical direction) become more sober and more integrated in the design as a whole. Gastoldi's balletti are cruder than the imitations by Morley or Weelkes, whose musical structures are more satisfying than their models. The Italian madrigal was grounded in a literary movement, whereas the English madrigalists were literati at one remove; as noted earlier, the heading 'apt for voices and viols' was no idle boast, for the working out of many an English madrigal was as carefully done as in a fantazia, quite apart from the words being set 'with just note and accent' in several parts simultaneously. Some idea of the complexities involved may be gleaned from the following example:

Ex. 12

(Morley, 1595, no. XVII)

The accents of 'Ámaríllis' do not correspond with the beat: this technique, already noted in the lute-song, is used simultaneously in five parts.

The stock figures of the madrigal, whereby the words are literally illustrated in the music (eg. Wilbye's '*Long* have I made these hills', in which the first note is stretched out) were used somewhat more subtly by the majority of the English, as opposed to their Italian counterparts. Perhaps the most hackneyed cliché was the translated joke whereby the word 'sigh' was preceded by a rest: the Italian word *sospiro* means both a rest and a 'sigh'. The most characteristically English figure, however, was the 'weeping' motive adopted by Dowland in his 'lachrymae' pavan, to which he subsequently added the words 'Flow my tears':

Ex. 13

This figure was used, often with great subtlety, in countless English madrigals, making Dowland's musical 'weeping' trademark the only serious rival to the other famous four-note signature 'B-A-C-H'. Incidentally, his Latin pun *semper Dowland semper dolens* (Dowland always sad) shows that the name was pronounced something like 'Doe-land'.

The number of examples which might be drawn upon to demonstrate the care which the English madrigalists lavished on their settings is so large as to make even a representative selection difficult. Gibbons' 1612 collection is the most serious and consistently high quality contribution to the English madrigal. Kerman's contention (1962, pp. 122–4) that some of the pieces in the volume were originally solo songs is not without its difficulties. Although it seems likely that Gibbons had the possibility of performance by one voice with instruments much in mind — and thus was careful to allow the top (or second) part to proceed without verbal incongruity within itself — the often abrupt beginnings, some of the repetitions involved, and the difficulty of discerning which of the voice parts is to be regarded as the 'first singing part', do not confirm Kerman's argument satisfactorily, particularly when Byrd's solo songs are closely compared. On the contrary, the skill with which Gibbons reconciles the 'instrumental' and 'vocal' approach to his madrigals, merely presses the point that in these works the literary and musical elements have been carried to their furthest, and crucial, extremes.

After Gibbons, the most serious of the madrigalists were Weelkes and Wilbye, who together with Tomkins made outstanding contributions to the genre, as did the lesser George Kirbye and Ward. Wilbye's music has been admirably commented upon by David Brown (1974) and the position of Wilbye in relation to his patrons, the Kytson family of Hengrave Hall, has been treated by Price (1980). Wilbye is an unusual Tudor musician in that he held no appointment other than with one patron family, and composed virtually nothing but madrigals (in two sets of 1598 and 1601). His two contributions to Sir William Leighton's *Teares or Lamentacions of a Sorrowful Soule* of 1614 were settings of sacred words, it is true, but 'O God the rock' is merely a rewriting of his famous madrigal 'Draw on sweet night' from the 1609 set.

Wilbye's music is consistently finely wrought, from the lighter madrigals such as 'Flora gave me fairest flowers' through the artless 'Adieu, sweet Amaryllis', to the more complex and Italianate 'Of joys and pleasing pains'. His textures are rich, as in 'Weep, O weep mine eyes', or light and rhythmic, as in 'Sweet honey sucking bees'; but above all, the formal ordering of his musical ideas is carefully considered, with the result that (as with Gibbons, and indeed many of the English madrigalists) his madrigals are musically successful when performed by instruments alone.

Due to the indefatigible labours of E. H. Fellowes, who edited most of the madrigalian collections in the series *English Madrigal School (EMS)*, many of the outstanding examples of the genre are tolerably well known; indeed several of the contributions by lesser figures such as Thomas Bateson, John Bennet, Michael East and Giles Farnaby are justly popular. One name must, nonetheless, be mentioned, for Weelkes' bold inventiveness and brilliant handling of large-scale textures (in, for example, 'Like two proud armies') cannot be passed over; and his magical word painting, as found in 'Thule, the period of cosmography', deserves special comment. In the latter, his portrayal of the 'sulphureous fire' is truly volcanic, and the chromaticism at 'how strangely Fogo burns' is indeed strangely caustic. The deftness of his musical portraiture is not, however, confined to his large-scale works: the three-part 'Cease, sorrows now' is highly inventive, and daringly chromatic. Yet the means with which Weelkes and his English colleagues carefully fused words and music are often disarmingly subtle; of the many such instances which might be adduced, I will content myself with the opening of Weelkes' 'Take here my heart' from his 1600 collection (Ex. 14).

The whole of the opening, stretching for the equivalent of 13 bars, is a mere alternation of the chords of C and G knit together with a descending scale passage. It is nevertheless carefully contrived, and hardly dull, and the static effect reinforces the unwavering promise 'I give it thee for ever'; indeed perhaps the scales are in imitation of a ring of wedding bells.

The 'fuguing' of the concerted song and madrigal was not, as we have seen, to the taste of Campion. His ayres, in common with those of Dowland and others, were often issued in such a way that a four-part format was given as an alternative to the lute-song; this dual-purpose arrangement was unashamedly commercial. Often these lower parts were constructed and underlaid in an awkward and makeshift way, thus seeming to have some-

Ex. 14

thing in common with the published versions of Byrd's songs. Although commercial pressure may have appeared to forge a link between ayre, concerted song and madrigal, their intentions were worlds apart, the style of the lute-song being nearest to the principles of the *nuove musiche* of Count Bardi and the Florentine *camerata*. These apostles of the New Music, eschewing the literal word painting of the madrigal, and being opposed to polyphony in general, would nevertheless have found the lute-song far too elaborate musically, yet not extreme enough in declamation for their taste. The lute-song was peculiarly English in its ethos, whatever the apparent parallels. Campion's prolific output of songs is first seen in Rosseter's *Booke of Ayres* which contains twenty-one songs by Campion, including the Sapphic experiment mentioned earlier. Rosseter was probably responsible for writing out the lute parts from sketches by Campion, while the latter doubtless provided many or all of the lyrics which Rosseter set. This friendship was life-long, and indeed extended beyond the grave, for Campion left his entire estate to Rosseter, who was subsequently buried in the same church. By profession Campion was a doctor; but his verses and music, to use Rosseter's words, were the 'superfluous blossoms of his deeper studies.' Uniquely amongst the lutenist song-writers, Campion wrote all his own lyrics, and also provided texts for other song-writers such as John Coprario (who was born plain Cooper, but took on the Italianate form Coprario or Coperario). The songbooks which Campion issued on his own account contain a remarkable variety of moods. His *First Booke of Ayres* (c. 1613) are mostly religious, moving between the hymn-like 'Never weather-beaten sail' and the more elaborate and intense 'Author of light':

Ex. 15

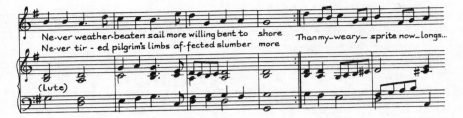

Ne-ver weather-beaten sail more willing bent to shore Than my-weary- sprite now-longs...
Ne-ver tir - ed pilgrim's limbs af-fected slumber more

(Lute)

Ex. 16

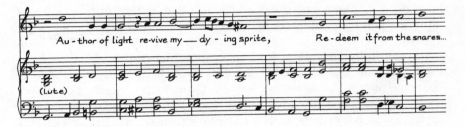

Au-thor of light revive my—dy - ing sprite, Re-deem it from the snares...

(Lute)

His style remains engagingly simple throughout most of his *Second, Third* and *Fourth* Books. Less prolific, but equally remarkable, was John Daniel, the brother of the poet Samuel. His *Songs for the Lute, Viol and Voice* (1606) contain the most intensely chromatic of all the English lute-songs and his declamatory passages often have a strangely Purcellian look to them. The song sequence beginning 'Grief keep within' is a remarkable demonstration of the application of rhetorical figures to music, discussed in a publication of Joachim Burmeister (1601) and possibly read by Daniel. The repetition of words for dramatic purposes was part and parcel of the choirboy-song style, but it is much used by Daniel ('Grief, grief, grief, grief keep within'), apparently as the figure *abruptio* of the rhetoricians. Further figures such as *syncope, heterolepsis,* and *gradatio* (a full list may be found in Buelow's article 'Rhetoric and Music' in the *New Grove*) seem clearly to be employed, perhaps somewhat artificially, by Daniel. It is not unlikely that these matters were the subject of much discussion between the Daniel brothers; Samuel's interest in poetics is of course evident in his *Defence of Ryme* (1603). The rhetorical figures are perhaps more successfully introduced in the song sequence 'Can doleful notes' with its famous second part, beginning 'No, let chromatic tunes . . .' (Ex. 17).

Whether the texts of these songs were by John, or by his brother Samuel (who certainly wrote some of the words used in the song book) remains problematic; but their content was clearly designed to allow the demonstration of somewhat mannered gestures of word painting.

As with the madrigalists, the lutenist song-writers such as Robert Jones

Ex. 17

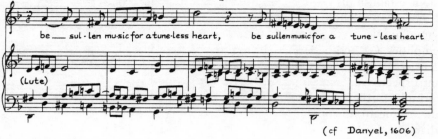

... No, let chromatic tunes, harsh without ground

be — sul-len mu-sic for a tune-less heart, be sullen music for a tune-less heart

(cf Danyel, 1606)

and William Corkine left so much of worth that it is difficult to do them justice without mentioning a bewildering number of songs and composers, most of whose work was published by Fellowes in the series *The English Lute-Songs*. Even those who, like Daniel, issued only one book of songs left an unmistakable mark: Rosseter, Thomas Ford, John Bartlett and Francis Pilkington all deserve more than honourable mention. Morley's tablatures show a perfunctory knowledge of lute technique, and there is more than a suspicion that many of his songs were arrangements: 'It was a lover and his lass' for example, which Shakespeare uses in *As You Like It* clearly had common currency, as did the 'Willow song'. Nor should the many other anonymous song-writers be forgotten — as this setting of 'Miserere my maker' shows:

Ex. 18

to hear my cease-less cry ing: Mi-se - re - re, mi-se-

-re - re, mi-se-re-re I ———— am dy - - ing

(Cambridge, King's Coll, Rowe 2 no. 8)

Dowland, however, stands peerless amongst the lutenist song-writers. 'Sorrow stay' from his *Second Booke of Songes or Ayres* (1600) would alone establish his claim to immortality. In the same book 'Fine knacks for ladies' shows that he is not *semper dolens*; 'White as lilies was her face' has the same simple grace of many of Campion's settings and 'Shall I sue' exemplifies yet another tone. 'In darkness let me dwell', from *A Musicall Banquet* (1610) is perhaps one of the gloomiest songs ever written. After an introspective opening, the 'jarring, jarring sounds' strike a more passionate attitude, furthered in the declamatory 'O let me living, let me living, living, die, till death do come.' The 'affect' is nearer that of the Italian monodists than the death-song of the choirboy plays; yet none but Dowland could have penned it. The master stroke is the resignation of the beginning exactly echoed at the end of the song: the listener is left hanging by a thread, music and verse ending in suspension (Ex. 19).

Fig. 4 Canon by John Dowland with signature (from *Album Amicorum* or Cellarius: BL Add. 27 579 f.88)

The Italianate influence is most obvious in 'Lasso vita mia mi fa morire.' Everywhere the syllables *mi* or *fa* appear in the text, the appropriate notes are given to them. Nor is this all, for the words *Deh* or *Ahi me* are set to the figures demanded by Caccini in his *Nuove Musiche* (1602). Two songs from

Ex. 19

in dark - ness let me dwell

(Lute)

the latter collection appear in the *Musicall Banquet* of 1610, so it seems obvious that Dowland's essay, found in *A Pilgrimes Solace* (1612), is to be read as a manifesto that he is not to be outdone by an Italian. Indeed he is not, as the two companion pieces of the volume (all are for obbligato treble and bass instruments together with voice and lute) show even more clearly. 'Go nightly cares' and 'From silent night' are amongst the most characteristic compositions of a commandingly individual composer.

The preface to *A Pilgrimes Solace* refers to his sojourn in Denmark as lutenist to King Christian IV, to the accusation that he was old-fashioned and to the impertinence of Tobias Hume (in his . . *Musicall Humours*, 1605) for averring that the lyra viol was the equal of the lute:

Worthy Gentlemen, and my loving Countrymen: mooved by your many and fore-tasted courtesies, I am constrained to appeare againe unto you. True it is, I have lien long obscured from your sight, because I have received a Kingly entertainment in a forraine climate, which could not attaine to any (though never so meane) place at home, yet have I held up my head within this Horizon, and not altogether been unaffected else where. Some part of my poore labours have found favour in the greatest part of Europe, and been printed in eight most famous Cities beyond the seas, viz: *Paris, Antwerpe, Collein, Nurenberge, Franckfort, Leipsig, Amsterdam*, and *Hamburge*: (yea, and some of them also authorized under the Emperours royall priviledge,) yet I must tell you, as I have beene a stranger; so have I againe found strange entertainment since my returne: especially by the opposition of two sorts of people that shroude themselves under the title of Musitians. The first are some simple Cantors, or vocall singers, who though they seeme excellent in their blinde Division-making, are meerely ignorant, even in the first elements of Musicke, and also in the true order of the mutation of the *Hexachord* in the Systeme, (which hath ben approved by all the learned and skillful men of Christendome, this 800 yeares,) yet doe these fellowes give their verdict of me behind my backe, and say, what I doe is after the old manner: but I will speake openly to them, and would have them know that the proudest Cantor of them dares not oppose himselfe face to face against me. The second are young-men, professers of the Lute, who vaunt themselves, to the disparagement of such as have beene before their time (wherein I my selfe am a party) that there never was the like of them. To these men I say little, because of my love and hope to see some deedes ensue their brave wordes, and also being that here under their owne noses hath beene published a Booke in defence of the Viol de Gamba, wherein not onely all other the best and principall Instruments have been abased, but especially the Lute by name, the words, to satisfie thee Reader I have here thought good to insert, and are as followeth: *From henceforth, the statefull instrument Gambo Violl, shall with ease yeeld full various, and devicefull Musicke as the Lute: for here I protest the Trinitie of Musicke, Parts, Passion, and Devision, to be as gracefully united in the Gambo Viol, as in the most receiurd (sic) instrument that is, &c.* Which Imputation, methinkes, the learneder sort of Musitians ought not to let passe unanswered . . .

Hume's eccentricities eventually developed into madness. As to his baseless charge that Dowland was unable to compose in the new style, 'Go nightly cares' and 'From silent night' together with 'Lasso vita mia' are an emphatic refutation. 'From silent night' has the obligatory rest before the word 'sighs', and the plangent ascent of a chromatic semitone, doubtless performed as John Galliard's translation of Pier Francesco Tosi (1723) suggests (1743, pp. 38, 191) 'with a *Messa di Voce*, the Voice always rising till he reaches it':

Ex. 20

my— wail - ing Muse

nought— else but sor - - row, grief— and care

N⁰ 15.

per Meſse di Voce

(cf Dowland, 1612 & Tosi, 1743)

The words of the second and third verses demand minor alterations to the printed music by the singer. Here again is cogent illustration of the way verse and music have been extended to their technical limits. In a strophic setting each repeated, or otherwise isolated word of the first verse must be matched by a compatible phrase in the others: and if the sense of a subsequent verse requires a longer note in place of a rest, the music must allow this modification, for the 'chiefe Pauses' must be 'carefully reduced unto the same place in the line . . . which they have in the first stanza.' This virtuosity is the *ultimum vale* not only of Dowland, but of the 'sister and the brother' of the lyric: Milton and Lawes were to come after.

The same complexity is found in 'Go nightly cares'. At the words 'O give me time to draw my weary breath' there is an elaborate musical pun: the voice sings on in a monotone, denoting the tolling of the death knell, while the passing bells (a conventional three-note figure found in many songs) figure in the lute and bass parts. One setting (BL Add. 15117, f3) of 'O death rock me on sleep' has the three-note figure at the words 'toll on the passing-bell', another has a bell-like clash (unfortunately suppressed in *MB* XXII, no.I—the second highest instrumental part should have flats to each E in bars 20–24) to illustrate the tolling. Dowland has both, and also contrives to insert his musical 'lachrymae' trademark in both 'Go nightly cares' and 'From silent night', just as he manages to quote the beginning of his 'Sorrow, stay' at the opening of 'Lasso vita mia'.

In Dowland is found the epitome of the age of the silver swan. The spur of competition and criticism caused Dowland to compose some of his most memorable and evocative songs; but in common with Gibbons and others, the simultaneous exploration of the limits of poetry and music was to achieve a brilliance which must burn itself out. Dowland was exhausted: 'Thy yeares', as Peacham (1612) said of him, 'have made thee white'. This phrase, written more than a decade before Dowland's death, is part of a peculiarly melancholy portrait, beginning:

> Heere, *Philomel,* in silence sits alone,
> In depth of winter, on the bared brier . . .

Thus he sang, and sung no more.

CHAPTER 3

Small and Popular Musickes

In 1613 the poet Michael Drayton published a long poem entitled *Poly-Olbion*: this, a rhyming gazeteer, contains a lively portrait of life in the England of the time. Drayton is possibly the 'Mr M. D.' of Morley's 1595 set of *Balletts* and may have been responsible for the translations of some or all of the texts in that collection. Whatever the truth of this, the 'Fourth song' of his *Poly-Olbion* seems to be a first-hand description of English music–making during that era, in which the poet comments that:

> the English that repyn'd to be delay'd so long
> All quicklie at the hint as with one free consent,
> Strooke up at once and sung each to the Instrument
> (of sundry sorts that were, as the Musician likes)
> On which the practic'd hand with perfect'st fingring strikes
> Whereby their height of skill might liveliest be exprest
> (1622 ed., p. 63)

Drayton goes on to list stringed and wind instruments in such profusion as to suggest that town and country rang to the sound of instrumental music, played by performers of the calibre of the London waits; indeed, many such quotations (see Woodfill, 1953, ch. ix passim) tend to foster the irresistible impression that music flowed through London like the Thames, and that town and country, courtiers and commonfolk alike, were bathed in its melodious waters.

This romantic view of 'Merrie England' is, sadly, far from the truth. Most of the populace could not read anything, let alone music. And even amongst the literate class, music was frequently ill-esteemed and often incompetently practised. Puttenham (1589) says 'it is hard to find in these dayes of noblemen or gentlemen any good *Mathematician*, or excellent *Musitian*'.

The prefaces to the madrigal collections take up this theme. In 1598, Weelkes speaks of the task of professional musicians attempting 'Amongst so many men dayly labouring to call home againe the banished Philomele, whose purest blood the impure Minstralsie hath strained' (Weelkes, 1598). Wilbye (1609) says that: 'Musicke sits solitary amongst sister Sciences and . . . often wants the fortune to be esteemed (for so she is worthy) even amongst the worthyest.' In his autobiography (c. 1576) Thomas Whythorne writes in a similar vein. He finds that church music is 'slenderly maintained', so that soon 'when the old store of the musicians be worn out' there will be few or none left to 'make good lesson of descant'. He continues:

> I cannot here leave out or let pass to speak of an other sort that do live by music and yet are no musicians at all. And those there be they, who after they have learned a little to sing pricksong, or else have either learned by hand, or by ear, or else by tablature, to play or sound on musical instruments, such music as hath been and is made by others and not by them; by and by they will usurp on music, and account and call themselves musicians; of the which pettifoggers of music, there be both schoolmasters, singing-men and minstrels.
>
> (Osborn, 1961 p. 246, modernized)

Whythorne goes on to compare England with the Continent, where music was more highly esteemed, and where in most houses of any reputation or importance were found 'not only instruments of music, but also all sorts of music in print . . . where there be many in one company together who can sing pricksong perfectly.' (ibid. p. 247)

In truth, therefore, most people's interest in music — then as now — extended to a few catchy tunes. In Puttenham's words, they preferred:

> small & popular Musickes song by these *Cantabanqui* [itinerant singers] and barrelsheads where they have none other audience than boys or countrey fellowes that passe by them in the streete, or else by blind harpers or such like taverne minstrels that give a fit of mirth for a groat . . . also they be used in Carols and rounds and such light or lascivious Poems, which are commonly more commodiously uttered by these buffons or vices in playes then by any other person. Such were the *rimes* of *Skelton* (usurping the name of a Poet Laureat); being in deede but a rude rayling rimer and all his doings ridiculous, he used both short distaunces [stanzas] and short measures [metres] pleasing onely the popular eare: in our courtly maker we banish them utterly.
>
> (Puttenham, 1589 p. 69)

The 'small and popular musickes' which Puttenham had in mind included the type of songs published by Thomas Ravenscroft in 1609, under the title

Pammelia, containing catches which, as his introduction states, 'are so consonant to all ordinaryie musicall capacity'. *Deuteromelia*, published in the same year, emphasized that they were suitable for '*almost* all men' who are '*capable*, that are not *altogether* immusicall'.

Yet even if the common people were indeed illiterate (see Cressy, 1980) in both the proper and musical senses of the word, music nevertheless played a substantial part in their world. Since most people could not read, merchants had to have symbolic trademarks such as the three balls of the pawnbroker or the barleysugar pole of the barber-surgeon, and pedlars would similarly identify their wares by shouting a type of signature tune far more enduring than that of its modern-day equivalent — the commercial television jingle. Having no clock, the people relied upon the night-watchman to call the time, as they relied upon the town-crier for the parish news.

Fig. 5 A bellman (from *The Belman of London*, 1608)

The bellman's cries or those of the street vendors, were probably no less raucous than the barely intelligible shouts of the modern newsboy; but some of the pedlars' songs were decidedly tuneful, as for example 'Will you buy my sweet lavender?'. The latter was heard in the streets of London until comparatively recently, and although few of the old cries (apart from one or two like 'Any old iron?') have survived in their original usage, many are remembered in the form of the folksongs (eg. 'Lavender's blue', 'Cherry-ripe' and 'Hot cross buns') which enshrined them.

The street-beggars, too, had their cries, of which the pleadings of the Abram man, let out of Bedlam to beg for food for the inmates of the asylum, is perhaps the best known. Bethlehem (Bedlam) house, which was then outside Bishopsgate, was given as a lunatic hospital to the City of London by Henry VIII. Its inmates were often the figures of coarse fun, but were sometimes the subjects of touching portraits in the literature and balladry of the period. There is a moving song called 'Tom a Bedlam' in *Musicks Delight on the Cithren* (1666):

> That of your five sound senses you never be forsaken
> Nor wander from yourselves with Tom abroad to begg your
> bacon
> . . .
> Come dame or maide,
> be not afraid
> poore Tom will injure nothing.

While the day was full of the songs of pedlars, watermen and beggars, the night air was often pierced by the sound of the City waits, a group of instrumentalists praised by no less a critic than Morley. There is a curious bilingual tract entitled *The French Schoolemaister* by Claude de Sainliens (who also called himself Claudius Hollyband), published in 1573. Although the purpose of the book was to teach French to the English (Sainliens, incidentally, must have been one of the first guardians of his tongue to warn against 'Franglais'), its chief interest today lies in its vivid pictures of London life.

In one dialogue, the host has apparently slept through the din of the waits:

[Gossip] What, have you not heard the minstrels and players of instruments, which did play so sweetly before the Cities stoarehouse, from midnight even unto the breaking of the day?

[Host] Verily I have not heard them

[Gossip] Truely you sleape very soundly . . . [perhaps, he implies, through over-imbibing]

[Host] . . . who were those singers and players of instrumentes?

[Gossip] I cannot tell truly: except perchaunce they were the minstrels of the towne, with those of the Queenes, mingled with voices of Italians and Englishmen, which did singe very harmoniously.

[Host] Would god I had herde them, and it had cost mee a quarte of wyne.

[Gossip]   I would you had for your sake: for it would seeme unto you to be ravished in an earthly paradise: you had heard first and formost the Viols, Cornets, Harpes, Hobois, Trumpets, with four Flutes the which did triumphe.

(1573 ed., f 38)

The word 'waits' comes from the Anglo-Saxon 'to guard' (*wacian*) through Norman French, and is allied to the word 'watch'. The function of the waits was officially to serve as night-watchmen, and their shawms would signal the time at various hours. In their role as minstrels, however, they would provide the 'band' for entertainments such as wedding feasts, plays and masques; or for ceremonial occasions they might act as the musical equivalent of a coat of arms. Five waits from Norwich went on an expedition with Francis Drake in 1589, when 'three new howboyes and one treble recorder' together with a 'saquebut' were issued for their use. The waits' livery was strikingly colourful (the London waits had blue gowns with red sleeves and caps) and banners would often be hung from the shawms or trumpets (see Woodfill, 1953, pp. 86, 89–90). One of the tunes of the London waits survives in *Apollos Banquet* of 1669. Unfortunately, its words have been garbled and bowdlerized; it has become the victim of the vogue for pseudo Christmas carols, a curious form of literary ullage emanating from our ancient universities. The waits' song survives intact only in the refrain of this carol: 'Past three o'clock and a cold frosty morning/Past three o'clock, good morrow masters all.'

A more genuine survival is the bellman's carol 'The moon shines bright' (cf. p. 68). Since it has an apparent reference to 'How that a life is but a flower' it is possible that Shakespeare had the song in mind when writing the final song in *As You Like It* (see p. 59). The combined weather forecast and time-signal of the bellman or waits, which started the Elizabethan day, is recorded in several quodlibets for voices and instruments by Richard Deering, Gibbons, Weelkes, Ravenscroft and anonymous composers, in which the cries of London are immortalized. They are mostly for five instruments accompanying various combinations of voices, although Whythorne's 'Buy new broom' and Weelkes' 'Cry' are for solo voice and four instruments, whereas the songs printed by Ravenscroft (1611) — such as 'A belmans song' — are for soloist and three accompanimental parts.

Rounds or catches based upon the cries were also common: some early examples are found in a King's College, Cambridge, manuscript dated 1580 (Rowe Lib. 1), and versions of these were later printed by Ravenscroft in various publications. Two rather later catches by Luffman Atterbury on the cry 'Hot cross buns', and by Nelham on 'Have you any work for a tinker' (BL Add. 29386), are so exquisite as to demand mention. Ravenscroft's publications were reprinted in facsimile in 1961 by the American Folklore

Society; the modern versions can thereby be checked. The cries by Gibbons and others are conveniently available in *MB* XXII.

Since the versions of the cries given in the various Jacobean settings are similar, but not identical (indeed, they can be conspicuously different on occasions), it seems likely that here we have a genuine record of London street-cries of Shakespearean times. These songs were not, of course, unique to London. Doubtless similar cries were heard in the Roman forum, when 'salt' meant almost the same thing as 'salary'; the cry 'strawberries ripe' features in a thirteenth-century Parisian composition; and a century later, a caccia by Zaccaria provides an Italian equivalent of the cries of London. Of the sizable number of this kind of composition, the English examples stand out, nonetheless, as the most elaborate and charming.

Joseph Addison's *The Spectator* of December 1711 opined that: 'There is nothing which more astonishes a Foreigner, and frights a Country Squire, than the *Cries of London.*' The ambuscade of pedlars' shouts in Gibbons' composition seems to bear out this impression of noisy streets and to echo the fifteenth-century poem (to which Lydgate's name is pseudepigraphically attached) entitled 'London Lykpenny':

> Then unto London I dyd me hye
> Of all the land it beareth the pryse:
> 'Hot peascodes', one began to crye
> 'Strabery rype' and 'cherryes in the ryse'
> One bad me come nere and by some spyce,
> Peper and saffaron they gan me bede,
> But for lack of mony I myght not spede

(cf. Robbins, 1959)

Gibbon's 'Cries' are perhaps the finest example of the genre. Although musically very different, this evocation of London life may be compared with Vaughan Williams' 'A London Symphony' — which incidentally records the cry 'Sweet lavender'. Gibbons' work is elaborately constructed, since it uses an In Nomine cantus firmus, whose long notes act as a ground-plan for the listener as he is taken on a musical journey of a London day. If this kaleidoscope of pedlars' songs records the letter of London street music, it seems also to breathe the very spirit of the early seventeenth-century city.

Gibbons begins with four somnolent chords suggestive of an early morning calm, soon to be shattered by the bellman's monotonous chant: 'God give you good morrow my masters;/past three o'clock; and a fair morning.' Without further ado, a mêlée of pedlars' cries bursts forth: 'New mussels, new lillywhite mussels' are early for sale, and so is a great variety of fish, together with vegetables and household articles. There is a comic skit on the town crier: he advertises the loss of a horse which 'halts down right behind, and is stark lame before; and was lost this thirtieth day of February.'

After the town crier has gone on his way, various commodities are offered for sale, including 'a barrel of samphire' — something long since vanished from the London streets. Pedlars of various trinkets of the kind summed up by Dowland in his song 'Fine knacks for ladies' sing next, but soon a more melancholy aspect of London life comes to the fore: 'Poor naked Bedlam' says 'Tom's a-cold' and asks for 'a small cut of thy bacon, or a piece of thy sow's side good Bess' ending with the rueful benediction 'God Almighty bless thy wits'. And it is not long before yet another beggar asks the passer-by to 'pity the poor women who lie cold and comfortless on the bare boards in the dark dungeon in great misery'. This scene, outside the women's prison, is the last one of the night, for the watchman returns, abjuring 'lanthorns and candlelight; hang out, maids for all night'. The reference is to the legal requirement to provide what amounted to street lighting. All of the voices join in singing, 'And so we make an end' to close the first part of this musical microcosm. At the second part of Gibbons' 'Cries', the In Nomine theme is begun afresh, over which is heard the tuneful song of the sausage-seller:

Ex. 21

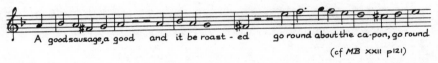

A good sausage, a good   and it be roast-ed   go round about the ca-pon, go round

(cf *MB* XXII p121)

The words are sung to almost, but not exactly, the same tune in Deering's 'City Cries'. Such concordances, as already noted, indicate that for the most part these snatches of melody were neither manufactured by the composers nor copied from each other, but are generally authentic records of the music of the streets. Certainly the next cry 'Oysters' is found elsewhere in catches and in cries, in much the same form:

Ex. 22i

New oy-sters, new!   Fresh plaice, fresh!   (ibid)

Ex. 22ii

1 New oy- - -sters, _____ new oy- - -

2 at a groat a peck, _____ at a groat a

3 Fetch us bread and wine that we may eat, let us lose no time with

(cf 'The oyster girl', Kennedy, 1975, no. 234)   (Ravenscroft, *Pammelia*)

It is interesting to note that various MSS of these pieces include the dialect forms 'firmenty' (for 'frumenty'), 'parsnips', and so forth, which are clearly an attempt to add to the air of authenticity. Doubtless different individual tradesmen had variant or even quite different songs: for example, Gibbons' tinker seems to have had a rather dull cry, whereas Weelkes records a distinctly more catchy tune:

Ex. 23

(cf *MB* XXII p108)

So, too, Deering's cooper is more adventurous than Gibbons'; whereas the latter intones a plain statement of his trade, the former prefaces his by a charming quatrain to the tune 'Heartsease':

Ex. 24

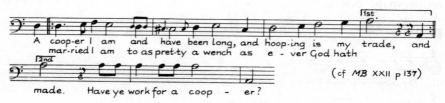

(cf *MB* XXII p 137)

Gibbons' coney-skin collector is also more matter-of-fact than Deering's, and an attempt by a scribe to insert the cry for 'Rosasolis' (a perfumed cordial) is also mundane; Deering's version of 'Rosasolis' is much more tuneful and its authenticity is attested in the *Fitzwilliam Virginal Book* (hencefor-ward *FWVB*) CXLIII. On the other hand 'Bread and meat for the poor pris'ners of the Marshalsea [the debtors' prison] for Christ Jesus' sake: bread and meat' is more heartrending in Gibbons' version than in Deering's. However, the next cry, that of the sweep, is virtually identical in both composer's versions: it is one of the most amusing cameos in the genre (next, perhaps, to that of 'Kindheart the toothdrawer' in Deering's 'City Cries'). The spelling of sweep as 'soop' seems to be intended to convey that sweeps were country bumpkins:

Ex. 25

Soop, chim-ney soop, soop, chimney soop, soop chim-ney soop misteress with a
soop derry derry derry soop; from the bottom to the top soop chimney soop;
then shall no soot fall in your porridge pot with a soop derry derry derry soop

(cf *MB* XXII pp124-5)

(cf. the folksong 'Sweep chim-nie sweep', Kennedy, 1975, no. 240)

The sweep is virtually the last character in Gibbons' composition, for soon the watchman is back, singing:

> Twelve o'clock
> look well to your lock
> your'fire and your light
> and so: goodnight.

Half a century later, the Great Fire was to prove how much London relied upon householders damping down their fires at night.

In common with other contemporary settings, Deering's includes several interesting cries not recorded by Gibbons, including a waterman's song, and a cry for 'oranges and lemons' recorded by an anonymous composer is clearly a relative of the 'Bells of St Clement's':

Ex. 26

O-ran-ges, o-ran-ges fine Seville oranges, Por-tin-gal oranges, fine Seville oranges;
le-mons and o-ran-ges I have to sell

(cf *MB* XXII pp 130-1)

Deering's setting was clearly worked over before being copied into his surviving MSS: his town crier's horse has a 'hole in her *ear*', (*arse* in other versions) and another polite anatomical change is made at the cry 'rosemary and bays', where the substituted 'bones' fails to rhyme:

> Tis good, tis good, to lay upon their bones
> which climbeth over walls to steal your plums
> so trim and trick
> that gentle is, yet very quick.

The solo song 'Buy new broom' by Whythorne is a literary and musical development on the 'broom' cry; the main outlines of the tune are attested, however, in Weelkes' 'Cries'. These, also for solo voice, end with the excruciating pun:

> White lettuce, white young lettuce
> Now let us sing:
> 'And so we make an end'; with Alleluia

This rich vocabulary of London cries finds its way, as we have seen, into various forms of music, especially rounds; and quotations are found in virginals music, in madrigals and lute-songs. Morley's lute-song (1600) 'Will ye buy a fine dog' (the second part of the lost 'What lack ye sir?') is a bawdy medley of cries similar in nature to those already described.

In plays and masques too, the cries are used as background colour to various dramatic situations. A whole scene of *The Winter's Tale* (IV, iii) is built around a variety of pedlars' songs and ballads, and the famous lyric 'Lawn as white as driven snow' is nothing but a series of these cries. John Wilson's *Cheerful Ayres and Ballads* (1689) includes a tune which may have been the version sung in the production of 1611. Wilson may have been the boy Jack Wilson, who seems to have sung 'Sigh no more ladies' in one of the early productions of *As You Like It*. Certainly he composed and arranged the music for *The Maske of Flowers* of 1613. Fletcher's *The Beggar's Bush* also has a scene centred, as in *The Winter's Tale*, about a pedlar's cries. His coney-skin seller, as in the setting recorded with music in D'Urfey's *Wit and Mirth* (1698), makes much play of the double meaning, common to many languages, of 'coney'.

Quite apart from the songs of the pedlars, the watchmen and criers, beggars and boatmen, the streets of London were full of the sounds of bells, for which the English had an extraordinary proclivity. Paul Hentzer, on a visit to Britain, wrote in 1598: 'The English . . . are vastly fond of great noises that fill the air, such as the firing of cannon, drums, and the ringing of bells, so that in London it is common for a number of them when drunk to go up into some belfry and ring the bells for hours together' (Rye, 1865, p. 111).

Although the noise may have seemed to the German visitor to be little short of a drunken cacophony, it is probable that what he heard was an early form of change-ringing, a peculiarly English pastime which was fully developed by the end of the seventeenth century.

The practical and magical properties of bells have been bound together for centuries, although nowadays the efficacy of a warning bell in the fog is more obvious than the possibility of a storm being dissipated by similar means. Yet, this kind of function was frequently alluded to on bell inscriptions (as witness that of 'Schiller's bell' in Münster, bearing the legend *vivos voco mortuos plango, fulgura frango*); the secular, superstitious and religious chimes combined to tell of war or victory, to ward off lightning, or to bid prayers for the dying and dead.

The merging of sacred and secular ringing customs (the belfry existed some distance apart from many early churches) is evident in the night curfew bell attributed to William the Conqueror which later became the Gabriel bell; and when the Angelus fell into desuetude, the secular use of the night bell came once again to the fore — in 1583 Queen Elizabeth ordained (or rather reaffirmed) that public houses should turn out their drinkers at curfew, a canonical hour still hallowed, by bells, according to the licensing laws of twentieth-century Britain. The knell of parting day also survives at Christ Church, Oxford, where Great Tom still rings 101 strokes to warn of what used to be lock-up time, even though the collegers greatly outnumber the 101 members provided for by its founder, and few of its present complement would take kindly to a nine o'clock curfew.

Tudor England, however, went early to bed; to rise, if only reasonably healthy and wise at dawn, beginning work when the Ave bell rang at five—or six in the winter months. Other bells would signal the beginning of the market (so that vendors could not 'forestall' each other), initiate the hiring of casual labour, or proclaim the commencement of the school day. Bell-ringing had countless functions, not least of which was to warn of danger, particularly war and conflagration.

Until recently the bells of fire engines retained the rhythm (short–short– long) of the Tudor fire bell, as captured in the opening of Morley's madrigal 'Fire, fire' (the first word being pronounced as a disyllable), or the well-known round 'London's burning' (in which, originally, the words were similarly pronounced).

The passing-bell and death knell, originating in the desire to ward off evil spirits, are well attested in literature and music. Executions were accompanied by the ballad 'Fortune my foe' whose mournful tune was intoned to the baleful burden of the passing-bell. Customs relating to the passing-bell differed widely: the sex or status of the person *in extremis* was identified by a code, commonly three bells for a man, two for a woman, one for a child. Each of these signals was often struck thrice (the sign for a man thus becoming the 'Nine tailors' [sc. tellers] made famous in detective fiction by Dorothy Sayers); or each signal might, in certain localities, be struck on three bells successively of descending pitch. The opening of 'Three blind mice' (there are many rounds similarly constructed upon the sounds of bells) may thus relate to the death of an infant — adding a further touch to the absurdity of the scene.

After the sex of the departing person had been identified, the bell was perhaps tolled every minute, or a three-bell toll was sometimes sounded. This latter figure is recorded in the lute part of 'O death rock me asleep' fancifully attributed to Ann Boleyn:

Ex. 27

(cf BL Add 15117 f 3ᵛ)

The passing-bell ceased when the soul had departed this life. In one of his *Meditations*, John Donne refers to the transition from passing-bell to the death knell when: 'The bell rings out, the pulse thereof is changed; the tolling was a faint and intermitting pulse, upon one side; this stronger, and argues a better life. His soule is gone out'. Donne is here referring to the practice of *ringing* (as opposed to *tolling* 'on one side' of the bell) the knell: the intermittent toll was succeeded by the quicker and louder ringing of the age of the deceased on the tenor bell. This was often succeeded (or preceded) by the identification of the sex, as before. The change of timbre between the passing-bell and death knell is also noted by Thomas Dekker in his *Lanthorne & Candlelight* (1608, xxii) and the three-note passing-bells and the knell of the tenor are taken up by Dowland in his song 'Go nightly cares' (1612).

A form of the 'winding bell' is commemorated in 'The burying of the dead' in some versions of Byrd's 'Battell'. A two-note knell is heard in the bass, as if from one bell-tower, while a six-note peal, as if from another, is heard against it. A similar figure is found in John Bull's 'Batell':

Ex. 28

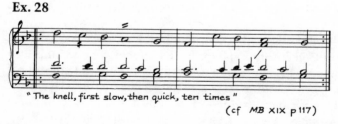

"The knell, first slow, then quick, ten times"

(cf MB XIX p 117)

This sequence of six bells was presumably rung muffled (the clappers being encased in leather). At New Year, the death of the old year was rung out on a muffled peal, the birth of New Year being welcomed in on 'open' bells. Similar customs prevailed at Christmas. The chime named 'Whittington' is essentially that of the six-bell burial peal quoted in D'Urfey's *Wit and Mirth* (1707, iii, p. 40), called 'alarum' in Bartlet's 'Surcharged with discontent':

Ex. 29

It is an intriguing coincidence that part of this chime is found in the round 'Turn again Whittington'. Legend has it that the young Dick paused on Highgate Hill for a last look at London, and heard Bow bells telling him to return. The round, however, originated as a waterman's song, which is appropriate enough in view of Whittington's supposed maritime adventures. In Ravenscroft's *Pammelia* (1609) the ending is 'row to thy leman', but John Hilton's *Catch that catch can* (1652) preserves the words as below: the first two lines were quoted earlier by Skelton in his *Bowge of Court* (printed 1568).

Ex. 30

Playford later substituted the word 'Whittington' for 'Norman' (a nautical term), presumably because of the uncanny resemblance between chime and catch. The six-bell chime was certainly known as 'Whittington' by 1640, since James Shirley's *Constant Maid* of that year refers to the 'Six bells in every steeple' which 'all go to the *city-tune* — *Turn again*, Whittington' (II, ii).

The ringing of large numbers of muffled bells could be used as a signal of danger, or war, whereas the 'open' ringing of a peal was associated with victory or other celebrations. Legend has it that Queen Elizabeth never passed the bells of Shoreditch without stopping to listen to them; at St Michael's, Cornhill, moreover, her procession happened to pass as the bells were ringing in a sequence of thirds, called 'Queens'; supposedly on account of this incident:

Ex. 31

The chimes of several of the London churches resembled, as the nursery rhyme tells us, the cry of 'oranges and lemons', as is confirmed by the tune quoted on p. 47. Sarah Cobbold has pointed out that several passages in the 'Euge bone' and 'Cantate' Masses of Tye and Sheppard resemble chimes of a similar nature (eg. those of Ex. 32) the significance of which is not yet clear.

The normal ring of six bells was soon enlarged to eight, which required a larger number of ringers. Although several chimed bells could be managed by one sexton, the new fashion of double-handed ringing required one man's skilled and undivided attention for each bell. It was now mounted on a wheel to which was attached a circumambient rope. The bell would ring once as the wheel revolved in one direction, and then again when it was allowed to travel in reverse. This two-stroke method gave rise to the elaborate and peculiarly English 'science' of change-ringing. John Jenkins' consort 'The sixe bells' (Oxford, Bodleian Mus. Sch. c 84) is an early representation of a ring of this kind (here each change is rung twice, once on each stroke):

Ex. 32

('The Sixe Bells' for violin, lyra viol, bass & harpsichord : Oxford Bodl Mus Sch c 84)

Others of Jenkins' consorts (eg. the 'Bell pavin' and the 'Five bell consorte') represent chimes, however, in which the bell was struck without involving the full use of the wheel.

Bells were frequently the subject of catches, which reflected the life of the times to a remarkable extent. Besides preserving bell-chimes and cries of London, psalm-tunes and folk melodies were also incorporated into rounds. The round is a perpetual canon, each successive voice beginning when another has reached the marshalling point, each subsequent line being sung in the same way. When all the voices have entered, the first returns to the beginning, and the sequence continues. The earlier method of ending the round was to determine beforehand the number of times each voice would sing the complete round; the singers, having completed the agreed number of repetitions, would then drop out one by one, thereby reversing the procedure of the start. The skilled composer had thus to take these events into account in order to make the melodic and harmonic texture satisfactory throughout the performance. The following example (from Ravenscroft's *Pammelia* of 1609) is based upon a Sternhold and Hopkins hymn tune (Ex. 33).

As can be seen a second verse is printed by Ravenscroft; since the words of the hymn were well known, additional stanzas could easily have been added by the singers: it is possible that after the first, subsequent verses were sung without repetition.

Later rounds were constructed so that the voices ceased, say after the first

Canons in the vnison. 3 Voc:

Ex. 33
48

Lord turne not away thy face from him that lieth proftrate,

.S.

lamenting fore his finnefull life before thy mercies gate, which gate

thou openeft wide to thofe that doe lament their finne, Shut not that gate

againft me Lord, but let me enter in.   O Lord *vt fupra*.

2 And call me not to mine accounts
how I haue liued here:
For then I know right well O Lord,
how vile I fhall appeare.
I need not to confeffe my life
I am fure thou canft tell,
What I haue beene, and what I am,
I know thou knoweft it well.

Transcription of the above

1   O   Lord, turn not a-way thy face from him that lieth prostrate

la - ment-ing sore his sin-ful life be-fore thy mer-cy's gate

which gate thou openest wide to those that do la-ment their sin

shut   not that gate against me Lord, but let me ent-er in

✱ misprinted in *Pammelia*

53

singer had completed the round three times and had reached the end of a line or a special pause note. The composition thus ended in harmony, rather than tailing off to a single voice. This advantage, however, was outweighed by a loss of contrapuntal interest, and the irregular interlocking phrase lengths of many of the earlier rounds was lost.

The earliest known round (called a *rota* in the source) is the famous thirteenth-century 'Sumer is icumen in'; however, the medieval rondellus was also, in effect, a round. The equivalent English word 'roundelay', forms part of the subtitle of Ravenscroft's publications of 1609, (eg. *Pammelia, Musicks Miscellanie. Or, Mixed Varietie of Pleasant Roundelayes, and delightfull Catches*), and the word is often found in poetry: the introduction to Drayton's *Poly-Olbion* (1613), for example, speaks of 'Shepheards . . . singing roundelaies'. It might seem far-fetched that the medieval rondellus should survive as rustic folk polyphony, but several instances of the pre-servation of medieval rondellus by oral tradition can be traced. The high art of an earlier age, though banished from the pages of written history, can survive with remarkable tenacity in this manner. This musical substrate has preserved instruments such as the rebec, shawm and hurdy-gurdy; and the ballate and madrigale of the Italian trecento turn up again in the sixteenth century, if only in name. As has been noted, one example of the caccia (the canonic trecento madrigal) consists of a tapestry of pedlars' cries inter-spersed with ribald comments; another caccia has a distant affinity with Morley's 'Fire, fire!'. In general, however, their subject was the hunt (the name caccia — 'chase' — being thus doubly appropriate); and the *double entendre* of what was being hunted, together with the significance of the weapons of the chase and the 'dying' of the quarry, was made more explicit in the ritornello ('turning round') at the end of the caccia. These features of the Italian trecento are echoed in seventeenth-century England to the extent that coincidence can hardly be envisaged, in spite of the lack of intermediate written evidence. The name of the seventeenth-century 'catch' (merely the alternative title for a humorous round), coupled with the fact that it was a canon, and that its subject was often 'hunting' of one sort and another strongly suggests a remarkable capacity for folk tradition to preserve archaic polyphonic devices.

It should not come as a surprise, therefore, that the catch 'What shall he have that killed the deer' mentioned by Shakespeare in *As You Like It* (IV, ii) apparently survived until 1652 when a version of it was printed by Hilton, or that the hunting catch (eg. 'Blow thy horn jolly hunter' in *Pammelia*) has an analogue of something like a century earlier (Ex. 34).

It seems likely that the tenor part of this setting was a popular tune which served both as the middle part of the refrain and as the melody for the verse; the latter is not given in the polyphonic source (BL Add. 31922), but appears in another MS (BL Roy. App. 58) as the tune (or tenor part — this MS is a sole surviving partbook) for the whole song. Here the two versions

Ex. 34

[REFRAIN]

Blow thy horn, hun ter, come blow thy horn on high! There is a doe in yonder wood, in

faith she will not die. Come blow J blow thy horn, hun-ter, come blow thy horn jolly hun — ter

[VERSE]

Sure this deer stricken is and yet she bleeds no whit She lay so fair, I could not miss, lord,

I was glad of it. Come blow thy horn, hun-ter, come blow thy horn jolly hun — ter Come

* and } in Add 31922
† now

[dal $, then Refrain]

(BL Add 31922 ff 39ᵛ-40 & Roy App 58 f 7; cf MB XVIII no. 35)

have been collated. What seems to have happened in several instances is that a popular, monophonic, song was converted from a straightforward strophic pattern into the more complex courtly carol, by the addition of a polyphonic refrain having the song tune as its tenor. It is probable that the final bars of the refrain of 'Blow thy horn, hunter' were sung at the end of each solo verse, as a link into the refrain proper. A *signum congruentiae* (see Ex. 33 — the same sign was used in rounds to denote the entry of successive voices) appears in many compositions of this kind in BL Add. 31922, an early Tudor source known as *King Henry VIII's MS* (printed in *MB* XVIII).

The suspicion that popular tunes were employed in *King Henry VIII's MS* is confirmed in songs such as 'You and I and Amyas' and 'Green growth the holly'. Here the polyphonic music of the refrain cannot be fitted to the verse, which has no music, since the metres differ too widely.

Ravenscroft's *Deuteromelia* (1609) was subtitled *or The Second part of Musicks melodie, or melodius Musicke. Of Pleasant Roundelaies; K. H. mirth, or Freemens Songs. And such delightfull Catches.* 'K. H.' is widely supposed to have been King Henry, and 'Freemens songs' is likely to be a corruption of 'Three men's songs'. The compositions which Ravenscroft prints under this heading are three-part songs of a very similar kind to those found in *King Henry VIII's MS*. The latter includes several rounds and canons, although most are of a courtly nature. One of its canonic pieces, however, entitled 'A Robin' (alluded to in *Twelfth Night* IV, ii), is apparently based on a well-known song tune, whose words also formed the basis of a poem by Wyatt (Ex. 35).

The use of snatches of popular tune in musical compositions, or to provide allusions in plays, was widespread; one of Ravenscroft's rounds (*Pammelia* no. 30) is on a two-note bell-ground, and is a quodlibet of a waterman's song

Ex. 35

(BL Add 31922 ff 53ᵛ-54; cf *MB* XVIII no.49)

and several folk songs, including 'Shall I go walk the woods so wild' which turns up again in Dowland's 'Can she excuse my wrongs'. 'The leaves be green' was also a popular ground — a ground being an ostinato usually, but not necessarily, found in the bass — and is found as the basis of several compositions called 'Brownings', which were founded on 'The leaves be green', one of which is an extended and ironic quodlibet by William Cobbold (printed in *MB* XXII, no. 71) beginning 'New fashions now do bear the sway'. However, by the time of Hilton (1652) who used 'The leaves be green' in an earthy round commencing 'Here is an old ground', it was clearly old-fashioned.

Imitations of bells were popular as grounds—'The great bells of Osney', 'Let's have a peal' being well-known examples of rounds based on peals, some of which merely employ the two-note 'ting tang' of the clock. The 'bome bome' of a single tenor bell is called for in Ravenscroft's 'Ut re mi' (*Pammelia* no. 71); the instruction for the voice having the tenor is 'The fourth must sing the Fa burthen'. Since the note is *F* (Fa) there is a double pun: burthen means a bass part, often of a somewhat primitive nature, whereas

> *Enter Ferdinand & Ariel, inuisible playing & singing.*
> *Ariel* Song. *Come vnto these yellow sands,*
> *and then take hands:*
> *Curtsied when you haue, and kist*
> *the wilde waues whist:*
> *Foote it featly heere, and there, and sweete Sprights beare*
> *the burthen.* . Burthen disperfedly.
> *Harke, harke, bowgh wawgh: the watch-Dogges barke,*
> *bowgh-wawgh.*
> Ar. *Hark, hark, I heare, the straine of strutting Chanticlere*
> *cry cockadidle-dowe.*
> Fer. Where shold this Musick be? I'th aire, or th'earth?
> It founds no more: and sure it waytes vpon
> Some God 'oth'Iland, sitting on a banke,
> Weeping againe the King my Fathers wracke.
> This Musicke crept by me vpon the waters,
> Allaying both their fury, and my paffion
> With it's sweet ayre: thence I haue follow'd it
> (Or it hath drawne me rather) but tis gone.
> No, it begins againe.
> *Ariell* Song. *Full fadom fiue thy Father lies,*
> *Of his bones are Corrall made:*
> *Those are pearles that were his eies,*
> *Nothing of him that doth fade,*
> *But doth suffer a Sea-change*
> *Into something rich, & strange:*
> *Sea-Nimphs hourly ring his knell.*
>   Burthen: ding dong.
> *Harke now I heare them, ding-dong bell.*
> Fer. The Ditty do's remember my drown'd father,
> This is no mortall busines, nor no found

Fig. 6 The Tempest, Act I, scene ii (First Folio edition, page 5)

the professional singer's technique of faburden was likely to be beyond the technique of most singers of rounds.

Unfortunately, the word 'burden' or 'burthen' is frequently misconstrued as the equivalent of 'refrain': its correct meaning is simply a bass part, especially an insistent formula of the 'ground' type. When Shakespeare says 'the rest shall bear the burthen', he is using a pun on the word which goes back at least to Chaucer: the burthen 'bowgh waw' in 'Come unto these yellow sands' (*The Tempest* I, ii) was an obbligato barking (the stage dir..ction is 'dispersedly'). In the same scene the burthen 'ding dong' to 'Full fathom five' should be an insistent death knell, similar to the 'bome bome' of Ravenscroft, or the two or three-note equivalents discussed earlier.

The popularity of the 'ding dong bell' burden gives a clue to the music of 'Tell me where is fancy bred' (*The Merchant of Venice* III, ii). The singer enjoins 'Let us all ring fancy's knell' and begins the 'ding dong bell' taken up by the company. In all probability the whole song — not merely the knell — was built on a two- or three-note formula, whose monotonous burden would have given added point to the rhymes *bred, head, nourishèd*, perhaps sung in such a way as to convey a heavy hint to Bassano to open the casket of *lead*.

The round 'What shall he have that killed the deer' has already been mentioned; Shakespeare's direction (*As You Like It* IV, ii) that 'The rest shall bear this burthen' implies that the concluding lines 'Take thou no scorn . . .' are sung as a bass to the Foresters' song, a somewhat un-orthodox method of singing a round.

The interpretation of the word 'burthen' as a refrain would falsify Shakespeare's intentions, since a burthen or burden is sung simultaneously with the verse, whereas a refrain is sung consecutively: the correct word for a refrain (in Middle- and Elizabethan English) was 'foot'. Indeed, a whole scene of an otherwise unremarkable comedy by Wager entitled *The Longer Thou Livest* (registered in 1569) introduced a fool called Moras, 'synging the foote of many songs, as fooles were wont'. His lines then consist of a string of refrains, many of which are well-known songs and catches: 'Robin lend to me thy bow', 'By a bank as I lay', 'Come o'er the bourne, Bessie', and so forth.

The tracing of these allusions to popular snatches is often a difficult matter. One of the most intriguing concerns a reference in *Henry V* (IV, iv) to the tune 'Calen o custare me'. The spelling of the printed texts ('Calmie custare me') and of the musical sources which have the tune, is clearly corrupt. *A Handfull of Pleasant Delites* of 1584 has 'A Sonet of a lover in praise of his lady, to Calen o custare, sung at everie line's end'. A bowdlerized version of the tune is found in the *FWVB* (CLVII), but a more authentic intabulation of the tune is found bound into *Ballet's Lute Book* (Dublin, Trinity College D. 1.21/ii), dating from the end of the sixteenth century, an important source of ballad tunes and other popular music:

Ex. 36

The words have long been suspected to be Irish, the 'Calen' obviously being equivalent to 'Colleen', an anglicizing of *Cailín*, a girl; but it was not until half a century ago that a proper identification was made when Murphy (1939, pp. 125–9) noted a quotation from a popular song in a seventeenth-century Fermanagh poem, which cites the title as *Cailín Ó chois tSiúre [mé]* (I am a girl from the banks of the river Suir). References to this tune are found in fifteen or more plays of the period.

The circulation of popular tunes was, of course, oral; but new and topical words were printed on ballad sheets (the first appears to have been one by Skelton on the battle of Flodden in 1515) and hawked about by ballad mongers. Shakespeare's portrait of Autolycus as an all-purpose pedlar shows him as a more successful pickpocket than sheet seller: in *The Winter's Tale* (IV, ii/iii) he fails to sell any ballads to the shepherds who are 'three-man song-men, all' and have 'one puritan amongst them, and he sings Psalmes to hornepipes'. Later (IV, iii/iv) he has more success with his 'delicate burthens of Dildo's and Fadings: "Jump-her, and thump-her"', to which a maid might well answer 'Whoop, doe me no harme good man' (cf. pp. 64 and 123):

Ex. 37

Whoop, do me no harm good— man
(cf Corkine, 1610)

Popular songs were a large part of the musical culture of the common folk, as playwrights were well aware, inserting references to them, or employing them as songs, at strategic intervals. Though the gallery may have laughed at the Latin tags, the dances, ballads and catches were the Vergil of the groundlings, whose taste was more for 'a Iigge or a tale of Baudry'.

The threads of musical allusion running through *The Tempest, Twelfth Night* and *As you Like It* would have been appreciated by the whole audience, who would have known the catch: 'Hold thy peace, I prithee hold they peace/Thou knave' (Ravenscroft *Deuteromelia* no. 10: see *Twelfth Night* II, ii). His audience would also know the 'Carrol they began that houre/ how that a life was but a flower' (*As You Like It* V, iii); but only comparatively few would have known what Orsino (*Twelfth Night* I, i) meant by a 'dying fall' or would have been able to master the intricate rhythms of Morley's setting (1600) of 'It was a lover and his lass' (*As You Like It* V, iii).

In Morley's *Consort Lessons* of 1599 is found, amongst other Shakespearean tunes, a setting of 'O mistress mine' (*Twelfth Night*). The *Lessons* were dedicated to the City waits, reminding us that they would have supplied the music for the more lavish stage productions. Morley's pieces are scored for a distinctive mixed consort which was employed at wedding celebrations, played to Queen Elizabeth on her 'progresses' and used to accompany sacred songs. This combination of lute, bandora, cittern, treble and bass viol and (transverse) flute seems to have become extraordinarily popular, to judge by the collections, compiled by Rosseter and others, which appeared in manuscript and print round about the turn of the century. There is more than a suspicion that Morley had some help in arranging the parts for plucked instruments: his *First Booke of Ayres* (1600) shows a very awkward understanding of the lute. The surviving items of his *Consort Lessons* of a year earlier, however, show no such shortcomings: it is possible that they were edited and improved by the dedicatees, the City waits.

The waits would also have provided the 'Musicke of the Hoboyes' and 'Loud Musicke' of *Anthony and Cleopatra* and many other plays, together with the various trumpet flourishes and 'alarums' of that play. Typical trumpet calls of the period may be seen in Byrd's 'Battle' piece already cited; as for the drums, the same marches would have served for a battlefield march, as called for in *King Henry VI Part 1*, III, iii ('*Here sound an English March*', followed by a French March) or for the funeral march as at the end of *King Lear* or *Hamlet*. The distinction was probably only that the funerary drums (like the passing-bell peals) were muffled:

Ex. 38

'The March of Footmen'

(cf *MB* XXVIII p175)

The signals for 'Alarum', 'Parley', 'Retreat' and 'Excursions' were often merely performed by drummers and fifers; and although the trumpet was used increasingly for this purpose, its sounds were standardized only comparatively recently, in this century. The distinction between 'Tucket' and 'Sennet', both of which are mentioned by Shakespeare, seems to have caused some difficulty to commentators. 'Tucket' is actually the Italian Toccata, (an onomatopoeic word, which incidentally has nothing to do with *toccare*) and means a long drawn out fanfare (a 'flourish' being less considerable). The 'Sennet', on the other hand, is a Sonata which is more complex musically, and might indeed be for more than one instrument.

This distinction is made clear in an early trumpet manual by Fantini published in 1638, entitled *Modo per imperare a sonare di Tromba*.

The 'Soft Musicke' called for in various plays would indicate instruments other than the trumpets and hoboyes, while 'Solemne Musicke' implies the organ: 'Solemne and strange musicke' (*The Tempest* III, iii) uses the word 'strange' in the sense of foreign and exotic. (For further references to Shakespearean music, see especially Sternfeld, 1963; 1971 and s.v. 'Shakespeare' in the *New Grove*.)

The waits bridged the gap between popular and more learned music, playing both in the playhouse and in the street, at court and at weddings. Most of the street musicians were, however, the 'pettifoggers of music' condemned by Whythorne, the 'cantabanqui' vilified by Puttenham. These would scratch a tune on a fiddle, or perhaps play on pipe and drum, hoping to initiate a tavern dance and earn a few groats for their pains. Most dance music which comes down to us from the period is of course stylized, as for example the elegant pavans and galliards of the virginalists. In the written sources, even the crudest dance music — consciously imitating that of the itinerant minstrel — is probably a good deal more polished than that of the village strummer. The minstrel's music was often constructed on a crude harmonic skeleton, which fleshed out in a lute, virginal, or even a treble and bass fiddle (see Figure 7) could provide quite varied music.

Fig. 7 Fiddlers at a tavern (from *The Two Fervent Lovers*, British Library, Roxburghe Ballads I.417)

The simplest harmonic skeleton was the tonic–dominant 'Dump' formula, which possibly took on its funereal meaning by being associated with one of the many varieties of death knell. The figure is found in 'My lady careys Dompe' (BL Roy. App. 58) and many other instrumental pieces of the period. This harmonic kernel could be expanded in countless ways, from the few simple chords of the anonymous 'Watkins Ale' (*FWVB* CLXXX) or Bull's 'Bonny Peg O' Ramsey' (*MB* XIX no. 75) and several 'Lavolta' settings, to the more complex grounds in vogue both in England and the Continent.

Using capital letters to denote major $\frac{5}{3}$ chords and small letters for minor $\frac{5}{3}$ chords, one common formula can be represented thus:

$$\| : g \: D \: g \: F : \| \: g \: D \: G$$

The tonic–dominant kernel is identified by the slurs. This sequence is the basis for the 'Spanish pavan' and its probable parent 'La folia'. Bull's setting of the 'Spanish pavan' (*MB* XIX no. 76) shows how the formula may be varied by the addition and subtraction of chords.

A reordering of the chord sequence above gives rise to the following pattern:

$$\| : g \: F \: g \: \overset{d}{D} : \| \: g$$

This is the harmonic skeleton for King Henry VIII's 'Pastime, with good company' (based on a song found in several continental collections — see Ward, 1960). Several other songs in *King Henry VIII's MS* appear to have been modelled upon this bass or upon the closely related Romanesca and Passamezzo antico basses: notable examples are Cornish's canonic arrangement of 'A robin' and his 'You and I and Amyas'.

The Romanesca generally consisted of the following chord sequence (which, like the others under discussion, may of course be transposed):

$$\| : B\flat \: F \: g \: D : \| \: g$$

The four-chord sequence could also be played in reverse, and chords could be omitted and added making for endless possibilities: one of several examples of the loose employment of the formula is found in the first strain of Byrd's 'Alman' (*MB* XXVIII no. 89). The Romanesca was combined with the patterns discussed earlier, for example in the later Folia, as used by Corelli. Similarly, the Passemezzo antico employed the Romanesca, which was tonally ambivalent, within a wholly minor formula:

$$\| : g \: F \: g \: \overset{d}{D} : \| \: B\flat \: F \: g \: D \: \| \: g$$

In this ground, which was particularly popular in England, the first strain was often repeated. A large number of keyboard dances (eg. pavans and galliards) were founded upon it, and it provided the bass for many songs and ballads:

Ex. 39

   (i)   'Fortune my foe' (Dublin, Trinity College D.1.21/ii — many collations, conflated)
   (ii) 'Greensleeves' (Dublin, Trinity College D.1.21/ii — many collations, conflated)
 (iii) 'Quodling's delight' (Set by Farnaby, *FWVB* CXIV.)
 (iv) 'Robin Hood' (Conflated between Ravenscroft *Pammelia* Cambridge UL Dd. 9.
     33 etc.)

The Passamezzo moderno, was in a major key, involving the *B natural* (*B
quadrata* in Italian — hence the name 'quadran' in England). Although having
some relationship with the Passamezzo antico, it can be seen as an extension
of the Bergomask bass G C D G, on which 'The Hunt's up' (Touchstone's 'O
Sweet Oliver' quoted in *As you like it* III, ii, and the basis of various settings of
'The King's Hunt') and many other tunes such as 'Up tails all' were founded.
Arbeau's 'Branle d'Official' (*Orchésographie*, 1589) and his 'Canaries'
(mentioned in *Love's Labour Lost* III i and *All's well* II i) were also founded
upon the Bergomask, which itself is specified in *A Midsummer Night's Dream*
(Vi). The 'quadran' or 'Passamezzo moderno had the following basis:

$$\|: G\ C\ G\ D :\| G$$

This ground gave rise to a large variety of songs and dances, of which a few may be seen in the following example:

Ex. 40

(i) 'Malt's come down' (Ravenscroft, *Pammelia*; also set by 'Byrd' in *FWVB* CL)
(ii) 'Jhon come kiss me now' (set by Byrd — *FWVB* X)
(iii) *Danse de bouffons* (cf. also *Danse de chevaux* etc.) — Arbeau *Orchésographie* 1589.
(iv) 'Whoop do me no harm' (cf. Corkine, 1610; set by Gibbons etc.)

An important key variant of the Romanesca sequence was associated with the chacona in Spain and the gagliarda in Italy (also known as the Aria, or Ballo, de Granduca).

ie. transposed ‖· B♭ F g d ·‖ E♭ F ‖ B♭
              ‖· G D e b ·‖ C D ‖ G

This pattern, together with the 'quadran' sequence, provided the framework of the 'Frog galliard' to which Dowland wrote his song 'Now O, now I needs must part':

Ex. 41

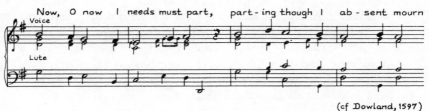

(cf Dowland, 1597)

The multiplicity of songs and dances, written to popular tunes and grounds, is commented upon in Webbe's *Discourse of English Poetry* (1586):

> Neither is there anie time or stroke which may be sung or plaide on instruments, which hath not some poetical ditties framed according to the numbers thereof, some Rogero, some to Trenchmore, to downe right Squire, to Galliardes, to Pauines, to Iygges, to Brawls, to all manner of tunes which euerie Fidler knows better then myself.

The persistence of the cruder ground bass formulas was partly due to their use by the hack dance musicians and partly to the challenge which they offered to more sophisticated composers. In their more elegant guises they were remarkably popular for several centuries: it is worth mentioning in passing that derivatives of the Romanesca bass remained in use throughout the Baroque period, being employed as a chaconne bass by Purcell, Handel and Bach (in the 'Goldberg Variations'). In a minor key variant, the sequence was also used by Purcell many times — such as in his well-known 'Chacony' for strings — and a close relative of the 'Frog galliard' was a favourite formula of Corelli and Handel. In all of these cases, however, an important modification is evident, which exemplifies a significant difference between Baroque and Renaissance harmony: all of the Baroque basses use a leading-note $^6_3$ chord (rather than the dominant) as the second element of the sequence and an additional $^6_3$ chord elsewhere; hence the Renaissance progression, with its emphasis on $^5_3$ chords, is made smoother in the Baroque equivalent:

Ex. 42

The grounds of the fiddlers allowed the common folk to imitate, at a distance, the dances of the court, just as the country imitated court manners and clothing. By the time this happened (this was Malvolio's mistake) such fashions meanwhile were decidedly *démodées* at court:

> All manners of attire came first into the City and Countrey from the court, which, being once received by the common people, and by very Stage-players them selves, the Courtiers justly cast off, and take new fashions (though somewhat too curiously); and whosoever weares the old, men looke upon him as a picture in Arras hangings. . . . In like sort, many daunces and measures are used in Court, but when they come to be vulgar and to be used upon very stages, Courtiers and Gentlemen think them uncomely to be used, yet is it no r[e]proach to any man who formerly had skill therein.
>
> (Fynes Moryson, *An itinerary* . . . 1617, I, p. 199)

The 'country bumpkin' atmosphere is coyly portrayed in Deering's 'Country Cries' (*MB XXII*, no. 70) a bucolic equivalent of his 'City Cries'. The composition has only an incidental interest: for its use of *col legno* ('drum with the back-side of the bowe') in imitation of bees; for its whistled quotation of the country dance 'The shaking of the sheets'; the bells ringing 'harvest home'; and for the cries of the hunters. Ravenscroft's 'Country Pastimes' printed in *Melismata* (1611) are far more interesting, including 'There were three ravens', 'It was a frogge in the well' and others, in addition to the well-known 'Wooing song' of the Kent yeoman's son. These were the kind of three-men's songs mentioned in *The Winter's Tale* (IV ii–iii). In *Pammelia* (1609) Ravenscroft had already printed 'A round of three Country dances in one' including 'Robin Hood', 'The crampe' and 'Tomboy Tom'. In a later publication (*Briefe Discourse*, 1614) Ravenscroft printed 'A hunting song' by Edward Pierce (or Pearce) which has a splendid imitation of the hunting horns and the dogs:

Ex. 43

Gervase Markham, in his *Countrey Contentments* (1611, I, p. 7) advised:

If you would have your Kennell for sweetness of cry, then you must compound it of some large dogges that have deepe solempe mouthes and are swift in spending, which must as it were beare the base in the consort, then a double number of roaring, and loud ringing mouthes which must beare the counter-tenor, then som hollow plain sweete mouthes which must bear the meane or middle part: and so with these three parts of musique you shall make your cry perfect . . . and you shall understand that this composition is best to be made of the swiftest and largest deep-mouthed dog, the slowest middle sizd dog, and the shortest legd slender dog, and if amongst these you cast in a couple or two of small slinging Beagles, which as small trebles may warble amongst them: the cry will bee a great deale the sweeter . . .

Cobbold's *New Fashions* (*MB* XXII no. 71) includes several country dances, though the guise is the polyphony of the waits, rather than the cruder minstrelsy of the itinerant fiddler.

As already noted, the waits to some extent bridged the social gap between the classes. Similarly, becoming a chorister or a Gentleman of the Chapel Royal was a method of climbing up the social ladder. The latter, however, were perfectly capable of slipping a rung or two in the estimation of at least one critic:

The Common Singing-men in Cathedrall Churches are a bad Society, and yet a Company of good Fellowes, that roare deep in the Quire, deeper in the Taverne. [Sainliens' musician regarded this as a necessary professional qualification] . . . Their pastime or recreation is prayers, their exercise drinking, yet herein so religiously addicted that they serve God oftest when they are drunke . . . Their skill in melody makes them the better companions abroad, and their Anthemes abler to sing Catches.
(Earle, 1628, p. 32)

The fashion for catches persisted into the eighteenth century, when the catch clubs merged into the glee clubs. Folk songs and ballads, many of which may be traced to Tudor times, also often led long and healthy lives — 'Greensleeves' is an obvious example, and 'Quodling's delight' survives as 'The oak and the ash'; similarly the ballad carol 'God rest you merry, gentlemen', found in a garbled sixteenth- or seventeenth-century version ('Sit yow merry gentlemen') in Oxford Bodleian Eng. poet. b 5, is nothing but a Chaucerian ballade. The waits' wassail at the end of the anonymous cry printed in *MB* XXII no. 68 strongly resembles the Somerset version recorded by Cecil Sharp in 1903 (see Karpeles, 1974 no. 373 D). Tunes from metrical psalters, too, passed into the music of the common people; they survived, albeit in bowdlerized form, into the age of Thomas Hardy who described the accompaniment of psalm-tunes by a 'gallery band' — a curious survival of the waits — in several novels. *Under the Greenwood Tree* records the continued use of 'Remember thou, O man' first printed by Ravenscroft in 1611: as with the 'Bellmans carol' which has also remained popular in various versions, this tune was based upon the Passamezzo, the same ground which fathered Ravenscroft's 'We be soldiers three', the folk ballads 'I am the Duke of Norfolk', 'Paul's steeple', 'Oak and the ash' and of course 'Greensleeves'.

Thus, the music of the Tudor people lived on in the musical substrate through catch and glee, psalm and hymn-tune, cries, dances, chimes, hanging-tunes and nursery rhymes, to reappear and perhaps to perish in the present century. Sadly there is today a divergence, even opposition, of cultures; but the Tudor age saw an unselfconscious confluence of popular and learned heritages. This coexistence is witnessed in the plays of Shakespeare, with their hundred or so songs and something like four hundred other musical directions and allusions: it was, *pace* Puttenham, the 'small and popular musickes' which gave birth to Gibbons' 'Cries of London' and many other compositions which allow a remarkable glimpse into the life and times of the sixteenth- and early seventeenth-century citizens.

CHAPTER 4

Private Musick

A song in the *Fayrfax MS* entreats the King: 'Enforce yourself as Goddis knyght/To strenkyth your comyns in ther ryght' (cf. *MB* XXXVI, no. 67). While Henry VII 'strengthened the commons in their right', music and poetry flourished under the welcome stability brought about by the union of the rival Lancastrian and Yorkist houses. The *Fayrfax MS* indeed celebrates the end of the Wars of the Roses in a lyric having the refrain 'O rote of trouth, o princess to my pay'. (cf. *MB* XXXVI no. 46). The song enquires what is the most fragrant and colourful flower, and rehearses various claims in a somewhat conventional list of marjoram, lavender and columbine, the primrose, violet and daisy, 'gelofyr' (gillyflower — a clove-scented pink still found in some country gardens), rosemary, camomile, borage and savoury. But above all these herbs and flowers, the rose is 'This fayre fressh floure full of beaute' and as to its colour, the poet diplomatically disposes his favours equally: 'I love the rose, both red and white.'

The relationship of the manuscript with the family of the composer Fayrfax is obvious, but whether or not he was its copyist is obscure. He was made a Doctor of Music in 1504, but since this title does not occur in connection with the items bearing his name, the songbook must be earlier, perhaps dating from about the turn of the century. The songs and carols found in this source display a complex musical style, coupled with studiedly rhetorical lyrics. The medieval diction and elaborate word-play of Lydgate still pervades, and the highly ornamented melodic style of its luxuriantly long passion carols is not far removed from that of Guillaume de Machaut. The unity of words and music is thus false, for each element goes its own way; this divergence had taken place in the fourteenth century when Deschamps lauded, as *musique naturelle*, poetry having its own Miltonic music and which was sufficient unto itself. Deschamps considered *musique artificièle*, in which words were married to music in a more or less equal partnership, to be inferior; and this unity disappeared from the fifteenth-century courtly lyric, to survive only in popular songs. In the sixteenth century a return to a simpler diction was urged (if somewhat eccentrically) by Skelton, and was eventually brought about by the mid century: at the same time, the revival of the influence of popular music moved the music of the courtly songs in the direction of simplicity. This can be seen in the largely secular songs and carols of *King Henry VIII's MS* (*MB* XVIII) which are set in a more pithy and four-square strophic style. Richard Pygott's 'Quid petis, O fili' (the only piece in *King Henry VIII's MS* with sacred words) is remarkable in that its musical style moves one step further, prefiguring the later madrigalian techniques of highly organized imitation matched by a concomitant use of characteristic verbal repetition.

Ritson's MS (printed in part in *MB* IV and partly in *MB* XXXVI) straddles the time of the two Henrys, and of the two sources already noted. Its contents probably date from 1480 to 1530 and include paraliturgical carols with sacred words in a more archaic and chordal style than is found in the passion carols of the *Fayrfax MS* — those of *Ritson's MS* may well have been used in church, whereas those of the *Fayrfax MS* appear to be purely domestic devotional music. *Ritson's MS* also contains compositions in a Burgundian ballade style together with racy secular songs and carols of the less melismatic kind found in *King Henry VIII's MS*. The songs and carols of *Ritson's MS* appear to have been copied somewhat incompetently, which suggests that a professional repertory was later added to by an amateur scribe. The *Fayrfax* (BL Add. 5465) and *King Henry VIII* (BL Add. 31922) manuscripts are courtly both in origin and destination, whereas *Ritson's MS* (BL Add. 5665) appears to be a provincial collection of courtly and west country music representing the repertory of a Devon country house. All three MSS have been admirably edited by John Stevens in the volumes of *MB* already mentioned, who has also explored the whole background of the Tudor lyric in his invaluable book *Music and Poetry in the Early Tudor Court* (1961).

Although the *Fayrfax MS* contains several political and occasional pieces referring to events in the reign of Henry VIII, *King Henry VIII's MS*, presents a far more vivid picture of courtly music making, reflecting the musical taste of the second decade of the sixteenth century. The songbook is a miscellany of canons, 'threemen's songs' and instrumental consorts, some of which were composed by the king himself — which emanated directly from his court and provide an invaluable record of his musical taste.

Henry VIII's prowess as a composer has often been exaggerated, partly because of the romantic view of King Hal espoused by former historians of music, and partly because his subjects were doubtless obliged to be generous in their estimate of the king's abilities. The 'Service' which he is supposed to have composed for his chapel, mentioned by Peacham (1622, p. 99) no longer survives; if works of this kind ever existed, their musical worth is not likely to be much greater than those which survive in the manuscript in question. Leaving aside a few barely competent parts added to the work of previous composers, the king's musical vocabulary seems to have been decidedly limited. The famous 'Pastime with good company' starts off with exactly the same phrase as many of his other compositions, and in any case the tune seems to have been borrowed from a French theatrical chanson, 'De mon triste et desplaisir'. But although the musical interest of Henry's efforts is small, the words which he and the court composers set are an interesting testimony to the prevailing atmosphere in his household during these years. True, there are many ribald 'forester' songs, and indeed at least one pageant involved the representation of six foresters who blew their horns 'when the pageaunt rested before the Quene' (Stevens, 1961, p. 249). But the tone of most of the songs is only lightly ribald; the lusty songs by the same composers in the only slightly earlier *Fayrfax MS* are markedly different. In the court of Henry and his newly wed Catherine, the extremes of amorous and divine sentiments seem to have been set aside, and were not to return until the days of Anne Boleyn.

Instead, *King Henry VIII's MS* reflects the pomp and revelry of the early years of his reign. The New Year celebrations of 1511, when the birth of Henry's son was much in the news, seem to have been concluded thus:

> Adew, adew, le company
> I trust we shall mete oftener.
> Vive le Katerine et noble Henry!
> Vive le prince, le infant rosary!
>
> (no. 68)

Later songs in the book speak of Henry's campaigns against the French:

> England be glad! Pluk up thy lusty hart!
> Help now thi kyng, and take his part!
> Ageynst the Frenchmen in the feld to fyght
> In the quarell of the church and in the ryght,
> With spers and sheldys on goodly horsys lyght,
> Bowys and arows to put them all to flyght:
>
> (no. 96)

and this three-part round:

> Pray we to God that all may gyde
> That for our kyng so to provid,
> To send hym power to hys corage
> He may acheffe this gret viage:
> Now let us syng this rownd all thre;
> Sent George, graunt hym the victory!
>
> (no. 97)

The satirical tone of many of the songs of the *Fayrfax MS* is replaced by this artificial chivalry; and gone, for a few years, is the ale-swilling vulgarity of

71

Cornish's 'Hoyda, jolly rutterkin' which contrasts so vividly with the poignant passion carols by the same composer.

Cornish succeeded William Newark as Master of the Children of the Chapel Royal in 1509. In this post he would have been responsible for many of the revels which occupied courtly life at the time: several of the songs in the collections under discussion were doubtless sung at these 'devisings'. His association with the poet Skelton, the implacable critic of Wolsey, possibly resulted in some collaboration from time to time, but Skelton's poetical contribution to settings of the period is often grossly exaggerated; thus Cornish's supposed involvement in treasonable satire is extremely dubious. Nonetheless, a questionable incident brought Cornish to the Fleet prison in 1504. There he wrote *A treatise betwene Trouth and Enformation*, which is incidentally remarkable for its use of musical terminology. According to this long poetic tract, his imprisonment was due to false witness. At all events, he was soon released.

Fig. 8 Bass part of a partsong by John Gwynneth (from *XX Songes*, 1530)

In 1513 Cornish journeyed to France with the Chapel Royal, winning great acclaim for himself through its singing, and in 1520 at the Field of the Cloth of Gold the Chapel again performed on French soil with great splendour (see Anglo, 1969). Fayrfax, from St Alban's Abbey, John Browne (apparently an Oxford composer) and Richard Davy (from Magdalen College, Oxford) are the outstanding colleagues of Cornish; ample testimony to their ability is found in the elaborate antiphons, Magnificats and other music which they wrote for the church, and in the carols and similar pieces found in the songbooks. But the most versatile of these composers was undoubtedly Cornish himself. Several of his major compositions (including Masses — see Harrison, 1958) have perished, and others are fragmentary. Among the compositions known to have been lost are a Pater noster and the carol 'Pleasure it is', both printed in the *XX Songes* of 1530, of which only the mutilated bass part survives. What does remain, however, gives the impression that Cornish often had virtuoso singers in mind:

Ex. 44

(cf *MB* XVIII no. 38)

The carols of the *Fayrfax MS* are mostly through-set, each verse having different music. Those of the *King Henry VIII's MS* are strophic: in some cases, moreover, the same melodic material does duty for both the verse and refrain. As noted in the previous chapter, the modern use of the word 'burden' to indicate the refrain is both misleading and anachronistic; the relationship with other refrain forms is obscured by giving currency to a word which was used in a very different sense in the fifteenth and sixteenth centuries.

The carol, together with the rondeau, virelai and ballade, began as a dance. Since these dance songs were extremely popular, the Franciscans took over the tunes for their own purposes, substituting loftier Latin sentiments for what were often lascivious vernacular texts. The power of this music was not so easily tamed, however, for although dances soon evolved into static songs, and although now clothed in respectable Latinity, their association with pagan festivals such as that of the mid-winter solstice persisted. Thus these songs became embedded in the liturgy, particularly at Christmas, when the Church found it hard to resist the pressures of the old customs, and so gave way to such festivities as the Feast of Fools, the Boy Bishop, and so forth. As Harrison (1958) has shown, carols were frequently used as Benedicamus substitutes, hence the frequent occurrence of the phrase *Deo gratias*. Occasionally the tables were turned, and ungodly 'goliardic' skits on the church carols artificially restored the genre to the secular sphere; but the earlier carol had not been banished entirely: as with other forms such as the ballade, it lingered on in the folk memory.

The paraliturgical carols, even the late examples found in *Ritson's MS*, affected a fairly simple chordal style, and so were not wholly divorced from the simplicity of the folk carol. This was because it had proceeded on different lines of development to the other 'fixed forms'. The fourteenth-century rondeau and ballade (and to a more modified extent, the virelai) were absolutely removed from their rustic origins; the courtly rondeaux and ballades of the age of Chaucer and Machaut were exceedingly complex, both musically and verbally, to the extent that the two elements eventually became divorced at the time of Deschamps. One of Chaucer's ballades, 'Hide Absalom' in the *Legende of Good Women*, was intended to be sung 'as it were in carole-wyse'. But in general the ballade degenerated into the narrative ballad, eventually shedding its refrain.

73

The distinction between the fixed forms became blurred as time passed. Originally their identity was a question of dance-steps and musical structure; the formal characteristics recognizable in the earliest recorded musical sources, however, concern the inter-relationship between the music of the refrain and the verse. In the following diagram using numbers to indicate the lines of the text and italics to identify the refrain, the typical virelai and carol appear to be identical as far as their textual characteristics are concerned:

1 2   3456   *1 2*

The distinction between the two kinds of lyric, however, lay in the relationship between the refrain music and that of the verse. If the various sections of the music are now represented by being marked off by double bars, and the numbers signifying lines are disposed vertically according to the musical phrases to which they are sung, then a typical virelai displays this kind of form:

(music for refrain and dependent lines of verses)		(music for independent lines of verses)
	1 *2*	
		3
		4
'tierce' 5 6		
	1 *2*	

Thus, the refrain is prefigured musically by the closing part of the verse. The same technique may be recognized in the earliest carols, as found in the Franciscan *laude* and other contrafact lyrics of the same kind. Here however, the independent lines are sung to two separate strains, thus:

	1 *2*		
		3 ‖ 4	
'tierce' 5 6			
	1 *2*		

The tierce section was often modified to the extent that its musical links with the refrain concerned the last line only, or even the last bar or so.

It should be noted that what are generally regarded as the typical rondeau, virelai and carol forms tended to commence with a refrain; but this consistency is illusory, however, for the appearance of the refrain was frequently delayed until after the opening verse, as in the typical ballade. The presence or absence of an initial refrain cannot therefore be held to be a necessary formal quality of these fixed forms, particularly the carol.

The fixed formal patterns of the earliest lyrics rapidly became modified. In

English sources there are few virelai and carol forms answering exactly to those illustrated above. *MB* IV no. 11a, 'As I lay upon a night', is in unmodified virelai form, and no. 63, 'Ecce quod natura', has the old carol structure; but both are rare examples. The Franciscan friar James Ryman, in a late fifteenth-century carol, takes the tune and refrain of 'Ecce quod natura' and adds English verses; but here the carol form is modified, since the verse has no tierce. By an interesting coincidence, the version of 'Ecce quod natura' in Oxford Bodleian Arch. Selden b 26 (cf. *MB* IV no. 37) also lacks this section. It is not unlikely that Ryman's structure was due to working from such a source, where the scribe had misunderstood the form. Misunderstandings of this nature often led to unwitting innovations, notably the modified rondeau refrain ('rentrement') of Christine de Pisan, initiating a fashion which persisted to the time of Wyatt. Ryman's English version of 'Ecce quod natura' doubtless belongs to the same category of accidental innovation:

Ex. 45

Ec - ce quod na-tu - ra — mu-tat su-a ju - ra Vir-go pa-rit pu - ra —

De - i fi-li - um —— Bothe yonge and olde, take hede of this: The cours of na-ture

changèd is; A mayde that ne-ver did a - mys Hath — borne oure Sa-vy - oure

(Bodl Arch Selden b 26 f 27 & CUL Ee i 12)

In other carols, there is only a vestigial link between refrain and verse; and the breakdown of the established formal pattern often makes it difficult to discern how the piece was to be performed. The rondeau also suffered from breakdown of its complex construction; originally its typical structure was:

1	2	3	4
5	6		
7	8		
9	10	11	12
13	14	15	16

Here, lines 7 and 8 are identical with the first half of the refrain; 5 and 6 have the same music, but sung to different words; the final four lines are exactly the same (words and music) as the opening refrain, and are prefigured by lines 9–12, whose music is the same as that of the ensuing refrain. This elaborate structure was called for by van Ghizeghem in his rondeau 'De tous bien plane' found in *King Henry VIII's MS* (no. 36) and a similar anonymous rondeau found at no. 37. Since, however, the words are lacking, and there is little or no indication of where the first strain should end (merely a solitary *signum congruentiae* in one part of no. 37) it is evident that these pieces were performed without the elaborate system of repeats typical of the rondeau, and were probably played by instruments alone.

The songs in carol form found in the early Tudor songbooks also show signs of formal degeneration, but the extent of the modification is not always clear: as a consequence, several performance problems arise. The long passion carols of the *Fayrfax MS* have through-set stanzas, preceded by a long refrain. The words of the refrain are taken up at the end of each verse, in which the music of the refrain is also prefigured. Cornish's 'Woefully arrayed' (*MB* XXXVI, no. 53) is a good example of this technique; since the repetition of the full refrain is not specifically indicated, it would be pardonable if the performer substituted the smaller for the larger refrain. Yet Browne's 'Jesu mercy' (no. 51) has clear directions for the repetition of the long refrain, which thus clarifies the structure of 'Woefully arrayed'. Similarly, the form of the carol-style compositions of *King Henry VIII's MS* is perhaps better understood if this tendency towards prolixity is kept in mind.

In common with several similar compositions in this songbook, 'If I had wit for to endite' (*MB* XVIII no. 29) seems to be a popular courtly song converted into a carol; the transformation was achieved by taking the first verse of the original song and using this, in a polyphonically disguised form, as a refrain. As in other instances, the original version of the tune can be traced in another incomplete court songbook. In the polyphonic version it is hidden in the refrain as the tenor part of a 'threemen's' texture. Following this refrain, the subsequent verse (actually the second stanza of the original song) is then sung to the unadorned tune, followed by the three-part refrain, then another verse, and so on. Occasionally, the disguising of the original tune was taken to greater lengths than merely by placing it in the tenor. In the carol 'This enders night' (see Ex. 8) the music of the refrain runs in the equivalent of modern $\frac{4}{4}$ time, effectively concealing the true nature of the triple-time melody.

The popularity of the carol form is attested by the fact that well-known courtly tunes were frequently converted into carols. Ironically, these tunes may themselves often have been derived from older carols, whose refrains had fallen away with the passage of time, and which had become modified by the change in fashion from performance by soloist and chorus to a merely soloistic rendering. The musical and poetical link which was characteristic of the carol seems often to have been indicated in *King Henry VIII's MS* by a *signum congruentiae* or *signum intimationis*, a sign answering somewhat to the *dal segno* mark found in modern music. If this is taken to indicate the appearance of the link line, supplied by repeating the last line of the polyphonic refrain after each solo verse, the form of 'If I had wit' would be as follows (the asterisk here represents the *signum* of the MS):

[Refrain: à 3]

> *Iff I had wytt for to endyght*
> *Of my lady, both fayre and fre*
> *Of her godnes than wold I wryght;*
> *Shall no man know her name for me*
> *[*Shall no man know her name for me]*

[Verse: Solo]

> I love her well with hart and mynd
> She ys right trew, I do it se.
> My hart to have she doth me bynd
> Shall no mane know her name for me
> [*Shall no man know her name for me]

[Refrain à 3
   . . . etc.]

'A the sighs' (no. 27 in *King Henry VIII's MS*) is by Cornish, but is once again an arrangement of a tune found in another source. Here, however, the *signum* indicates that the last line of each verse should be sung by the soloist and then repeated to the three-part version, to provide the link between verse and chorus. Although Cornish's 'Blow thy horn hunter' (see Ex. 34) lacks the *signum*, it seems likely that the same method of performance would have been adopted as a matter of course. King Henry's own 'The time of youth' (no. 23) was presumably sung in a similar manner. It is reasonable to suppose that the tune for the couplets is the same as the tenor part of the first two lines of the refrain; but the latter portion — from the *signum* onwards — is obviously intended as the link-line. In his 'Whereto should I express' (no. 47) there is no *signum*: here the most appropriate link would be the repetition of 'No myrth can make me fayn/Tyl that we mete agayne.' That the scribe was inconsistent in writing the sign is of little consequence compared with his failure to supply the music, or indeed the words, for the verses of many of the pieces. Doubtless Cornish based his 'You and I and Amyas' (no. 41) on a pre-existing tune. Possibly the stanza and the refrain were linked in the manner already described, but the verses cannot be fitted comfortably to any part of the refrain music; it seems therefore that this is a different type of song. In common with King Henry's 'Green grow'th the holly' (no. 33), and others of the same format, the refrain must have been either wholly original or an arrangement of a pre-existing refrain whose music differed from that of the stanzas. The probability that well-known songs were involved would explain why Cornish's 'Adieu, courage, adieu' (no. 38) has neither words nor music for the verses; yet even here the *signum* is present, apparently indicating a link between stanza and refrain.

To the performers of the time, these ambiguities and omissions would have mattered little, since word of mouth could quickly make up for the deficiencies of script; today, however, these inadequacies can often cause considerable difficulties for the performer. Particularly unclear are sources up to the end of the fifteenth century containing paraliturgical carols where there often appear to be two refrains, existing side by side. One of these, however, is more often than not a prelude, which is dispensed with once all the voices have entered. This use of a prelude is clearly evident in Cornish's arrangement of 'A Robin' (no. 49 — cf. Ex. 35) and his 'My love she mourneth for me' (no. 25). The same is true of Browne's 'Jesu mercy how may this be' (*MB* XXXVI, no. 51) whose refrain proper is preceded by a prelude. We may suspect that his 'Woefully arrayed' (ibid. no. 55) was intended to be performed in a similar manner, in common with Cornish's setting (ibid. no. 53) of the same words. The editorial attempts to make a false distinction between 'burden' and 'refrain' in *MB* and a failure to identify the 'prelude', where present, complicate rather than simplify the problem.

In addition to the structural difficulties outlined above, the sources are also unhelpful as to the types of voices and instruments envisaged. Cornish's 'A the sighs' is a fifth higher in one source than in another. Which, if either, of these pitches is correct? Some of the 'threemen's songs' seem impossibly high, others improbably low; but since none of the parts bears any indication of the name of a voice, there is no guide as to what singers were required, much less the pitch at which they sang. This problem will be addressed, in connection with church music, in a later chapter (8); but it is obvious that since the composers and singers of sacred and secular music were often the same, the vocal ranges, which are reasonably easy to establish for church music, would have been similar in both cases. Thus the compasses printed on page 212 should doubtless apply to the courtly repertory; after all, the singers and clergy of the King's Chapel took part in the court pageants and other entertainments. At one pageant there were: 'viii mynstrells with strange [ie. foreign] instrements, and befoor un the steps stood dyvers persoons dysgysyd [in costume], as Master Sub Deen, Master Kornyche, Master Kaan [sc. Crane] and other, and un the top wer the chylldyrn of the chappell syngyng . . .' (see Stevens, 1961, p. 249)

Although the question of voices may be laid aside for the present, the problem of instrumentation cannot be avoided, even in what at first sight appears to be vocal music. Several wordless passages occur in the songs, and although it would be reasonable to regard some of them as melismas, others are lengthy enough to imply instrumental participation. Earlier music presents similar problems: longish wordless passages suggest the use of instruments to a modern eye, but the suspicion cannot lightly be cast aside that the contemporary view might have been different. In the Elizabethan period fantazias, called 'solfaing songs', were vocalized, instead of being performed instrumentally.

Nonetheless there were many instruments at King Henry's disposal: it is not unreasonable to suppose that the entirely wordless compositions found in *King Henry VIII's MS* were instrumental, as for example no. 60:

Ex. 46

This composition by Cornish, beginning and ending thus, is a reminder of an additional difficulty concerning the extempore addition of flats and sharps, a practice commonly called musica ficta. Here, however, the lack of information seems to be deliberate, the piece being a relative of the puzzle canons found elsewhere in the collection. Renaissance musicians would delight in writing out canons in such a form that it took longer to work out the pitch and order of the parts than to perform the canon itself; the later 'Non nobis domine', formerly attributed to Byrd, is a well–known example of this genre. The puzzle canons of *King Henry VIII's MS* are not particularly abstruse (no. 87, three in one, gives the solution away *gratis*: 'the secund parte restes iij and begynnyth in alamire underneth; the iij^d part rest[s] v and begynnith in gesolreut beneth'). Cornish's piece is written out, and canonic to the extent that the lowest part has two sections in *cancrizans* (palindrome) canon; the real puzzle is whether the piece is a joke, demonstrating the absurdity of the 'Locrian mode' (soon to be discussed, with due solemnity, in Glarean's *Dodecachordon* of 1547), or whether, in common with Ockeghem's Mass 'Cuiusvis toni' the piece is a *catholicon*, in which the key can be altered by reading off different combinations of clefs and accidentals. This ingenious composition is one of the most intriguing of the whole collection, and its secrets would probably have taxed many an instrumentalist. The more fundamental puzzle, however, remains: what kind of instruments would have performed this piece, and others like it?

In the absence of rubrics, the obvious course would be to play these compositions on the sorts of instruments known to have been in Henry VIII's possession. There would have been abundant choice since the inventory in BL Harl 1419 printed by Galpin (1910, p. 292) extends for several pages. The king owned countless boxes of recorders, flutes of glass and wood, crumhorns, bagpipes, lutes, clavichords, virginals, regals and organs, viols, cornetts, shawms and so forth; this collection was not merely for the use of minstrels, for the king himself is known to have played various instruments (cf. eg. *Calendar of State Papers . . .* Venice ii no. 328).

So far as can be gathered, the tendency was for instruments to play in homogeneous groups of viols or recorders, flutes or crumhorns or in established combinations such as cornetts, shawms and sackbuts. The king did not lack players for these instruments: in 1540 there were eight viol players (all foreign), seven sackbut players and five flute players, besides many others. In 1547 his musicians numbered something like fifty-eight (Woodfill, 1953, pp. 178, 197). The choice of instruments would have depended on the occasion: cornetts, sackbuts and shawms outdoors, flutes or recorders indoors. The mixing of one type with another would have depended on considerations of tone and also of pitch.

Much early polyphonic instrumental music was merely vocal music played without words. The cruder sort of 'minstrel music' played by rebecs was dance music, hardly ever written down, and mostly improvized upon well-worn harmonic patterns such as the Passamezzo (Shakespeare's 'Passy-measures') noted in the previous chapter. By the middle of the sixteenth century, however, these two extremes had come together to some degree, and the instrumental music took on an increasingly independent character.

Taverner's Mass 'Gloria tibi Trinitas' has the plainchant melody of that name running through the Benedictus, in which the section 'In nomine domini' begins thus:

Ex. 47

(original note values and pitch)

It is difficult to explain the particular attraction of these bars and why they should have begun such a fashion for the In Nomine, but this passage from Taverner's Benedictus was transcribed, played, added to and widely imitated, becoming a standard exercise in composition and playing (see Woodfield, 1984, p. 217). The 'Gloria tibi trinitas' cantus became so popular that the In Nomine may be regarded as the most characteristic English instrumental form of the late sixteenth century.

Puzzle canons continued to be composed, and other cantus firmi such as 'Salvator mundi', 'Christe qui lux' and 'Miserere' (all appropriate to evening music making, since they are hymns and an antiphon from Compline), were used widely: also popular was the formula 'ut re mi fa sol la', in which the cantus firmus was merely a scale passage. Christopher Tye and others incorporated street cries into their fantazias, and songs such as 'The leaves be green' (commonly known as 'Browning' see p. 56) began to rival, if at a distance, the popularity of the In Nomine theme.

The *Mulliner Book* (*MB* I) gives some idea of musical taste in the middle of the century: it charts the progress of instrumental polyphony evolving from mere arrangements of vocal music towards a more genuinely instrumental texture. Thomas Mulliner's collection is a musical scrapbook, mostly for keyboard: besides the earliest keyboard arrangement of Taverner's 'In Nomine', it contains partsong arrangements, dances, anthems and liturgical pieces, and several fantazias. His arrangements are important sources of several partsongs by Tallis, Sheppard and others; there are arrangements of anthems (including 'Rejoice in the Lord alway', erroneously attributed to John Redford); and there are many organ pieces by William Blitheman who appears to have had some connection with Mulliner. Among the gems of the collection are an instrumental fantazia and 'A pavyon' by the virtually unknown Newman; numerous other works, such as the partsong 'In going to my naked bed' (words, and presumably music, by Richard Edwards) are uniquely preserved in Mulliner's MS. Edwards' name is mentioned in a scene from Sainliens' previously quoted book (1573):

[Host]	Roland, shall we have a songe?
[Roland]	Sir: where be your bookes of musicke? For they bee the best corrected.
[Host]	They bee in my chest: Katherin, take the key of my closet, you shal finde them in a little till at the left hand: [Katherine fetches the books] beholde, there be faire songes at foure partes.
[Roland]	Who shall sing with me?
[Host]	You shal have company enough: David shall make the base: John, the tenor: and James the treble. Begin: James, take your tune: go to: for what do you tarry?
[James]	I have but a rest.
[Host]	Roland, drinke afore you begin, you will singe with a better courage.
[Roland]	It is wel said: geve me some white wine: that wil cause me to sing clearer.
[Host]	You must drink greene wine.
[Roland]	Yea truly to cause me to lose my voice.
[Host]	Oh, see what a fonell, for he hath powred downe a quart of wine without any taking of his breath.

[Roland]	I should not bee a singing man ex-cept I drinke well: . . .
[Guest]	There is a good songe. I do marvell who hath made it.
[Host]	It is the maister of the children of the Queenes chappell.
[Guest]	What is his name?
[Host]	Maister Edward.
[Guest]	Is hee alive?
[Host]	I heard say that hee was dead.
[Roland]	It is already a good while a go: it is at the least five yeeres and a halfe.
[Host]	Truly, it is a pitie: he was a man of good wit, and a good poet: and a great player of playes.

(f 28v)

Edwards' fame was substantial, particularly as a producer of choirboy plays; even Shakespeare, that severe critic of the choristers, was moved to quote from one of his songs ('When griping griefs') in *Romeo and Juliet* (IV, v).

The considerable partsong repertory of the period between the Henrician collections discussed earlier and the rise of the madrigal is only fragmentarily represented by the extant sources. Something like one-sixth of the *Mulliner Book* is made up of keyboard arrangements of these songs which, unlike their earlier Tudor equivalents, were regularly in four parts. The words of these songs can often be recovered from collections such as *The Paradyse of Dainty Devises* (1576), which contained heavily alliterative verses by poets associated with the choirboy plays, Edwards, William Hunnis, Francis Kinwelmarsh and others. Curiously, although Jasper Heywood's 'The bitter sweet' is included by Mulliner (the text is found in *A Gorgious Gallery of Gallant Inventions* of 1578), nothing of his more illustrious namesake, John Heywood, is included. Mulliner's connection with this famous Tudor gentleman of music and letters was evidently intimate, as an inscription in the *Mulliner Book* bears witness: 'Sum liber thomae mullineri, johanne heywood teste.'

In about 1549, Whythorne mentioned that he had 'learned to play on the Gyttern, and Sittern which ij instruments were then strange in England' (Osborn, 1961, p. 19). Mulliner's anthology includes a number of pieces for these newly fashionable instruments, printed by Stevens (1952). Since the cittern was of a very limited compass, its capacity for playing full chords was severely restricted, with the result that much of the music, from Mulliner's to Antony Holborne's collection (1597), consists of strings of $\frac{6}{4}$ chords and other harmonic peculiarities. Although some players may have been content to strum in this fashion, it is hard not to suppose that a bass viol completed the harmony. In Holborne's collection a viol part is indeed provided for the more complex pieces, though for the pieces constructed on ground basses, the viol player was clearly expected to improvise. Mulliner's pieces, similarly, are on ground basses, and it must be supposed that these were supplied in all but the most crudely amateurish performances:

Ex. 48

(f 122; cf Stevens, 1952)

In addition to his discussion (Stevens, 1952) of the partsong repertory preserved in *Mulliner*, Denis Stevens has published (1950, 1955) valuable surveys of other, more fragmentary, sources of the mid-century partsong. Collation of these sources (see also Milsom, 1981) reveals the extreme popularity of certain of these songs, for example Sheppard's 'O happy dames':

Ex. 49

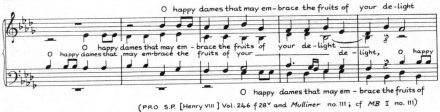

(PRO S.P. [Henry VIII] Vol. 246 f 28ᵛ and *Mulliner* no. 111; cf *MB* I no. 111)

Increased interest in amateur music making led to the rise of the partsong, and eventually to the madrigal, thus lending some veracity to Peacham's portrait of a civilized gentleman:

> I desire no more in you than to sing your part sure, and at the first sight, withall, to play the same upon your Violl, or the exercise of the Lute, privately to your selfe.

> (Peacham 1622)

The rise of amateur music-making is also testified in another remarkable anthology (BL Add. 31390), dating slightly later than the *Mulliner Book*. It is a 'table book', the parts being readable from four different angles: from the bottom of the book, upside-down, and from the two sides. Many of these pieces are merely arrangements of church music, but much is genuine instrumental music, in which the name of Tye figures largely. The volume is entitled *A Booke of In nomines & other solfainge songes of v: vj: vij: & viij parts for voyces or Instrumentes*. The practice of 'solfaing' was probably both a means of learning vocal sightreading and for non-instrumentalists to perform a wider repertory. Wordless singing was looked upon as a poor substitute by Morley who could not see that a motet can stir passions if 'sung as most men doe commonlie sing it: that is leaving out the dittie and singing onely the bare note, as it were a musicke made onelie for instruments. . . .' (Morley, 1597, p. 179)

The instruments which were involved in the music of BL Add. 31390, as with those of the earlier age, cannot be identified with absolute certainty, although viols may be assumed. In spite of the impression left by Peacham, Drayton and others, the English gentleman did not take to the viol as an everyday instrument until comparatively late in its history. The number of amateur musicians in a household capable of playing upon such instruments would have been small; most of this music, at least until the closing years of the century, would have been played by professionals.

Whythorne may lay claim to a minor place in the history of instrumental music: he also occupies a niche in the development of the partsong. As Fellowes (1948, p. 34) pointed out, he was to Dowland or Wilbye what Wyatt and Surrey were to Shakespeare, Spencer and Sydney. Whythorne was sent to be a chorister at Magdalen College by his uncle, a priest living near Oxford, he left the College in 1545 at the age of 17 to become the 'servant and scholar' of John Heywood. Whythorne's subsequent career ranged widely: after a sojourn abroad during Mary's reign, his most distinguished post was that of master of music in the Archbishop of Canterbury's Chapel. Matthew Parker, who successfully navigated the rocks of being chaplain to Anne Boleyn, the storms of Henry's Reformation and Mary's bloody reaction to it, reached the Archbishopric in the haven of the Elizabethan settlement, to die in peace in 1575. Whythorne himself died in 1596, having published two sets of compositions, and leaving behind him a manuscript autobiography which affords a considerable insight into the status of differing classes of musician of Whythorne's era.

Whythorne's autobiography, unpublished until modern times, records his career as a private musician struggling to climb the social scale from the status of mere servant to that of a gentleman. His ambitions were often hampered by the entreaties of amorous females which, had he succumbed to them, would have done nothing to further his social aims. The book is incidentally significant in that it is written in a more or less phonetic orthography: it is one of a small number of works of this kind which may be assumed to provide a reasonably accurate record of the pronunciation of Elizabethan English. Whythorne (his orthography shows the pronunciation of his name to have been 'White-horn') was anxious not to have been thought a mere 'rascal and off-scum of that profession, who be, or ought to be called minstrels (although nowadays many do name themselves musi-

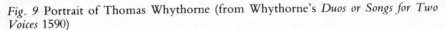

Fig. 9 Portrait of Thomas Whythorne (from Whythorne's *Duos or Songs for Two Voices* 1590)

cians); these I say did and do make it common' (Osborn, 1961, p. 244, modern spelling). He goes on to recount, by way of illustration, an anecdote in which a beggar compared himself with a minstrel, saying that the only difference was that the one was allowed into the house, the other not. In the same passage Whythorne says that:

> when the old store of the music[i]ans be worn out the which were bred when the music of the church [was] maintained (which is like to be in a short time) ye shall have few or n[one] remaining, except it be a few singingmen and players on musi[cal] instruments of the which ye shall find a very few or none that [can] make a good lesson of descant, and yet these would be named and accou[nted] musicians although there be

none worthy of that name except they can make songs of ij, iij, iiij parts and so upward according to the true rules thereof . . . There be another sort of musicians that be named *speculators*. That is to say, they that do become musicians by study without [any] practice thereof. There have been of such who have made songs and have pric[ked ie. written] them out, and yet could not sing a part of them, themselves. There be another sort of lovers of music who do either learn the science as afore[said], or to play and sound upon musical instruments, or else to sing prickson[g], for that they would therewith, either set forth God's glory in the Church, or else use it for the same purpose in private houses or else for their own recreation; and do not otherwise seek to live by or to further their livings thereby . . . (Osborn, 1961, pp 245–6).

These latter, he says, are those 'which the book named *The Courtier* [by Castiglione] doth will to learn music' (ibid. p. 246).

It is clear that Whythorne classes himself both as a 'speculative musician' — the phrase used by Morley (1597) — and as a practical musician 'worthy of that name': similarly, it is evident that his publications were intended not as a source of income, but to 'further his living' by enhancing his reputation. The first publication of instrumental, and nearly the first publication of vocal music in England, is thus owed to Whythorne's ambition. His *Songes for three, fower, and five Voyces* were published in 1571, the only secular partmusic to appear between the virtually lost set of *XX Songes* (1530) and Byrd's 1588 collection. He commends them as being 'some hard, some easier to be songe, and some betweene both . . . according to the skill of the singers (not being Musitians) and disposition and delite of the hearers' — making a clear distinction between gentlemen and players.

Whythorne's songs remain largely unpublished. Some of them were edited half a century ago by Peter Warlock, who also wrote a short appreciation of him, but have long since been out of print. They are remarkable not only for their priority in the field but also for their slavish application of the characteristically English off-beat underlay, of which more will be said in due course. For the present, its essence may be defined thus: if a sequence of syllables were to be sung to twice that number of notes, the most obvious method of underlay would be to group pairs of notes to the syllables, corresponding with the beat; English composers, however, would often slur a syllable to two or more notes across the beat, a practice carried to an extreme by Whythorne. Another point of interest in his *Songes* is that many of them feature in his autobiography; 'Buy new broom', we are told (ibid. p. 90), was the result of an unsatisfactory relationship with one of his several woman-friends, the moral of which was,

"Tis not good to trust overmuch at the first show.' This *mise en scène* heightens the interest of this particular song (based, as noted earlier, on the familiar street 'cry' of the broom-seller) for solo voice and unspecified instruments. Unfortunately, the musical quality of most of his songs is well below this example.

The same uneven quality has to be admitted in respect of his *Duos or Songs for two voices* of 1590 (imitated by Farmer in a publication of 1591 and by Morley in 1595). The interest of these duos is that the first twenty-two of the fifty-two items are for 'young beginners' or 'a man and a childe', or indeed for voices or

Fig. 10 Cornetts, sackbuts and other instruments with voices shown at the funeral of Charles III Duke of Lorraine at Nancy, 1608. (from Ruelle, *Decem insignes tabulae*, 1611)

instruments 'that be of the like compasse or distance in sound' (this latter rubric is intended as a warning against those who might play or sing an octave too low relative to the other, thus inverting the harmony and perverting the counterpoint). The final fifteen songs of the collection are canons 'for voices and instruments of divers compasses and distance'; but the previous fifteen, although specified 'for two children to sing' are also 'aptly made for two treble Cornets'. Here, remarkably, is the first unequivocal reference to specific instruments attached to an example of English polyphony.

Apart from these pieces, John Hingston's suites for one and two cornetts, sackbut and organ (Bodleian Mus. Sch. e 382) are among the very few surviving pieces which specifically mention the use of the cornett, although several collections envisage its employment: Holborne's *Pavans, Galliards, Almains* . . . of 1599 were for 'Viols, Violins, or other Musicall Winde Instruments', and John Adson's *Courtly Masquing Ayres* (1621) were for 'Violins, Consorts and Cornets'. A 'Verse' for cornett, sackbut and organ by Coprario survives in fragmentary form. Only the organ score of this movement remains, doubtless the opening of what was once a suite continued by an alman and ayre or galliard; and since, to judge from other similar organ scores, the cornett part is presumably hidden and disguised within the organ score, sometimes transferred from octave to octave, its recovery is a problematic task. According to Aubrey (cf. Britton, 1847) Coprario composed 'Fansies which were for a sagbot, a violin and organ, equivalent to five parts.' Several of his fantasy suites could be played like this, but none specifically mentions this instrumentation, which is unusual in that a cornett would normally be partnered by a sackbut. It may be that Aubrey was mistaken, but it is a curious coincidence that the MS containing Coprario's fragmentary Verse for cornett, sackbut and organ (New York PL Drexel 5469) also includes a companion piece for violin, cornett, sackbut and organ by its copyist Henry Loosemore.

Loosemore (the true composer of 'O Lord, increase our faith', often attributed to Gibbons) was organist of King's College, Cambridge, from 1627 until 1670, and so lies somewhat outside the 'Tudor' period, as does William Lawes, the composer of 'Before the mountains were brought forth'. Tantalizingly, the music of Lawes' anthem, with 'verses for cornetts and Sackbutts' no longer survives; the words alone are given in BL Harleian 6346, but the specific reference to voices being used together with wind instruments is remarkable in itself.

Instruments are frequently mentioned in connection with royal music, both of a funereal and of a celebratory nature. Shawms and trumpets were often used, in common with bells, when Te Deum was sung; these practices, dating from the Middle Ages, continued well into the sixteenth century. In Wolsey's time, Te Deum was sung at St Paul's in 1525 with 'mynstrelles on every side', and two years later with 'the kings trumpetts and shalmes'. In 1566 Queen Elizabeth visited Oxford when the 'Quyer sang and play'd with Cornetts, Te Deum' (see Dugdale, 1818, p. 217 and 433; Plummer, 1887, p. 199).

At the funeral of the universally mourned Prince Henry in 1612 there were 'sung divers excellent Anthems, together with the organs, and other wind Instruments.' One of these anthems was probably 'Know ye not' by Tomkins (see James, 1971, p. 156). Cornetts and sackbuts were also in use at Durham, due to the influence of John Cosin, and much against the puritanical tenets of the Prebendary Peter Smart (see Ornsby, 1869, p. 166; Smart, 1642, p. 9 and 1628).

Such references to wind instruments, or to the less specific 'musicall instruments' recorded in connection with Princess Mary's christening in 1605 (Rimbault, 1872, p. 68), are often vague, particularly in regard to whether or not voices and instruments actually performed together. When they did, as one or two references unambiguously indicate, the circumstances were special. It is probably no coincidence that Lawes' 'Before the mountains were brought forth' is funereal, or that the most frequent references to wind instruments concern the Te Deum. Indeed, that such instruments are mentioned in these connections leaves the strong impression that the use of wind instruments was unusual in church, and more particularly so in direct connection with voices, where pitch and balance might have posed special problems.

Since viol players are recorded as being used for royal occasions, it is reasonable to suppose that they took part in royal anthems such as 'Great King of Gods', 'O all true faithful hearts' and 'Thou God of wisdom' by Gibbons, or his 'Do not repine, fair Sun' (Brett, 1961) — all of which were occasional pieces for King James. One or two anthems by Edmund Hooper — 'Hearken ye nations' (for November 5th) and 'O God of Gods' (for the 'King's Day') — might possibly have been accompanied by the cornetts and sackbuts; these instruments had earlier been the subject of special payments to Hooper, on the 'Queen's Day' at Westminster in 1599 (Treasury accounts, 33653–4). But the scoring is not the six-part texture typical of 'The King's Musicke' (see p. 97). The unspecified parts found in many anthems by Byrd, Gibbons, Tomkins and other composers associated with Chapel Royal may be assumed to have been intended for viols, since their connection with royal music is established (see Woodfield, 1984, p. 216) and these are the only instruments mentioned in connection with the printed anthems of composers such as East and John Amner. East's *Third Set of Bookes* (1610) has the usual 'Apt both for Viols and Voyces' rubric, and consists of 'Pastorals, Anthemes, Neopolitanes, Fancies, and Madrigales . . .'. His *Fourth Set of Bookes* (1618) also contains 'Anthemes for *Versus and Chorus* . . . Apt for viols and voyces'. Amner's *Sacred Hymnes of 3, 4, 5 and 6 parts for Voyces and vyols* appeared earlier, in 1615. Although it is reasonable to argue that these publications were meant for private music making, or that East and Amner were both associated with Ely (East was Amner's pupil for a short time), the use of viols can hardly have been confined to these composers, and certainly not to one cathedral. At Exeter there was a 'delicate, rich and lofty organ . . . which with their viols and other sweet instruments and tunable voices, and the rare organist . . . ravish the hearer's ears', according to the diary of Lieutenant Hammond (Legg, 1936), in which he records a tour of cathedrals between 1634 and 1635. Since the viols were by then becoming old-fashioned, and displaced by 'other sweet instruments', and since Edward Gibbons, the brother of Orlando, was succentor of Exeter and himself a composer of Verse anthems with instrumental accompaniment, viols can hardly have been a novelty when Hammond heard them, nor peculiar to Exeter. Indeed, Edward may well have imitated his more illustrious brother, transporting from the Chapel Royal to the west country a fashion for anthems accompanied by viols. A significantly large portion of Gibbons' Verse anthems have instrumental accompaniment (and there is reason to suppose that many more, if not all, were originally conceived in this way): they seem to have been intended for four, or perhaps five, viols. The repertory for voices and viols during the first half of the seventeenth century is discussed in Monson (1982).

It should be noted that in compositions where both instrumental and organ accompaniments are extant, the two forms of accompaniment should not be mixed; no source gives both forms, and in many cases the versions are incompatible. The sources of songs and anthems with concerted accompaniments do not make clear whether the instruments should be silent in the chorus passages, or whether they should double the voice parts; if the latter, it would be logical for all voice parts, solo or chorus, to be doubled. This procedure would obviously pose problems where there is division of the vocal parts; and although rule-of-thumb solutions may be worked out, and doubtless were, there is no certainty in the matter. One source (Oxford Ch Ch 56–60) has *corona* marks appearing before the vocal entries; the contexts do not allow these signs to be interpreted as pauses, yet although they might be taken to imply the cessation of instrumental participation, they are far from being unequivocal, and probably merely serve as a reminder of an incipient vocal entry. The Verse anthems of Gibbons — unique to Oxford Ch Ch 21 — also pose several problems of scoring and doubling; and even in the case of 'See, see, the word is incarnate', found elsewhere in a concordant set of partbooks (see below), the intentions of the composer are not always obvious.

The anthems of Byrd published with instrumental accompaniment in his 1589 and 1611 collections were presumably arrangements for private use. There is no doubt that works of this kind were popular forms of household music making (see Monson, 1982) and that several examples were expressly composed for this purpose. It is significant, however, that only one anthem by Gibbons ('See, see, the word is incarnate', in Myriell's collection of 1616) exists in a set of secular partbooks, and Gibbons did not follow Byrd's example by publishing any anthems of this kind in his madrigalian collection of 1612. It must therefore be concluded that Gibbons' instrumental anthems were designed for church, rather than private, use.

In the realm of purely instrumental music, Gibbons' contribution is outstanding, even when compared with many of his illustrious contemporaries. Although Byrd's instrumental music (discussed in Neighbour, 1978) is not of a consistently high standard, several of his fantazias, pavans and so forth have the fluency and expressive range found in his other music, especially his two great six-part fantazias, which are magisterial in their technical prowess. There is also much to admire in the instrumental music of Alfonso Ferrabosco II, Tomkins, Peerson, Lupo, Ward and Coprario (some of which are printed in *MB* IX); yet the concentrated range of Gibbons' *Fantazies of three parts* (printed about 1620, and incidentally the first music to be engraved — 'cut in copper' — rather than set from moveable type) is unequalled until the three-part fantazias of Purcell. Gibbons' careful treatment of the fantazia, particularly in regard to his fastidiously worked counterpoint, allows him to move easily between vocal and instrumental music; his avowedly instrumental style is nonetheless unmistakable. The authenticated (see Hobbs, 1982) six-part fantazias with organ are among the most important contributions to the repertory.

Ex. 50

(cf *MB* XLVIII no. 33)

In his In Nomine compositions, Gibbons shows an enviable disregard for any constraint which the cantus firmus might have been assumed to exercise. The five-part In Nomine admirably demonstrates this freedom, but incidentally emphasizes an important facet of performance practice; towards the end Gibbons apparently wrote the following passage(cf. *MB* IX no. 52):

Ex. 51

Christ Church & Tenbury MSS

It is almost inconceivable that this section, lacking any particular rhythmic vitality, should act as the climax to a work which begins with syncopated entries and develops through a complex web of downward scale passages met by upward ranging 'divisions'. If we were to believe the sources in general, Gibbons would have been guilty of a curious lapse of rhythmical judgement; but as one particular source confirms, the players would automatically have added 'divisions', ornamenting the passage thus:

Ex. 52

Marsh's MS & others

This is a dramatic reminder of the extent to which a composer may be at the mercy of the performer; to use Gibbons' own words, compositions are often 'esteemed as they are well or ill performed': the quality of the performance, including the choice of the voices or instruments, the consideration of matters concerning pitch, ornamentation and so forth, have a vital role to play in the recreation of this music.

The conventions of division can be learnt, in part, from sources such as dalla Casa's *Il vero modo di diminuir* (1584), and the *Trattado de glosas* (1553) by Ortiz; and English treatises, Coprario's *Rules how to Compose* (c. 1610) and Morley's *Plaine and Easie Introduction* (1597) have useful information. Caution is needed, however, since the wrong kind of ornamentation, or too much, is as inimical to the composer's intentions as none at all. Charles Butler (1636, p. 116) warned against 'Too much quaint Division, too much shaking and quavering of the Notes, all harsh straining of the Voices beyond their natural pitch, as they are odious and offensive to the ear' (spelling modernized). Nevertheless, some vocal sources of the early seventeenth century have comparatively extravagant written-out divisions:

Ex. 53

The art of division was particularly important to the dance musician, for otherwise banal dance music could be utterly transformed by 'quaint Division', as in the following excerpt from BL Roy. App. 76, in which the ornamental part is apparently destined for the violin:

Ex. 54

Some of these divisions would doubtless have been taken under one bow; the absence of slurs need not necessarily indicate that the bow was changed for every note, for the use of the slur gained ground rather slowly in the early part of the seventeenth century. Nevertheless, slurred bowing was the exception rather than the rule, as Silvestro di Ganassi's fully bowed music (1543) shows, although for quick notes ('semiminimas') a slur was permissible (see Ortiz, 1553, f 3r). There is, however, no evidence to show that the elaborate mixtures of bowing employed by modern string players is appropriate to viol music. There is, on the contrary, much to be said against anything but the most subtle bowing and accentuation of the notes: indeed the underhand bowing of the viol does not permit harsh accentuation, and the distinction between the stronger 'up' and weaker 'down' bow is relatively small. The galliard frequently features the *hemiola*, in which $\frac{3}{2}$ and $\frac{6}{4}$ time is juxtaposed, as in the following example (*MB* IX, no. 92) by Tomkins. It would be mistaken to bring out this conflict by exaggerated accentuation and articulation, since the interplay of rhythms is implicit in the note-values:

Ex. 55

By the same token, swellings of tone, unremitting vibrato and similar anachronisms must be rejected. The vibrato (known as the 'close shake' on the viol, or 'sting' on the lute) was no more than an incidental ornament (see Simpson, 1667, section 16 and Mace, 1676, p. 109). As for the swelling of tone, or *messa di voce*, it is inappropriate except for 'pathetic' passages of the kind quoted on p. 37.

The same strictures apply to wind playing. The cornett, after all, was supposed to be able to vie with, and imitate, the human voice (cf. North, apud Wilson, 1959, p. 40). It is a mistake to suppose that articulation necessarily required staccato tonguing; on the contrary, it is as inappropriate as off-the-string bowing. Double tonguing in the 't–k t–k' fashion was regarded as a crudity until the nineteenth century (Baines, 1957, p. 42). The articulation of cornetts and sackbuts should resemble the articulation which results from the proper pronunciation of consonants in vocal music. Subtlety in ornamentation, expression and articulation is the best way to allow this music to express itself, unencumbered by the accretions of later styles. It is well to remember that one of the most popular instruments was the lute, whose range of expression was particularly subtle.

The music of Thomas Cutting, Daniel Bacheler, Dowland and other lutenist composers has not generally received its deserved attention, although much of it exists in other, more well-known versions. The interchange between instrumental and lute music is found throughout the period from the mid fifteenth century to the time of Byrd and his contemporaries. The restrained tone of the lute should thus be borne in mind when playing on other instruments, even in the most exuberant galliards and almans. In spite of its title, Dowland's *Lachrimae or Seaven Teares figured in Seaven Passionate Pavans . . . for the Lute, Viols, or Violons* (c. 1605; see Warlock, 1927) contain some decidedly undolorous dances (Ex. 56.).

The earliest source of English lute music is BL Roy. App. 58 (about 1540) containing eight pieces — the *Bowles Lute Book* (1558) also contains the same number; but the largest sources are the *Dallis Lute Book* (Dublin, Trinity College D.3.30) and the important *Cambridge Lute Book* (UL Dd.2.11). A good selection of lute music may be found in David Lumsden's anthology (1954); and the music of several composers such as Dowland are now available complete in modern editions. Many of the lute MSS contain music for

Ex. 56

('M. George Whitehead His Almand')

bandora, cittern and various groupings, but it is worth mentioning that some of the most charming pieces of the repertory are lute duets: the *Jane Pickering Lute Book* (BL Egerton 2046), the *Sampson Lute Book* (Robert Spencer Collection) and the *Brogyntyn Lute Book* (Brogyntyn NLW, 27) all contain several examples. Nordstrom (1976) has pointed out that the lute duet appears to have begun as an ornamented treble played to a ground on a second lute or other instrument, evolving towards the consort lesson for mixed ensemble. In turn, the style of the consort lesson, developing in the 1580's, gave rise to the fully fledged lute duets of the 1590s and onwards, as found in the MSS previously mentioned.

Gibbons is almost the only composer of instrumental music whose work is not represented in lute transcriptions. This circumstance may be explained partly, but not wholly, by the fact that his instrumental compositions date from the declining years of the lute. Under the championship of Hume, the spectacular division viol was undermining the long supremacy of the lute as a solo instrument. The intabulations of songs, fantazias and church music found in the Paston lute sources (Brett, 1964) and several earlier MSS bear witness to the long, largely unwritten, history of the lute in private music; but the trend in solo music was towards the virginal or division viol, and at the same time there was a greater interest in ensemble music. The fantazia, dominated in its earlier years by the In Nomine, developed at the hands of Parsons, Tye and White, together with the elder and younger Ferraboscos, to become enormously fashionable by the beginning of the seventeenth century.

By this time, the vocal origins of instrumental music had become decidedly less obvious; the music of Ward, for example, with its many repeated-note figures, is unmistakably instrumental; and extreme chromaticisms abound in the works of Tomkins and his contemporaries. The monothematic fancies of Tomkins and, even more particularly, of Jenkins who frequently employs augmentation and diminution, developed instrumental music in different directions, ensuring a vigour which was to be undiminished by the time of Christopher Simpson, who in his treatise of 1667 described the fantazia thus:

> beginning commonly with some *Fuge,* and then falling into Points of *Division;* answering one another; sometimes two against one, and sometimes all engaged at once in a contest of *Division:* But (after all) ending commonly in grave and harmonious Musick.

Monothematic fantazias were comparatively unusual; in general the fantazia consisted of a series of these 'points' or subjects worked in fugal style, which were then passed over in favour of a fresh point. Several fantazias by Byrd and Gibbons incorporate snatches of popular tunes, echoing earlier compositions such as the 'Cry' by Tye and 'Johnsons knell' found in BL Add. 31390. These lighter episodes, often in a different metre, provided a foil to the surrounding more stately points. Fanciful or programmatic titles – 'Myself' in Holborne's collection of 1599, Tye's 'Hold fast' in $\frac{5}{4}$ time, *The XII Wonders of the World* by John Maynard, or the *Monthes* and *Seasons* of Simpson — are often found, testifying to the emancipation of instrumental music from its vocal origins. To view the phrase 'apt for viols and voices' as denoting that instrumental music returned full circle into the realm of vocal music would be to be hoodwinked by the commercial instincts of the composers of these collections: it is only rarely, as in Gibbons' madrigalian publication, that a madrigal might truly do double duty as a fantazia.

The sectional character of Gibbons' fantazias, the nature of his contribution to the repertory of instrumental pavans, galliards, almans and other dances, and his espousal of the organ in several of these works, may have led to the development of the suite. Indeed, some of Gibbons' three-part works seem closely connected with the fantasy suites of Coprario. As observed previously, the suites of the latter composer comprise a fantazia, followed by an alman and an ayre or galliard. The scoring — as with some of Gibbons' pieces — was often for two treble instruments and a bass, with an organ doubling 'Evenly, softly and sweetly acchording to all' (Mace, 1676, p. 234). Several fantazias of Gibbons, and one of his galliards, call for the 'Great Dooble Bass' viol, (tuned in *A,* a fourth below the ordinary *D* bass viol) and organ (See *MB* [2]IX nos. 9 and 17, and pp. 220, 229). These pieces represent the germs, or possibly the remains, of an early fantasy suite. The markedly sectional character — almost amounting to separate short movements — of the fantazia in question (*MB* IX, no. 9) suggests a close link with Lupo and Coprario, members of the King's 'Private Musick'. So, too, the last five of Gibbons' printed three-part fantazias (c. 1620) have both this sectional character and the 'two treble' scoring of the fantasy suite, the earlier works of the set being formally and instrumentally more homogeneous. There is no need, however, to suppose with Dart (1956) that Gibbons was the imitator; indeed it seems more likely that Lupo and Coprario built on his innovations. It is noteworthy that Gibbons' instrumental music seems to have circulated particularly at Oxford, where most of the MSS now survive; several unique sources, however, are now preserved at Dublin, in Archbishop Marsh's Library. From 1666 to 1678, when he left for Dublin, Marsh was active in Oxford keeping 'a weekly consort (of instrumental musick and sometimes vocal) in my chamber on Wednesday in the afternoon, and then on Thursday, as long as I lived in Oxford' (*Diary* — Dublin, Marsh MS Z2.2. 3a p. 9). How it came about that so much music by Gibbons was circulating in Oxford (Benjamin Rogers owned Oxford Ch Ch 21, a unique score of Gibbons' instrumental music and anthems) is not clear at present. Although Gibbons' father was an Oxford wait, the family moved to Cambridge soon after Orlando's birth in 1583; since there is no evidence that the son performed on anything but the organ and virginals, he is unlikely to have been a member of the king's band, as has sometimes been suggested.

The royal music of King James' day recaptured some of the richness and variety of Henrician times (see Woodfill, 1953, pp. 300–3). Music for strings and organ, much of which was doubtless written for the court, has already been touched upon, but a distinctive repertory for wind instruments has come to light, which Thurston Dart recognized in 1958 as belonging to the royal wind players between 1603 and 1665. The manuscript set of partbooks, Cambridge, Fitzwilliam Museum 24. E. 13–17, bears the arms of James I, and contains music by Bassano, Coprario, Ferrabosco, Guy, Harding, Johnson and Lupo, all of whom were members of the 'Kings Musicke'. Although many items are anonymous and one book is missing, concordances yield further identifications and supply, or help to supply, the missing part, the restoration of which in any case is not a matter of insuperable difficulty. The complete six–part texture, although it could be played by recorders, or various combinations of other instruments, is clearly most suited to an ensemble of cornetts and sackbuts; generally, the upper parts have cornett range, the lower three appear to be for two tenors and one bass sackbut, and the missing part would probably have had an alto sackbut range. The following excerpt is from an 'Almande' which although anonymous in the MSS is attributed to Coprario in *Parthenia In-violata* (c. 1614). In the latter source most of the pairs of quavers are dotted; the wind players would presumably have played an alman in this way as a matter of course (Ex. 57):

It should perhaps be mentioned that although drums are used in military music, and possibly with trumpets and shawms, there is nothing to suggest that percussion instruments were used with cornetts and sackbuts. In poly-phonic dance music the use of drums is probably fanciful; and even the itinerant fiddlers apparently played without such an accompaniment (see p.

Ex. 57

61). The pipe and tabor is the only such combination readily supported by English iconographical evidence. The use of percussion instruments in vocal music such as the Tudor carol is, needless to say, wholly out of place.

Although the specific repertory for cornetts and sackbuts is small, other appropriate music is found in Whythorne's 1590 collection of duos, already mentioned; and it is likely that the instrumental duets in Morley's *First Booke of Canzonets to Two Voyces* (1595) owe something to Whythorne's example. Holborne's 1599 set of *Pavans, Galliards, Almains . . . for Viols, Violins, or Other Musicall Winde Instruments* included a pavan 'The Funerals' (*MB* IX no. 66) which may have been designed for wind instruments, although the disposition of this piece (requiring a second alto sackbut in place of a second cornett) and of Holborne's music generally, does not have the typical six–part texture discussed earlier. Adson's *Courtly Masquing Ayres composed to. 5 and 6. Parts, for Violins, Consorts and Cornets* (1621) however, contains six-part music by several of the king's musicians, among which are pieces which seem particularly appropriate to wind instruments.

The mention of 'Consorts' in Adson's publication is noteworthy. It seems that the phrase 'broken consort', nowadays used to define a mixture of instruments (as opposed to a 'whole consort'), is a misnomer (see Edwards, 1971). It was the word 'consort' which referred to a mixture of instruments, and specifically to the viol or violin, flute or recorder, bass viol, lute, bandora and cittern — the combination mentioned in the previous chapter in connection with the London waits. It was for these waits that Morley compiled his *First Booke of Consort Lessons* (1599) addressing himself to the Lord Mayor of London, a city whose custom 'hath beene ever, to retaine and maintaine excellent and expert Musitians, to adorne your Honours favours, Feasts and solemne meetings: to those your Lordships Wayts, after the commending these my labors to your Honorable patronage: I recommend the same to your servants carefull and skilfull handling.'

Morley's enterprise in issuing this collection, particularly since he may have had little to do with the arranging of the pieces for 'consort', caused Rosseter to put forward his own collection of *Lessons for Consort* (1609); these were issued, as Rosseter found it necessary to observe, because of the 'good successe and francke entertainment which the late set of consort bookes generally received . . . The Authors names have I severally pre-fixed, that every man might obtain his right'. The anonymity of Morley's *Lessons* was the occasion for the jibe concerning 'Authors names'. Both Morley's and Rosseter's collections now survive imperfectly, but a set of books used by the Oxford waits (and perhaps their Cambridge counterparts), together with other sources, including a set of consort books compiled for Sir Francis Walsingham, allow some identifications and res-torations to be made. A selection of these pieces is printed in *MB* XL, which together with Beck's reconstruction of Morley's set (1959) gives some idea of this fascinating repertory. It should be remarked, however, that much of the waits' repertory would have been improvised, often on a ground, the tunes being 'broken' (ie. played with divisions, the correct meaning of the word) extemporaneously. This practice led Burney to speak slightingly of Morley's *Consort Lessons*, saying in his *History* that Morley 'was not so very nice in setting parts to these tunes, which are so very far from correct, that almost any one of the city waits would, in musical cant, have *vamped* as good an accompaniment.'

The mixing of diverse instruments in these specific 'consorts', or indeed the combination of any group of instruments and perhaps voices, raises a serious performance problem in regard to the compatibility of pitch levels. It is often assumed that lutes, viols and other stringed instruments of the time were able to play at a variety of pitches simply by tuning flat or sharp. This notion is far from the truth, however, since the method of instrument construction, allied with the use of comparatively thick gut strings (though the bandora and cittern were wire strung) made it necessary for the strings to be of maximum tension, so that the instrument might 'speak' properly. This explains why Thomas Robinson (1603) made the apparently absurd remark that the treble string of a viol should be tightened 'so high as you dare venter for breaking' [sc. 'venture before breaking']. Mace (1676) uses almost exactly the same words, in common with Playford, who says: 'When you begin to Tune, raise your *Treble* or smallest string as high as conveniently it will bear without breaking' (1674, p. 93).

This maximum tension is an audible condition; it therefore effectively fixes the pitch of the instrument. This property has been shown by im-portant research undertaken by Abbott and Segerman (1974) who concluded that English viols would have responded to tuning 'at least a tone below the modern standard'. It is interesting to note that Martin Mersenne speaking of the viol (1636, VII, 4th book) observed that 'the English ordinarily play their pieces lower than the French', explaining that French *C* is thus English *D*. Although this statement depends on the pitch Mersenne took as his point of reference, it accords with Praetorius' assertion (1618, XX) that the English play their viols a fourth or fifth lower (ie. than his high pitch — see below). Michael Prynne (*Grove* 5, s.v. 'lute') has concluded that lutes were also tuned to a pitch of 'no higher than three quarters of a tone lower than modern pitch'. Since viols and lutes, and indeed other instruments, were often played together, the standard English Elizabethan string pitch seems to have been a tone lower than the modern standard of *a* = 440.

This lower pitch, henceforward denoted as *B flat* pitch, has a considerable significance for singers, since songs with viols or the lute would have been sung a tone lower than appears at first sight. There seems to have been more than one standard of instrumental pitch, however: Michael Lowe suggested to me some years ago that lutes and viols were made in two different pitch ranges, and recent evidence seems to confirm that there were small, high pitch viols, and lutes standing a fourth higher than the pitch of a range of larger instruments. Thus, by using a small or large instrument, a lutenist could offer a singer a choice of two pitches, a fourth apart. The larger 'mean' lute would play at *B flat* pitch, whereas the same accompaniment played on the smaller 'treble' lute would sound a fourth higher, at *E flat* pitch, a minor third above present–day pitch.

Ex. 58

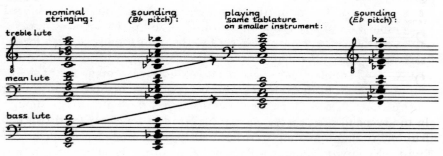

The lutenist would be unaware of the transposition, since his tablature was merely a set of symbols denoting on which fret to place his fingers. The singer, for his part, would treat the written notes in a manner similar to 'tonic solfa', and would understand relative, rather than absolute pitch. The chosen pitch would depend upon the singer's range and the clef of the voice part: C clef parts would suit a low or medium voice if accompanied upon the mean or treble lute respectively, whereas G clef vocal parts would suit, respectively, a medium or high voice.

It is possible that some songs were transposed to a low *F* pitch by using a bass lute, whose pitch was a fourth below *B flat* pitch. Dowland's 'Come when I call' (1603) employs two unspecified lutes pitched a fourth apart; for this song the choice of singing pitches would thus be limited to two, the lutes being tuned to *F* and *B flat*, or *B flat* and *E flat*. Campion's 1601 collection contains 'The cypress curtain of the night' which is remarkable in that the voice part is printed a tone higher than the key implied by the tablature. The voice part would thus have sounded a major third lower or a semitone higher in relation to modern pitch, depending on the choice of lute; the use of the bass lute, which would result in the voice part being heard a major sixth lower, seems unlikely.

Since a bass, viol part was regularly included in lute-song publications, it is clear that the viols must have been compatibly pitched. Ian Harwood (1981) has argued that *B flat* pitch viols, in bass, tenor and treble sizes, were complemented by *E flat* pitch sizes. Since the treble was pitched an octave above the bass, and the tenor a fifth below the treble, there were thus five sizes in all. The high pitch tenor is the origin of the fictitious 'alto viol'.

Ex. 59

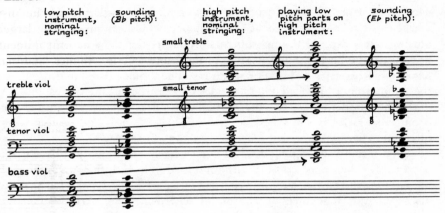

In the event that the lowest part of a concerted song was written with a baritone (F₃) clef, the use of low-pitch instruments would be indicated. Byrd's 'Ye sacred muses' is in 'd minor' in one source and could have been read at *B flat* or *E flat* pitch, sounding in c or f minor respectively; in another source, however, the notation is transposed up a fourth ('g minor') so at *B flat* pitch this version comes to the same thing as the 'f minor' alternative in the other version. The clefs of the higher source warn against a further upward transposition, however, since the lowest part has an F₃ clef. A further source, for lute alone, displays yet another nominal pitch, which would have sounded in 'e flat minor' at *B flat* pitch or 'a flat minor' at *E flat* pitch.

In music for viols alone, the pitch standard chosen would be less crucial than when vocal participation was involved. There are, nonetheless, several instances of purely instrumental music where one standard of pitch rather than the other is clearly required. Taverner's 'Quemadmodum' (BL Add 31390) can hardly be played at the low pitch: its tessitura is about a fourth below the norm for instrumental music of this kind: the use of the low clefs confirms that the high *E flat* pitch was envisaged. On the other hand, the music of Alfonso Ferrabosco I regularly employs the continental 'high clefs' in common with Deering (see for example his fantazia, *MB* IX, no. 38): here the high tessitura and clefs clearly indicate that *B flat* pitch was intended.

Ian Harwood (1981) has pointed out that Morley's *Consort Lessons* and other works for the characteristic waits ensemble pose several problems, notably in connection with the flute part. The latter stands a fourth lower than is feasibly playable; such a part demands a flute so large as to be cumbersome in divisions and which would be unable to achieve a satisfactory tonal balance. If the bandora, cittern, lute, treble and bass viols are assumed, however, to have played at *E flat* pitch, the problem is solved by the flute part being played on a smaller instrument a fourth higher. Morley's *Consort Lessons* indeed specify a 'treble' (ie. high pitch) lute. The whole ensemble is pictured at the foot of the Unton mural (see cover illustration) where all the instruments are clearly of the small size. Here, however, a violin is shown, in spite of the express designation of a viol in Morley's, Rosseter's and other collections. The violin existed in three sizes; the countertenor, pitched like a modern viola; the mean, corresponding with the modern instrument; and the treble, an octave above the countertenor. As is shown by several title pages, viols and violins were often interchangeable.

Many of the items in Leighton's *Teares or Lamentacions* of 1614 have parts specified for the mixed consort, although the treble viol, flute and bass viol merely play the cantus, altus and bassus voice parts. The *E flat* pitch already discussed suits the voices in the pieces where they are accompanied by instruments. Robert Tailour's *Fifti Select Psalms* of 1615, however, demand a different pitch; here, the music 'set to be sung in Five parts, as also to the Viole and Lute or Orph-arion' has a rather high tessitura. The *B flat* pitch would be more suitable for Tailour's *Psalms*, though the bass part would then be rather low. Leighton's 'unaccompanied' pieces also pose problems, for both the *E flat* and *B flat* pitches are less than ideal. The pitch which best suits the voice ranges of these items is, curiously, modern pitch. Both Leighton's and Tailour's collections are domestic rather than church music, so if a *C* pitch is to be envisaged for the purely vocal performance of both of these anthologies, then a third chamber pitch must have been in use, roughly corresponding with the modern standard of *a* = 440 Hz.

There is some evidence for this third chamber pitch. Praetorius, who mentions the 'English consort' of the waits also remarks (1618, p. 16) that 'most English wind instruments were formerly tuned a minor third lower than our present chamber pitch' (sc. *E flat* pitch — see Chapter 8 for further discussion of this question). This statement matches the evidence of the early seventeenth-century cornetts in the possession of Christ Church, Oxford, which are approximately at modern pitch. Since cornetts played together with sackbuts, it must be presumed that sackbuts were also capable of playing at this *C* pitch. If this were so, however, there is the problem of reconciling what must have been the *E flat* pitch of the organ and violin in Loosemore's 'Verse' with the pitch of the cornett and sackbut. The mechanism by which this was achieved is not at present clear, but since Coprario used the organ in connection with all of the foregoing instruments, and indeed the viol, it is obvious that some method of transposition must have been employed. Similarly, Peerson's publications indicate some kind of compatibility of pitch. His *Mottects or Graue Chamber Musique* (1630) are 'fit for voyces and vials, with an organ part' and his *Priuate Musicke* (1620) is also for 'voyces and viols. And for want of viols, they may be performed to either the virginall or lute'.

The *Walsingham* partbooks of the waits repertory specify a recorder; this instrument must therefore have been capable of playing at *E flat* pitch. Peter Holman (1981) has argued that the fantazias by Jerome Bassano in Oxford Ch Ch 716–20 are for recorders. The compasses suggest that, like the viols, recorders were able to move between *B flat* and *E flat* pitches by using a smaller range of instruments a fourth higher.

The pitch of the lyra viol was extremely variable. It gained increasing popularity as the first quarter of the seventeenth century progressed, and was built to be tuned in a bewildering number of *scordature*, and thus employed tablature notation. Its repertory, which consists largely of variations, is represented in Hume's publications of 1605 and 1607 and also Thomas Ford's *Musicke of Sundrie Kinds* (1607).

Another important collection for lyra viol is by Alfonso Ferrabosco II (Anthony Wood called him 'most excellent at the lyraviol') entitled *Lessons for 1, 2 and 3 Viols*, printed in 1609; Maynard's *The XII Wonders of the World* (1611) is also noteworthy. Music for cittern was published in Holborne's *The Cittharn Schoole* (1597) and Robinson's *New Citharen Lessons* (1609), and the bandora and orpharion were catered for in two separate publications of William Barley in 1596. Surprisingly, however, the vast repertory for solo lute (which extends to roughly four times the surviving amount of virginal music) hardly appeared in print: Barley's *A New Booke of Tabliture* (1596) and Robert Dowland's *Varietie of Lute Lessons* (1610) are the only printed collections solely devoted to lute music. The lute compositions of John Dowland were only sporadically printed, in spite of their enormous popularity both at home and abroad. His 'Lachrimae', however, was published in several versions; since it was perhaps the most well-known piece of the time it is an appropriate conclusion to this brief survey:

Ex. 60

(cf Poulton & Lam, 1974, no. 15)

CHAPTER 5

With Fingers and with Penne

A long eulogy in John Baldwin's commonplace book (BL RM 24. d. 2) gives pride of place to Byrd, 'Whose greater skill and knowledge dothe excelle all at this time'. He specifically praises Byrd's playing, thus: 'With fingers and with penne he hathe not now his peere,/For in this worlde so wide is none can him come neere'. Orlando Gibbons was to stake a rival claim as a player, for he was reputed to have 'the best Finger of that Age', and it must be supposed that John Bull, the composer of the most highly virtuoso music of the period, was also a formidable executant. That these were the three principal composers of virginals music of the Jacobean period is reflected in their appearance as the 'three famous Masters' whose music was printed in *Parthenia or the Maydenhead . . .* (1613).

Although Baldwin's eulogy is partisan doggerel, there is no doubt that the compositions and playing technique of the English virginalists and organists exerted a profound effect upon keyboard composition and execution on the Continent. The development of Tudor keyboard music was extraordinarily rapid. There is little or no sign of a distinctive keyboard style until the late fifteenth century, but many of the idiomatic figurations found in *Parthenia* are evident by the mid sixteenth century. Transcriptions of vocal or instrumental music do not loom so large as the repertory develops, although there is still a heavy reliance on ground basses and cantus firmi. That cantus firmus should predominate in early organ music is perfectly natural, since the organ played a purely liturgical role. The Te Deum and Magnificat were frequently performed *alternatim*, the organ providing the polyphonic verses, the choir singing alternate verses in plainchant; and office hymns, responds and antiphons were also treated in this way, with the organ acting in the stead of the select part of the choir. In the Mass both Propers and Ordinary were frequently set, though the Kyrie, Alleluia, Sanctus and Agnus Dei were the most usual items, together with the Offertory 'Felix namque', which seems to have had a vogue as an independent piece, after the manner of the In Nomine. An early sixteenth-century, possibly earlier, Felix namque occurs in BL Roy. App. 56; it makes much use of complex rhythmical proportions, including

Fig. 11 Organ Screen of King's College, Cambridge, showing Dallam organ case, similar to that of Tomkins' organ at Worcester

quintuple time and eight in the time of three. Another Felix namque in the same source appears to require two players and, since the intonation is included in the organ setting, is probably one of the earliest non-liturgical treatments of this cantus firmus. The same MS also contains a florid Kyrie on a 'square' cantus firmus, which enshrines a primarily improvisatory technique of organ playing.

A later MS, BL Add. 15233, contains several pieces by Redford, together with some of his literary efforts; he is also represented in the *Mulliner Book* and in Oxford Ch Ch 371, dating from 1560 or so. Unlike the foregoing sources, BL Add. 29996 preserves a systematic repertory of liturgical organ music. As it stands, it is a compilation of various music manuscripts of different periods bound together — it was owned by Thomas Tomkins and indexed by his son, Nathaniel. The three earliest sections of this MS are devoted to liturgical organ music, the first representing an early Henrician repertory, including a Mass by Philip ap Rhys. Had the Creed been finished, this would have been the only surviving complete British setting of an Organ Mass. The second section of the MS comprises music solely by Thomas Preston, and appears to be of Marian date (one of the notable works is his setting of the Propers for Easter Day). Preston's music is often technically difficult, frequently employing chains of left-hand thirds, and lines of differing metrical proportions, but there is also a contrapuntal assurance which prevents the virtuoso element getting out of hand. Preston's music tends to avoid the somewhat mechanical impression left by Redford's over-use of sequences of ostinato figures:

Ex. 61

(Redford, 'Eterne rex altissime'; cf *MB* I no.26)

The corpus of liturgical organ music found in this and other sources is printed in *Early English Church Music* (*EECM*) 6 and 10, although there are several important pieces of the genre scattered in Mulliner's anthology (*MB* I) probably dating from the Marian period. Besides works by other composers, principally Redford, the *Mulliner Book* contains liturgical organ works by Tallis and Blitheman, whose compositions represent something of a climax of the style. In common with the other sources, the chanted verses are not given by Mulliner, so the organ hymns are twice as long as they appear to be in *MB* I; thus Tallis' 'Ecce tempus idoneum' is a five-verse hymn whose two organ verses, separated as nos. 100 and 105 in the *Mulliner Book*, represent verses 2 and 4 of the hymn, the odd numbered verses being chanted. Similarly, Blitheman's 'Gloria tibi trinitas' (a hymn having no connection with the antiphon which gave rise to the In Nomine) is thirteen verses in length, the six of *MB* I nos. 91–96 requiring to be complemented by seven plainchant verses.

These hymns, together with Blitheman's 'Eterne rerum conditor', represent an excellent cross-section of the best pieces of the genre. The latter admirably demonstrates the technique of the organ hymn. As usual, the even-numbered verses are set polyphonically. The opening verse is therefore chanted, and the organ plays verse 2 as a bicinium in which the cantus firmus is barely recognizable in the left hand. The setting sustains a remarkable rhythmic development ending in a brilliant coloratura passage for the right hand. Verse 4 (the second in which the organ is heard) has the cantus firmus mostly in long notes in the bass, with a development, in two upper parts, of the ostinato type of theme favoured by Redford. The sixth verse of the hymn provides a contrast of texture, and probably of tempo. This exquisite working of the cantus firmus in the tenor is entitled *melos suave* in the MS. How sweetly indeed it flows, ending with the familiar 'English cadence', which in Blitheman's time had not yet quite become the cliché vilified by Morley as 'robde out of the capcase of some olde Organist . . . though it fit the fingers as that the deformitie whereof may be hidden by flurrish . . . where as it might well enough be left out, though it be very usuall with our *Organists*' (Morley, 1597, pp. 164 and 154):

Ex. 62

[chant, disguised]

(Blitheman, 'Eterne rerum'; cf *MB* I no.51)

In the eighth verse the cantus firmus has risen to the treble; a two-part texture of unceasing rhythmic vitality is set against it, providing a fitting conclusion to one of the most perfect sets of 'chorale variations' prior to, and indeed including, Bach.

Of Blitheman's career little is known. According to Anthony Wood, he was supposed to have been a member of the choir at Christ Church, Oxford, but this cannot be substantiated. He died on Whitsunday 1591, and was buried at St Nicholas, Coleabbey, where the following epitaph (Stow, 1618) mentions that Bull was his pupil:

Heere *Blitheman* lyes, a worthy wight,
   Who feared God above;
A friend to all, a foe to none,
   Whom rich and poor did love.
Of Princes Chappell Gentleman,
   Unto his dying day;
Whom all tooke great delight to heare
   Him on the Organs play.

Whose passing skill in Musicks art,
   A Scholler left behind;
John Bull (by name) his Masters vaine
   Expressing in each kind.
But nothing here continues long,
   Nor resting place can have;
His soule departed hence to Heaven,
   His body here in grave.

With the exception of Blitheman's hymns and Te Deum, Mulliner was somewhat off-hand about the manner in which liturgical organ music was copied into his book, perhaps reflecting that the genre had fallen out of use by his day. Various verses were scattered about its contents, to the extent that Redford's setting of the Te Deum and the Mass are in a hopelessly dismembered state, as are many liturgical organ works by other composers.

Liturgical cantus firmi such as the Miserere, Felix namque and especially the In Nomine became divorced from their original functions and served as the framework of purely secular pieces. The brevity of the Miserere was suitable for succinct movements, whereas the prolixity of the Felix namque chant allowed all manner of canonic and proportional devices to be explored, often to an intolerable length, of which even Tallis himself was guilty (see *FWVB* CIX-CX). In general, the In Nomine cantus firmus was developed in instrumental music, alongside popular tunes such as the Browning theme; but contrived cantus firmi also came into use, as is evident in the enchanting 'Uppon la mi re' found in BL Add. 29996, which Denis Stevens has plausibly attributed to Preston. Even here, however, the first three notes appear to be derived from the 'Spagna' (an earlier *bassadanza* theme later pressed into service for didactic and other purposes):

Ex. 63

(lower part transposed an octave higher than written: see p.154)

Robert White (if he is the 'Mr. Whight' of Oxford Ch Ch 371) is the composer of a pithy 'Ut re me fa sol la':

Ex. 64

The *Mulliner Book* includes several keyboard works which are independent of pre-existing material. At least two of these — the voluntary by Richard Allwood and a similar composition by Farrant — may be assumed to be for organ. Although in the strictest sense the organ ceased to have a precise ritual role after the establishment of the English liturgy, the playing of voluntaries (ie. pieces not bound by a cantus firmus) was customary at various points of the service. James Clifford (1663) records the continued use of an Offertory voluntary, and an organ piece was usual after the collects and before the anthem at Matins and Evensong. What seem to be earlier precursors of the voluntary are found in BL Roy. App. 56 whose contents may be as early as 1530, and a similar composition by John Ambrose occurs in Oxford Ch Ch 1034A (dated about 1570).

The earliest sixteenth-century source of secular keyboard music is BL Roy. App. 58. In common with BL Roy. App. 56 it dates from the 1530s or 1540s, and both have apparently a west country provenance. BL Roy. App. 58 includes an arrangement of a vocal piece 'Heven & earth' (which later occurs in more elaborate forms elsewhere, notably in *FWVB*), as well as 'The emperorse pavyn', 'A galyarde', 'The Kyngs pavin' (alternatively titled 'Kyng Harry the VIIIth Pavyn'), 'The crocke', 'The Kyngs marke' (perhaps *recte* 'maske') and another 'galyard'. These pieces are probably arrangements of vocal and instrumental pieces of continental origin, brought over when Charles V of France visited England in 1522; most of them can be traced in continental sources. 'A hornepype' by Hugh Aston, 'My lady careys dompe' and 'The short mesure off my lady wynkfylds rownde' are, however, idiomatic English keyboard works, and display many of the characteristics of the Elizabethan and Jacobean virginalist style.

Aston and his contemporaries still cling, nonetheless, to pre-existing material: a ground, or something like it, is present in all three works by Aston. 'My lady careys dompe' has a remorseless tonic-tonic-dominant-dominant bass in the minor key, whereas 'my lady wynkfylds rownde' is in C major having the bass C-G-C-B [flat]-B [flat]-C-G-C, interspersed with a plain tonic and dominant bass. Aston's 'hornepype' is more adventurous in that the basic tonic and dominant pattern is ingeniously varied. But for all this, 'My lady careys dompe', whose left-hand broken-chord bass and

109

right-hand embellishments prefigure the later virginalist style, has an extraordinary telling impetus, in spite of its uncompromisingly primitive
harmonic structure:

Ex. 65

(BL Roy App 56)

A few pieces are found in early MSS described by Dart (1964) and Blezzard
(1981) — see also Ward (1983). There is a more substantial amount of
secular keyboard music in the *Mulliner Book*. The left-hand broken-chord
bass is again evident in 'O ye happy dames', a somewhat bumbling setting
of 'The maiden's song' (untitled in the MS but later more majestically
treated by Byrd) and the use of a ground bass is again evident in the
associated galliard (also untitled). What seem to be French dance songs
appear under the titles 'La bounette', 'La doune cella' and 'La shy myze'; but
these trifles are overshadowed by Newman's 'Pavyon', which takes pride of
place in Mulliner's anthology:

Ex. 66

[etc.]

The *Dublin Virginal Book* (see Ward, 1957 and 1983) is an entirely secular
repertory dating from 1570 or so. It appears to have been copied by John
Tayler who succeeded Robert White at Westminster; one of White's works
is the basis of the pavan no. 21 (see p. 305). The MS testifies to a continued
reliance on Italianate ground basses, and to the influence of continental
music in general, for much of its contents can be traced to French and other
sources. The book also evinces the growing popularity of the paired pavan
and galliard, of which there are five examples in the MS. Besides these,
there are almans, and other dances, including independent galliards.

   My Ladye Nevells Booke (copied by Baldwin and completed in 1591)
contains music exclusively by Byrd; once again, the penchant of virginalists
for a ground bass is signified by the first item of the MS, 'My ladye Nevels
grownde'. There follows a miscellaneous collection of pieces, including a

curious piece of programme music centering upon 'The battell' after which there is a sequence of pavans and galliards followed by another miscellany of variations, voluntaries and so forth.

Alan Brown has argued that the elaborately descriptive 'Battell' sequence (*MB* XXVIII) was probably prompted by John Derricke's *The Image of Irelaunde* (1581), in which various skirmishes between the English and the Irish are described, notably the defeat of O'Neill, Earl of Tyrone, in 1578. 'The Irishe marche' with 'The bagpipe and the drone' is contrasted by Byrd with the English sounds of 'flute and the droome'; and in the 'marche to the fighte', the section before 'the battels be joyned' has a clear representation of the 'charge'—a trumpet call which remained the same up to the present century:

Ex. 67

the battles be joined

Byrd's connection with the Sidney family (Sir Henry Sidney was Lord Deputy for Ireland and Derricke's book was dedicated to Sir Philip) doubtless lay behind Byrd's contribution to this curious genre; battle pieces have been written by several composers from Jannequin onwards, but it must be said that most (including Byrd's setting and Beethoven's Op. 91) have only modest musical interest.

My Ladye Nevells Book (henceforward *Nevell*) also contains several dances reflecting country pastimes, and variations on popular tunes. 'The barelye breake' (Byrd's setting quotes the tune 'The leaves be green') was an energetic dance for three couples, described by Sidney in 'Lamon'. The same dance is mentioned in Morley's well-known ballett 'Now is the month of maying' where one finds the line 'Say dainty nymphs and speak — Shall we play barley break?' Incidentally, the words *speak* and *break*, then pronounced in what would seem to our ears after a somewhat northern fashion, would of course have rhymed.

The ground bass of 'Hugh Ashtons grownde' has been ingeniously traced by Nick Sandon (1981) to 'Hugh Ashtons maske', an early instrumental composition whose bass part, though missing, is clearly the same ground. In turn, this bass was used in several other compositions, notably a Mass which must now be attributed to Aston. Ground basses, as was seen in an earlier chapter, were the stock-in-trade of the itinerant musician, allowing him to improvise on a ground which was being played by another not particularly gifted player, or to 'vamp' an extempore dance on the virginals after the fashion of the Bergomask settings entitled 'Dr Bull's Ground' (*MB* XIX — see also the 'New Bergomask' and 'The King's Hunt', and cf. p. 63).

The Bergomask ground features in Morley's Alman (*FWVB* CLII), Farnaby's 'Up tails all' (*FWVB* CCXLIII) and many other songs and dances. Even more popular basses were the Passamezzo antico, upon which Byrd composed his 'Ninth', or 'Passinge Mesures' pavan and galliard, and the Passamezzo moderno upon which Bull and Byrd wrote 'Quadran' pavans and galliards. 'Quadran' referred to the B *quadro* or 'natural' which distinguished it from the b *molle* of the 'flat' *antico* ground:

Ex. 68

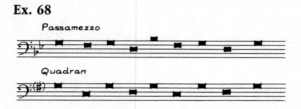

Byrd's Passamezzo pavan and galliard (*FWVB* LVI-LVII) begin thus:

Ex. 69

Commonly, the melodic ideas of the duple-time pavan were taken over into the triple-time galliard. One of the most curious transmutations is Dowland's 'Galliard to lachrimae' for lute, printed in 1612. Here the duple-time 'lachrymae' theme is fitted into the triple-time willy-nilly, with little or no modification of time values. With one exception, Byrd does not derive the melodic material of the galliard from the pavan. This emphasizes the harmonic standpoint from which the English viewed the process of variation. It is notable that even where variation sets are composed upon melodies such as 'The carman's whistle' or 'Go from my window', several individual variations are based upon the harmonic rather than the melodic implications of the opening theme — it is perhaps no coincidence that 'ground' was applied to both kinds of variations. This makes for a variety of technique which far transcends that of the somewhat mechanical melodic-based continental variations of the same period. It is noteworthy that in Italy even the ground bass variations tended to follow a melodic line of derivation, perhaps reflecting that improvised dances were loath to leave entirely their earlier, melodically generated, methods of extemporization. Thus, the English use of ground basses and of variation form is often more sophisticated than might appear at first sight; in turn, the harmonic aspect was intimately related to the rise of a new kind of tonality, shortly to be discussed, a movement in which the English virginalists were in the vanguard.

Amongst examples of their ingenious use of ground bass, Byrd and Bull often indulge in deliberate crudity, apparently to pillory the efforts of hack musicians; several of their works are larded with 'vamped' consecutives, as for example in 'Dr Bull's ground'. Here, the erudite sound of the title is belied by the music:

Ex. 70

(cf *MB* XIX no. 102)

Byrd and Bull also contributed, if only in small measure, to the duet literature. Bull's 'A battle, and no battle' (*MB* XIX, no. 108, doubtless inspired by Byrd's essay) requires two players, the second to play the ground; similarly, Byrd's 'Ut re mi' (*MB* XXVIII, no. 58) requires 'The playnesong Breifes to Be playd By a second person'. The latter includes quotations from the song 'The woods so wild' (a popular tune which is found in countless pieces of various types including Byrd's own variations of the same title); also quoted is 'The shaking of the sheets', which occurs in Deering's 'Country Cries'.

As would be expected, Byrd lavished much contrapuntal skill on his fantazias and voluntaries. Although one or two of these are merely adaptations from instrumental fantazias, most — such as the brilliant 'Verse' (*MB* XXVII, no. 28) — are original keyboard compositions. The word 'Verse' derives from the practice of playing *alternatim* verses in liturgical organ music: later it came to mean the same as 'fantazia', 'fantasy', 'fancy' and 'voluntary', the last implying that an organ piece is paraliturgical, rather than strictly liturgical (as in the case of Byrd's settings of the hymn 'Salvator mundi' and antiphon 'Miserere', both for Compline). The voluntary, nevertheless, was often an important part of the Anglican service. Edward Gibbons' 'Prelude upon the organ as was usual before the Anthem' (BL Harley 7340) doubtless established the key for the choir (as similar pieces, eg. the 'Versus' by Sheppard in the *Mulliner Book*, may have done earlier). The short preludes and fantazias by his brother Orlando Gibbons (*MB* XX, nos. 3–6, 46–7) might have served a similar function and not only for Full anthems and services, for Verse anthems and services occasionally begin without introduction (eg. the Nunc Dimittis to Gibbons' Second service and 'Almighty God who by Thy Son', if the editorial reconstruction of *EECM* 3 is accepted).

In common with Bull, Byrd occasionally prefixed a prelude before a fantazia:, as in *MB* XXVII, nos. 12–13. This fantazia is a substantial piece, of many varied moods, and includes a triple-time section in which the chime motive (more fully worked out in 'The bells' — *MB* XXVII, no. 38) appears. The 'Ut re mi' pieces by Byrd found in *FWVB* were intended as a pair, as is indicated by the copyist's Latin direction *perge* inserted between them. Although pairings of this kind were comparatively infrequent, the pavan and galliard were by now more regularly composed together as a pair, particularly by Byrd.

The central part of *Nevell* is occupied by a splendid sequence of nine pavans and galliards, with a tenth coming towards the end of the manuscript. The ordering is clearly not the copyist's whim, but appears to be a sequence authorized, or indeed dictated, by Byrd: 'The firste pavian', for example, is described in *FWVB* as 'The first t[hat] ever hee m[ade]', and it is clear that 'The tennthe pavian' is a later work. The fact that 'The firste pavian' is also found in an instrumental version is a reminder that dance music was often transferred from concerted instruments to lute and keyboard settings. Byrd's pavans and galliards, nonetheless, are further removed from the dance floor, and belong to the realm of abstract music. The almans, corantos, jigs and voltas are more nearly related to the dance, as their use of popular tunes confirms; indeed, many are simply short variations on well-known tunes. Byrd's contribution to the variation form proper is much more eloquent, evincing an elaboration of the improvisatory methods of the 'cantabanqui' by a master contrapuntist. The resulting techniques are far beyond the ken of 'pettifoggers of music'. Some of the earlier variations, the 'Gipsies round' for example, are perhaps closer to the world of the 'small musickes'; but 'O mistress mine', 'The carman's whistle' and many other compositions of this genre command a range of expression and ingenuity which characterized English virginalist variations, and which drew forth admiration and imitation by continental composers such as Sweelinck.

Apart from *Nevell*, whose contents are wholly by Byrd, there are many other important sources of his music, of which the most wide ranging and important is *FWVB*; this MS is also noteworthy in that it also contains the bulk of Bull's extant keyboard music. *FWVB* was copied between 1609 and 1619 by the Cornishman Francis Tregian, an entrenched recusant. He was one of eighteen children, and educated at Douai (the College in Flanders for Roman Catholic exiles from Britain) until 1592, when he became chamberlain to Cardinal Allen in Rome. In 1605, however, he returned to Britain in an attempt to regain his confiscated estates. This led to a conviction for recusancy and subsequent imprisonment in the Fleet: there he remained from 1613 until 1619, the year of his death. Tregian was heavily in debt, so the prison warden frequently attempted to take away his possessions by way of repayment. Tregian's own efforts to repay his debts led him to become a commercial scribe; but he was already an avid copyist of music on his own account, and it is clear that he was anxious that the more precious MSS copied for his own use should not be involved in any financial transactions. Thus, as Elisabeth Cole pointed out (1953), *FWVB* bears the signs of having been rolled up and smuggled in and out of the Fleet, being bound up only on completion of the collection. The originals were doubtless to be found among the 'many hundreds' of his books which the warden attempted to sequester, but which his sisters managed to retain by conveying them to a friend and fellow prisoner, Sir Francis Englefield.

Tregian's choice of composers, both in the *FWVB* and in his two major collections of partmusic (BL Egerton 3665 and NY PL Drexel 4302), was biased to a certain extent towards fellow recusants such as Philips, Byrd, Alfonso Ferrabosco I, and indeed Bull, if his avowals are to be regarded as genuine. But it would be a mistake to think that the compilation of these MSS was sectarian, since Farnaby, whose work occupies a considerable portion of the *FWVB*, was of Huguenot descent, and a staunch Puritan Anglican.

The lavish representation of Bull in *FWVB*, on the contrary, was on grounds of merit alone; his bravura style, highly influential in respect of continental music, is technically the most formidable among the English virginalists. A portrait of Bull, now in the Faculty of Music at Oxford, shows him surrounded by the following motto:

> The Bull by force
> In field doth Raigne
> But Bull by Skill
> Good will doth Gayne.

In spite of this disclaimer he seems to have steered a remarkably bovine course through a veritable china shop of a career. Although his early years were marked by poverty, his fortunes had changed by 1597, when he was appointed Gresham Professor of Music. He was allowed to lecture in English (his colleagues had to do so in Latin) and, as a further concession, to depart from the appointed timetable (Stow, 1618, p. 123).

In spite of this generosity shown towards him, Bull seems to have fallen foul of almost every other statute governing his post at Gresham. His College rooms were still occupied by the late Sir Thomas Gresham's stepson, but Bull was anxious not to lose his lectureship by failing to reside there. His solution, to gain entry by battering down the wall of one of the rooms was without subtlety, and it may well have been behaviour of this sort which failed to secure him any substantial preferment in Elizabeth's or James' Court. The Gresham statutes obliged the holders of Professorships to remain bachelors: Bull's tenuous grip on his post was thus lost when he was forced to marry in 1607.

In 1612 or 1613 the 'three famous masters' — Bull, Byrd and Gibbons — issued the collection of virginals music entitled *Parthenia* (full title was *Parthenia or the Maydenhead of the first musicke that ever was printed for the virginalls*). At this time Bull was music teacher to Princess Elizabeth (for whose marriage to the Elector Palatine he composed an anthem, now lost); but these brief halcyon days were soon followed by a final disaster. He was arraigned in 1613 for various 'grievous crimes', especially adultery. King James' dislike of Bull thereupon grew to open hate. The composer fled to Antwerp, joining his fellow exile and friend Peter Philips in the service of the Archduke Albert. The British envoy at Brussels knew perfectly well the circumstances leading up to Bull's arrival, since he had received a letter from the Archbishop of Canterbury in which Bull was described as having 'more music than honesty and is as famous for marying of virginity as he is for fingering of organs and virginals'. The recipient of this Shakespearean *double entendre*, Sir William Trumble, was blamed by the King for concealing Bull's whereabouts. At the insistence of King James, Trumble therefore persuaded the Archduke to dismiss Bull. But the kindly Archduke continued to support the composer in a roundabout financial fashion, and Bull finally became organist of the cathedral at Antwerp in 1617. He achieved this by declaring that his allegiance to the Roman Catholic faith was the true reason for his fleeing from the King. Although it is unlikely to have had much truth, the explanation seems to have sufficed, for Bull remained in Antwerp until his death in 1628.

Bull's output consisted of a large number of pavans, galliards and other dances and many ingenious canonic pieces. He wrote at least 120 canons, most of which are based on the plainchant 'Miserere'. One or two canons are for keyboard, and are printed in *MB* XIV.

In common with Byrd's, Bull's fantazias were sometimes preceded by a prelude, thus forming what to all intents and purposes is a prelude and fugue, though Bull's fantazias are perhaps more like toccatas. Much of his later keyboard music was liturgical: he set several hymns, including 'Salvator mundi', 'Jam lucis' and other plainsongs, which date from his years at Antwerp. The prelude and carol 'Laet ons met herten rejne' have the distinction of being the earliest organ music to contain directions for registration; but they are for a Flemish rather than an English organ.

Bull's music is often highly chromatic: one of his settings of 'Ut re mi' (*MB* XIV, no. 17) modulates into extreme flat and sharp keys. Nicholas Carleton (in a later layer of Tomkins' MS — BL Add. 29996) also wrote two highly chromatic pieces — 'Upon the sharpe' (centering on c sharp minor) and 'A verse of four parts' beginning and ending in c minor, but going through the cycle of sharp and flat keys. These are works in which *A sharps* and *B flats*, *D sharps* and *E flats* require a keyboard temperament not unlike that of today.

Theoretical discussions of the time give the impression that Pythagorean intonation, founded upon perfect fourths and fifths, was current during the Renaissance. A circle of perfect fifths cannot be closed, for a yawning gap inevitably opens between enharmonic notes which might otherwise meet. Because of this, Pythagorean temperament was impracticable, even for the mildest chromaticism; and since its thirds were extremely sharp, the temperament was also unflattering where chords with thirds were emphasized. 'Just intonation', which takes several of the 'natural harmonics' as its starting point, was also discussed by Renaissance theorists; it, too, is equally problematic. The true major third (eg. as found on the natural harmonics of the horn) is rather flatter than that of equal temperament and flatter still than the Pythagorean third. There is thus an irresoluble conflict between a temperament with perfect fifths, in which the thirds are sharp, and one in which the thirds are perfect. The latter temperament has another disadvantage, in that the natural harmonics making up the progression *CDE* produce two different sized tones, the major tone *CD* being considerably larger than the minor tone *DE*. Thus, although these tones and the third *CE* are perfect in the key of C major, the tone *CD* must be adjusted for the key of B flat, and *DE* similarly for the key of D, making modulation impossible.

A solution to the dilemma was to have a 'mean-tone' temperament, in which the major and minor tones were averaged out. In one kind of meantone temperament, the perfect third was retained (cf. Zarlino, 1571): this and its variants persisted until the nineteenth century. It, too, was not without problems, and was unsuitable for extreme keys. By abandoning perfect thirds and sharpening them so that they lay between the acoustical and Pythagorean third, various kinds of intonation, approaching equal temperament, were achieved (cf. Cerone, 1613). Doubtless, it was for this kind of temperament, where neither fifths nor thirds were perfect, but were variously adjusted, that the English chromatic pieces were written. Perfect third temperament was nonetheless more popular in general; only viols and lutes used what amounted to equal temperament proper, in which all the thirds and fifths are roughly of the same dimensions. For this reason keyboard and fretted instruments were not readily compatible. The problem appears to have been solved by the time of Gibbons' fantazias for viols and organ: if these instruments were reconciled by adjusting the temperament of the organ, then the latter must have been able to accommodate the chromaticisms of Bull, Carleton and others.

It is plain that in these pieces tonality has little to do with the so-called 'modes'. Much ink has been wasted on irrelevant discussion of the modes: they had remained aridly theoretical concepts since the Middle Ages, when Hermanus Contractus and others tried to embrace the ethical and formulistic characteristics of the chant within eight scale patterns (see Wulstan, 1971a). Attempts to link polyphonic music with the modes are doubly unwise in view of the fact that the Renaissance theorist Tinctoris (1476) denied any possibility of polyphonic modality.

Much of the misunderstanding of the question lies in the ambiguity of our terminology; it is obvious that tonal music of the Baroque era seems to behave differently from the music say, of Vaughan Williams or of Palestrina, and it is natural that the two latter composers should be described equally as 'modal'. Indeed, Vaughan Williams and his generation thought that modality had to do with the lack of accidentals; hence the belief, still current, that the addition of accidentals would ruin the 'modality' of Renaissance music. This misapprehension leads to the curious view that the Renaissance musicians were 'shackled by the modal system' only later to be released into the freedom of Baroque tonality. Actually, the reverse is true, for Baroque composers deliberately limited themselves to the two key types which we call major and minor keys, whereas Renaissance composers, in common with composers of this century, were less tramelled in the matter of keys and accidentals. It is easier to designate the technical differences by using the word 'duotonal' to describe the major-minor system of the Baroque, Classical and early Romantic eras, and 'diatonal' to describe much of the music of other periods. Twelve-note music has a large number of semitones; sixteenth-century music also displays freedom in its deployment of semitones; pentatonic and so-called whole-tone music has no semitones. Many of these kinds of music are tonal as opposed to atonal; but because of the variety in the positions of the semitones, they are not tonal in the Baroque sense.

Plainchant was diatonal: one of the especial features which confirmed its diatonality was the avoidance of the subsemitonal cadence. This characteristic is also found in many types of folk music, including the pentatonic styles; it is not, however, true of medieval secular music, as for example the music of the trobadors and trouvères, which did not necessarily avoid the leading-note. The secular leading-note infiltrated sacred polyphony during the Middle Ages, so that long before the Renaissance the battle for the preservation of diatonic 'modality' had been lost: only by the fiction of musica ficta could an illusion of 'modality' be contrived. The tonal flavour of Renaissance music was not due to its lack of accidentals but to their profusion, or rather, their freedom of usage. Too few or too many accidentals come to the same thing: in pentatonic and twelve-note music alike, the tonal boundaries are indistinct.

These tonal boundaries were carefully defined in Baroque music by a deliberate restriction of the use of accidentals. At the one extreme the key was bounded by its sharpest note, the leading-note: at the other extreme the key was bounded by its flattest note (the fourth in the major key; in a minor key it was essentially the flattened sixth). Thus the secular leading-note finally triumphed, since it was now an essential pointer to key recognition. The duotonal system, although it was necessarily confined to two key types, nonetheless allowed Baroque composers to develop the harmonic advantages, especially the structural use of modulation, inherent in the system. In turn, structural modulation demanded more even systems of temperament, as already discussed.

Renaissance composers, then, were hardly 'shackled': their use of variant inflections was comparatively free. The presence or absence of accidentals had a much more portentous effect in the Baroque era, for in the duotonal system a change in the equilibrium of accidentals tended to lead to a shift of key centre.

Music of the Middle Ages often displays tonal patterns not dissimilar from those of Baroque music. During the Renaissance, however, the movement towards a duotonal system gathered momentum: this was especially notable in secular music, and particularly evident in the music for lute and keyboard. As a result, theorists were at a loss to reconcile the new developments with the old technical vocabulary. Morley, in a discussion concerning 'going out of the key', explains that certain modulations are admissable (such as starting in G and ending in C or D or perhaps then returning to G); but he is at a loss to give a 'generall rule' for 'keeping of the key', saying that 'it must proceede only of the judgement of the composer' (Morley, 1597, p. 147).

Morley goes on to describe the 'eight tunes' [tones] used by 'the church men for keeping their keyes': these, the psalm tones, are merely 'some shadow of the ancient *modi* whereof *Boethius* and *Glareanus* have written so much'. But the secular tones, which differ considerably, are often referred to in manuscripts of keyboard music. A list is given in a manuscript containing music by Bull (Vienna NL 17771 — dating from c. 1621). The tones are numbered one to eight, of which the first are minor keys (d g a e) and the last four major (C F D G). Only tones 2 and 6 (g minor and F major) have key signatures, both of one flat; other signatures (eg. g minor with two flats, or d minor with one flat) indicate transposed tones. Gerald Hendrie (1963) has investigated the use of accidentals in these tones and concludes that the extreme accidentals were *B flat* and *G sharp* for tone 1; *E flat* and *C sharp* for tone 2 and so on (though not precisely in this pattern). Thus, Morley's appeal to the 'judgement of the composer' seems to be heeded in the music. The complete table of tones is set out below:

TONE	FINAL	SIGNATURE	EXTREME ACCIDENTALS IN NORMAL USE		MODERN EQUIVA-LENT
1	d		b flat	g sharp	★ d minor
2	g	1 flat	e flat	c sharp	g minor
3	a		(f natural)/ b flat	g sharp/ d sharp	a minor
4	e	(rare)	(c natural)	d sharp	e minor
5	C		b flat	f sharp	C major
6	F	1 flat	e flat	(b natural)	F major
7	D		(f natural)	g sharp	D major
8	G		(f natural)	c sharp	G major

★ The contemporary descriptions were *D sol re* (with the lesser third) and so forth, by which the pieces were sometimes named and grouped in the sources.

The tonality of Bull's music, in common with other English keyboard music, was thus far divorced from widely-held notions of 'modality'. On the contrary, Bull's use of the words 'Phrygian' or 'Dorick' relate to Platonic Greek ideas, and have something to do with the ethical concepts of the *harmoniae*, with which modality was originally related. The resemblance of the virginalist tones with the 'modes' invented by Glarean is small. The instrumental tones used by Andrea and Giovanni Gabrieli are nearer to Glarean's, but also have a clear connection with the psalmodic tones from which they eventually derive. But the 'tones' of the virginalists were more nearly related to the modern keys, showing the English keyboard school to be, as in other respects, in the vanguard of tonal development. Apart from excursions into chromaticism, Bull's music shows a strong sense of key balance; indeed the tonal architecture of English keyboard music is manifestly more advanced than in continental music of the same period.

Technically, too, the English virginalists were more advanced. Bull's passage-work often demands the same sort of technique required of a Bach player; and in devices such as crossing the hands and the repetition of notes he considerably antedates Scarlatti with whom these devices are often associated.

Ex. 71

(Bull, 'Walsingham'; cf *MB* XIX no.85)

These passage-work techniques (together with broken octaves, arpeggio formations and so on) were closely imitated by Sweelinck. The Flemish composer may have met Bull in 1601, but the influence could well have been indirect at first, through his fellow exile Peter Philips. Since Bull's passage-work owes much to his teacher Blitheman, and also to Tallis, and since north-German keyboard composers were greatly influenced by Sweelinck, it is possible to trace a line of development from the time of the *Mulliner Book* through Bull and Sweelinck, and through Scheidemann, Scheidt, Pachelbel and others, to J. S. Bach.

Bull's 'Walsingham' variations contain some of his most technically demanding pages; unfortunately, the musical interest is often slight. His obsession for the bravura style and his fondness for canonic writing led him to write several intricate canonic and cantus firmus pieces, many of which are decorated with brilliant divisions. Equally diverting, however, are his character-pieces such as 'My self', 'Dr Bull's goodnight' and 'My grief'. The more overtly descriptive pieces, including 'The King's hunt' and 'Battle', are vigorous, yet not devoid of subtlety. His 'Country dance' (*MB* XIX, no. 111), is also an amusing descriptive piece: the variations are apparently based upon a bucolic tune of some sort, but the divisions conjure up a stylized picture of rustic life not dissimilar from that evoked by Edward Pierce's 'A hunting song' printed by Ravenscroft (1614) — see Ex. 43 — or Deering's 'Country Cries'. The blare of the hunting horns and barking of the dogs are splendidly portrayed in music by Bull, and provide a perfect counterpart to the description of the hunt in Gervase Markham's *Countrey Contentments* printed on page 67.

The character-piece is also represented elsewhere in *FWVB*, in works by Giles Farnaby and others. Tregian's texts sometimes give the impression that Farnaby was a slapdash composer, but it is likely that the scribe himself was to blame for at least some of the evident infelicities, for there are palpable errors in Tregian's versions of several works by Byrd. Apart from fantazias, pavans and galliards, the majority of Farnaby's pieces are dances, settings of popular tunes, and titles such as 'His humour' or 'His rest'. Fanciful titles are often found in the virginalists (some earlier examples are found among Tye's instrumental music); Peerson's 'The fall of the leafe' and 'The primerose' (*FWVB* CCLXXI-II) are among the most charming. Mundy's *Fantazia* (*FWVB* III) is perhaps the most descriptive, moving from 'Faire wether' through 'Lightning', 'Thunder' and 'Calme wether' by turns, eventually breaking out into 'A cleare day'.

Richard Farnaby is also represented in *FWVB* by a handful of pieces; his style is virtually a parody of his father's. Giles (who was by trade a joiner, and only an amateur musician) left a considerable amount of vocal music (including several contributions to metrical psalters and volumes of canzonets printed in 1598). His lack of training is manifest in that his canvas is often conspicuously greater than his limited palette can cover. At the same time his colours are often fresher, more spontaneous, than some of his more distinguished colleagues. His duet 'For two virginals' appears to be the first of its kind. Duets for two players at one instrument are less remarkable: Byrd and Bull contributed duets of a sort, but the earliest fully-fledged duets are by Carleton and Thomas Tomkins. Carleton, of whom little is known, wrote two (one of which is incomplete), doubtless inspiring his friend Tomkins to write 'A Fancy for two to play': all are found in the latter's own manuscript (BL Add. 29996). Since continental examples date from considerably later, it is interesting to note the primacy of the English duet.

As already mentioned, Carleton composed two highly chromatic pieces. The 'Pavana chromatica' (*FWVB* CCXIV, subtitled 'Mrs Katherin Tregians paven') by William Tisdall is in the rare 'fourth tone' but ending on a chord of B major. In spite of this, it can hardly be called extravagantly chromatic, although there are several piquant harmonies in this pleasing work.

Tregian's anthology includes several pieces by Bull's expatriate colleague Philips. One of these (LXXXVIII) is dated 1582, the year of his exile. This, and the more elaborate no. LXXXIV, despite its title 'Fantazia', are sets of variations, the latter treating the theme in diminution and augmentation. Although Philips' pieces are often intabulations of vocal pieces or arrangements of other instrumental works, they show considerable sophistication and musical interest. It is interesting to note that the Pavana and Galiarda 'Dolorosa' (LXXX-I) have stretches in the left hand which imply a split F sharp and G sharp key, the front portion of which would have sounded low D and E. On the other hand, Gibbons and others require the low A_1 and B_1 which implies a short octave (possibly with split keys) in which the low C sharp and D sharp keys actually sounded the notes A_1 and B_1, as on the Knowle chamber organ of 1623.

Although Flemish instruments survive which had the compass $C-a''$ (less than four octaves), some English compositions, such as Farnaby's

'Lachrymae pavan' (*FWVB* CCXC), require high *c''*. Most virginalists, however, were more conservative; it is noteworthy that neither *Parthenia or the Maydenhead . . .* nor *Parthenia In-violata* call for a note above *a''*. Incidentally, the term 'virginals' subsumed any plucked keyboard instrument, of whatever shape.

The contents of the *FWVB* also include one or two Italian works, as would be expected from Tregian's stay in Rome. Some native composers, notably Tomkins and Gibbons, are poorly represented, suggesting that they were not in Tregian's immediate circle of musical contact. Gibbons was at the time rather young, which perhaps also explains why the *FWVB* includes only two of his compositions, one incomplete, and both unascribed.

Gibbons had been appointed organist of the Chapel Royal in 1604–5 at the early age of twenty-one, and to Westminster Abbey in 1623. In 1619, meanwhile, he had been made 'One of His Ma[jesties] Musicians for the virginalles'. In 1612–13, in the company of the much more senior Bull and Byrd, he contributed to *Parthenia*.

Gibbons' comparatively small output includes several impressive fantazias, pavans and galliards, and various dances. In spite of his prowess as a player, he does not allow his passage-work to run riot, as often it does in Bull's (and occasionally even in Byrd's) music. In common with Bull, however, his use of passage-work in pavans and galliards slowed down the tempo to a more sedate speed, wholly inappropriate to dancing: functional music has given way to art music. Gibbons, however, can hardly be said to be an innovator, and curiously, the most arresting novelty apparently emanating from his pen is probably due to the imagination of the scribe. The so-called 'Fantazia for double organ' (*MB* XX, no. 7) bears clumsy attempts by that inveterate meddler, Benjamin Cosyn, to make an ordinary fantazia into a piece for two manuals in alternation. These directions for the manuals ('ten[or]' and 'base') are so inept that they are unlikely to have any authority.

The idea of using the manuals in this manner, or of exploiting the divided registers found on some contemporary organs — such as that at Staunton Harold, Leicestershire — to provide similar effects, does not seem to have occurred to composers until some time later; Cosyn's adaptation, gratuitous and incompetent though it may have been, was therefore nonetheless an innovation.

Gibbons, in common with most of his contemporaries, was conservative in his demand for an extended upper register. His elaborate variations on 'Peascod time' (*MB* XX, no. 30) often reach high *a''*, but no higher. The same is true of his variations on 'The woods so wild' (*MB* XX, no. 29 — a title sometimes mistakenly copied 'Wolseys wild' by scribes) much quoted in the music of the time, and a favourite of King Henry VIII. Another popular tune set by Gibbons was 'Whoop, do me no harm good man' (*MB* XX, no. 31) which the bawdy Autolycus in *The Winter's Tale* put into the mouth of a pedlar at the door who sang 'several tunes faster than you'll tell money'. In common with Byrd, however, Gibbons' métier lay more with weightier forms than with variations on popular tunes. As in his madrigals, he tended to steer a course some way removed from the lighter vein of many of his contemporaries. This is not to say that his works are heavy — far from it, as many of the keyboard preludes, variations and dances testify. But as his somewhat stern portrait (a later copy of which is in the Faculty of Music at Oxford, together with Bull's portrait) seems to indicate, Gibbons' nature tended to incline towards the grave rather than the trivial. His impressive 'Fantazia of foure parts' (*MB* XX, no. 12) with its close-knit, carefully worked polyphony, is quintessential of its composer. It appears to have been adapted from a concerted fantazia; and the same is doubtless true of the three-part fantazia printed as *MB* XX, no. 8. It is perhaps no coincidence that at least three of Gibbons' pavans are founded on the 'lachrymae' theme (*MB* XX, nos. 16–18). Nonetheless, Gibbons was often exuberant, as is shown at the opening of a galliard printed in *Parthenia* (cf. *MB* XX, no. 25):

Ex. 72

Gibbons' death in 1625 marked the end of the English virginalists' era. The style continued to flourish on the Continent with Bull and in isolation at Worcester in the hands of Tomkins, of whom more will be said later; but in general, the palm had passed to continental composers, now in the ascendancy. Although Gibbons' influence on Blow is palpable, that of Froberger and Fischer, of the Italians and of the French *clavecinistes* upon Purcell is more fundamental, even if the detailed penmanship of his music is often clearly English. Thus, although the composers of the virginalist era were in the vanguard of many developments, their English successors became content once more to follow, at a discreet distance, behind continental fashions.

CHAPTER 6

Graces in Play

The performance of virginalist and organ music poses several problems of pitch, tempo, articulation and so forth, all of which will be discussed in the course of this chapter. The most obvious and intriguing performance problem in connection with the keyboard music of the period, however, concerns the meaning of the strokes often found in profusion in English virginalist sources. A distinction should perhaps be drawn between short formal ornaments, usually known as 'graces' at that time, and the more complex improvised ornamentation called 'divisions'. It is to the former class that these strokes belong. Written-out graces are found in England as early as the thirteenth century, among the dances contained in BL Harley 979; this is the manuscript which contains the famous 'Reading rota'. Here a number of written-out on-the-beat mordents (lower auxiliary) are found; similar figures occur in the monophonic dances of the 'Manuscrit du Roy' (Paris BN f. fr. 844). In the Robertsbridge Codex (BL Add. 28550, though it is unlikely to be of English provenance) a circle over some of the notes seems to indicate an ornament. In the German organ tablatures (Buxheim, Kleber, etc.) a stroke or hook through the stem presumably serves a similar purpose.

In the works of the English virginalists, however, two factors make the signs unusual: their profusion, and that there are two (sometimes three) apparently distinctive signs. Since there are many contrary theories as to their meaning, and since there is sometimes a tendency to disregard them on the grounds that their interpretation is dubious, it is worth devoting some attention to the problem. The notion that the signs are arbitrarily applied by the copyists may occasionally appear to be borne out by the sources; but closer scrutiny shows that more often than not the signs were carefully applied, and *a priori* it is unlikely that a working copyist would waste his time adding useless signs.

On the contrary, the disparity between the strokes of one manuscript and another is often no greater than the disparity between the notes themselves. When there are substantial differences, the divergences, far from being arbitrary, often appear to be systematic in character. Corrections and alterations in single sources can be detected too; such as where the cancellation (thus #) or repositioning of signs has occurred. The modifications would hardly have been made if the signs had no meaning; such changes must therefore be of evidential interest in any attempt to solve the problem of the meaning of the strokes. Apart from this evidence, the testimony of fingering found in early sources may be adduced, together with that of ornament tables (most of which are unfortunately of secondary relevance, since they differ in time or place), and of theoretical statements (to which similar strictures apply). The large amount of often marginally relevant evidence has been distilled as much as possible in the following pages in order to keep the subject within reasonable bounds; and an attempt has been made to steer a mid course between too exhaustive and too cursory a treatment.

THE ORNAMENT SIGNS IN SIXTEENTH- AND EARLY SEVENTEENTH-CENTURY SOURCES

The earliest sources of English sixteenth–century keyboard music tend to have few, if any, signs. The liturgical organ music of BL Add. 29996 contains several passages of the following nature, in which the double stroke seems to do duty for a particular figure (similar to that seen in Ex. 52), the first occurrence being fully written out, after which the sign appears to be some variety of shorthand for subsequent repetitions:

Ex. 73

(Redford 'Eterne rerum conditor'; BL Add 29996 f 11ᵛ)

This evidence is not, however, paralleled in later sources and may be peculiar to this MS. Similarly, Blitheman's use of the triple stroke (see *MB* I no. 91) involves short note-values in contexts quite different from those involving the triple stroke found in manuscripts copied by the seventeenth-century Benjamin Cosyn. The use of the triple stroke is almost exclusively to be associated with these two names, though there are instances of its use in *FWVB* and *Priscilla Bunbury's Virginal Book*. The earliest instances of the single stroke (discounting the cancellation signs of BL Roy. App. 58) are in the *Mulliner Book*, followed by the *Dublin Virginal Book*, after which both single and double strokes are found in abundance. Unfortunately, various numbers of strokes are often used to cancel a stem, to denote the crossing of parts, or sometimes apparently as a scribal flourish; not all strokes are therefore to be interpreted as grace signs. In music written specifically for the organ (whether in a soloistic or accompanimental role) the signs are comparatively rare. This might be taken to indicate that graces were unusual in liturgical music; but equally their absence (as with the absence of fingerings) may be taken to reflect the professional as opposed to amateur milieu of the sources, and should not be taken to mean that ornaments were characteristic of virginals rather than of organ playing. After all, a 'fantazia' does not shed its ornaments when it is alternatively entitled 'voluntary' (cf. Ex. 74, named either 'Fancy' or 'Voluntary' in the sources).

The problem of the significance of these signs is underlined by the various conflicting usages of sources, already alluded to. These conflicts, however, are a useful starting-point in the discussion. The following extract typifies the appearance of manuscripts copied by Cosyn (working in the second quarter of the seventeenth century) and those of other copyists:

Ex. 74

Some of the variants between the sources, such as accidentals or where notes are ornamented in one MS and not the other, are of a general nature. The two sources differ specifically, nonetheless, in their application of the two signs, Cosyn using far more single strokes than Bevin. That this divergence is intentional is borne out by the regular substitution of the one sign for the other in certain contexts. It is noteworthy that Baldwin's single strokes in *Nevell* were altered to double strokes by a corrector, presumably Byrd. Few single strokes survive in this MS, and it is also striking that the figuration commonly found at the strain ends of a pavan is unmarked by Byrd in *Parthenia* or *Nevell*: the same figure, however, is marked with single strokes by Cosyn; whereas other sources, such as *Parthenia,* or 'Bevin' in BL Add. 31403, give double strokes:

Ex. 75

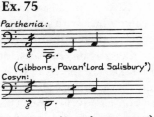

Parthenia:

(Gibbons, Pavan 'Lord Salisbury')

Cosyn:

(Gibbons, 'Pavan'; *MB* XX no. 15)

It seems, therefore, that Cosyn either deliberately edited his text, altering the intention of the composer, or that his understanding of the signs differed from scribes such as 'Bevin' (whose identity will be discussed later). Although both of these possibilities must be reckoned with (the former since Cosyn was an indefatigable reviser of composers' music, and the latter because of the consistent differences already noted), it is not improbable that, for all intents and purposes, they come to the same thing. If the single stroke meant two things to Cosyn (which henceforward will be referred to as 1a and 1b) and the double stroke meant two things to 'Bevin' (henceforward 2b and 2c); and if we assume that the places where they agree concern meanings 1a and 2c; then when they conflict (1b and 2b) they probably concern meanings which were either identical, or at least similar enough to make them reasonable equivalents (one of which was apparently disliked by Byrd).

Further conflicts of sources reveal that one acceptable alternative significance of the double stroke was the trill. There are many instances where one manuscript has a double stroke while another gives a written-out trill:

Ex. 76

FWVB:

RM 24.d.3:

(Byrd, 'Lachrimae' Pavan; cf *MB* XXVIII no. 54 bar 68)

It must be stressed, however, that the carefully written-out trill, which normally occurs in cadential or similar positions, could hardly be wholly synonymous with the double stroke. If it were, there would be little point in carefully notating the many repercussions of the written-out trill, and even less in using written-out trills in alternation with double strokes (see page 132–4). In the latter case its meaning may have been a short trill, of the kind found in the following example:

Ex. 77

(Tisdall, 'Almand'; *FWVB* no.CCXIII)

Thus, the trill was either an equivalent, or sometimes a synonym, of the double stroke; but the synonymity was by no means total. It seems hardly necessary to point out that written-out trills were notated conventionally, the number of repercussions being shown arbitrarily: this is clear from many collations between MSS. Since the exact number of trill-notes written in the sources has no importance, the use of slurs in *MB* and elsewhere in this connection is redundant and misleading.

The proven equivalence of the trill as a particular meaning of the double stroke is paralleled, though in circumstances which are hardly unequivocal, by instances in which one source has a single stroke and another a written-out slide (before the beat). Although this evidence is too vague to be considered as conclusive, it might also be mentioned that several passages (in the *Mulliner Book* and elsewhere) have three or more single strokes in a chord — precluding any reasonable possibility of interpreting them as slides.

This evidence may be followed up by the testimony of those sources containing fingering. Extreme fingers show that the double stroke must have meant both an upper- and lower-note ornament and that the single stroke meant a lower-note ornament. The following example illustrates these points. (Note that the fingerings of the sources have not been trans- lated into modern equivalents: those of the left hand must therefore be reversed). Ex. 78, in Tomkins' handwriting, is the opening of an untitled piece occurring on f 80 of Oxford Bodl. Mus Sch c. 93:

Ex. 78

In bar 3 (L. H.), 5 implies a lower-note ornament for the double stroke, whereas in the R. H., 2 above 1 indicates an upper-note ornament. In bar 4 (L. H.) the single stroke carries the thumb, implying a lower-note ornament. Evidence of this kind fails to reveal any case where a single stroke must mean an upper-note ornament; but although this *argumentum ex silentio* cannot be taken as conclusive, it is nevertheless suggestive. If the single stroke may sometimes have meant a slide, there are also occasions when considerations of fingering often make it improbable. The above example (bar 2, R. H.) shows the fourth finger involved in a single stroke, preceded by a second finger: taking a slide on the fourth finger would involve using the second finger on two consecutive notes, which is perhaps unlikely. The skipping of fingers may well imply a repeated appoggiatura D on the beat, played by the third finger.

The foregoing discussion allows the following (highly provisional) conclusions to be drawn in relation to Cosyn's and 'Bevin's' signs: 1a might have meant a slide; 1b a rising appoggiatura; while 2b might have meant a lower-note ornament; and 2c an upper-note ornament, resembling a trill.

Figure 12 shows part of the table 'Graces in play' from the *Bevin MS* (BL Add. 31403 f.5). Robert Ford (1982) has shown that the copyist of the relevant part of this MS was Edward Bevin, son of the more famous Elway. The table of graces thus belongs to the second quarter of the seventeenth century, but since the contents of Bevin's section of the MS are clearly archaistic, the signs found in the table, although late and idiosyncratic, may be seen as a bridge between the virginalist signs and those of Restoration sources. The peculiarity of the signs, coupled with the presence of an otiose and clearly erroneous sharp in the antepenultimate note of the right-hand part has tended to emphasize the eccentricity of Bevin's table; yet it would be a mistake to dismiss its evidence entirely.

Fig. 12 'Graces in play' from Bevin's MS (BL Add. 31403 f.5)

It is true that the signs are idiosyncratic; but they are not wholly so, since they represent modifications of the signs normally encountered in virginalist music. The first is a single stroke explained as a slide, here in a dotted-note version. The second is the same sign, with a hook 'exprest' as an upper returning-note termination. The third sign appears to be a combination of a single and double stroke: the explanation is a slide plus a trill (if we ignore the two final notes, perhaps inserted to link with the next ornament). Lastly, the double stroke denotes a trill; and although the significance of the preparatory hook is not immediately transparent, it might denote that a long trill (the equivalent of the written-out trill) is required; or the hook may perhaps call attention to the termination of the trill.

Essentially, therefore, the Bevin table agrees with what is known from other sources: that the single stroke could mean a slide; the double stroke a trill; and the two together (as will be seen shortly, these are written elsewhere as three parallel strokes) a combination of slide and trill. The weakness of the table as evidence is that it apparently implies exclusive meanings to signs which are largely idiosyncratic and indeed hardly figure elsewhere in the same MS. There is, nonetheless, some use of one or two of these signs in the *Bevin MS*: the stroke followed by a hook occurs once or twice, together with frequent use of the single stroke (though in contexts which nevertheless do not easily accommodate the slide); and several times the hooked form of double stroke is found (twice in Gibbons' 'Fancy' of which the beginning is given as Ex. 74, and half a dozen or so appearances elsewhere). The latter instances are mostly off-beat, or else they occur on cadences or semibreves, which come to much the same thing, as they subsume the off-beat position. This point is of some significance since in this context Purcell and Blow regularly use the 'shake turned', that is to say, a trill with closing note termination. Since considerations of fingering suggest that the double stroke without hook, (the most common sign in the music of the *Bevin MS*), indicates an ornament commencing on the written note, the context of the hooked double stroke sign, sometimes cadential, and virtually always off-beat, suggests that it was intended to denote a full trill with closing notes.

Although at first sight it would seem reasonable to suppose that ornament tables should have the status of a cypher book, anyone who has puzzled over Bach's ornament table, that attributed to Purcell, or many other such 'explications' will have disabused himself of this pious hope. Composers took for granted that the omissions and ambiguities of their jottings, hardly ever meant for publication, would be obvious to the contemporary player. Thus the rhythmic details, the apparent exclusivity of the forms and numerous other characteristics of their tables, must be taken together with other evidence before coming to firm conclusions.

Viewed in this light, the Bevin table corroborates the use of the double stroke for a trill — with termination in the off-beat position; the single stroke for a slide; and the triple stroke as some kind of compound ornament. It also suggests a slide plus upper returning-note termination as a possible interpretation of some single slide ornaments. The table also shows that the fingerings given above the 'graced' notes correspond with the written note, not with other component notes of the explanation. Thus, it is reasonable to interpret the testimony of extreme fingers in the manner already discussed.

What the 'Graces in play' fail to tell us is how the signs should be interpreted in a rapid context when trills would be out of the question, or in a harmonic context when a slide is an unlikely explanation for a single stroke. So far as the latter problem is concerned, the dotted-note formula, if abbreviated by suppressing the lowermost note of the slide, gives an ornament corresponding graphically and interpretatively with the Restoration 'forefall', that is to say, the ornament is the rising appoggiatura already tentatively adduced. Thus in spite of its lateness and idiosyncratic appearance, the Bevin table has considerable value, since it generally confirms or interlinks with other evidence. Although it fails to hint at a lower- note interpretation of the double stroke, this omission is made good in Bevin's 'Preludium' (no. 3 of his MS), where the double stroke coincides with the fingering R. H. 5, and must therefore represent a lower-note ornament.

It has already been noted that the double stroke is often an equivalent for the long written-out trill; but that it is not a consistent synonym is clear from passages such as the following (Farnaby's arrangement of the alman quoted at Ex. 57):

Ex. 79

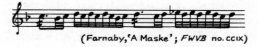

(Farnaby, 'A Maske'; *FWVB* no. ccix)

Here an ascending off-beat trill, written out *in extenso*, is manifestly intended to be distinguished from an on-beat figure carrying a double stroke. This latter figure ends with an off-beat slide, which prepares the succeeding written-out trill. A very similar progression is found in Gibbons' 'The temple mask' in one of Cosyn's MSS (BL RM 23. 1. 4); but in another of his MSS (Paris Cons. Rés. 1185) the same passage is abbreviated thus:

Ex. 80

In this instance, therefore, Cosyn's triple stroke has every appearance of meaning a 'prepared trill' consisting of an off-beat slide plus normal trill. The

question is complicated by the repetition of the passage in Ex. 80, which
appears as follows:

Ex. 81

(Gibbons, 'The Temple Mask', in Rés 1185)

The same figure in Farnaby's 'The New Sa hoo', however, is repeated thus:

Ex. 82

At the end of Gibbons' 'Temple mask' one MS has the double stroke plus
termination, where another has a turned preparation before a similar figure:

Ex. 83

The implication of these examples is that the figure, which in a Baroque
context would have the appearance of a shorthand trill with closing notes,
does not signify an ordinary trill but is either part of a 'prepared trill' (where
it is followed by a written-out trill) or is in itself a 'prepared trill'. Considerations of fingering also favour this interpretation, since the fingered instances of this figure almost invariably indicate the third finger. The 'good'
finger, applied to the note on the beat, would necessarily imply the written
note. The music of Bull and Byrd frequently carries trills of this type, which
begin on the principal note, but continue, rhythmically speaking, as
appoggiatura trills (since the latter is present on each odd-numbered fraction
of the beat). They represent an extension of the 'turn' found in some of the
early sources (see below): indeed in the third strain of Byrd's 'Ninth pavan'
there are cadence figures written with a turn in *Nevell*, and as an extended
turn in *FWVB*; the figure frequently occurs in parallel sources as a substitute
for the normal trill starting on the appoggiatura. The extended turn is
found, side by side with the written-out trill, in *Intabolatura nova di Balli*,
printed in 1551.

The relationship of the prepared trills under discussion may be seen in the following table:

Ex. 84

It is to be noted that the essential progression, shorn of ornaments, involves the repetition of two notes, ascending on the next beat to the higher adjacent degree of the scale. Cosyn frequently uses the triple stroke in this context; but he also uses it in a descending context where repeated notes are involved, thus:

Ex. 85

(Cosyn, 'The Goldfinch'; RM 23.l.4 f94)

Either form of prepared trill (ie. beginning with a slide or with a turn) has the effect of avoiding, as Baroque composers also often avoided, the repetition of notes caused by the appoggiatura of a normal upper-note trill. Thus, Cosyn's use of the triple stroke probably subsumed both forms of prepared trill. Using 1, 2 and 3 to denote the number of strokes, the discussion so far suggests the following possible meanings for the signs:

1a	=	slide
1b	=	rising appoggiatura
2b	=	lower-note ornament, eg. an undershake
2c	=	short trill
2d	=	3c
3a	=	slide plus trill
3b	=	extended turn
3c	=	turn, plus trill or reverse turn plus trill

The question of context is clearly important for the choice of interpretation of the signs, but before examining the matter further, it would be as well to consider briefly some further kinds of evidence, in spite of the fact that some of it apparently lies well outside the periphery of the virginalist sources.

CONTINENTAL AND LATER ENGLISH TREATISES

In his *Musical Ornamentation* (1893–5) Dannreuther collected several documentary sources, including continental and later English ornament tables, which have some bearing on the problem of the virginalists' signs. These, together with sources more recently discovered, strengthen some of the conclusions reached so far. The tables printed by Locke (*Melothesia* 1673) and Purcell in 1696 (appearing also, virtually unaltered, in *A Choice Collection of Ayres* . . . printed in 1700 by John Blow and others) show what appear to be a final evolution of virginalist signs, cross-fertilized by French influences. Locke merely gives five signs and their names: the forefall, backfall, shake, forefall and shake, and beat are, respectively, an upward sloping single stroke; its downward equivalent; a double stroke (upward sloping); a combination of the latter preceded by the first of these signs; and a wavy line, similar to the German sign for a trill. These signs are explained in *A Choice Collection of Lessons* . . . (1696, attributed to Purcell) as an upward and downward appoggiatura respectively, in the rhythm of a 'Scotch snap'; an eight-note trill beginning on the upper auxiliary without termination (a special sign ℘ indicating the 'shake turned'); an upper appoggiatura and shake, plain note and shake; and the following explanation of the 'beat':

Ex. 86

Christopher Simpson calls the ornament a 'shaked beat', his beat proper being what Purcell and others call a 'forefall'. There is some ambiguity here: it seems that the word 'beat' meant several things, and it is more than probable that the wavy lines sometimes meant a prepared undershake as given by Purcell and Blow, or an unprepared undershake (as with North), or sometimes, particularly in quicker tempi, it may have meant a short undershake resembling a mordent.

For the early history of ornaments, Diruta and Praetorius are often taken as important sources; but their usage is somewhat removed from that of the English virginalists, particularly in their reluctance to use upper-note trills. The Spanish treatise *Libro llamado Arte de Tañer Fantasia* (1565) however, is considerably earlier and bears rather more directly upon the English virginalists. In his book, Fray Tomás de Santa María shows that the English, in starting their trills on the upper note, are in the 'new fashion':

Ex. 87

Estas maneras... son muy nuevos y muy galanos

described as follows:

ff 48 – 48ᵛ)

His *quiebro reyterado* shown above is simply a trill starting on the principal note (third finger), but in the 'new fashion' it begins on the upper-note (fourth finger). The *redoble* differs only in that after the first principal note the ornament momentarily descends a note lower to form a reversed turn prior to the trill proper: but the preferred 'new fashion' again begins on the upper-note. The *redoble* and 'short *reyterado*' are both turns, the first being a reversed turn commencing on the principal note, the second being a normal turn beginning on the upper-note. The first is used in a rapid tempo, the second, in a moderate tempo; but the first is allowed only when one of the auxiliaries is a semitone apart, and the second only when the lower auxiliary is a subsemitone — in the latter case a supersemitone is specifically forbidden. The long *redoble* and *quiebro reyterado* are both used in rapid tempo, the former on semibreves, the latter on minims. On crotchets, but sometimes on minims, the *quiebro senzillo* is employed. This latter consists of either a lower or an upper auxiliary note interposed between two principal notes, the first alternative being used in an ascending context, the second descending. On quavers, 'seldom on semiquavers', in 'very fast' tempi the *senzillo* is adapted by playing the principal note then touching and releasing the auxiliary while the principal note is sustained. The effect (though not notated by Fray Tomás) is as follows:

Ex. 88

and

(cf f48ᵛ–49ᵛ)

Quite apart from the question of the relevance of a Spanish treatise to English virginalist ornaments, Fray Tomás' notation cannot be taken any more literally than other ornament tables. Yet the fact that the English upper-note trill is in the 'new fashion' is interesting, and his *quiebros senzillos* conform with Diruta's usage of lower-note ornaments in ascending passages and vice versa. The concern of Fray Tomás with the semitone in ornaments of the 'turn' variety is of some interest; the use of this kind of ornament in virginalist music seems to imply a similar regard for the semitone without, however, attaching quite so much importance to its position — the following examples, from the *Mulliner Book* and BL Roy. App. 58, are typical:

Ex. 89

(Hugh Aston, 'A Hornpype'; Roy App 58)

(Allwood, 'Voluntary'; *MB* I no. 17)

Since turn figures appear to prefer or require a semitone above or below the principal note, musica ficta sharps are clearly implied in these positions in 'My Lady Carey's dompe' (BL Roy. App. 58) and in similar passages elsewhere.

Fray Tomás, in common with other theoretical treatises, does not mention signs for ornaments, nor does he mention the slide. Apart from the ornament tables of Purcell, Blow and Locke, already noted, the most informative sources concerning ornament signs and the status of the slide are reviewed in the following paragraphs.

The slide

The decline in popularity of the slide is attested by Caccini (*Nuove Musiche*, 1602). The relevant passage, as it appears in Playford's translation under the title *Introduction to the Skill of Musick* (1655) is given below:

> There are some . . . that in the *Tuning* of the first *Note*, Tune it a *Third* under . . .
>
> . . . Since it is not a general Rule, because it agrees not in many Cords, although in such places as it may be used, it is now become so ordinary, that instead of being a Grace (because some stay too long on the third note under, [as in the dotted form advocated by Bevin] whereas it should be but lightly touched) it is rather tedious to the ear; and that for Beginners it ought seldom to be used . . .
>
> (1674 ed. pp. 42–3)

Simpson (*Division Violist* 1659, p. 11) says the same thing:

> Sometimes a Note is Graced by sliding up to it from a Third below, called an *Elevation, now something obsolete.*

Mace (*Musick's Monument*, 1676, p. 105) describes the 'wholefall' (which from his detailed description turns out to be what Simpson and others call an 'elevation') as 'a Grace much out of use in these our days'.

Examples of written-out slides are found in works dealing with division techniques, notably Praetorius, *Syntagma Musicum* III (1618).

The single stroke

The tables of Locke and Purcell agree in using the upward sloping single stroke to indicate a 'forefall' (rising appoggiatura). In some instances, the virginalist single stroke may thus have meant something similar, for it is not unreasonable to suppose a connection between the two signs. The backfall, or falling appoggiatura, was represented at the Restoration by a downward sloping single stroke; it occurs mostly in descending progressions. A large number of significances, many of them quite contradictory, are given for the single stroke in seventeenth-century writings. L'Affilard's *Principes . . .* (1694) are only relatively early, and give the slide as the meaning of the single stroke, while Marpurg's *Principes . . .* (1756 — an enlarged translation of *Die Kunst das Klavier zu Spielen*, 1750) gives a rising on-the-beat slide for the upward sloping single stroke and a falling slide for the downward stroke. Prencourt (c. 1700) gives an interesting discussion of various ornament signs; among them he mentions the slide and its sign, and taken with North's comments upon his ornament table, he offers perhaps the least unequivocal evidence of all. He also discusses the double stroke. The following passage is quoted from *Roger North on Music* (ed. Wilson, 1959, p. 62):

Prencourt: They also put two little strokes over the note, when a shake must be made.

North: He means the English, but that is not his use.

. . .

[Here follows a discussion of a mark like a reversed figure 3 that signifies a 'slurr' (slide), upon which North comments:]

North: To understand this excellent grace well, required some knowledge of composition, for it is (properly) harmonious, and mixeth the sound of the 3rd below with the note played.

Prencourt: They make a short stroke thro' the tail of a note where this slurr is to be made:

North: That is, the English; . . .

[The forefall and backfall are then discussed: they are represented by a single stroke before and detached from the note. From this it seems that North distinguished between the stroke through the tail of the note, meaning a slide, and the Restoration forefall or backfall, signified by a detached stroke previous to the note.]

It should be noted that the single stroke *within* two notes —

Ex. 90

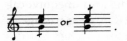

is found in tables such as Purcell (1696) and Chambonnières (*Les Pièces de Clavessin I*, 1670). This represents a *coulé* which, although in some ways is equivalent to a slide, differs from the virginalists and Prencourt's sign in being between two sustained notes, rather than applying to a single note. Similarly, the French sign applied to the tail of a chord —

Ex. 91

is not related to the English single stroke but indicates a *coulé* on two following notes' (D'Anglebert, *Pièces de clavecin* . . . 1689), ie. a sustained arpeggio.

The double stroke

Restoration usage (cf. Locke, Purcell and Prencourt, cited previously) consistently equates the double stroke with the shake. On the Continent the double stroke occasionally means a mordent, as in Kuhnau's *Clavier-Übung*. So too in Walther (*Musicalisches Lexicon*, 1732), though the strokes sloping downward indicate a short trill. These sources may owe something to earlier English usage. Geminiani (*The Art of Playing on the Violin*, 1751) is also likely to have taken the equivalence of a 'beat' (undershake) for the double stroke from English tradition; but he uses the single stroke (horizontal) in a different significance, to mean 'holding the note'.

The triple stroke

According to Restoration usage the sign for a forefall and shake consists of three strokes, the first to the left of the other two. In some sources (eg. in Portman's works in the *Wimborne MS* [unnumbered]) the three strokes may be carelessly aligned so that they resemble the virginalists' triple stroke. In

139

the first note of *Parthenia In-violata* the single stroke is printed separately above a double stroke, clearly indicating a compound of the two. As has been noted, the true triple stroke is virtually confined to Blitheman and Cosyn — the meaning implied by the former (since the sign occurs on quick notes) may well have differed from that of the latter, for whom it appeared to mean a prepared trill: this, too, is possibly the meaning of the same sign found in van Noordt's *Tabulatuur-Boeck* (1659).

Returning to the period of the virginalists, it should be mentioned that several lutenist sources contain signs different from those of keyboard music, but which seem to represent parallel usage. Correspondence indicates that the lutenist sign resembling the sharp is the equivalent of the virginalists' double stroke, whose single stroke is paralleled by an upright cross in lute music. The latter never occurs on an open string, which (corresponding with the fingering evidence of virginalist sources) indicates that a lower-note ornament is involved. A source described by Dart (1961) explains the 'sharp' as a shake and the cross as a 'fall'.

The cross is explained as a 'whole-fall' or slide by Mace (1676); it is notable that his upward sloping single stroke before the note is called a 'half-fall' (ie. the upward appoggiatura — Purcell's 'forefall'). For the 'shake' and 'beat' (undershake) the single stroke is inclined further, being more or less vertical in the latter case. Simpson (1659) has the 'forefall' sign and meaning, but calls it a 'beat'; the cross (signifying a slide) is called an 'elevation'. Simpson's most interesting mark is the dot, explained as a 'close shake', ie. *vibrato* (for this Mace gives a wavy line and calls it a 'sting'). Dots are sometimes found in earlier lute music, where the interpretation of a 'close shake' is indeed suitable. The other signs in these treatises belong to Restoration usage, and seem to have little relevance to virginalist ornaments.

MODIFICATIONS OF VIRGINALIST SIGNS

Turning once again to the virginalist sources themselves, there are several instances of apparently significant modifications of signs, either by repositioning or by the use of auxiliary signs. In his 1957 edition of *Clement Matchett's Virginal Book* (1612) and his edition of *Parthenia In-violata* (originally printed c. 1625), Dart noted several instances — Matchett often placed the double stroke ornament carefully below the note, instead of in its normal position above; and an early owner of *Parthenia Inviolata* crossed out several double signs above the note, and placed them below, in one case adding a small note, apparently signifying a lower appoggiatura. Desmond Hunter (1983) has found several instances of positions below the note (where otherwise the double stroke would be expected above) in *Will Forster's Virginal Book* (BL RM 24. d. 3) and elsewhere. In all of these cases a lower-note ornament seems indicated (often further enforced by considerations of fingering); and whether or not the opinions of the scribes merit much credence is not so important as the evident care with which they sought to elucidate the signs.

Similarly, in *Elizabeth Rogers' Virginal Book* (BL Add. 10337, c. 1656–7) care is taken to distinguish between a single stroke before the note (presumably a forefall) and through the stem. (See also Hunter, 1983, for other idiosyncratic positions of the single stroke). Since elsewhere the forefall sign occurs in conjunction with the slide (written out in small notes), it is possible to equate the latter with the single stroke through the stem. The double stroke with an additional cross is sometimes found in *Rogers* and elsewhere. Although the cross usually indicated an undefined ornament in some continental conventions its more specific meaning was a mordent. The transition from 'virginalist' to 'Restoration' usage is particularly striking in Playford's *Musick's Handmaid*. In Part one (1663) the alignment of the double strokes changes apparently with the engraver from above and below to before the notes. In Part two (1689) new, specifically Restoration, signs (ᴡᴡ and ᴠᵧ) occur.

In all cases, Restoration ornaments appear to come on the beat. In the following passages the double stroke ornament can hardly come before the beat:

Ex. 92

(Blow [Prelude]; ChCh 47 p56)

The sixteenth-century mechanical virginal in the Charles van Raalte collection, housed in Dean Castle, Kilmarnock, plays its solitary slide on the beat. The evidence of Cosyn and of written-out slides, however, indicates that the slide came before the beat, at least in some instances: the 'forefall', therefore, may have followed suit. But it is unlikely that the single stroke indicated an ornament before the beat, as distinct from the double stroke indicating an ornament upon the beat, as was argued by Clutton (1956, p. 99). His argument rests on the difficulty of playing different ornaments appearing simultaneously in the same chord; but it is invalidated by the frequent occurrence of the *same* sign simultaneously — in Oxford Ch Ch 431 f.3v the single stroke occurs on all four notes of a chord. Rapid execution demands, nevertheless, that ornaments should be modified, as is evident from writers such as Tomás de Santa María, already cited, to C.P.E. Bach in the eighteenth century. In such contexts the principal and auxiliary notes would have been sounded as simultaneous acciaccaturas, particularly in the bass: this is also suggested by several passages in Scarlatti's sonatas, together with statements by Marpurg (ibid.) and Roger North (apud Wilson, p. 171).

141

In sum, therefore, the evidence so far discussed confirms the equivalences noted on page 134, bearing in mind that ornaments on short notes will demand modifications of the single and double stroke. As to the precise ornament to be used the question of context is of particular importance, and is a matter requiring some detailed discussion.

CONTEXT

The difference between the application of signs in the *Cosyn* and *Bevin* *MSS* has been noted earlier. In a given piece, the number of signs in each source tends to be similar; Cosyn, however, uses the single stroke significantly more than Bevin; and even more striking is Bevin's reluctance to use a single stroke in the left hand. Since the double stroke may well have signified both an upper- and a lower-note ornament, it is desirable to know under what contexts it is possible to distinguish the two meanings. Since the Restoration ornament signs are not ambiguous in this way, a study of their contexts is a likely source of information. In a survey of the suites of Purcell, Beer (1952) investigated the frequencies of ornament signs according to their contexts and applied his conclusions to the virginalist strokes. He established that several contexts seemed to influence the choice of ornament: that starting, final and cadence notes had their characteristic ornaments; and that the ornament also varied according to whether its principal note was the same, lower, or higher than the note preceding. He also considered the application of graces to dotted-notes. The following summary of Beer's findings shows the melodic context of each sign in relation to the general character of the ornament (upper- or lower-note, rather than its precise structure, which Beer also considered in detail):

MELODIC CONTEXT OF ORNAMENTED NOTE IN RELATION TO PREVIOUS NOTE	NUMBER OF UPPER-NOTE ORNAMENTS IN THIS CONTEXT	NUMBER OF LOWER-NOTE ORNAMENTS IN THIS CONTEXT
Descending	200	1
The same note	86	34
Ascending	16	142
Initial note of piece	–	9
Penultimate or cadence note	27	0
Final note of piece	–	11
Totals	329	197

The dotted-note class is omitted here, for it does not seem to provide a particularly useful demarcation; Beer's proportions for this class were 190: 50 in favour of an upper-note grace. This is in excess of the general preference, but when it is remembered that dotted-notes are frequently cadence notes, then there seems little reason to suspect any distinctive treatment for dotted-notes in general. One aspect which Beer's analysis did not consider was the position of the semitone; as Desmond Hunter has pointed out (1983) a high proportion of written-out virginalist shakes involve a semitone alternation.

From the table printed above, and from Beer's more detailed analysis, the following conclusions are apparent: the proportion of upper- to lower-note ornaments is roughly 2:1. Of individual ornaments those most consistently used are the 'beat' for the initial and final notes; and shakes (with or without appoggiatura preparation) for cadential notes. Shakes, or backfall with shake, or the plain 'backfall' (short appoggiatura from above) occur in the proportions:- shake 123: backfall and shake 43: backfall 33, in a descending context, whereas in an ascending context there are 89 occurrences of the 'beat' (9 of which are actually preceded by a forefall) and 50 occurrences of a plain forefall.

These findings are extremely instructive, but open to two criticisms: the Frenchified suites of Purcell are perhaps not a very good standpoint from which to evaluate the possible ornament practice of the English virginalists, and also the choice of contextual criteria leave something to be desired. A wider choice of contextual possibilities investigated in the organ works of John Blow (which have much in common with the earlier 'voluntary') has shown that Beer's general conclusions are valid, but with certain modifications. The salient points arising from this investigation are as follows:

(i) Beer's conclusion that upper-note ornaments predominate over lower-note ornaments by 2:1 is reinforced; indeed Blow's preference appears to be for a still higher proportion.

(ii) Although ascending motion generally requires a lower-note ornament, an off-beat note forming the middle of three in ascending conjunct motion requires a shake (or a 'shake turned').

(iii) There was no discernible consideration of the position of the semitone in the choice of ornaments.

In Cosyn's version of the Gibbons Fancy whose opening is quoted at Ex. 74, the majority of double strokes appear either in a descending context or on an off-beat rising crotchet. (Although Cosyn's triple stroke fails to occur here, it appears on off-beat ascending crotchets in his MS at p. 110.) In most cases the single strokes come on the beat and in an ascending context. The Bevin version of the same piece, however, contains more double strokes applied to downbeat notes, and fewer single strokes. There are less ascending off-beat crotchet double strokes in Bevin (though the hooked double stroke occurs here once in this context).

SUMMARY

The contexts indicate that the differences between the Cosyn and Bevin versions of the Fancy cited above generally relate to the ornaments found on ascending notes on the beat: very likely this conflict merely expresses a preference for various kinds of forefalls, undershakes and so forth, a distinction which was in any case blurred in a rapid context. Thus, the virginalists' signs, far from being arbitrarily placed, seem to have been carefully considered, and at least some of their ambiguities may be resolved by recourse to consideration of the usage of Restoration ornaments. Indeed, the Restoration signs represent what appears to be a development of the virginalist ornaments.

The earliest virginalist sources (eg. BL Roy. App. 58) employ the double stroke alongside written-out graces of the 'turn' type. The *Mulliner Book* includes Blitheman's triple stroke, and, together with the *Dublin Virginal Book*, shows an early use of the single stroke. Most probably these signs originally represented degrees of rapidity, much as the same signs today convey various speeds of *tremolando*. Blitheman's triple stroke would thus represent a very rapid ornament; since the double stroke probably represented all but the most rapid practical ornaments, the triple stroke would be correspondingly rare. The single stroke represented slower, lower-note graces; when the slide fell into disuse, the single stroke eventually meant something like a forefall. John Harley (1970) has shown that the single stroke ascended, and finally left, the stem of the note. This doubtless led to the introduction, by analogy, of the downward sloping backfall. The gradual evolution of the single stroke towards the exclusive meaning of a forefall eventually ousted a second meaning of the double stroke, namely a lower-note ornament — by the Restoration, the double stroke was used exclusively for the upper-note shake, its former meanings being taken over by the Restoration signs for the beat and backfall. Cosyn's use of the triple stroke and Bevin's idiosyncratic signs seem to indicate that slide preparations of a trill could sometimes become synonymous with the turn of a previous trill; although the slide itself fell into disuse, the 'shake turned' was important enough to the Restoration composer to be given a separate sign.

If this summary development of the signs be accepted, together with the evidence adduced earlier, the following interpretation of the virginalist grace signs may be set forth. The number of strokes is represented numerically, letters being used, as earlier in the discussion, for different meanings:

	CONTEXT	MEANING:	
		SLOW TO MODERATE NOTES	RAPID NOTES
1a	in earlier music, where harmony permits (eg. where third below is present or implied): fell from fashion in the first quarter of the seventeenth century.	dotted (?) or plain slide, (the latter sometimes before the beat, especially when followed by trill or double stroke = shake)	(= 1b)
1b	otherwise than above	forefall (rising appoggiatura)	simultaneous forefall = 'lower acciaccatura'
2b	down-beat, especially where previous note is lower	undershake or mordent	as above

NB — Some or all of the above disliked by Byrd: cf. *Nevell* (finished in 1591) and *Parthenia* (1612/3).

	CONTEXT	SLOW TO MODERATE NOTES	RAPID NOTES
2c (i)	where the previous note is higher	short shake	simultaneous backfall = 'upper acciaccatura'
2c (ii)	ascending off-beat patterns	short shake plus turn	short shake or as above
2d	ascending; with closing notes, but not when followed by written-out trill; when written-out trill follows, especially in almans, short shake, 'closing notes' as preparation to ensuing trill	= 3b or 3c	—
(3	Blitheman — c. 1560		= 2)
3a	ascending by step	prepared trill, especially slide plus trill	
3b } 3c }	ascending; and descending (especially to avoid repetition of previous note)	extended turn; turn plus trill; reverse turn plus trill	

There is some evidence (eg. Fray Tomás) that the choice of ornament could be influenced by the availability of a semitone above or below the note: in particular, long trills, usually written out, appear to favour the semitone position. All of the English written-out trills, whatever the figuration of the preparatory opening notes, eventually emphasize the upper-note on the fractions of the beat according to the 'new fashion'. This feature had a considerable influence upon the development of Baroque ornamentation, where the harmonic importance of the appoggiatura and its associated ornaments marked it off from other, purely melodic, ornaments. This aspect of the matter is frequently misunderstood, but is clearly demonstrated in the English virginalist graces. It is notable that the written-out trills are sometimes appoggiatura trills, but sometimes undershakes in which the lower auxiliary (returning-note) is dissonant with the principal harmony. That the undershake (extended mordent) is indistinguishable from the trill proper emphasizes that these two figures should not be regarded as opposites: the Baroque trill is essentially an appoggiatura decorated by a series of returning-notes forming its undershake. The fact that the appoggiatura tends to be dissonant, but that the upper-note of the mordent is consonant, merely emphasizes the increasing importance of the appoggiatura in the harmonic vocabulary.

OTHER ASPECTS OF KEYBOARD INTERPRETATION

Hilda Andrews, in her preface to her edition (1926) of *My Ladye Nevells Booke* remarked that the ornaments 'destroy the melodic line and burden the piece with unnecessary elaboration'; even Thurston Dart on at least one occasion advised that 'they are sometimes best omitted'. On the contrary, they are a vital part of the texture; often they bring cross-rhythms into relief, as in the galliard and similar dances; and their presence, taken together with contemporary fingering patterns, frequently proscribes the choice of too fast a tempo. They also articulate the music: there is no point in introducing anachronistic 'phrasing' and yet ignoring the articulative function of the ornaments. The cross-rhythms engendered by the ornaments written in Byrd's 'Ninth pavan' are illustrative:

Ex. 93

(Byrd, Ninth [Passamezzo] Pavan; *Nevell*)

Nor should it be forgotten that ornamentation of the 'division' type is often required in keyboard music where compulsory repetitions were the rule. Some of these matters are most conveniently dealt with by discussing the forms involved, the principal ones being pavan, galliard, alman and coranto.

The pavan, according to Morley (1597, p. 181), was 'a kind of staide musicke, ordained for grave dauncing, and most commonlie made of three straines, whereof everie straine is plaid or song twice'. In this connection it is important to remember that double bars and repetition marks are indistinguishable in this period. Thus, a pavan having only three sections needs to have each of these 'strains' repeated, with more elaborate gracing and divisions. The 'Salisbury' pavans by Byrd and Gibbons in *Parthenia* are printed without repetitions, and therefore require ornamented reprises to each strain. The style appropriate to these additional divisions is best seen in the six-section pavans (ie. those with written-out divisions) by the same composers; but as Tisdall's 'Pavana chromatica' (*FWVB* CCXIV) shows, these divisions were not necessarily complex.

Several of Gibbons' pavans are based upon the 'lachrymae' theme. One

146

Fig. 13 Gibbons: Lord of Salisbury Pavan (from *Parthenia* . . . 1612).
The first two sharps in the piece are probably a misreading on the part of the
engraver.

(*MB* XX no. 17) was partially adapted in one of his Verse anthems ('Behold, thou hast made my days'). The printed version of his 'Lord Salisbury' pavan has otiose sharps in the second and third notes of the treble part, which distorts the 'lachrymae' theme. The accidentals printed in *Parthenia* arise from a confusion on the part of the engraver between the sharp and the double stroke grace sign. The publication has several other instances of this misunderstanding; often, as in this case, the correct readings are revealed by collations with other sources: *MB* XX no. 18 should thus be amended.

The pavan was often used for a processional entry, particularly suited to its 'staide' swaying steps. 'After every pavan [is] usually set a galliard' says Morley (ibid), which is a 'lighter and more stirring kinde of dauncing then the pavane consisting of the same number of straines'. The total number of sections in the galliard is thus six, as in the pavan. The written-out divisions of Gibbons and others make it clear that the speed of three minims in the galliard was the same as that of four minims of the previous pavan — resulting in a slower tempo. It had dance steps which were of a 'lighter and more stirring kinde' — being considerably more elaborate in the galliard than in the pavan, and usually left to the younger dancers. The tempo, on the other hard, was as Mace says (1676), 'in a *Slow and Large Triple-Time*'. The alternations of $\frac{3}{2}$ and $\frac{6}{4}$ time inherent in the galliard adds a piquancy to its tempo, and this cross-rhythm is often underlined by the ornaments:

Ex. 94

(Byrd, Galliard 'Mistress Mary Brownlow' *Parthenia*)

The alman, according to Morley, was a 'more heavie daunce'; but again he seems to have had the music less in mind than its steps, which had 'no extraordinarie motions used in dauncing of it'. On the contrary, its music was 'very *Ayrey* and *Lively*; and Generally of Two *Strains*' (Mace). The tempo was effectively as fast as that of the pavan, since the time units moved in four crotchets rather than four minims. Morley says that 'foure of the pavan measure is in *dupla* proportion to the foure of the *Alman*' (so that sixteen pavan semibreves are in the time of eight in the alman). This is hardly likely to be correct: in fact the time taken by the semibreve was probably the same in both cases.

The characteristic rhythm of the alman was the dotted-note figuration: concordances show that even quavers were probably dotted in performance (see Chapter 4, Ex. 57). The trill figurations discussed in Examples 79–84 of this chapter are also particularly characteristic of almans, so much so that here again, a plain-written version was probably ornamented as a matter of course with the typical alman trills. Thus Byrd's 'Munsers almaine', which in the *FWVB* (LXI) is written out in a plain version, is given in *Nevell* with the figuration indicated (cf. also Ex. 79):

Ex. 95

In common with the dances already discussed, the alman was repeated; thus each of the strains of a two-strain alman should therefore have an ornamented reprise. Often, however, the repetition began with an upbeat written at the end of the first strain, but which was not intended to be part of the second strain (see *FWVB* CCII — note, too, the dotted-notes which should be extended). The ambiguity arises because of the lack of a proper scribal convention for marking first time and second time bars. In two almans by Gibbons, however, the reverse happens: the upbeat belongs to the second strain and not to the first (*MB* XX nos. 34 and 35: note the characteristic alman trills). *MB* XX no. 36 (subtitled 'The King's juell') is provided with written-out divisions; again there are upbeats which are slightly ambiguous in the sources. Its form is what might be termed a 'double alman': the complete alman (with repetitions marked, but not varied) is followed by another of the foregoing two strains, this time with written-out divisions. This arrangement seems to have confused one of Gibbons' scribes a good deal, resulting in the sections being copied in a jumbled order. Byrd's 'Munsers almain' is also a 'double alman' in the *FWVB* version (with written-out repetitions), and a 'triple alman' in *Nevell* and *Will Forster's Book* versions. From this it appears that the alman was frequently repeated several times for the dancers, although 'Munsers almain' was unlikely to have been intended for dancing.

Tregian frequently adds a final chord at the end of a piece: often this is a mere scribal peccadillo, as in the alman *FWVB* CCII; in *FWVB* CC, however, it is possible that the chord is either the 'second time' chord, or indeed an additional final chord (see Ferguson, 1962).

A similar difficulty arises in the corantos of the *FWVB*: in CCI, CCIII and

CCIV this chord seems gratuitous; in CCV, however, it seems to complete the movement more satisfactorily than would otherwise be the case.

The tempo of the coranto was quick: the notation denotes tempo a third faster again than the alman. Morley is not particularly helpful as to the coranto: Mace calls it 'full of *Sprightfulness*, and *Vigour, Lively, Brisk*, and *Cheerful*'. Its two strains were presumably repeated, as Byrd's 'double corantos' indicate. The volta (or la volta) was musically similar to the coranto, but danced differently; in Morley's words 'the *voltes* and *courantes* which being both of a measure, [are] notwithstanding daunced after sundrie fashions, the *volte* rising and leaping, the *courante* travising and running . . .'. An anonymous painting at Penshurst Place, Kent, apparently a copy of a French picture, shows Queen Elizabeth dancing the volta with her then favourite, Robert Dudley, Earl of Leicester. Byrd's setting of 'La volta' (*FWVB* CLV) is a 'double volta', running twice through and including reprises with written-out divisions.

The 'Daunce' found at *FWVB* CCVI is the tune 'Dulcina' found in Giles Earle's book and elsewhere. It seems to be a combination of an alman and coranto, with a striking change from slower duple to faster triple time. Time changes were often inaccurately notated in England (and indeed on the Continent) from which a measure of confusion has ensued. The problem arises partly because 'ordinary time' was sometimes reckoned in breves (eg. in most church music) and sometimes in minims (as in secular music generally); but the two were often confused, so that the 'whole stroke' of a semibreve with a time signature of C was the same as that of a semibreve in ₵. The latter, properly, should be 'The More Stroke . . . when the stroke comprehendeth the time of a Briefe' (Morley); that is *alla breve*. But as Ravenscroft says in his *Brief Discourse* (1614) 'the ignorance of our times is such, not knowing the differences of this imperfect prolation (C) and the diminutions thereof (₵) . . .'; as a result, a transition from C to triple time with the same 'whole stroke', and thus apparently slower, may actually imply a quicker 'half stroke' tempo, since the basic tempo was the equivalent of C: as Morley says, 'that rule bee not so generally kept; but that the composers set the same signe [₵] before songs of the *semibriefe* time' (1597, p. 23).

Triple time signatures reflect the same confusion. Different madrigal part books will have ₵, C, C3 and ϕ indifferently (as in Byrd's 1588 collection); furthermore, English triple notation was in black semibreve units as opposed to the white breves of continental 'true tripla' (see Morley pp. 36–68, esp. pp. 39 and 51). Both forms of tripla could be faster or slower than the preceding tempo, depending on whether ₵ or C was understood as the basic speed. To complicate matters still further, English tripla was sometimes given the signature $\frac{C}{32}$ and sometimes $\frac{C}{31}$ though the second is probably twice as fast as the first, it was often used to mean the same thing (see also p. 185).

In practice, all that is needed is a measure of common sense. Most changes from duple to triple time involve a speed change whose result is that the latter *sounds* (whatever the notation) a third faster than the former. A regression to duple time will normally operate in the reverse direction. Thus the 'Daunce' at *FWVB* CCVI should be performed so that the bars of the first strain as printed in the edition are equal to those of the second strain.

In toccata-style preludes, considerable freedom of tempo, as demanded by Frescobaldi (1615), is appropriate; the tempi of the sections may be varied, he says, as 'in modern madrigals'. Ritenutos are also specified by Frescobaldi 'as the performer approaches the end of a *passaggio*' (ie. division). Unfortunately this statement and others of a similar nature have been interpreted to mean that the performer should take his fingers off the keys prior to the final chord: this curious and loathsome practice has no authority.

The rhythmic alterations discussed in connection with almans are described by Tomás de Santa María (1565) and other writers, in such a way that the *notes inégales* of the French clavecinistes seem to be prefigured. Certain sources indeed seem to indicate that, as in the Baroque era, conjunct downward pairs of notes could often be played in *coulé* rhythm:

Ex. 96

(BL Add 29996 f9; cf *EECM* 6 no.54)

The keyboard dances, especially the more elaborate settings, were not necessarily intended to accompany dancing; but it is likely that the tempi of the simpler dances were roughly the same as those required in the ballroom. And though the types mentioned were clearly the most popular, many other dance forms must have existed, some suddenly becoming the craze of the year, to be as old-fashioned as Malvolio's yellow cross-garters the next. As Moryson wrote in his *Itinerary* of 1617, 'many daunces and measures are used in Court, but when they come to be vulgar and to be used upon very stages, Courtiers and gentlemen think them uncomely to be used . . . .'.

Some of these new-fangled 'dances and measures' are enshrined in the 'Masks' found in the virginal manuscripts. These tunes, made popular in the court masques, are often almans; occasionally, however, something more individual is found, as in Gibbons' Mask 'Welcom home':

Ex. 97

(Gibbons, Mask 'Welcom Home'; BL Add 36661)

Apart from the third instance (doubtless an error) each $\frac{6}{4}$ bar of this Mask has a double stroke on the second beat, signifying a short shake only: together with the ornaments on the fourth beat this gives a curious lilting rhythm to the dance, whose steps were probably correspondingly dainty. Note the alman style trills; the fingering of the last bar in particular indicating an extended turn since an immediately repeated 'bad' 4 would be unlikely on the *C sharp*. It is also noteworthy that English fingering is designed to secure a mainly legato touch (crossing over the fourth finger of the right hand in ascent, and over the second in descent). This method of fingering, as Fray Tomás' book shows, had much in common with Spanish technique; it ensured that a strong finger (or 'good' finger as Diruta termed it) should occur on the beat. This was in order that any involuntary gaps come before, rather than across the beat, as they might with the Italian style of fingering. The following chart gives the main differences between the Italian system and that of the English virginalists:

Ex. 98

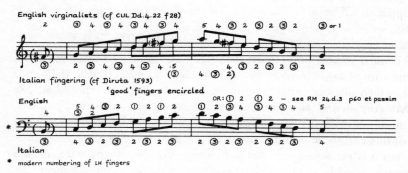

English virginalists (cf CUL Dd.4.22 f28)

Italian fingering (cf Diruta 1593)
'good' fingers encircled

English

Italian

* modern numbering of LH fingers

To assume that either style of fingering implied on- or off-beat articulation is simplistic (*pace* le Huray, 1981). Even where the fingerings given in the virginalist sources do appear inevitably to result in some form of articulation (usually, as already noted, before — but not across — the beat), it should not be emphasized unduly. Diruta (1593) vilified dance musicians who played 'striking the keys' rather than in a smooth fashion. The fingerings of the English virginalists were designed to achieve a smoothness of line, particularly by the use of the third finger of the right hand, and of the third and thumb in the left, which was the essence of Bach's fingering and whose style of playing was described as *cantabile* by one of his listeners. Thus the English virginalists, through Bull, Sweelinck, Scheidemann and Reincken, had a considerable influence on keyboard technique, replacing the erratic Italian system with one in which the thumb played a fuller part, the particular use of which became associated with Bach's style of organ playing.

In the fancy or voluntary and kindred cantus firmus forms the cohesion of the parts is of the utmost importance. It is with the ornamentation of voices rather than by a misguided attempt at 'phrasing' that the performer should seek to heighten the interlocking quality of the strands of polyphony. Graces should be added, in conformity with similar passages elsewhere, rather than subtracted; it would nonetheless be a mistake to suppose that every repetition of the 'point' should be identically graced, for the sources indicate a good deal of freedom in this regard. The role of contemporary fingering and the graces in preventing too fast a tempo being chosen by the modern performer must again be emphasized. In short, the amount of attention devoted in this chapter to the problem of ornamentation might at first appear to be disproportionate, but in truth, the role of the 'graces in play' has considerable significance.

Although unrelated to the foregoing discussion, the question of keyboard compasses requires some treatment here, since it too bears upon the question of the interpretation of the music of the virginalist school. As mentioned in the previous chapter, the highest note on English keyboards seems generally to have been *a″*; but many early organ pieces, nonetheless have upper-notes of *c‴ d‴* or *e‴*, well outside the normal keyboard compass, so from this it is obvious that some form of transposition must have been employed. Redford's 'Iste confessor with a meane' (*MB* I — 'mean' being a middle part) is obviously an octave too high; and similarly, the same composer's 'A solus ortus cardine' in BL Add. 29996 (*EECM* 6, no. 25), which ascends to a written *e‴*, clearly demands transposition. The same MS contains an anonymous organ Magnificat (printed in *EECM* 6, no. 4), and here there is a rubric: 'play bothe parts viij nots lower heer'. The editor of this volume appears to have found it difficult to take the hint of the scribe, but it is plain that here and elsewhere, impossibly high parts should be played an octave lower. It should be noted that sometimes only one part requires transposition; hence the 'bothe parts' of the above rubric.

Transposition of a fourth was also effected as a matter of course in certain circumstances. In earlier times, chanted passages had to be sung at a pitch comfortable for the voices, and the organ had to conform. On some instruments there were two keyboards, one a fourth apart from the other (see Mendel, 1949). Thus, for certain plainchant tones whose notation apparently indicated a high range, the lower pitch would be chosen; and a low range tone would be played at a higher pitch. The problem is discussed by Schlick (1511), Praetorius (1618) and other theorists. The Ruckers instrument of 1638 in the Russell Collection, Edinburgh, has a transposing lower manual aligned so that the lower manual *F* plays the same string as *C* (a fourth lower) on the upper manual.

A consequence of the use of transposing keyboards will be explored more fully in a later chapter, but it is worth mentioning here that church organs frequently appear to have been pitched as though at the *C* manual of the virginals, but sounding at what the choir would regard as *F*. Organists were sometimes required to transpose down a fourth in order to reconcile these two pitches. It may be that the reverse of this transposition is required by the 'Uppon la mi re' of BL Add. 29996 (see Ex. 63) whose upper range is too high for the normal organ compass, and clearly requires downward transposition; but the bass part is written in the D clef, which, as will be seen in the next chapter, normally signifies an upward transposition of a fourth. Thus, if the bass part were transposed up a fourth and the treble part down a fifth (both transpositions were achieved by clef substitution), the piece would be in 'd minor' rather than 'a minor'.

An added difficulty when discussing these transpositions is that the pitch of organs, in addition to being nominally a fourth above vocal pitch, was also a minor third higher relative to our own nominal pitch. *C* at choir pitch would have to be played as *G* at high organ pitch, but both would be at *E flat* pitch in relation to the standard of our own times. This problem will be discussed at length in Chapter 8.

In conclusion, it is perhaps necessary to mention that there is no evidence that English organs had pedals at this period. This notion is based upon the misapprehension of the words 'playne keyes' and 'Bassys' in the Duddington specification of 1519:

> of double Ce-fa-ut that is to saye, xxvij, playne keyes, and the pryncipale to conteyne the length of v foote, so following with Bassys called Diapason to the same conteyening length of x foot or more: . . .

> (Hopkins & Rimbault, 1855)

The 'playne keyes' are, however, what are now called the 'white notes', and the 'Bassys' are simply the pipes of the 'Diapason', a rank equivalent to our 16 foot stop. The 5 foot principal was nominally equivalent to our 8 foot stop (sounding to us at *E flat* pitch in respect of the contemporary choir pitch) and the diapasons were used in connection with the transposition outlined earlier. For this reason the principal was sometimes the lowest stop in use; otherwise, the organist would transpose up a fifth by clef and down an octave by drawing the diapason as the lowest stop. Thus, on this kind of organ the principal was sometimes equivalent to our 8 foot stop, sometimes to our 4 foot (as now); and in order to achieve a proper tonal balance many organs had two ranks of principals, one louder than the other. This explains the provision in the Duddington specification (cf. the Tomkins organ whose specification is given on p. 202) of 'double pryncipalls thoroweout'. The elaborate misunderstanding of this and other phrases has often clouded the interpretation of what are essentially straightforward organ specifications of the period.

CHAPTER 7

The Meaning of the Author

It is hardly necessary to say that music properly exists only as sound, but it is commonly forgotten that the printed or written note, also loosely called 'music', is but a cypher whose significance must be interpreted by the performer: the notation is merely a link in the chain by which the message of the composer is eventually passed on to the listener. There is little wonder that the message is often garbled, for since sound cannot accurately be expressed on paper its recreation is often a matter of difficulty, particularly if several centuries have elapsed since the music was first composed.

Even comparatively recent music can be problematic in its interpretation. A great deal is taken for granted in notation, for instance a composer may not trouble to indicate a rallentando, and many other vital rhythmic conventions — as with the characteristic Viennese waltz rhythm — often find no place in the score, yet a performance which ignored these matters would be unthinkable. And how loud is loud; how slow is slow? The inadequacies of musical notation are self-evident, even in the music of Elgar and Bartók. These composers, furthermore, were not above making fundamental errors in the calculation of metronome marks, or failing to correct misprints in printed scores; and partly missing or incompleted music by these composers adds to our problems.

Such considerations become even more crucial in regard to the music of nearly five hundred years ago. Defective manuscripts or lost partbooks, coupled with a failure to explain conventions and the generally misleading impression which musical notation can often convey, all conspire to offer difficulties to the present-day editor and performer of Tudor music. Several of these difficulties have been touched upon already; and the particular problem of the pitch and scoring of vocal music is dealt with in a separate chapter. Some of the remaining points of interpretation which confront the performer and his editor — if they are to achieve a faithful representation of the composer's intentions — will be the concern of the following pages. Although this chapter deals principally with the editing and performance of vocal music, the general principles involved apply to Tudor music as a whole.

The recognition of a problem must necessarily precede its solution — modern editions and performances are sometimes unaware that some polyphonic works require the necessary addition of plainchants; these were hardly ever copied into polyphonic sources, but often account for something like half of the music. Similarly, it is important to recognize that sources may contain scribal errors. Merely to select the earliest MS (which is not necess-arily the most reliable) as a 'primary' source, and to consign all other readings to the critical commentary is an abrogation of scholarly responsibilities. Housman, with characteristic irony, dealt with this notion in his preface to his edition of Manilius: 'An editor of no judgement, perpetually confronted with a couple of MSS to choose from, cannot but feel in every fibre of his being a donkey between two bundles of hay . . . he confusedly imagines that if one bundle of hay is removed he will cease to be a donkey.' If, moreover, the ravages of time have removed all the other bundles, it is important that the scholar should not mimic Buridan's ass by regarding the extant version as sacrosanct by survival. A facsimile or diplomatic text should be a means, rather than an end, to editorship.

Assuming, however, that the editor arrives at an edited text which can lay some claim to be near to the composer's own intentions, he must help to bridge the centuries; for if the unwary performer is misled into thinking that the composer's written pitch and note-values have the same meaning as those of today, the edition will have the shortcomings of a facsimile without its virtues. The editor should thus guide the performer in various matters such as tempo and so forth and, from his knowledge of the conventions of the period, he should make the interpreters aware of the extent of the gap between the notation and the composer's intention. That the two are frequently confused is evident in this extract from an article in the journal *Early Music*; for although the author is trying to demonstrate the curious notion that the pitch of the written note is absolute, it is clear that his literalism is deeply ingrained and general:

> Directions for tempo and dynamics, and frequently for underlay also, are absent from manuscript and printed sources alike; this suggests that whatever the contemporary approaches to such aspects of performance may have been, they were quite alien from any which we might understand and appreciate. In the absence of 15th-century gramophone records and tape recordings, idiomatic restoration of contemporary practices . . . can barely even be contemplated.

The absence of these directions suggests nothing of the sort, but it is more curious that the writer will not allow the restoration of contemporary practice even when confronted by evidence from the period, dismissing such evidence elsewhere by saying that it 'cannot stand up to informed scrutiny'. This nugatory attitude is hardly likely to lead to an authentic interpretation of old music, or indeed of the music of our own century. Hindemith's symphony *Die Harmonie der Welt* ends without a ritenuto direction in the score: yet that some form of slowing down was intended is confirmed by the composer's own recording, which ends in a massively underlined ritenuto: it may be wondered if this evidence would 'stand up to informed scrutiny'.

The natural slowing down at the end of a section or of a piece is taken for granted, as in good reading; but nonetheless, it is useful to have the confirmation of one or two contemporary theorists on this point. Some conventions are more difficult, though not impossible, to recover. Still other aspects of performance practice may, alas, be lost to us; but this does not justify our refusing to look for solutions to problems of interpretation. Few of these are intractable, given a mind open to evidence and performers willing to listen for those moments of revelation when the true utterance of the composer is sometimes self-evidently unfolded. It is essential to keep faith with the composer if the freshness and vitality of his music is to be preserved, for although in some cases it is perhaps only its bloom which is rubbed off by rough handling, in others its very essence is destroyed by the ignorance of editors and performers: as Gibbons remarked, 'Songs . . . are usually esteemed as they are well or ill performed' (1612, Preface).

Editors and performers then, must act as the joint trustees of a musical heritage, a heritage which must not be squandered or debased. To this end, as has been noted, the editor must restore and refurbish, making good the ravages of time, and he must bring to light what has become obscured by age. The extent of his responsibilities can be gauged in a sizeable majority of Sheppard's music. The responds, hymns and psalms of Sheppard mostly survive in a set of books whose tenor part is missing. Where the tenor is a cantus firmus on which a plainchant is sung in long notes, its restoration is a fairly simple matter, but elsewhere, the problem of restoration is more formidable. Additional plainchant must also be supplied for the hymns (only alternate verses being set in polyphony) and for the incipits and verses of the responds. Thus the editor must know that the polyphony which appears in the sources as 'Cor vestrum' must be preceded by the plainchant incipit 'Non conturbetur', which begins the Vespers respond at the Vigil of the Ascension. He must also identify 'Adesto nunc propitius' as the second verse of the Compline hymn 'Salvator mundi, domine', and supply the plainchant verses: moreover, since the hymn was used for two distinct Christmas feasts, and at Epiphany, Easter and Ascensiontide, five different doxologies are possible. The plainchant source also supplies the missing tenor part in the second setting of 'Non conturbetur', but since the first setting of this respond has the cantus firmus in the treble the plainchant does not aid the reconstruction of the tenor.

The chants are found in the printed or manuscript Sarum Service books which give the music for the Offices, Mass, and other Services. Nonetheless, it sometimes appears that Sheppard and others used chants which varied somewhat from the standard form. Occasionally the differences might be attributable to scribal error, or to the composer deliberately altering the chant; but it must often be concluded that the local plainsong books were themselves the source of variant forms of the chant.

Various other problems arise in regard to plainchant. Sometimes the key relationship between polyphony and chant is unclear — even a simple Credo intonation can be troublesome. The liturgical position of the piece often has an effect on the choice and use of the plainchant: thus, in deciding upon the celebrant's incipit for the Gloria or Credo of a Mass, the question as to whether it is a ferial or festal Mass, and its 'tone', must both be taken into account. Several Masses require extensive plainchant sections to be added to the surviving polyphony, but apart from the intonations, most Masses were set entirely in polyphony. Occasionally, parts of the Credo are missing which were not actually intended to be sung — their omission was originally due to an accident of history which had become hallowed as a tradition (see p. 259).

Liturgical considerations are only one facet of the problems of editing an apparently straightforward piece of church music. As an illustration of the magnitude of the undertaking, Taverner's 'Leroy' Kyrie may be followed from manuscript to edition. As Figure 14 shows, the four parts are separate, and exist in archaically long note-values without bar-lines or voice-names. A performing edition must unite the separate parts in score; modern note-values, clefs and pitch, together with bar-lines and other aids to the performer, should also be provided by the editor with the proviso that his interpretation of the composer's wishes should be readily distinguishable, where necessary, from the letter of the manuscript.

English polyphonic Masses rarely have attached Kyries, since the Sarum Kyries were frequently troped (ie. with an extensive added text) on certain feast days; and on other days they were often sung to 'squares', which apparently originated as the bass parts of earlier polyphonic settings. In turn, these 'squares' were used as a kind of cantus firmus to provide the basis of a primitive form of improvised polyphony for organ or voices; and a few written-out Masses (notably two by William Mundy) were based throughout on 'squares'.

The 'Leroy' Kyrie of Taverner is also based upon a 'square': the polyphony, as the illustration of the *Gyffard* partbooks (BL Add. 17802–5) shows, is in three sections: Kyrie, Christe, Kyrie. The top part has a long note 'square' cantus firmus, traceable in another partbook (BL Roy. App. 58). The voices required by Taverner are not immediately clear, but the ranges of the two top parts correspond with the boys' voices discussed in the next chapter, and the bottom part clearly requires the bass voice. The

(a)

(b)

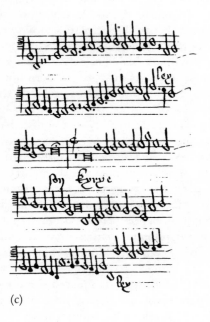

(c)

(d)

Fig. 14 Taverner's 'Leroy Kyrie' in the *Gyffard* partbooks. (BL Add. 17802–5, no. 7)
(a) Treble (b) Mean (c) Alto (d) Bass
The extract discussed in the text begins with the signature ₵

range of the remaining part might equally represent Taverner's typically low alto compass, or a high ranging tenor part. A sizeable corpus of four-part music exists (of which the 'Western wind' Masses found in the same MSS are typical), which confirms that the tenor voice was frequently dropped. In this particular instance it seems unlikely that the tenors sang the alternate sections of the Kyrie to the 'squares' but were otherwise silent: since the trebles have the 'squares' as cantus firmi in the polyphony, it seems reasonable that they should also chant the cantus firmus in the other sections; but there is no contemporary evidence on this point. Boys were specifically allotted certain chants, such as the 'Audivi' at Matins for All Saints and the 'Gloria', the verse of 'Hodie nobis' at Christmas Matins; but elsewhere their role in the chant, especially as 'beginners', is prob-lematical; the Sarum use more often specifies clerks of varying seniority for this task. In the 'Leroy' Kyrie, however, the problem subsumes a more basic difficulty relating to the order of polyphonic and chanted sections.

In Machaut's 'Messe de Nostre Dame', the Kyrie is based on a plainchant cantus firmus which can be recognized as the Kyrie 'Cunctipotens genitor'. Many plainchant Kyries have only three sections, each of which is repeated thrice to form a nine-fold Kyrie; but 'Cunctipotens' has a variant, and longer, ninth Kyrie. Accordingly, Machaut composed four polyphonic sections: Kyrie, Christe, Kyrie, Kyrie; of which the last is clearly the ninth. Thus the nine sections of the work obviously alternate between polyphony (*P*) and chant (*c*) in this fashion:

	Kyrie			Christe			Kyrie	
P	*c*	*P*	*c*	*P*	*c*	*P*	*c*	*P*

In compositions making use of this kind of alternation, composers seem to have avoided successive sections of chant or of polyphony. Thus, although organ and polyphonic hymns normally begin with a chanted verse, whether the ending is polyphonic or chanted depends on the number of polyphonic verses provided by the composer. Byrd's 'Christe qui lux' is an exceptional case, outside the Sarum system; unlike White (who set this hymn several times), Byrd treated almost the whole hymn polyphonically, framed by chanted opening and final verses together with a polyphonic 'Amen' at the close. William Whitbroke's Mass 'Apon the square' is through-set (apart from one 'Christe' too few, which was presumably made good by a repeat). Mundy's Masses of the same name have two Kyries, two Christes and two Kyries — it is not clear whether a repeat of the polyphony or an inserted chant is required in each case.

A separate, untitled, Kyrie by Mundy has four sections: Kyrie, Christe, Christe, Kyrie: this demands a pattern of alternation which is the opposite of Machaut's Kyrie 'Cunctipotens' (upon which chant Mundy's setting also appears to be based). Tye's Kyrie is on the same lines: the 'key' indicates the chant 'Orbis factor' to be appropriate; and the pattern of alternation would allow the variant ninth Kyrie to be chanted, as in Mundy's setting. Sheppard's Paschal Kyrie has only three polyphonic sections, but since the cantus firmus is 'Lux et origo' (in which the ninth Kyrie differs from the preceding chants) the repeats must be made according to the pattern of Tye's setting:

Kyrie	Christe	Kyrie
c P *c*	P *c* P	*c* P *c*

The three sections of Taverner's 'Leroy' Kyrie could be treated in the same fashion; and this was probably the intention of the composer since the 'Machaut' pattern shown earlier would result in five fairly lengthy polyphonic sections.

The first Kyrie and the Christe have the mensuration sign $\mathbb{C}$: if the original note-values are reduced by half in the edition, the time signature $\frac{6}{4}$ is appropriate. For the final polyphonic Kyrie the sign is $\mathbb{C}$, which theoretically produces a faster tempo: in reduced note-values a $\frac{4}{4}$ bar would occupy the same time as the previous $\frac{6}{4}$ bar. Such a time-change is appropriate in view of the fact that Mass movements tended in general to take a faster tempo as they progressed; thus, it is advisable that the editor should indicate the faster tempo verbally. It is improbable that the monophonic 'squares' were sung at the same tempo as the polyphony. Since plainsong was sung more quickly than polyphony (this matter will be discussed in due course), it is likely that the 'squares' were treated as measured plainchant.

Before completing the transcription of the 'Leroy' Kyrie, however, the manner in which the words are set to the music must be considered. The MS clearly has the last syllable of *Kyrie* elided with the first syllable of *eleison*; another possibility was the elided pronunciation of the last syllable of *Kyrie* which was common in many settings of the period. Taverner (or his scribe) appears to be consistent in this detail, but other composers varied their practice between works, and indeed within works. The word *eleison* was often given a disyllabic *ei*; and its first vowel was sometimes elided with the last vowel of *Kyrie* or *Christe*. Thus the words *Kyrie eleison* could have as few as four syllables or as many as seven:

Ky-ri'e-lei-son

or Ky-ri-e-e-le-i-son

The word *alleluia* was also set with an intrusive *i* sound in several compositions but, again, with considerable inconsistency. Unfortunately these inconsistencies, compounded by scribal vagaries, have misled more than one editor: the spelling *alleluy-a* (or the archaic symbol ẏ, which had no peculiar significance) has drawn forth the fictitious pronunciation *a-lle-lwee-ya*. This patent absurdity need not detain us here, though it serves as a reminder that the MSS should not be taken too literally.

In final form, therefore, the transcription of a sample section of the piece under discussion will appear thus, beginning with the added monophonic 'square':

Ex. 99

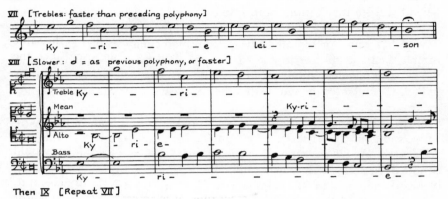

A discussion of the underlay and the significance of the ligatures would be included in the commentary, together with a note on the source of the 'square'. The prefatory clefs at the left of the polyphony would normally be given at the beginning of the transcription rather than as here — they indicate the original key and time signatures, clefs and first note from which the transposition and degree of reduction may be determined. The important editorial considerations concern (a) pitch and vocal scoring (to be discussed in due course), (b) liturgical position and therefore (c) necessary additional material, (d) tempo and (e) underlay. Thus the transposition and allocation of voices, the liturgical structure, the insertion of the 'squares', the reduction of note-values, together with the addition of bar-lines, and marks clarifying the underlay, are matters where the editor's decision might well affect the performance to a considerable extent. If the interpreter is to disagree on any of these matters, his knowledge must equal that of the editor's. Ideally, the performer should concern himself with comparatively subtle points of interpretation, leaving the more basic decisions to the skill of the editor; but since there are many traps for the unwary, the performer needs to know how much he can rely upon his editor, and, when he cannot, to be able to make the necessary emendations.

Sheppard's Paschal Kyrie has been touched upon earlier; although it raises editorial problems similar to those presented by Taverner's setting, there are some additional matters which require consideration. The correct plainchant is easily identified and inserted, since Sheppard used it as a cantus firmus in the polyphony; similarly, as mentioned earlier, the pattern of alternation between chant and polyphony is pre-empted by the exigencies of the chant. The mensuration sign is the same throughout, and there are no difficulties of transposition and scoring; but there are, however, problems of underlay, since some sources have virtually no words and others have them haphazardly placed; and there are errors and inconsistencies regarding the notes themselves.

The underlay presents no difficulties in the tenor part, since the words can be added from the Sarum chant, found in the *Antiphonale ad usum ecclesiae Sarum* (printed 1519–20). As to the other parts, the words apparently change where the 'point' or repeated musical motive begins, so that each recognizable thematic unit carries the same word in all parts. This, in general, is the practice manifest in most sources, but some manuscripts are so careless in their treatment of the words that their evidence is of comparatively little value.

Sheppard's Paschal Kyrie requires editorial attention both in the matter of possible pitch errors in the sources, and in regard to additional accidentals. As to the latter, the term 'musica ficta' is commonly used to denote those accidentals which, unlike Victorian children, were supposed to be heard and not seen. Indeed, Galliard (1743, p. 17) defines 'Alla Capella' simply as 'Church-Musick where the Flats and Sharps are not mark'd'. The use of unmarked accidentals arose partly out of a guild secrecy perpetuated by the singers; partly because the system of solmization (rather like tonic solfa, see p. 213) did not readily encompass unusual inflexions; and partly out of a desire to preserve a 'modal' appearance in the music. Because these accidentals were added in performance according to rule-of-thumb conventions, it is sometimes difficult to divine the exact nature of these conventions. The evidence of theoretical statements, and the large number of 'cautionary' accidentals (ie. apparently otiose signs which prevent an extempore sharpening or flattening) have nevertheless allowed some progress to be made in this subject in recent years. However, the path of this progress has not always been straight; indeed, a reverse or crab-wise movement is often evident. For example, more than one editor of Tudor music has felt obliged to suppress most of the accidentals found in the sources; equally curiously, another scholar has argued that a sharp means a flat, and vice-versa. In the middle of these fringes, other workers have been patiently unravelling the evidence in an attempt to establish the truth of the matter (eg. Bray 1971, 1978). According to the medieval theorists, accidentals were added *causa necessitatis* and *causa pulchritudinis*. 'By reason of necessity' includes the avoidance of a harmonic 'tritone' fifth between the bass (which might be flattened) and another note (which alternatively might be sharpened); melodic tritones were also avoided in a similar manner; and a minor third on the last chord of a piece or section would be automatically sharpened. 'For the sake of beauty' the lowermost note of cadential figures of patterns such as *G F G* would be sharpened, to form a 'leading note'. The reverse pattern, *D E D* might have its apical note flattened. This principle was followed with considerable consistency in English music, and indeed extended so that the sharpened leading note might clash with, or narrowly avoid, a falling flattened seventh. This progression, known as the 'English cadence', was the object of Morley's scorn when, in spite of his own considerable usage of the idiom, he wrote that 'such closings have beene in too much estimation heretofore amongst the verie chiefest of our musicians, whereof amongst many evil this one is the worst' (Morley, 1597, p. 164):

Ex. 100

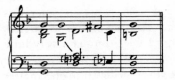

This cadence appears to be the ending of Tallis' 'O nata lux': if so, it was quoted from memory, since it differs slightly in the print of 1597. In spite of Morley's mock horror of this progression, this clash was frequent in English music and far from being suppressed, its ubiquity should be recognized with the appropriate musica ficta.

Thus, in Sheppard's first polyphonic Kyrie (number II in sequence cf. Wulstan 1978, p. 77), the last note of the second alto should form a major rather than a minor third (*causa necessitatis* — in any case the treble already has the accidental written). In Kyrie VIII the *A naturals* written in bar 31 of the first alto (clashing with *A flat* in another part) should be extended to bars 30 and 32 of the second highest part (here shown below the stave), *causa pulchritudinis*:

Ex. 101

The problems of musica ficta arise not only from a sixteenth-century disinclination to commit accidentals to paper, but from a different understanding of the function of accidentals. Unlike ourselves, the Tudor composer regarded *F* and *F sharp* as variants of the same note, rather than as two essentially different notes. The supposed diatonic purity of 'modality' was frequently subverted by the use of accidentals in plainchant cantus firmi; and there are several such examples in the works of Tallis (cf. especially 'Te lucis' in the 1575 *Cantiones Sacrae*), White and others. Thus, a failure to insert musica ficta into polyphony (cf. Tallis' 'Videte miraculum') in the mistaken belief that the shibboleth of 'modality' were thereby to be served, would be perverse (cf. p. 118) Some accidentals, nonetheless, arise from scribal or printers' errors; and although cases of erroneous accidentals in the sources are surprisingly few, their excision is normally a matter of common sense. Where, however, an editor suspends all belief in the accidentals of the sources, belief in him should likewise be suspended.

In modern notation, an inflection remains operative throughout the bar unless countermanded; this convention was of course impossible prior to the advent of the modern usage of bar-lines. The earliest custom was for the accidental or 'key signature' to last for the whole line (but applying to the specified octave only). In his 1571 collection, Whythorne reversed this convention, carefully explaining that accidentals applied to the succeeding note only: Whythorne's repeated notes thus carried reiterated accidentals. Unfortunately, both practices often co-exist; sometimes an accidental functions for one note only, sometimes it is operative for longer, and occasionally it is even retrospective in force. In order that the performer may derive as clear a picture of the sources as possible, the following editorial convention is useful:

Ex. 102

Wholly editorial (or retrospective) accidentals are shown above or below the note, or in square brackets; only those appearing specifically in the MS are printed normally; if an editor wishes to appeal to the original key signature a dotted accidental may be used, while a small accidental sign calls attention to the continued force of an incidental sign in the source; the use of round brackets is independent of all the above usages. Thus:

> 1 editorial (retrospective); 2 ditto (continued according to modern convention); 3 implied by original signature; 4 authentic; 5 cautionary (implied by signature in MS); 6 not in MS: editorial — and thus shown in spite of modernized signature; 7 authentic; 8 cautionary (but given in MS); 9 continuation of 7.

This elaborate code may seem unnecessarily complex, but until the problems of musica ficta are satisfactorily solved, the presence or absence of a source accidental is of a significance disproportionate to its size. An editor must supply the accidentals as he thinks the composer intended them, but at the same time, lest he be wrong, he must provide as much evidence of the true state of the sources as is possible.

The necessity for the insertion of the appopriate chants and the restoration of other missing material has already been touched upon. It is self-evident that if a respond such as Tallis' 'Videte miraculum' were sung without its plainchant or repeated sections, then the work would be severelytruncated, as would a performance of his organ hymn 'Ecce tempus idoneum', robbed of its chant: both would lack the length and formal plan envisaged by Tallis. Yet not all hymns and responds are properly liturgical — both Tallis' hymn 'O nata lux' and his respond 'In jejunio' were intended to be sung as 'anthems', since their structure does not admit of the insertion of the additional chants. As the sixteenth century progressed, liturgical texts were often set in a paraliturgical manner, that is, as compositions for optional insertion into the liturgy. On the Continent, the word 'motet' was used for this type of composition, but the indiscriminate use of this term is unfortunate, especially for England, where the word had a different meaning. It is particularly misleading when applied to responds and antiphons, for in common with Masses and Magnificats, these far outnumber paraliturgical pieces and have a radically different form and function.

Liturgical considerations point to the possibility that Sheppard's Kyrie and 'Haec dies' are for the Office, and not, as might be expected, for the Mass. Similar considerations govern whether or not a lesser doxology was added after an Office respond, since the Gloria is proper only to the third, sixth and ninth responds.

The largest single source of Sheppard's music lacks the tenor book. Although, as already noted, the tenor was frequently a cantus firmus which can be restored by recourse to the appropriate Sarum Service books, the tenor is often also freely composed; here, the problem of reconstruction is more severe. The difficulties of restoration are hardly simplified by the peculiarities of Sheppard's style. In some instances, it is true, the process of restitution is so simple as to be almost mechanical. For example, where the bass is silent, particularly where the texture has an apparently dissonant fourth requiring a lower note to complete the harmony, the shadow of the missing tenor may often be glimpsed, if fleetingly, and the imitative texture of the surviving parts often allows its outlines to be discerned. Elsewhere, the clues towards a definitive reconstruction may be less helpful. A consistent composer (and it must be noted that even Palestrina was only a relatively consistent composer) is manifestly easier to imitate than Sheppard, whose attitude to consecutives is difficult to judge and whose use of ornamental dissonances is often idiosyncratic.

167

An illustration of the problem is clearly seen in the following extract, a setting of 'Christe qui lux' by White — probably for instruments. Sixteenth-century polyphony regularly adhered to the practice whereby suspensions are prepared on a consonance on a weak beat: that is to say, the note occurring on a strong beat which causes a vertical dissonance of a second, or is a fourth or seventh dissonant with the bass, should be carried over from a $\frac{5}{3}$, $\frac{6}{3}$ or a 'consonant' $\frac{6}{4}$ chord on the previous beat. In several instances White (if indeed the piece is by him) ignores this convention:

Ex. 103

(cf *TCM* V p191)

A study of each composer's style, often very different from the common notion of 'sixteenth-century counterpoint', is thus a necessary prerequisite before any attempt is made to restore missing parts. The task is fraught with difficulties from the editor's point of view, since as soon as the reconstruction is published, he or his public will immediately detect errors and suggest better alternatives; and the labour is thankless, since if his reconstruction resembles the obvious intentions of the composer, the restorer is but faintly commended for his faithfulness.

The reconstruction of a somewhat later work, Weelkes' 'Ninth' service, provides further and different illustrations of the problems of restoration. The Magnificat and Nunc Dimittis of this Service (Wulstan, 1979a) exist principally in a Durham-related source at Peterhouse, Cambridge, comprising seven partbooks — two means, three altos and two basses — one alto and two tenor books being missing. The post-Reformation choir was usually disposed into two half choirs: the right side — as seen looking towards the altar — being the Dean's side (*Decani*) and the left being the Precentor's (*Cantoris*), though at Durham, since there had been a mitred Abbot, the sides were reversed. The boys sat in the front row of stalls on either side of the chancel, while the men sat in the second row. In a properly disposed choir there would have been at least two altos to each tenor or bass on each side of the choir, because the alto part was frequently divided. Since each side of the choir often sang independently as *Decani* and *Cantoris*, the altos were distributed both as first and second altos, and as *Dec* and *Can*. If the principal voice on each side were allocated to the first alto part in the Full sections, the second alto part would possibly be less well-balanced: the solution to this dilemma is manifest in the partbooks, since the first *Dec* alto is normally the same as the second *Can* (and so with the second *Dec* and first *Can*) in the Full sections.

A missing partbook may thus have varied consequences. In a pre-Reformation set of parts, it means the whole of that part is lost; indeed two parts may be lost if, as in one instance in White's Latin Magnificat, the missing part divided into a 'gimel' (the contemporary word for *divisi*). After the Reformation, certain kinds of sources continued to be disposed in a similar fashion; thus in Gibbons' 'I am the resurrection', which exists only in a 'madrigalian' set, the loss of two out of five original books is substantial. Music found in post-Reformation liturgical sources, however, is somewhat less vulnerable — the Venite of Byrd's Service survives intact apart from the first *Dec* out of four alto parts, and only the *Dec* bass part is missing in Sheppard's First service.

Weelkes' 'Ninth' service poses slightly more severe problems, since both tenor books are missing, and the second *Can* alto is also wanting. Unfortunately, concordant sources at Durham involve two parts already accounted for at Peterhouse. The sources for this Service have no directions indicating 'Full' and 'Verse', but presumably where the parts are the same on both sides the choir sang Full, and where different, soloists (or in the case of the boys, perhaps a duet) sang each part. Although the tenor part must be restored throughout, together with the second *Can* alto in *Can* Verse sections, the closeness of Weelkes' imitation lessens the difficulty of reconstruction. In some Verse sections both sides of the choir are involved. Sometimes, as in 'He hath shewed strength' the texture appears to be complete, but elsewhere, as in the Amen of the Magnificat and in the section of the Nunc Dimittis printed here, both the second *Can* alto and two tenor parts are clearly required:

Ex. 104

The underdotting of some of the words in the previous example is a convenient symbol, indicating a degree of dubiety concerning the underlay of the source. Such cases arise when the positioning of the words is unclear and no other sources give any help, or where there is a repetition mark (·//· or ij) whose expansion is dubious. Repetition marks are often perfectly straightforward in their meaning, in which case there is no point in calling the performer's attention to them; but where there is reasonable doubt, sublinear dots may serve to indicate the state of the MSS. Sometimes, however, the editor may well alter the underlay of the source entirely, believing it to be corrupt; for if the 'point' in one part is underlaid in a wholly contradictory manner from the others, there is a good case for emendation, the manuscript reading being consigned to the fastness of the critical commentary. Occasionally, as in bars 47–68 of the Nunc Dimittis of the 'Ninth' service, a more drastic revision must be carried out. In this particular instance, the mistake appears to arise from *homoioteleuton*, a process by which the scribe seems to have confused two similar passages. In the edition (Wulstan, 1979a) the *Dec* and *Can* 'means' have been reversed as a consequence of emendation. This apparently bold step is justified by the frequent reversal of the parts in various sources; and differences of underlay (often with concomitant differences of note-values) are all too common between corresponding passages in partbooks of the same set. The following example, from Sheppard's Second service, is typical:

Ex. 105

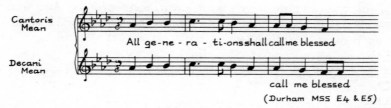

(Durham MSS E4 & E5)

Conflicts of this order must reflect either that the partbooks were used infrequently, if ever; or that the choir using them was a shambles. Whatever the correct explanation, the contradictory readings can hardly reflect the composer's intention. We know very little about the transmission of pieces from one establishment to another, but it is unlikely that books in daily use would be lent by one foundation to another while the contents were transcribed. Nor would a copyist be likely to lavish such care upon an intermediate rough copy as he would upon fair copy stall-books. It is probable, therefore, that some form of shorthand score was used to transmit church music, and indeed instrumental music, since both genres show similar signs of corruption. There is no direct evidence for these intermediate sources, although some extant organ scores are sufficiently elaborate to have served this function. The lack of such intermediate sources, or of composers' scores which must necessarily have existed, cannot be taken as a conclusive argument; a variety of *tabula rasa* is a plausible explanation for the scribal corruptions evident in many sources.

These corruptions give some comfort to the reconstructor, the enormity of whose task is underlined by the fact that half of Sheppard's hymns, responds and psalms would be unperformable without editorial reconstruction. Similarly, much of the music of Aston and his contemporaries, several of Weelkes' many Services and a considerable amount of Gibbons' music exist severally in varying stages of decrement. Since Gibbons' output of church music was not extensive, the comparatively large fraction which repines in incomplete sources is correspondingly significant. 'I am the resurrection' is obviously a magisterial work which demands the restitution of its missing voices. More difficult is the task involving 'Almighty God, which hast given' of which only a bass voice and organ score are extant, or the several Verse anthems of Gibbons which survive only in organ scores. Whether or not there is any point in undertaking their reconstruction is answered by the quality of 'Lord, we beseech thee' and 'Praise the Lord, O my soul', both of which are in the front rank of his compositions. The former is a setting of the Collect for the Annunciation, so the text itself

Ex. 106

poses no problem; the problems of restoration lie rather in identifying the parts in the organ score and in allocating the words. Since, as concordances for other works attest, this particular organ source is carelessly written, the task at times resembles a crossword puzzle. The extract in Ex. 106 (the reconstruction includes parts for viols) shows the extent of the problem. Although outlines of the voice parts are not faithfully echoed in the organ part of 'Lord we beseech thee', the source for 'Praise the Lord' is exemplary in this respect, and even gives the names of the voices involved in the Verse sections. Ironically, it is the words which here present major difficulties. The anthem clearly begins with Psalm 103, vv. 1–2, but unfortunately Gibbons was not content to compile his text solely from one psalm, but ranged with apparent freedom through the psalter. The pursuit of Gibbons among a hundred and fifty psalms is an energetic task, and although success can be recorded in several instances, failure must be admitted in at least one of the sections. The quality of 'Praise the Lord', however, justifies the labours of reconstruction and perhaps excuses the inevitable imperfections, and since the sources of complete works are so often unreliable, there is some comfort in the possibility that the restoration may well be little further from the composer's intentions than many a contemporary manuscript. Hardly, if ever, do organ scores agree entirely with the corresponding voice parts; and frequently they are irreconcilable, as is notable in parts of Gibbons' Second service, or in his anthem 'Glorious and powerful God'.

In addition to the responsibility of reconstruction, the editor must also correct extant sources when they are faulty. If two sources conflict, and one is clearly wrong (as happens in one or two instances in the Sheppard Paschal Kyrie) then the choice is clear; but if only one source survives and this, too, contains an obvious error, the obligation of the editor must be the same. If there are a hundred sources they could still, equally, be wrong — there is no sacerdotal principle in mass testimony. As Bentley, the seventeenth-century critic, wrote *ratio et res ipsa centum codicibus potiores sunt*: a hundred MSS cannot be held up as proof against common sense; and as Morley (1597, p. 151) said:

> . . . for copies passing from hand to hand a smal oversight committed by the first writer, by the second will bee made worse, which will give occasion to the third to alter much both in the wordes and notes, according as shall seeme best to his owne judgement, though (God knowes) it will be far enough from the meaning of the author . . .

Morley went on to assert that printed copies will contain 'no such thing' and Byrd felt able to say in the preface to his 1588 collection 'If ther be any jarre or dissonance, blame not the printer who . . . doth heere deliver to thee a perfect and true Coppie . . .'. Although it may be true that printed copies are often more reliable, they are by no means wholly so: the task of the editor must always be to recover what the composer intended, rather than to place his faith utterly in the MSS or printed sources.

The possibility of scribal error must be envisaged in Sheppard's Paschal Kyrie (Wulstan, 1978, p. 77). In bar 9 of the second alto, consecutive octaves arise with the mean — these may be avoided by a simple adjustment, no more adventurous than the correction of a misprint. At bar 6, the MSS impute consecutives between the treble and second alto. In my edition, this passage was emended, but as a reviewer pointed out, the alteration is not much better than the original, since consecutive fifths now arise between treble and second alto a beat later. Although consecutive fifths are more common in Sheppard, the criticism is just, for since no simple and obvious alteration is possible, the probability must be that Sheppard wrote the consecutives either in error, or not thinking them to be significant. Ironically, Morley, immediately prior to the quotation cited above, praises:

> . . . *Farefax, Taverner, Shepherde, Mundy, White, Persons, M. Birde*, and divers others, who never thought it greater sacrilidge to spurne against the Image of a Saint then [than] to take two perfect cordes of one kind together [ie. two consecutive perfect concords] . . .

In spite of this commendation, Sheppard was probably guilty of occasional solecisms of this nature (cf. 'In pace': Wulstan 1978, p. 43, bar 44), leaving to posterity the problems of deciding between possible lapses on the part of the composer or his scribe. Where the difference in sound is negligible, the editor may safely, and indeed more wisely, take the MS reading.

The majority of ordinary pitch errors committed by the sources are instantly detectable, however, and their emendation (by the excision or insertion of a dot, rest, and so on) is often a matter of common sense. It was therefore unfortunate that a much heralded series of church music contained, in its first volume, a display of excruciating dissonances resulting from blatant scribal errors, the emendation of which was obvious to everyone save the hapless editor. Nonetheless, the styles of some composers may raise particular difficulties since, as has been seen, an anomaly in the source might equally represent a mistake on the part of the scribe or an idiosyncracy on the part of the composer. To compound the problem, as Morley hints, a scribe may 'work over' the text, removing what he thinks to be a mistake. This means that the *lectio difficilior*, or more unusual possibility, is sometimes deliberate and to be preferred over one which is more conventional. For instance, the phrase 'All that glisters is not gold' is correct, the substitution of 'glitters' being an erroneous correction of the *lectio difficilior*.

The recognition of error (eg. dittography, or its opposite haplography, together with *homoioteleuton* and other kinds of scribal mistakes) is sometimes a simple matter; but often two readings will appear to be equally probable. The alternative variants sometimes have to be decided upon empirically; but sometimes they will allow a family tree to be constructed, where conjunctive variants unite branches of the stemma whose branches are separated by disjunctive variants. Unfortunately, collusion between sources, either real or apparent (eg. by sources making the same correction independently) introduces 'contamination', whereby the family relationships become falsified. In the following hypothetical stemma, contamination is indicated by a dotted line.

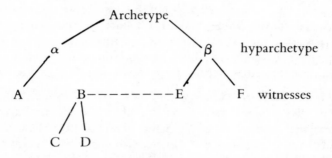

Ideally, some of the extant MSS (here, the 'witnesses' C and D) can be dismissed, as demonstrably deriving from a known exemplar, B. Here, B differs slightly from A, but agrees in conjunctive variants with which in turn they both differ from E and F. Leaving aside contamination between B and E, two or more lost exemplars ('hyparchetypes') are indicated by the evidence of the variants; and if all the disjunctive variants separating α and β are eliminated, then, theoretically, the 'archetype' (a much misused word, properly meaning 'the nearest possible relation to the author's text') can be reconstructed.

In reality the reconstruction of archetypes is a far from simple matter, due to contamination, incomplete evidence and so forth: an eclectic approach to the problem is frequently necessary. It is sometimes forgotten, however, that earlier sources are not necessarily better than later sources which might conceivably represent a still earlier and better tradition; nor should incomplete sources be regarded as the inferiors of the complete. Some of the problems of textual criticism have been illuminated recently (Rapson, 1981) by a method of evaluating sources by computer. Although the use of the computer in this connection frequently produces results as easily determined without its help, Mrs. Rapson's methods mark a signal technical advance and greatly contribute to the elimination of the difficulties of 'contamination'. An important conclusion of her work is that Tudor composers were inconsistent. This apparently gratuitous statement is considerably more far reaching than might appear at first blush. A composer was (and is) capable of writing two completely different versions of the same piece. The three redactions of *Piers Plowman* do not represent two which are incorrect and one which is correct; on the contrary, they must be regarded as three similar poems by Langland. By the same token, slavish consistency of musica ficta and underlay, for example, should not be sought: although a certain level of consistency may be part of a composer's style, anomalies cannot always be regarded as scribal errors.

Mrs. Rapson's study has shown that Tallis' underlay is frequently inconsistent, and thus that caution must be exercised in considering emendation. This having been said, the scribal treatment of underlay must often be regarded with healthy suspicion: Sheppard's 'Cantate' Mass, for example, abounds with instances where the underlay must be considered carefully. The Mass exists in a unique source (Oxford Bodleian Arch F. e. 19–24, *olim* Mus Sch e. 376–81), whose text seems generally reliable. In the Sanctus, however, the three uppermost voices begin the word *sanctus* syllabically, repeating it immediately in the same manner, after which its third appearance is melismatic. Since there are rests in the course of these melismata, and since after one such rest a new point appears to be initiated, should not all of these points be underlaid to the word *sanctus*, as it is on the first appearance of this point in the mean part? This course of action is taken by one modern editor; and he is in good company, for Baldwin (the copyist of most of Sheppard's other surviving music) was wont to introduce word repetition after a rest, perhaps sharing the dislike of Morley (1597, p. 178) for rests in the middle of words. It can be shown, nevertheless, that repetition is not a necessary consequence of rests, and that Baldwin was in many instances 'modernizing' his text, whether consciously or not. In the opening the underlay of the source can safely be followed: no extra repetition is demanded beyond the three occurrences of *sanctus* in each part. This threefold iteration, as Sheppard's other Masses confirm, answers to the liturgically correct *tersanctus*.

Ex. 107

Later in this passage, there should not be a repeat of the word *sabaoth* merely because of an intervening rest — the source makes it clear that the 'point' of *dominus deus* carries word repetition only where the whole phrase *dominus deus sabaoth* has been sung, and not otherwise. Yet the source exemplifies a palpable error in the tenor; at its entry (after the three upper voices have sung the *tersanctus*) it is underlaid with *sanctus*, while its companions are underlaid, to the same 'point', with the words *dominus deus*. Here the source requires emendation.

In Sheppard's music generally there are frequent problems as to the repetition or the displacement of 'points' (ie. where the same musical idea has different words in one or more parts). In solving these difficulties, the possible inconsistency of composers must be weighed against the probable corruption by scribes. In his responds, it seems generally to be the case that the underlay becomes more syllabic as the piece progresses: repetition is therefore less characteristic at the beginning than at the close of a movement. But often the correct placing of syllables is difficult to discern. Rules for underlay stated by continental theorists do not appear to have been adhered to by English composers. Finck (1556, V) and others stress the desirability of certain vowels for melismas; but there appears to be no such general preference in English music. Nevertheless, a rule that the melisma should be borne on the penultimate syllable at the end of a phrase does seem to be followed almost universally, particularly (as is normally the case in Latin) where this syllable carries the accent. Where the accent falls elsewhere, however, complications arise, to which the sources often add their own measure of confusion. In a word such as *dóminus* (where the accent is on the antepenult) Sheppard seems to follow any of three different courses:

(i) treating the word as though it were accented on the penult (which Morley — 1597, p. 178 — regarded as 'barbarisme'), but often alighting on the syllable with an off-beat slur, thus mitigating the effect of the 'false accent'.

(ii) alighting on the melisma at the last syllable, thus effectively throwing the accent back on to the correct syllable by the principle of the 'alternating accent'.

(iii) using a patterned system of underlay which allows the accented syllable to be treated melismatically. These possibilities are evident in Ex. 108.

Although the implications of the sources are obvious in these examples, patently representing the intentions of the composer, the correct underlay is frequently difficult to determine, since scribes' and composers' habits often differ widely between one another and are frequently inconsistent within themselves. Slurs in the MSS sometimes help, but are often ambiguous and contradictory (as in the repetitions of Sheppard's 'Gaude, gaude, gaude' in Baldwin's MSS — Oxford Ch Ch 979–83 — which show the same music with different underlay). Ligatures, an old-fashioned convention by which

Ex. 108

(Sheppard, 'In manus tuas' I, bars 19-21 (Mean))

(Sheppard, 'Christi virgo', consecutive statements of the point
subveni domina bars 34-42 (Alto I): MS (and correct) reading)

(Sheppard, 'In manus tuas' I, bars 1-6 (Alto I))

two or more notes were united together in a theoretically inseparable bond, should give some guide to underlay; but Sheppard's 'Laudem dicite' occurs twice in the same Baldwin sources, each version having different ligatures implying different underlay; thus the evidence of ligatures is clearly of limited value.

The manner in which Baldwin can be seen to tamper with Sheppard's underlay is nonetheless instructive, since it appears to reflect general changes in taste during the later half of the sixteenth century. Where a rest intervenes in a melisma Baldwin added a repetition to avoid the hiatus disliked by Morley, but which was common in earlier music. In copying Sheppard's psalms in Oxford Ch Ch 979–83 Baldwin seems to have been generally faithful to the composer's underlay, but by the time he came to copy responds many text repetitions are added; for although Sheppard frequently indulged in such repetitions at a climax, eg. at the last section of a respond, they are otherwise uncharacteristic.

Another alteration which appears to be made by Baldwin involves pattern (ii) above. Generally speaking the dotted-note pattern involving two notes of the same pitch is underlaid by Sheppard as at (ii), as Sarah Cobbold has pointed out. She also notes that the same device is prominent in the *Eton Choirbook* and, although it is not readily discernible in the work of Taverner and Tallis, it is common in Tye, White and Mundy. Copyists frequently altered pattern (ii) to (i) however, delaying the final syllable until the last note of the melisma (indeed, some examples of pattern (iii) may also be attributable to a similar alteration of what originally was pattern (ii)). In favouring off-beat slurring, Baldwin, and sometimes the Paston copyists, seem to reflect the increasing popularity of this device towards the end of the sixteenth century. This style of underlay is characteristic of the English madrigal collections and, as noted earlier, is used to excess in Whythorne's *Songes . . .* of 1571. Early seventeenth-century sources of church music also attest to an increase in the use of this kind of underlay, but at 1625 or so the increasing use of homophonic textures laid considerably less emphasis on off-beat underlay.

It is worth mentioning that since sixteenth-century composers wrote without bar-lines, tied notes were rarely used (those of modern trans-criptions normally represent whole or dotted notes in the original). Tallis is exceptional in this regard, for in at least one passage in 'Spem in alium' and probably elsewhere, he appears to make use of a short note-value tied to a long one, the sum of which cannot be expressed as one note. This is one of many instances where Tallis' underlay, and that of his compatriots gener-ally, has little in common with that of the Continent. Thus the pro-nouncements of continental theorists such as Zarlino, although they have considerable relevance for Palestrina, are of limited use in solving problems connected with English underlay.

Ideally, the editor will present the performer with an edition in which all of the foregoing problems, and many more, will have been solved, leaving the finer points of interpretation to emerge in performance. The edition will provide the performer with a clear modern equivalent of the obscure, incomplete and archaically written sources. At the same time, by using prefatory staves (which show the original pitch and note-value of the opening note, together with the mensuration sign and key signature of the source) and by distinguishing his own contribution by the use of square brackets and other conventions, the editor is able to convey as much information about the state of these sources as is possible without needless clutter.

The old *Tudor Church Music* editions with their expensive and large format, long note-values and untransposed pitches, were clearly im-practible, and omitted the necessary chants. The more practical editions by Fellowes and others made good some of these deficiencies, but sometimes failed to distinguish between the contributions of the editor and his manu-scripts. At the same time, a pseudo-facsimile is not helpful to the practical musician. Many modern editions have neither the advantages of a facsimile, nor of a practical format. The series *Corpus Mensurabilis Musicae*, for example, although reducing the note-values, often failed to supply con-ventional bar-lines and ties, so that one note can last for several bars; in this kind of notation a misprinted or misread dot can cause the performer to err for several bars, if not pages. The question of transposition is evaded by this and many other series, including several of the volumes of *Early English Church Music*. In the latter, however, the process of reduction is often embraced with such enthusiasm that the note-values assume almost bacterial proportions. The pendulum of time notation swings the other way in some recent Byrd volumes, where the tiresomely long note-values used by the old *Tudor Church Music* volumes have been resurrected.

The performer is not well served by these vacillations between pulicine and leviathan note-values; nor is it easy to read plainchants represented by tail-less blobs, minute notes and accidentals; and his task is also made harder by a failure to supply proper bar-lines, or by the music being printed in the wrong key. In the half-light of the choir stalls much is made obscure which should be patent; and a barrier, rather than a bridge, is constructed between the composer and his performer.

The performer's task, after all, is formidable enough. Matters of musica ficta and underlay, of pitch, additional plainchants and so on should properly have been dealt with before he begins to perform. In the unlikely event that he may dismiss such matters from his mind, there remain specific technical matters, as for example the problems of pronunciation and articulation, and more general matters such as the questions of dynamics and tempo.

In the consideration of all of these topics, one over-riding consideration needs to be borne in mind: music is best served when it is allowed to speak for itself. Exaggerated dynamics, tempi and 'expression', together with mannered pronunciation, or articulation are as inimical to the composer's intentions as lifeless performances in which words are uttered mechanically, or in which cadences come to a violent halt as though precipitated by a seizure.

The late nineteenth century has much to answer for, since it replaced subtlety of articulation with exaggerated modes of 'expression'. Most of all, it introduced the unremitting use of vibrato, coupled with the vowel distortion and suppression of consonants characteristic of most operatic singers today. The complex polyphonic textures of Tudor music would be imperspicuous if the parts were blurred, particularly by vibrato. Yet in spite of this, singers are reluctant to forsake wobbling, partly because it appears to amplify the voice, and partly because intonation problems are covered up by its obligingly wide margin of error. As in instrumental playing, vibrato was employed only as an occasional ornament in early vocal music. In the eighteenth century Geminiani, (1751) appears to have attempted to introduce a more pervasive style of vibrato into violin technique; it is interesting to note that this was resisted by his English publisher, who suppressed the relevant passage in the 1777 edition (cf. Hickman, 1983). It must, however, be stressed that any reference to vibrato prior to the late nineteenth century must be taken to indicate the subtle sense of the word; it was not until then, with the invention of the violin chin rest and 'cello spike, that the fingers of string players were able to perform a tireless twitch around the note. The operatic retracted larynx technique, with its concomitant vibrato, also began to gain ascendancy at about this time. It is obvious that Baroque singers could hardly have sung in such a way that trills were indis-

179

tinguishable from the surrounding gelatinous wobble, yet it is still woefully rare to hear a singer who has foresaken the nineteenth century mannerisms.

So entrenched is the use of vibrato that tremulous, if specious, arguments are advanced in its favour, in spite of the evidence. The surprising assertion has recently been made that vibrato is necessary for the psychological perception of sound (Donnington, 1982, p. 35). The notion is based upon a mistaken view of neurological phenomena: to say that the ear cannot tolerate a steady note (which in any case is more apparent than real) is tantamount to saying that the eye cannot perceive a stationary object. On the contrary, the brain has a highly developed system for reducing sensitivity to prolonged stimuli (cf. Blakemore, 1977).

The retracted larynx technique, as will be seen in the next chapter, also suppresses the distinctions between the vowels and makes the articulation of consonants more difficult. The resultant undifferentiated tone displays a complement of harmonics which is by turns dull and loud in at least two critical parts of the frequency spectrum. The necessity for clear vowel contrasts is emphasized by several passages of Tudor polyphony. Cornish and Sheppard, for example, make much use of the contrast between the *i* and *a* vowels in the section 'dimisit inanes' of their Magnificats (on the 8th tone, and 1st tone for men's voices, respectively). These instances of the exploitation of vowel colour are striking examples among many; the theorists make the matter equally clear. Bathe, in his *A Briefe Introduction to the skill of song* (1587, 'The ante rules') says: 'Practise to sunder the Vowels and Consonants, distinctly pronouncing them according to the manner of the place . . . to have the breath long to continue, and the tongue at liberty to runne . . . [and] to have your voice cleer . . .' Charles Butler (1636, p. 98) wrote that the words are 'half the grace of the Song'; and that singers should sing 'as plainly as they would speak: pronouncing every Syllable and letter (especially the Vowels) distinctly and treatably. And in their great variety of Tones to keep still an equal sound (except in a Point) that one voice drown not another' (spelling modernized). Morley also abjures 'Church men' to 'studie how to vowell and sing clean', reflecting the *Black Book* of Edward IV a century earlier, which called for singers 'shewing in descant, clean voysed, well relysed and pronouncing' (cf. Myers 1959, p. 135).

There is no comfort here for the operatic school of singing: continental writers confirm that articulate delivery, but even tone, is required. It is interesting to note that Butler urges restraint 'except in a Point', echoing Zacconi (1592) who calls for 'entries to be emphasised a little'. This general restraint, contrasted with occasional gentle emphasis, is one of the keys to good polyphonic singing. Butler (1636, p. 97) also calls for 'a decent erect posture of the Body, without all ridiculous and uncomely gesticulations of Head, or Hands, or any other part . . .'. Dowland (1609) translated the *Micrologus* of 'Ornithoparcus' thus: 'Let a Singer take heed, least he begin too loud braying like an Asse . . . For God is not pleased with loude cryes . . . The uncomely gaping of the mouth, and ungracefull motion of the body, is a signe of a mad Singer'.

The same defects, and many more, were pilloried by Finck (1556, V) who speaks of 'bleating and barbarous cries' of singers changing their tone colours and gaping mouths — a 'deplorable sight'. Basses are warned against making a raucous noise like 'a hornet trapped in a boot'. Singing does not come from bellowing, indeed 'the higher the voice rises, the quieter and lovelier the note should be sung'. Finck's treatise goes on to echo many points discussed by Conrad von Zabern in his *De modo bene cantandi* (1474), who says that singing through the nose is not beautiful, nor are 'intrusive aitches' anything but rustic, and vowels should be carefully differentiated so that one does not sing 'let us plough' rather than 'let us pray' (*aremus* for *oremus*): this disability sounds like 'fodder in the mouth'. Distortion of vowels during a long note, wobbling, squeezing out the voice, singing high notes with heavy voice ('bellowing like cattle in the field') are all crudities, he says. Instead, von Zabern calls for an even delivery, shading off towards the higher notes so that the gradation of tone is smooth. Although singing should not be loud, it should not be 'sluggish, without life or emotion, like the groans of an old woman close to death'. Not only many singers of the operatic school, but those purporting to sing in an 'authentic' style, would also do well to heed these strictures, echoed frequently in the sixteenth and early seventeenth centuries (eg. Mersenne, 1636).

The accentuation of words sometimes presents difficulties, since singers occasionally treat the bar-line as having an accentual significance, from which misaccentuation may often arise. Equally frequently, the self-conscious cross-accentuation of words is heard, arising from over-correction or from confusing notation. The simplest way to prevent these problems from coming to the fore is to provide the performer with normal groupings of notes in regular bars, with the occasional mark (⌣) to denote that a note or syllable should be light or (–) heavy.

Ex. 109

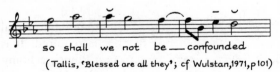

so shall we not be — confounded

(Tallis, 'Blessed are all they'; cf Wulstan, 1971, p 101)

It is particularly important not to crescendo, after the nineteenth century fashion, on notes tied over the bar; in any event, the ties of Tudor music result from the process of transcription. Equally, however, the habit of fading away on a suspension (whereby the musical grammar of dissonance and resolution is perverted) is to be avoided. 'Pushing and pulling the voice'

Cap.8. *in the Counter-point.* 89

1 When you defire to fing any thing, aboue all things marke the *Tone*, and his *Repercuſsion*. For he that fings a Song without knowing the *Tone*, doth like him that makes a fyllogifme without *Moode* and Figure.

2 Let him diligently marke the *Scale*, vnder which the Song runneth, leaft he make a *Flat* of a *Sharpe* or a *Sharpe* of a *Flat*.

3 Let euery Singer conforme his voyce to the words, that as much as he can he make the *Concent* fad when the words are fad;& merry,when they are merry. Wherein I cannot but wonder at the Saxons (the moft gallant people of all Germany, by whofe furtherance I was both brought vp, and drawne to write of Muficke) in that they vfe in their funerals, an high, merry and ioconde *Concent*, for no other caufe (I thinke) than that either they hold death to be the greateft good that can befall a man (as *Valerius* in his fift Booke writes of *Cleobis* and *Biton* two brothers) or in that they beleeue that the foules (as it is in *Macrobius* his fecond Booke *De ſomnio Scip.*) after this body doe returne to the original fweetnes of Muficke, that is to heauen. Which if it be the caufe, we may iudge them to be valiant in contemning death, and worthy defirers of the glory to come.

4 Aboue all things keepe the equalitie of meafure. For to fing without law and meafure, is an offence to God himfelfe, who hath made all things well, in number, weight, and meafure. Wherefore I would haue the Eafterly *Franci* (my countrey-men) to follow the beft manner, and not as before they haue done; fometime long; fometime to make fhort the Notes in Plain-fong, but take example of the noble Church of *Herbipolis*, their head, wherin they fing excellently. Which would alfo much profit, and honour the Church of *Prage*, becaufe in it alfo they make the Notes fometimes longer, fometime fhorter, than they fhould. Neither muft this be omitted, which that loue which we owe to the dead, doth require. Whofe *Vigils* (for fo are they commonly called) are performed with fuch confufion, haft, and mockery, (I know not what fury poffeffeth the mindes of thofe, to whom this charge is put o-uer) that neither one Voyce can be diftinguifhed from another, nor one fillable from another, nor one verfe fometimes throughout a whole Pfalme from another. An impious fafhion to be punifhed with the feuereft correcti-on. Think you that God is pleafed with fuch howling, fuch noife, fuch mumbling, in which is no deuotion, no expreffing of words, no articulating of fyllables?

5 The Songs of Authenticall *Tones* muft be timed deepe, of the fubiugall *Tones* high, of the neutrall, meanly. For thefe goe deep, thofe high, the other both high and low.

6 The changing of Vowels is a figne of an vnlearned Singer. Now, (though diuers people doe diuerfly offend in this kinde) yet doth not the multitude of offenders take away the fault. Here I would haue the *Francks* to take heede they pronounce not *u* for *o*, as they are wont, faying *nufter* for *nofter*. The countrey Church-men are alfo to be cenfured for pronouncing, *Aremus* in ftead of *Oremu s*. In like fort, doe all the *Renenſes* from *Spyre*

B b   to

Fig. 15 Description of undesirable qualities in singers. (from Dowland's translation of Ornithoparcus' *Micrologus*, 1609)

to *Confluentia* change the Vowel *i* into the dipthong *ei*, saying *Mareia* for *Maria*. The *Westphalians* for the vowel *a* pronounce *a* & *e* together, to wit, *Aebs te* for *Abs te*. The lower Saxons, & al the *Sueuians*, for the Vowel *e*, read *e* & *i*, saying, *Deius* for *Deus*. They of lower *Germany* doe all expresse *u* & *e*, in stead of the Vowel *u*. Which errours, though the *Germane* speech doe often require, yet doth the Latine tongue, which hath the affinitie with ours, exceedingly abhorre them.

7 Let a Singer take heed, least he begin too loud braying like an Asse, or when he hath begun with an vneuen height, disgrace the Song. For God is not pleased with loude cryes, but with louely sounds: it is not (saith our *Erasmus*) the noyse of the lips, but the ardent desire of the Art, which like the lowdest voice doth pierce Gods eares. *Moses* spake not, yet heard these words, *Why doest thou cry vnto me?* But why the Saxons, and those that dwell vpon the Balticke coast, should so delight in such clamouring, there is no reason, but either because they haue a deafe God, or because they thinke he is gone to the South-side of heauen, and therefore cannot so easily heare both the Easterlings, and the Southerlings.

8 Let euery Singer discerne the difference of one holiday from another, least on a sleight Holiday, he either make too solemne seruice, or too sleight on a great.

9 The vncomely gaping of the mouth, and vngracefull motion of the body, is a signe of a mad Singer.

10 Aboue all things, let the Singer study to please God, and not men; (saith *Guido*) there are foolish Singers; who contemne the deuotion they should seeke after? and affect the wantonnesse which they should shun: because they intend their singing to men, not to God: seeking for a little worldly fame, that so they may loose the eternall glory: pleasing men that thereby they may displease God: imparting to other that deuotion, which themselues want: seeking the fauour of the creature, contemning the loue of the Creatour: to whom is due all honour, and reuerence, and seruice. To whom I doe deuote my selfe, and all that is mine, to him will I sing as long as I haue being: for he hath raised me (poore Wretch) from the earth, and from the meanest basenesse. Therefore blessed be his Name world without end, *Amen.*

The end of the Worke.

is a common, and irritating, habit (instrumentally as well as vocally): the *messa di voce* is called for only in certain special effects (see p. 37).

Breaths naturally come at the end of a phrase or at a comma (others should be excised by the singer in order to lessen confusion); and by modern convention, the consonant of a final note before a rest will normally come upon that rest, as opposed to notes where the phrase ends without a rest. When a sibilant is involved in passages where some voices rest at the same time as others continue the phrase, unanimity is desirable. Similarly, an unintentional dissonance might ensue from a sonant (voiced) consonant fractionally extending the note; in these cases the offending consonants are best sounded before the rest. These cases may be marked by a dot over the note; the same device (perhaps in conjunction with some other sign) may be used for the several places where composers are unwilling to give a rest to the bass, while allowing it elsewhere. This peculiar mannerism is comparatively frequent: since the basses must take a breath at some point, they might as well synchronize with the other parts, in spite of the notation:

Ex. 110

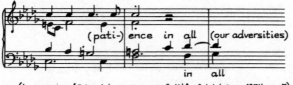

(Loosemore 'O Lord increase our faith'; cf Wulstan, 1971b, no. 7)

The pronunciation of English is of course a notorious difficulty, since its long vowels are actually diphthongs and sometimes vice versa; it is nevertheless important not to distort these sounds by introducing 'singers'' pronunciations. Similarly, words such as *tempta-ti-on, thor-ough-out, al-mes* or *spirit*, where the number of syllables has changed since Tudor times, are best sung without exaggeration (tempta-sĭ-on, tho-row-out, al-mes, spreet): nor is there any point in irritating the listeners by putting up a barrier of 'authentic' pronunciation between him and the composer. The same is true for Latin. If *excelsis* is pronounced 'exselsis', rather than 'ekshelsis' in the Italian fashion, then there will be no difficulty with *gracias* (which is *gratias* mis-spelled) or with rhymes in *-cio // -tio*. In other words, a generally 'continental' pronunciation of Latin, but pronouncing *c* before *e* or *i* as *s* rather than *ch*, is a tolerable compromise. The Italianate pronunciation is clearly inappropriate, as are attempts to restore a 'classical' or even 'contemporary' pronunciation. Erasmus commented that, next to the Italians, the English pronounced Latin the best; and contemporary *accentuaria* in Breviaries gave a guidance to the accentuation (and indeed to the quantities) of Latin. To espouse the hideous 'Anglian' pronunciation of Law-Latin, or to advocate a 'contemporary' Latin pronunciation (whether specious or otherwise) is to introduce an unnecessary obfuscation.

In matters of pronunciation, there should be an artlessness of delivery which hides a good deal of technique and thought. Similarly, the dynamics of a piece should not be over apparent, but should seem to grow out of the music itself. In addition to the recommendation that the 'point' should be fractionally louder than the rest of the texture, there is evidence that various sections of Masses, Magnificats and so forth, were conventionally somewhat louder or softer, as appropriate. An Amen would naturally be more vigorous than the 'et incarnatus' of the Credo, where something resembling a musical genuflexion is required. This is what Morley meant (1597, p. 179) by singers 'expressing their wordes with deuotion and passion': other writers express similar sentiments.

The dynamic contrasts of vocal music, like that of instrumental music (as in Gabrieli's 'Sonata pian' e forte') are frequently inherent in the scoring of the music. Reduced forces and Verse sections allow changes of intensity in the scoring. In the *Eton Choirbook* sections for reduced voices are apparently indicated by red underlay) in later pre-Reformation sources there are no such indications, but it is possible that *soli* might be used whenever there is a reduction of the number of parts.

The dynamic level of the music is often indicated by the high or low tessitura of the parts. A performance of Victoria's Requiem comes to mind, in which I mistakenly attempted to impose an English restraint upon certain passages. Only when the full-blooded Spanish texture was allowed to come into its own did the piece become more comfortable to sing and the performance achieve a more obvious reflection of the intentions of the composer.

Speeds, too, can often be suggested by open-minded experiment. Tempi, of course, may vary 'according to the manner of the place' and indeed the technique of the performers, but the tolerable extremes of speed are often not far apart. Tempo is widely regarded to have been regulated by the mensuration signs (which evolved into modern 'time signatures'), and although this is true to some degree, it cannot be pressed too far. The principal mensuration signs were originally a circle (which represented 'perfect' time, where a breve was subdivided into three 'semibreves') and a half circle (where the breve was divided into two semibreves). Each of the semibreve subdivisions was divided into minims, two when the prolation was imperfect and three when the prolation was perfect (marked by a dot in the circle or half circle). The relationship between these four types of time is often vague, for it depended upon whether the breve, semibreve or the minim was the value common to each. Taking the semibreve as the denominator, the relationships would be:

Ex. 111

These mensuration signs were by no means consistently used, and were frequently modified, along with the note-values themselves. A stroke through the sign, or its reversal, diminished the note-values by half. Thus a breve in ₵ (or Ɔ) had the same duration as a semibreve in C; similarly breves in Φ were equivalent to semibreves in O. A proportional change could also be expressed with a figure: ² or 2; double diminution was also possible (₵, ₵, Φ or Ɔ2 ; Φ2). Diminution by half as much again (semiquialtera) could be affected by appending ³₂ (or simply 3; diminution by twice as much (tripla) was indicated by the sign ³₁ .

These devices enormously complicated the system. Theoretically, the sign 'set with a stroke parting it thus ₵ causeth the song before which it is set to be song as a breefe or the value of a breefe in other notes, [which therefore will] make but one ful stroke and is proper to motetes specially when the song is prickt in great notes' (Morley, 1597, p. 23, italics and some commas omitted); but Morley continues 'that rule bee not so generally kept: but that the composers set the same signe before songs of the *semibriefe* time'. In other words, *alla breve* (used largely in church music) is confused with common time (used mostly in secular music). Morley's 'infalable rule' for sorting out conflicting mensuration signs is to abide by the quicker alternative; and when there is any doubt it is often safer to follow Morley in rejecting the slower of two possibilities. As Agricola (1532, VI) also points out, 'sesquialtera is used as triple or hemiola proportion when all voices have it'.

Normally, where a figure is appended to a change of mensuration sign, a strictly proportional change is indicated, bearing in mind, however, that ₵ and C, for instance, are often confused: thus ₵ followed by C3 (slower) may actually mean C→ C3 (faster) where in modern values ← o = ♩. →. Sheppard and others frequently use the signature Φ to imply a faster tempo, though not one twice as fast as ₵. This change of sign from ₵ to Φ and back occurs twice in his Te Deum; and the same change is found at the Gloria of the hymn 'Martyr Dei', reverting to ₵ at the Amen (see Bray, 1981). Comparable changes of signatures, or a variation of note-values, or both, indicate that Amen was regularly sung more broadly than the previous section (though where it joins on to the previous section, the slower tempo should be started earlier, rather than suddenly introduced). The same phenomena indicate that various sections of the Mass and Canticles were traditionally sung at different tempi, whether or not marked with changes of mensuration. As Glarean bears witness (1547, III, viii):

when musicians fear that the listeners might become weary, they quicken the beat by crossing the circle calling it a diminution. In fact this does not diminish the value or number of the notes, they merely quicken the beat . . . Thus the sections of a Kyrie in the Mass are often signed Ⲫ C Ⲫ to avoid weariness.

Vicentino (1555, IV, *42*) remarks that 'the tempo should move according to the words'. In addition to singing *piano* and *forte*, one must also sing *presto* and *tardo*, 'according to the words'. Zarlino (1588) makes it clear that tempo changes are extremely important and that when beating *alla breve* one should change tempo. By this he means that ₵ is not merely the same tempo as C in enlarged note-values. These things, he says, although un-written, are 'understood in practice'.

Thus, the various sections of the Mass and Canticles were probably sung at slightly differing tempi, whether or not there were different mensuration signs and whatever the 'correct' significance of the latter. Some Masses appear to have had many time changes, others rather fewer. The main sectional changes (slightly faster unless otherwise stated) were:

Kyrie   :   Christe   :   Kyrie
of which the Christe was probably little, if any, faster than the first Kyrie.

Gloria   :   Qui tollis (slower)   :   cum sancto

Credo : Et incarnatus slower : Et expecto : Et vitam (slower)

Sanctus & Osanna   :   Benedictus   :   Osanna — at speed of
                                                            previous Osanna.

Agnus I   :   Agnus II   :   Agnus III (? at tempo of Agnus II,
                                              but slightly faster at 'Dona nobis'.)

The Canticles apparently also had similar time changes:

Te Deum : Tu patris : Eterna fac (slower) : Et laudamus : In te domine (slower)

Magnificat : Fecit potentiam (slower) :
Sicut locutus : Amen (? slower)

Hymns — last verse (if polyphonic) faster : Amen (slower)

In regard to proportional time changes, a general rule of thumb is to increase the speed half as much again when a 3 is found in the second mensural sign, and revert to the previous time if the corresponding men-sural sign reappears within that section.

In English settings, equivalent sections of the Mass and Te Deum may have been treated similarly to their Latin counterparts. Since mensuration signs were less lavishly used after the Reformation there is little clear evidence of this, but mensuration changes in some settings indicate that the Magnificat in English appears to have had conventional time changes at 'He hath put down' and 'As he promised', the Gloria (taken either quicker, or at *tempo primo* after the rallentando of the previous section) finally slowing down at Amen. Similarly, the Nunc Dimittis had a quicker section at 'To be a light', slowing down before the Gloria, the latter being treated as in the Magnificat.

The evidence of time-signatures makes it clear that these sectional changes of time, when indicated, were not necessarily proportional: only when the numeral 3 is involved in the new signature is a strictly proportional change required. Otherwise, any section may be commenced at a slightly different tempo, with a ritenuto at least at the close of the movement (at Amen or at a corresponding point) when, according to Praetorius (1618, III, p. 80), there should be a considerable ritardation before the final note. Praetorius also stresses that according to the 'meaning of the words sometimes, but not too often' the beat will be 'now fast and now slow', and deals similarly with dynamic changes (ibid. III, p. 132). Church tempi, he says, will be more moderate than those of chamber music. A similar distinction in regard to dynamics, which were louder in church than in chamber music, is drawn by Zacconi and Zarlino.

In the sixteenth and early seventeenth centuries many attempts were made to relate absolute tempo to the heart beat, or to the pendulum. These indications are either too vague (depending on the indefinable notion of an 'average' heart beat) or contradictory; Mersenne (1636) describes the beat as 'very slow' if it occurs once a second, but ascribes the same tempo to a 'measure' of duple or triple time. This appears to give a tempi approximating with $\quarternote$ = 120 or $\quarternote$ = 180, both of which are rather fast. A note (presumably by Nathaniel Tomkins) in the Tenbury copy of *Musica Deo Sacra* (1668) gives this direction:

O : Sit mensura duorum humani corporis pulsum, vel globuli
penduli longitudine duorum pedum a centro motus

But Tomkins is many years later than Mersenne, and though this tempo, the equivalent of $\quarternote$ = 76, may be appropriate for some music of the end of the seventeenth century, it is far too slow as the basic beat for Tudor music. After careful consideration of the facts, the question of tempo must eventually be resolved pragmatically.

Plainchant was of course intoned at a quicker tempo, and more freely than polyphony. Although there were certain types of pseudo-chant, such as is found in the 'squares' and in Merbecke's settings in *The booke of Common praier noted* (1550), there is no evidence to suggest that plainchant was sung metrically. There have been some arguments put forward for metrical performance, based on the use of plainchant cantus firmi in polyphony. But since Tallis and Sheppard sometimes set the same chant as a cantus firmus in both duple and triple time in the same hymn, this proposition cannot be taken seriously, quite apart from the length of time which the complex Sarum liturgy would have taken if the plainchants were drawn out to the same speeds as those required for polyphony. A significant pause was made at the *metrum* or half way mark of a plainchant (cf. Frere, 1898); but the verses themselves followed on rapidly, apart from the slight ritenuto at the cadences (often marked by editorial dots in modern editions of the chant). A peculiarity of English Tudor chant was the *strene*, a liquescent neume which originally signified two notes, the second being lower; although by the time of the sixteenth century it was normally performed as one long note:

Ex. 112

The ornamentation of virginalist music has been discussed at length. In vocal music the Baroque use of divisions and graces was slow to take hold in England (some early examples are collected in Duckles, 1957). Charles Butler (1636) railed against 'too much shaking and quavering of the notes'. Several seventeenth-century sources include these novel vocal divisions, but perhaps the more remarkable occurrences of this type of ornamentation are in church music. Some solo passages of Gibbons are found in ornamental versions,

Ex. 113

(Sheppard, 'Cantate' Mass: Gloria & Credo)

(Gibbons, 'Glorious and powerful God')

and Sheppard's 'Cantate' Mass has sporadic turn-like figures in the alto parts, though whether these represent the winter of the florid style of Cornish and Taverner, or the spring of Gabrieli and Monteverdi, is not clear (Ex. 113).

The vocal agility required by these passages cannot be achieved by the technique of using a retracted larynx in which the attack is made more cumbersome — if there were no other evidence, this alone would rule out the heavy operatic voice from early music.

In recent years, there has been an attempt on the part of some singers to return to the lighter and more agile style of singing which had been current prior to the operatic method of production evolved in the nineteenth century. Similarly, instrumentalists are gradually coming away from entrenched Romanticisms, and giving their playing more clarity and subtlety. There is a danger, however, that one set of bad habits might be supplanted by another, in the guise of a new orthodoxy. The irritating *messa di voce* over-used by some 'early music' singers and instrumentalists alike is one of several new mannerisms which have taken the place of old; and if no more false, the new fads are hardly less irritating. One contributory problem is that, as with a Biblical quotation taken out of context, the evidence of theorists can be made to confirm several erroneous practices. The words 'loud' or 'soft', 'fast' or 'slow' and particularly 'expressive', can be taken to mean almost anything, with the result that the same passage can be cited to justify two utterly opposed performances.

In the face of these difficulties, it is understandable that a reaction should set in, when the possibility of any useful degree of authenticity, or indeed its very advisability, should be questioned. Yet the fact that we cannot achieve absolute truth and perfection does not absolve us from seeking them; we have a duty to endeavour to keep faith with the intentions of the composer. It is true that times and tastes have changed, and that an utterly accurate replica of original performances would defeat the spirit of these intentions as much as a wholly modernized version would transgress the letter of his wishes. An honest performance lies between the two extremes at a point which will necessarily vary from time to time. But life and death always exist, even if they are redefined: we should not allow a composer's work to meet a living death simply because of a difficulty of definition. And although we should not condemn outright a performance which has unobtrusive anachronisms, nor should we excuse another merely by completing the insidious phrase 'had the composer been alive today . . . .'. Such a composer, translated to our times, would have written music wholly different to that of his own age. His trammels would not have been the same: he would no longer have to compose for keyboard instruments incapable of a crescendo; but in his own age he solved this problem in relation to the instruments at hand. This is why overt modernization is self-defeating; the composer would no more take kindly to the artificial removal of his challenges than a footballer would welcome an enlarged goal; his skill would thereby be devalued.

The interpreter must not use excuses to bowdlerize the music of the past. If he wishes to express himself unencumbered by the conventions adopted by the composer, it is open to him to do so by composing his own music; if he does not like the way a composer intended to express himself, the only honourable course is not to perform the music. Once the trust has been accepted, his duty must be to efface himself rather than to offend the integrity of the author. The performer is the medium and not the message; his role is to conjure up the imaginative spirit of the composer before his audience. He will do this best by endeavouring to discover all that he can of the conventions and conditions of the past and to try to follow those which are most feasible and most necessary to an honest modern performance. Some of the specific problems which confront the editor and performer of Tudor music have been explored here, by following one or two works from manuscript to performance. Other problems, concerning pitch and vocal colour, remain to be considered in the following chapter. That so much space should be devoted to questions of performance needs no apology. 'Only this I desire', said Byrd in the preface to his 1611 *Psalmes, Songs, and Sonnets*, 'that you will be but as careful, to heare them well expressed, as I have beene both in the Composing and correcting of them . . . for that the well expressing of them, either by Voyces, or Instruments, is the life of our labours . . .'

CHAPTER 8

A High Clear Voice

The resplendent and complex style of polyphony developed by British composers in the first half of the sixteenth century is without parallel on the Continent. It is distinguished by a characteristic richness of sonority, resulting partly from an extension of the total vocal range, and partly from an exploitation of individual vocal tone-colour. In its wealth of detail and overall magnificence this polyphony is a worthy representative of the intricacies of Perpendicular tracery; it also reflects the no less intricate Sarum Rite. This late and most vivid flowering of medieval polyphony withered at the Reformation, but bore fruits in the more progressive style of succeeding generations. The English concern with the exploitation of individual vocal sonority accounts partly for the late adoption of more advanced imitative techniques from the Continent where the treatment of voices was less idiomatic, more attention being concentrated on the creation of an abstract choral sound.

These things being so, the rediscovery of the particular sonorities of Tudor church music is obviously an important matter; and although difficulties involved in investigating the vocal characteristics of four-and-a-half centuries ago are self-evident, the task is by no means impossible. The evidence, though fragmentary, may be pieced together from a wide variety of sources, the most obvious of which may be found in contemporary, or nearly contemporary, theoretical writings, and, of course, the music itself. The musical sources, however, display two of the most important facets of the problem of vocal colour. As will be seen in the course of this chapter, the intended voices are rarely designated in the original sources of the period: this lack of identification would not be so problematical if, as in modern music, the intended pitch standard were immediately obvious. The problems of vocal scoring and of pitch are thus fundamentally interrelated.

As far back as the nineteenth century, it was recognized that the implied pitch of Elizabethan and Jacobean church music was somewhat higher than had been hitherto assumed. Ouseley, in his 1873 edition of Gibbons, transposed the music a tone higher; other editors occasionally made similar transpositions. In the present century Fellowes, who printed all of Byrd's music and a vast amount by other composers, regularly transposed Tudor vocal music in order to bring it into conformity with what appeared to him to be the intentions of the composer. The majority of these adjustments were upward transpositions of a minor third, following the pitch level he had found indicated in the Tenbury copy of Tomkins' *Musica Deo Sacra* (1688); but where the pitches seemed to him to be too high, he transposed the music down; and where it appeared to be much too low (eg. in Tallis' 'In jejunio et fletu', which he transposed up a sixth) he did not hesitate to print the music in what he considered to be the appropriate key, irrespective of the pitch of the original. To his abiding credit, the majority of Fellowes decisions, most of which he made empirically, can now be seen to have been more or less correct. Mendel (1948) in a series of articles amassed a considerable amount of evidence on the subject. Unfortunately, in both these and in a later treatment (1978), he seemed to be bemused by the sheer range of his material, and failed to come to any practical conclusions. An advance was made by Andrews (1962) however, who showed that several of Fellowes' empirical transpositions could be justified by the transposing clefs mentioned by contemporary theorists and confirmed, as Andrews demonstrated, by the alternative sets of clefs in sources of Byrd's music.

In 1962 Peter le Huray published his reconstruction of Weelkes' Service 'for trebles', in which he argued that the 'treble' was a very high voice. At about the same time I myself had come to the same conclusion, and found that the use of this voice was very extensive indeed in sixteenth-century English vocal music. A preliminary treatment (Wulstan, 1967) was much extended and revised in subsequent lectures and broadcast talks, the substance of which was eventually published some years later (Wulstan, 1979b), now superseded by this present account. In the meantime, many outstanding problems had been solved, and editors and performers had begun to take into account the need for systematic transposition and correct vocal scoring, and thus to bring the work of Ouseley, Fellowes and others to its logical conclusion.

It has to be said, however, that these advances have left behind a nullifidian rearguard: whether this is to be regarded as a Newtonian reaction or merely as a recrudescence of fundamentalism, it is nonetheless a curious reverse. There appear to be three main creeds espoused: the first, despite the fact that pitch is know to have vacillated in previous centuries, nonetheless adheres to the conviction that Tudor pitch was coincidentally the same as the modern standard. As an alternative, an appeal is made to the supposed 'lack of evidence' (a phrase which has become the battle-cry of the scholarly conscientious objector). That the evidence is occasionally somewhat complex will be seen in the following pages; but it can hardly be said to be lacking.

The third point of view seems at first sight to be more rational, and only covertly fundamentalist: since there was no tuning fork, runs the argument, the pitch of vocal music would have been flexible, and would have been chosen to suit each piece. The absence of fixed pitch, however, is no more proved by the lack of tuning forks than the absence of fixed time must be assumed prior to the invention of the clock. On the contrary, since sixteenth- and seventeenth-century instruments were made to fine tolerances, pitches must have been crucial to the maker; and since contemporary English vocal compasses were also extremely carefully adhered to in sacred music, it is highly unlikely that the composers would impose this discipline on themselves and yet envisage the arbitrary transposition of their works according to the whim of the performers.

Vocal compasses are often prescribed nowadays in books dealing with the 'Rudiments of Music'. There is usually general agreement as to the lowest notes of each range, but even in this era of standard pitch there is less agreement in regard to the topmost permissible notes. In contrast, the sixteenth-century English composers were particularly careful in regard to the higher extreme of the tonal range, which they exploited to a considerable extent. Handel similarly made full use of the upper limits of each vocal range, meticulously writing alternative notes where these limits were exceeded. But his careful use of the high range — for example in the 'Halleluia chorus' or 'The trumpet shall sound' — is effectively sabotaged by the use of modern (New Philharmonic) pitch: only when sung at the intended pitch, nearly a semitone lower, does Handel's careful use of the voice become obvious. And if a semitone can make a crucial difference, what of the interval of a minor third?

RENAISSANCE PITCH STANDARDS

It is frequently argued that standards fluctuated so much that almost every town had a different pitch. Although it is true that on the Continent, for example, there were indeed several different standards, these differences often displayed a consistency which is not immediately apparent. It is instructive to examine the four main theorists of the seventeenth and eighteenth centuries who mention the matter of pitch in any detail: Praetorius and Doni in the seventeenth century, and Agricola and Quantz in the eighteenth. The latter were near contemporaries whose testimony, while disagreeing sufficiently to rule out collusion, nevertheless has a remarkable consistency.

Agricola's statement (1757, p. 45) may be translated thus:

In Lombardy, and especially in Venice, the harpsichords and other instruments were tuned very high. Their pitch is nearly a semitone lower than ordinary choir or trumpet pitch. The trumpet *C* is for them a *C sharp*. In Rome the tuning is very low, more or less equal to the former French pitch, a major third below choirpitch: so trumpet *C* corresponds with *E* of their other instruments. It is also a semitone lower than the standard so-called *A* chamber pitch of many districts of Germany. With them the *A* of choirpitch instruments is the same as *C* in chamber pitch. In Naples they have adopted a middle-of-the-road pitch between these high and low tunings.

Quantz (1752 XVI, vii, p. 6–7) speaks of the 'disagreeable choir pitch' which 'prevailed in Germany for several centuries, as the old organs prove'. This 'began to be supplanted by the chamber pitch, as is demonstrated by some of the most renowned organs'. The latter appears to have been *A* chamber pitch, a minor third below the old choir pitch: 'At the present time the Venetian pitch is the highest: it is virtually the same as our old choir pitch. The Roman pitch of about twenty years ago was low, and was the same as that of Paris.'

Doni, a century or so earlier (1635, p. 70, writing in Italian — the other theorists quoted wrote in German), observed that the pitch of organs ascended by a series of semitones from Naples through Rome, Florence and Lombardy to Venice. This is at variance with Agricola's statement that Neapolitan was a 'middle-of-the-road' pitch: by his day, perhaps, Neapolitan pitch had been raised. Quantz may have heard a particularly high version of Venetian pitch to think it 'nearly the same' as old choir pitch, whereas Lombardy pitch may have risen considerably if Agricola regarded it as 'nearly the same' as Venetian pitch. Taking these statements at face value, nevertheless, and for the present taking the intervals in their modern tempered equivalents (100 cents = 1 equal tempered semitone), the following equations result:

tones above or below 0 = A chamber pitch	pitches referred to 0 = C	pitch nomenclature	cents [0 = A chamber pitch] Agricola & Quantz	Doni
+ 1½	*E flat*	Old Choir (trumpet)	300	
+1	*D*	Venice	? 200+	200
+ ½	*D flat*	Lombardy	? 100+	100
0	*C*	A chamber, Florence	0	0
− ½	*B*	Rome (France, formerly)	− 100	− 100
− 1	*B flat*	Naples		− 200

The value of the statements made by Praetorius (1619, p. 14–16) concerning pitch is somewhat diminished by a polemical element in his nomenclature.

He says that what he prefers as, and terms, 'choir pitch' is commonly called 'chamber pitch' and vice versa; yet it is not always clear whether or not he consistently reversed the meanings. On p. 13 of his treatise he refers to low bass notes, apparently in terms approximating to modern pitch; yet his ranges on p. 19 he says are at 'chamber pitch' — his high pitch. On p. 14 he says that 'choir pitch' was formerly a tone lower but was:

> raised up to the point at which it now stands in Italy and England, as well as the princely choirs of Germany. English pitch, however, is somewhat, if only to a small degree, lower, which can be observed in their cornetts, shawms or *hoboyen* (as they call them) made there. There are some who have presumed to raise the present pitch by yet another semitone.

'In England formerly', he continues elsewhere (p. 16), 'as is the case in the Netherlands today, most of their wind instruments were tuned a minor third lower than our present chamber pitch, *F* being thus our chamber pitch *D*. . . . In Italy and various Catholic choirs of Germany, the said pitch, a minor third lower, is still in use.'

The clearest part of this exposition is that English instruments appear to have been pitched a minor third or so below Praetorius' high pitch, the low pitch being still used in 'Italy and various Catholic choirs'. Less clear are his descriptions of some other pitches: he states, for example that Prague 'chamber' pitch was the 'pitch to which almost all of our organs are tuned', but that their 'choir pitch is a whole tone lower'; and although 'used in churches', Prague 'chamber pitch' was the same as his own (high) 'chamber' pitch. Yet on p. 102, he describes the Halberstadt organ as being 'a good tone or tone and a half higher than our present-day organs suited to the choir'. Here, the 'present-day organs' are those of the high pitch which he dislikes.

Finally, (pp. 231–2) Praetorius discussed an ideal pitch, suitable for violins, so that their *E* strings would not snap. He specifies this standard by means of a pipe diagram. Since elsewhere in the volume there is a drawing of his unit of measure, doubts over paper shrinkage and the meaning of 'foot' are thereby dispelled. The diagram therefore allows the calculation of a frequency equivalent to $a = 425$ Hz, about 60 cents below modern ($a = 440$) pitch (cf. Thomas & Rhodes, 1971). This frequency is only a little sharp of Handel's Foundling Hospital organ ($a = 422$, 70 cents lower than 'New Philharmonic' pitch — observed by Ellis, 1880).

Several writers, including Thomas & Rhodes and Ellis, cite a large number of historical pitches; in common with many apparently authoritative statements (eg. the article 'Pitch' in the *New Grove*), many of these are dubious, being based on false premises, inaccuracies of calculation and other errors. The few instances discussed here, therefore, are confined to those which can be verified to a reasonable degree.

A large number of Renaissance wind instruments have been tested by Baines (1957) who found them to be pitched at around $a = 450$–470 (about 50–120 cents above modern pitch). However, the early sixteenth-century English cornetts at Christ Church, Oxford, are roughly at our pitch. It is possible to equate this pitch with the English instrumental pitch described by Praetorius; and it is obvious that his high ('chamber') pitch is to be identified with old German C choir pitch. Taking the fixed points of Agricola's and Quantz's major and minor thirds (now using the acoustically 'perfect' values of 386 and 318 cents), reconciled with Doni's series of 'semitones' (112 — diatonic, or 92 — chromatic), the following equivalents may be tabulated:

Hz A = (approx)	tones above or below A chamber pitch	pitches referred to $0 = C$	pitch nomenclature	cents above or below A chamber pitch
528	1½	$E\,flat$	Praetorius' high pitch = Prague. Old German C choir pitch (Agricola, Quantz)	316
494	1	D	Venice (Doni, Agricola)	204
450–470	½	$D\,flat$	Lombardy (Doni). Renaissance wind instruments (Baines). Prague low pitch (Praetorius)	92
440 (Modern 'New Philharmonic' pitch)	0	C	Praetorius' low pitch = 'English wind instruments, Italian and Catholic churches'	0
425	½ ⎱	$B+$	Praetorius' ideal pitch	−60
422	⎰		Handel's pitch	−70
		B	Roman pitch (Agricola, Quantz & Doni) = Old French (" " ")	−92
392	−1	$B\,flat$	Naples (Doni). English viol pitch (Mersenne)	−204

Although it would be unwise to attach too much importance to these figures, there emerges, nevertheless, a clear pattern, particularly in regard to the consistent difference between the old German high church pitch and the low chamber pitch. And if Mersenne's statement concerning English viols playing 'a tone lower' relates to the Renaissance A chamber pitch (our C pitch), then the E flat and B flat pitches discussed on pp. 99–103 may be identified with the two extreme pitches given in the above table.

Praetorius thus allows some insight to be gained into the differing pitch standards of his day. As will be seen shortly, he also discusses mechanisms by which pitch divergences may be achieved. Thirdly, he discusses the ranges of voices, which he prints on p. 20 of his treatise. Transposed up a minor third (to 'choir pitch', or 'chamber pitch' as he insists on calling it) his compasses may be set out as follows:

Ex. 114

Eunuchus, Falsettista, Discantista:

Altista:

Tenorista:

Bassista:

°Ordinary basses in schools can achieve this range':
[p. 17]

It should be noted that the use of the word 'falsettist' indicates a higher compass than that of an alto. The word 'falsetto' merely meant 'head voice' according to Italian usage.

Praetorius' compasses show that much the same voice ranges were common to Germany, Italy and Spain. Provided that the necessary transpositions are taken into account, the ranges employed by Lassus, Palestrina and Victoria are remarkably similar to those of Ex. 114.

Praetorius' evidence of pitch standards and vocal compasses may be compared with the evidence adduceable in regard to English music. As already noted, the problem of pitch is related to the problem of voice nomenclature, since choirbooks and early partbooks tended to be named according to a once notional order of composition: Tenor, Contratenor, Triplex, and so forth. Such a 'partitive' arrangement, as it might be termed, allows any disposition of voices to be included in a set of partbooks. Thus the part-names, although in many cases corresponding with voice-names (eg. *Triplex primus, triplex secundus*), are often misleading: in a composition for boys' voices, for example, the *Bassus* book would not be used by a man. Partitive sources do not therefore necessarily show which voices were intended, so there is no means of deducing the general pitch level of each voice simply from the name of the part. Many later sources of church music, however, are 'eponymous': that is, each book contains music for one specified voice alone. In a composition for boys' voices, the alto, tenor and bass books would contain no music. Partitive sources therefore indicate relative pitch since they might be allocated by turns to different voices, whereas eponymous books, since they were used by one voice only, more closely reflect voice names in relation to absolute pitch.

The eponymous partbooks thus establish a standard of vocal nomenclature together with recognizable compasses for each voice. With one or two exceptions, music in eponymous sources can be transposed up a minor third in conformity with the organ pitch of the period discussed in the following pages. The exceptions normally reveal differences in clef configuration. Theorists such as Praetorius mention the use of varying clefs to indicate different transpositions; these are confirmed by pieces which exist in two separate sources each exhibiting a different written pitch, and corresponding variant clefs. This evidence establishes the interdependence of clefs and pitch. The transpositions indicated by the clefs, in addition to the upward transpositions of a minor third, then reveal the consistency of compass already mentioned.

Fig. 16a

Fig. 16b
Weelkes, (a) First (Verse) service and (b) 'Five part' service
At (a) one direction 'Play it as it stands' is seen, whereas at (b) substitute clefs are given to the left.
(Tenbury, St. Michael's College, 791 f. 134ᵛ and 132)

ENGLISH ORGAN PITCH

The pitch of organs is known from several sources, in particular a note inserted into the Tenbury copy of Tomkins' *Musica Deo Sacra* (1668; cf. Fellowes, 1921), the Duddington specification (1519; cf. Hopkins and Rimbault, 1855 — the original is now lost), and a note from Nathaniel Tomkins dated May 1665 (Oxford, Bod. Lib., Add. C. 304a). These sources describe *F* or *C* in relation to a 10, 5 or 2 ½ foot pipe, which results in an *F* about a minor third (or perhaps between a tone and a minor third) higher than present pitch. The difference between the *F* and *C* pitch is explained in the Tomkins letter concerning the Dallam organ at Worcester to a similar design, he says, as those at St Paul's, London, and St John's College, Oxford 'double F fa ut of the quire pitch and according to Guido Aretine's scale (or as some term it double C fa ut according to the keys and musics)'.

As John Steele pointed out (1958) organs were built to sound a fourth higher than choir pitch, which explains why organ scores are often a fourth lower (or a fifth higher) than the vocal parts. They often have the rubric 'play this as it stands' (Fig. 16a). Other organ scores are at vocal pitch, in which case the organist transposed using a system of clef substitution evident in several sources. As Figure 16b shows, the alternative clefs (to the left) automatically transpose the music up a fifth. To regain the correct octave, the organist would have two options, the first being to make the simple shift of an octave. Directions such as 'play this viij notes lower' (whether for one or both hands) abound in manuscripts from the mid sixteenth-century source, London, B.L. Add. 29996, onwards; rubrics calling for changes of key or clefs are also found. The second possibility was to draw the 10 foot stop (the equivalent of a modern 16 foot stop, and present on most contemporary instruments). It is clear from the organ scores involving these rubrics (the data are collected in Clark, 1974) that most, if not all, English instruments were built at the higher, organ, pitch; the expensive pipework required for the bottom fourth of the compass of an organ built at choir pitch lay, in any case, below the normal voice range.

Earlier, when Magnificats and antiphons were sung unaccompanied, the note would be given on the organ, using the clef substitutions set out below (see p. 208). This is presumably the explanation of the curious rubrics in the *Caius Choirbook*: 'Ut in C fa ut' to Cornish's Magnificat, or 'C fa ut' to those of Turges and Ludford ('Benedicta'). Since all are in F, but only the Cornish starts (polyphony or presumed plainchant) on *C*, it seems that here is evidence of the organist's being reminded that choir-pitch 'F fa ut' (the key of these pieces) is organ 'C fa ut' and that the keynote *F*, appearing in the bass part against the F_4 clef, should be read in tenor clef (C_4) as *C*. Roger Bray has independently arrived at similar conclusions. The direction 'in A re' for Horwood's Magnificat (*Eton Choirbook*) remains unexplained, however.

During the seventeenth century, church pitch gradually dropped, and so the pipes were moved along. In sixteenth-century terminology the word 'diapason' meant a lower octave. Accordingly, the 10 foot stop (equivalent to the modern 16 foot) was called a diapason. The principal (5 foot) was equivalent to 8 foot or unison pitch, in conformity with the continental terminology of today. In moving the pipes in order to lower the pitch, the pipes were shifted upwards; instead of providing expensive new large pipes for the diapasons, the latter were converted into 8 foot stops. Thus the English principal is now a 4 foot stop, rather than, as on the Continent, an 8 foot stop.

Using the modern equivalents 16 foot and 8 foot for the 10 foot and 5 foot stops, Tomkins' specification is, effectively, as follows:

		'as it stands'	transposing
(Great)	2 diapasons	16'	8'
	2 principals	8'	4'
	a twelfth	5⅓'?	2⅔'?
	2 small principals		
	or fifteenths	4'	2'
	recorder (stopped)	4'?	2'?
(Choir)	stopped diapason		
	(wood)	16'	8'
	principal	8'	4'
	flute (wood)	8'?	4'?
	fifteenth	4'	2'
	twenty-second	2'	1'

The provision of pairs of principals and fifteenths on this and other organs of the period was presumably in order that a quieter alternative should be available when the 16 foot became, with transposition, the 8 foot pitch. This was the case with Chirk Castle's new organ of 1631, which had large and small principals on each manual. The *Chirk Organ Book* (Oxford, Ch Ch, 6) has transposition rubrics similar to those already described; it is also of interest that the *Chirk Castle* partbooks (now in the New York Public Library) contain some late examples of high treble music. The organ at Magdalen College, Oxford, was built by Chamberlain in 1508; it was rebuilt at various times, but still had double sets of pipes (its specification was similar to Worcester's) in 1686. The significance of the association of the organs of Magdalen and Eton (the latter had a smaller organ, designated at 5 foot pitch) will become apparent in due course.

The fifteenths of the Eton and Chirk organs (for details, see Clutton and Niland, 1963, pp. 53–61) were probably equivalent to the 'twenty-second' stops on the Dallam organs of Magdalen, York and Worcester. The specification of the latter organ, given in the Tomkins letter, is as follows:

The Great Organ which was built at Worcester 1614 consisted
of —
2 open diapasons of pure & massy mettle. Double F fa. ut (of
the Quire pitch & according to Guido Aretinos scale, or as
some terme it Double C. fa. ut according to the keyes &
musicks) an open pipe ten foote long, the diameter 7 inches (at
St Paul's London the diameter was 8 inches) 2 principalls of
mettle, octave to the diapason. All in sight
1 recorder of mettle a stopt pipe.
1 twelfth of mettle.
2 small principalls or fifteenths of mettle.
That which they call the soundboard (which the Antients called
the Hydrauls from the resemblance which it hath to mant
Conveyances of waters from on great Cistern) was 8 foot long
and 4 foot broad.
The Chayre organ consisted of —
1 principall of Mettle a five foot pipe in front
1 stopt diapason of wood
1 ffluit of wood unison to the principall
1 small principall of ffifteenth of Mettle
1 two & twentieth or squeelers of Mettle
(Oxford, Bod. Add. c 304a)

Since the yard has varied less than a millimetre since 1305, and is
documented for 1497 (the exchequer yard, foot and inch of Henry VIII)
and 1588 (Elizabeth I), there is little room for doubt that church pitch was
about a minor third higher than today's standard, and was similar to
Praetorius' 'high pitch'. In consequence, a Tudor choir singing written *C*
would sound what is to our ears a modern *E flat*, (the Tudor organist
playing a high-pitch instrument without correction would sound *A flat*).
Viols and other instruments often played at *E flat* pitch, and often at *B flat*
pitch; a third chamber pitch, *C* pitch, was also current. Thus the full range
of Tudor pitch standards was as follows:

Written *C* sounding as modern
A flat   high organ pitch
E flat   { choir pitch (low organ pitch)
            { high chamber pitch
C   chamber pitch
B flat   low chamber pitch

These pitch standards could be reconciled or modified by actual transposition, especially through the use of special combinations of clefs.

CLEF CONFIGURATIONS

Theorists

Praetorius (1618, iii, pp. 80–81) says that pieces with their lowermost parts written in the alto, tenor or baritone (C_3, C_4 or F_3) clefs must be transposed when written out for the organist: if there is a flat in the signature the organ part should be transposed down a fourth, otherwise, down a fifth. He also mentions the use of clef substitution, already outlined. A later and more obscure theorist Samber (1707; apud. Mendel, 1948, p. 347) rules that the tenor clef implies transposition down a fifth, the baritone down a fourth. The names *chiavette* or *chiavi transportati* are sometimes applied to these clefs; since they are both anachronistic and misleading, these terms are avoided here.

It seems that there were two slightly different systems in use: that of Praetorius certainly fits the music of Palestrina (though the key signature appears to have been irrelevant), while Samber's rules apply generally to English church music (in all cases the upward transposition of a minor third, to equate with modern pitch, must be added to the shift mentioned by the theorists). Morley (1597, pp. 156, 165–6) is the only English theorist to mention transposition; what he says is far from clear, but he recognizes a 'high key' (ie. high clefs) and a 'low key' (low clefs) whose implied pitches correspond.

Conflicting clefs and keys

Many pieces occur in more than one source with conflicting clefs and written pitches. Some are a fifth apart, the higher version having a tenor clef in the lowest part, and some a fourth, in which the higher version has a baritone clef. These occurrences confirm Samber's rules, and incidentally establish that the ordinary bass clef (F_4) indicated untransposed *E flat* church pitch. Other clefs had similar properties: the C_5 clef, although it is homologous with the F_3, seems to have indicated a transposition of a tone downwards, whereas the F_5 clef, indicated the upward transpositions of a fourth.

Examples of these conflicting keys and clefs are as follows:

Tomkins: 'When David heard'
appears in *Musica Deo Sacra* (1668) with normal bass clef; in *Songes of 3, 4, 5 and 6 parts* (1622) it was printed a fourth higher, with an F_3 clef in the lowest part.

White: 'Deus misereatur'
appears in London, BL., Add. 30810–5 with tenor clef (C_4) in the lowest part, a fifth higher than in Add. 17792–6, which has an F_4 clef.

Fayrfax: Magnificat 'O bone Jesu'
appears in the *Lambeth Choirbook* with an F_5 clef in the lowest part; its pitch lies a fourth below Tenbury, St Michael's Coll. 354–8, where the lowest part has F_4.

Hooper: 'Hearken ye nations'
appears in London, Royal Coll. of Music, 1045–51 with bass clef in the lowest part; the version in Oxford, Ch Ch 56–60 is a tone higher, with a C_5 clef in the lowest part.

Other clef configurations

The transposing function of the foregoing clefs can be determined by theoretical statements and by the study of works displaying conflicting clefs and keys in the sources. The vocal compasses then revealed by these transpositions exhibit a remarkable regularity to the extent that the functions of further clefs may be elucidated, despite the lack of evidence of the kinds already discussed. Similarly, ambiguities in the clef convention can be resolved in the light of the vocal compasses.

The continental gamut clef (Γ_3) appears to imply an upward transposition of a fourth (= modern minor sixth). The Requiem of Pierre de la Rue has this clef in one movement, the F_5 (implying overall transposition of an upward fourth in modern terms) in another, and elsewhere the normal F_4. The ranges of the various movements are brought into conformity when these transpositions are effected. In England the D_5 clef is the equivalent of

Sheppard's Te Deum displays the D_5 clef, indicating an overall upward transposition of a minor sixth. There is considerable ambiguity, however, in the English use of the F_5 clef. Sheppard's 'I give you a new commandment' clearly implies the continental transposition of an overall upward fourth; the homologous D_4 clef in Tallis' 'Mean' Mass has the same significance. But in Fayrfax's Magnificat 'O Bone Jesu' the F_5 clef demands an overall transposition of an upward minor sixth. Thus, amongst English scribes the function of the F_5, D_4 and D_5 clefs were apparently confounded.

Similarly, the homologue clefs F_3 and C_5 appear to have been confused. In the 1589 edition of Byrd's 'Aspice Domine', the printer used the F_3 clef, whereas the voice ranges demand the transposition implied by the C_5 clef, as correctly given in Oxford Ch Ch 979–83. There are several similar examples of mistaken identity.

Other ambiguities arise in regard to the function of the topmost clef. According to Praetorius the C_4 and F_3 clefs behave in the prescribed manner only when there is a G_2 clef in the upper part: Samber does not mention this point. In continental music there is little doubt that the topmost and the lowermost clefs have to be considered together; the combination $C_2 + F_3$ therefore has a different meaning from $G_2 + F_3$. The English use of these combinations seems similarly to imply different pitches. Fayrfax and Taverner often use the C_5 clef in place of the F_3, but only in combination with the G_1 clef is overall downward transposition of a tone demanded; otherwise, where the upper part has a C clef, the transposition appears to be that of an overall upward semitone.

In Mundy's anthems 'Let us now laud' and 'He that hath my commandments', however, the topmost clefs have no modifying function; since these pieces are for men's voices, the use of a G clef would in any case be difficult. The organ part confirms that the normal F_3 transposition is required, despite the C clefs in the uppermost part.

In BL Add. 29401–5, Byrd's madrigals often display the combinations $G_1 + F_3$ or $G_1 + F_5$: the downward transposition is confirmed by the printed versions, a fourth or fifth lower. The combination of $G_2 + F_4$, in his madrigals seems to indicate C chamber pitch; in 'Peccantem me' (1575) the combination $G_2 + C_5$ seems to have the same meaning. 'Infelix ego' (1591), on the other hand, requires the use of high voices; yet Byrd notates the uppermost part in the C clef (the lowermost having F_4) thus clearly indicating that normal church pitch is required. Had the combination $G + F_4$ been used, this would, according to his convention, have indicated chamber pitch. In the church music of most English composers, however, the $G + F_4$ combination indicated that normal church pitch was intended.

Chamber pitch

BL Add. 31390 is headed 'A book of In nomines & other solfainge songes of v: vj: vij: viij: parts for voyces or Instruments'. If some of these pieces were treated as 'solfaing songs', and sung at C chamber pitch, it would explain why some originally vocal works are written out at pitch levels apparently corresponding with modern pitch. Thus Byrd's 'Ad dominum cum tribularer', unique to this source, is obviously at C pitch (probably transposed from a source a tone higher, having an F_3 clef). Sheppard's 'Our Father', whose equivalent modern pitch is known from other sources to be in *E flat* pitch (see Wulstan, 1979b) is here written in the key of G — which seems to be the nearest plausible equivalent to the note *A flat* in *C* chamber pitch.

Several of the *Teares or Lamentacions* (1614) of Leighton call for *C* pitch, having ranges which do not readily correspond with *E flat* or *B flat* pitch (see p. 102). Madrigals, too, frequently appear to call for *C* rather than *B flat* pitch.

Facultative transposition

The evidence adduced earlier shows that church music was generally sung at a fixed pitch, and not transposed into a 'suitable' pitch. Madrigalian music and church music of less than four parts may, however, behave differently. It is hardly surprising that Byrd's madrigalian compositions, often simply transplanted church music, adopt church pitch and the concomitant transpositions demanded by the clefs: only the combinations G + F$_4$ or C + F$_3$/C$_4$ seem to call for the use of chamber pitch. Other church composers — eg. Gibbons and Tomkins — apparently adopt the same convention in their madrigals.

Byrd's 1588 set listed the 'Songs which are of the highest compasse', by which was meant those having the greatest overall range. This point was misunderstood by Andrews, 1962: 'highest' is used here with Latin ambiguity — *altus* also means 'deep'. The purpose of this list must have been to show that transposition was inadvisable for these songs; this in turn gives the impression that, elsewhere, transposition to various suitable pitches was envisaged, a process which I have termed facultative transposition. That this kind of transposition was part and parcel of madrigalian practice is emphasized both by the retention of the old 'partitive' arrangement of the books (in which voices were not precisely identified) and by the compasses of the voice parts. The latter frequently differ markedly from those found in church music. Bull's sacred madrigal 'Fraile man despise the pleasures of this lyfe' (Myriell, 1616) is perhaps an extreme example; it is nonetheless notable that each of the four parts have a range of virtually two octaves, in striking contrast to the unexceptionable ranges of his church music.

Composers outside the church music establishment generally use clefs with no discernible transposing significance. Madrigalian music by all composers, however, tends to be scored in a manner which often sharply contrasts with that of church music. Alto parts in church music (eg. the four of Byrd's Great service) are divided equally as regards compass. Madrigalian scoring, however, adopts the 'terraced' arrangement: apart from the 'ballet' style where the notion of equal-voiced antiphony is retained, the vocal compasses tend to have progressively lower ranges as they descend from the highest to lowermost parts of the texture. Thus, facultative transposition would allow simple reallocation of voices; where voices are of equal compass, as in church music, transposition would not be conducive to simple rescoring.

Church music in three parts may also have been subject to facultative transposition. Ludford's three-part Masses show traces of this possibility (see *CMM* XXVII) and Tomkins' *Musica Deo Sacra* has unmistakable alternative clefs which could hardly be interpreted as ordinary transposing clefs, since the F$_4$ would come to the same thing as the substitute C$_4$. Octave transposition whereby music for boys' and men's voices might be interchanged, is also a possibility, as will be mentioned later.

Ambiguities of clef convention

Several ambiguities have already been discussed. These difficulties arise principally because of scribal misunderstanding, but possible contradictions

inherent in the convention are occasionally responsible. Whythorne's collection of 1571 shows several ambiguities. Here, since the books are named
Primus and *Secundus Triplex* and so on, the scoring appears to be
eponymous; but it seems likely that Whythorne had more than one pitch in
mind, and thus the clefs are somewhat eccentric. His Song 33 has a C_3 clef
in the lowermost part and is clearly for boys' voices at *E flat* pitch. Taverner
and Sheppard use the same clef in their settings of 'Gloria in Excelsis'
('Hodie nobis'), also for boys at normal church pitch. Praetorius' assertion,
therefore, that a C_3 acts as a downward transposing clef configuration, is
clearly not borne out in English music, even where a G clef is present in the
top part. Similarly, the 'Gloria' of Cooper or 'Audivi' of Taverner have C_2
clefs in the lowest part; again normal pitch is called for. Knight's 'Sancta
Maria' is more problematical. The clefs are $G_1 + C_2$, but the ranges appear
to indicate C pitch. Tallis' 'Sancte Deus' (C_3 in lowest part) is also difficult:
the compasses appear to demand upward transposition of a fourth. Apart
from Whythorne's songs, all of the pieces mentioned are in the same source
(BL Add. 17802–5). There is therefore a possibility of scribal misunderstanding.

There are several further examples of palpable scribal errors in regard to
clefs, or eccentric transpositions. As Hofman (1973) has shown, however,
the number of wholly inexplicable ambiguities or errors in the clef convention is negligible.

Summary of clef configurations

As has been seen, sixteenth-century pitch was governed by two separate
factors, the pitch standard and the clef convention. Church pitch was
approximately a minor third higher than our own, at *E flat* pitch; some
organs played at *A flat* pitch, and chamber music, besides using *E flat* pitch,
also used C and B flat pitch. As to the clef convention, the information of
the theorists is ratified and extended by those sources which demonstrate
the use of conflicting keys and clefs. Even where this information is lacking,
the convention can be amplified by reference to the vocal ranges, whose
exceptional consistency also clarifies the ambiguities inherent in the clef
system. The chart given as Ex. 115 shows the working of the convention,
and the significance of the lowermost clef. On the left of the table is the
written clef of the source, on the right its modern equivalent. The two
central columns show the clef which would have been used by the organist
to effect the change from written to choir pitch (a) if he were playing an
organ-pitch (*A flat*) instrument, and (b) if he were playing a choir-pitch (*E
flat*) instrument. The equivalence of the two sets of organist's clefs is
tabulated by Cerone (1613, p. 494) but apart from this, there is little direct
evidence bearing on the question other than that quoted in connection with
Samber and Weelkes. Morley has a vague reference to high and low 'keys'
(ie. clef combinations) which, he says, 'come both to one pitch' (1597, p.

Ex. 115

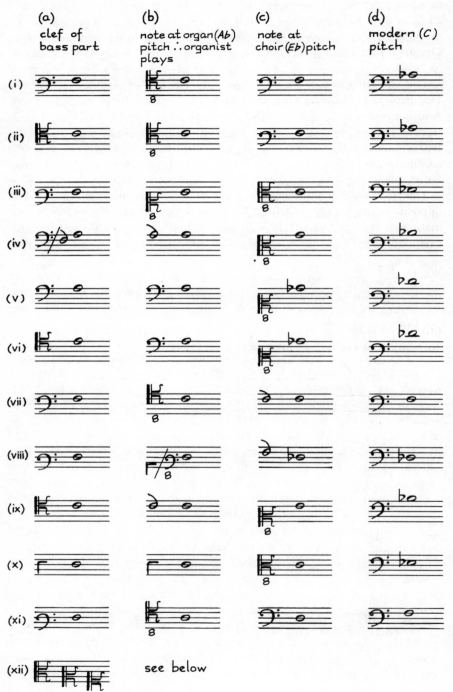

166). Apart from this, transposition is mentioned by him only in relation
to a piece which he considers to contain too many flats, being 'set in such
a key as no man would have done, except it had beene to have plaide it on
the Organes with a quier of singing men, for in deede such shiftes the
Organistes are many times compelled to make for ease of the singers . . .'
(p. 156).

The clef substitutions required to make these shifts, as set out in Ex.
115, explain the choice of clefs associated with the various transpositions.
Another noteworthy feature is that the vertical position of the note on the
stave in the first column is surprisingly stable, relative to its absolute pitch.
By remaining, therefore, within the confines of the clef in a given
configuration, the composer has a rough guide to the compass of the
voice, whatever the implied transposition. (See Ex. 115)

The following commentary on the twelve sets of clefs presented
opposite is necessarily an attempt to summarize a large amount of information; it is hoped nonetheless that the process of simplification has not
excluded mention of the more important details:

(i)   for (a), (b) and (c) see Weelkes (Fig. 16b); Cornish: Magnificat;
Taverner: 'Mater Christi' Sheppard: 'Gaude, gaude, gaude'; etc.

(ii)   for (a) and (c) see White: 'Deus misereatur', etc.; Weelkes (Fig.
16a) is equivalent to (b). See also (ix).

(iii)   Mundy: 'Let us now laud' and 'He that hath my commandments'
(both C_2 in top part) have voice-parts as at (a), organ as at (c).
Samber gives the transposing clef as at (c). C_5 equivalent in earlier
music is with G_1 in top part.

(iv)   this is the correct continental usage (eg. la Rue: Requiem, —
Sanctus); used, for example, by Taverner (eg. 'Ave Dei Patris'),
Tallis and Sheppard (eg. 'Media vita'). The only English example
of D_4 I can recall is found in Tallis' Mass à 4.

(v)   this is apparently the earlier implication of these clefs in English
pieces (eg. Fayrfax Mass and Magnificat 'O bone Jesu'). The D_5
clef (eg. in Sheppard's Te Deum) is used with the same meaning,
ie. like its continental homologue Γ_3 (see x). This usage of F_5
seems to have resulted from confusion of (iv) and (v).

(vi)   judging by the voice-ranges, earlier English usage appears to
imply (xi) when a C clef is present in the top part (eg. Taverner:
'O splendor'): otherwise the combination is invariably equivalent
to (iii). Later usage is always as here: Richard Farrant's Service in
'a minor' (many sources) has the bass in the C_5 clef, as (a); but the
organ part is in 'g minor', as at (c). These latter transpositions
may subsume the first case, in spite of the ranges. (The G_2 clef
associated with Taverner, 'Gaude plurimum' in Wulstan (1967) is
spurious.)

(vii)   with a G clef in the top part, continental music treated this as implying *A* chamber pitch, a minor third lower, rather than as at (i). This continental influence is found in Byrd's church music, and also confirmed by at least one organ part: Sheppard's 'O sing unto the Lord', where the organ pitch is as at (a), the voices implying (d). Very rare in church music apart from Byrd's; common in madrigals.

(viii)   Praetorius does not distinguish between the C_4 and F_3 clefs, treating (iii) or (viii) arbitrarily. In addition, according to Praetorius, these clefs operate as at (ii), (iii), (viii) and (ix) only when a G clef is present in the top part — not confirmed by English music or by Samber.

(ix)   see (viii); also (ii). Palestrina consistently uses this clef with this meaning, never as at (ii). This 'Italian' usage appears in England in one or two works: for instance by Sheppard ('Deus tuorum' for means: cp. ranges in setting for men) and Tallis ('Dum transisset'), but not Byrd.

(x)   normal continental equivalent of (v) (eg. la Rue: Requiem, — Introit). Not found in English music.

(xi)   Praetorius implies that F_3 or C_4 — ie. (ii), (iii)/(viii), (ix) — without G clefs in the top part have no transposing effect — ie. stand as (i) — which is not confirmed in any extant music. However, continental usage appears to indicate that F_3 or C_4 with C clefs in the top part have the same effect as English (vi), as here. For F_3 see (a); for C_4 see (b).

(xii)   Praetorius' implication that C_3 behaves as F_3 or C_4 is dubious in the extreme, though this clef might well be used if the bottom part were of tenor range: this circumstance rarely arises in English music (Byrd's 'Visita quaesumus', with C_3 as at (ii), is one example). High C clefs otherwise appear to imply (i), apart from one or two further exceptions, eg. Knight's 'Sancte Maria' (C_2 + G_1 = vii) and Tallis' 'Sancte Deus' (C_3 + C_1 = iv).

It should be emphasized that changes of clef within a movement are not significant; but between movements (as in Pierre de la Rue's Requiem) changes of transposition may occur.

The equivocations inherent in the clef convention (or rather conventions, since continental music differed) can normally be settled by reference to the voice ranges; the latter varied slightly during the course of the period, and between one composer and another; this should be borne in mind in connection with the samples of transpositions given in Ex. 116.

VOICE RANGES AND NAMES

The consistency of the voice ranges evident in Ex. 116 and elsewhere is further underlined by comparison with the ranges given by Morley and

Ex. 116

Taverner 'Mater Christi'

original   transposed

(Bodleian   Mus Sch e 1-5 etc)

'O splendor gloriae'

(ibid)

'Ave Dei patris'

(ibid)

Sheppard Mass à 6 'Cantate'

(Bodleian Mus Sch e 376-81)

Te Deum à 6

[chant]

(Ch. Ch. 979-83)

'Media vita'

[chant]

(ibid)

Fayrfax Mass (& Magnificat)
'O bone Jesu'

(low clef
version)

Tomkins 'When David heard' à 5

(high clef
version)

White 'Deus misereatur' à 6

Praetorius. The ranges given in column (i) of Ex. 117 are summarized from Ex. 116; these may be compared with Morley's compasses (ii), as set out in his book (1597, p. 166) and (iii) with those of Praetorius (1618, pp. 17 and 20). It should be emphasized that the latter two sources are theoretical, whereas the compasses under (i) are drawn from actual music. Both Morley's and Praetorius' ranges are given in normal clefs implying *E flat* pitch, and have therefore been transposed accordingly. The alternative compasses given by Morley are those which he says are appropriate to compositions for men only. He gives a further set of ranges in high clefs which are similar, but since two alto compasses are given, together with a range denoted 'Tenor and Quintus', it is clear that these refer to madrigalian scoring.

The ranges found in eponymous sources such as Barnard (1641) are similar (taking into account the evolutionary changes discussed in due course); and, although rare, pieces for the high treble range are occasionally found in this type of source — eg. the Magnificat and Nunc Dimittis 'in medio chori' by Mundy in the *Peterhouse MSS*. For the voice names see p. 233.

Ex. 117

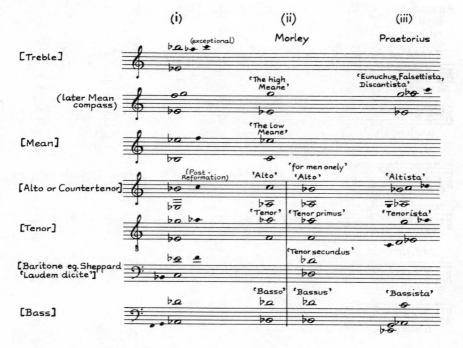

It remains to ask why this labyrinthine, cumbersome and often contradictory system of transposition came to be used. As with musica ficta, it arose in response to the notion that modality was somehow preserved if accidentals were left unwritten. This was hardly the true nature of modality, which originally had to do with melodic formulism, and had no place in harmonic music (cf. pp. 118–20). Be that as it may, the various modes or keys became associated with typical clef combinations, allied with transpositions made for practical purposes (see, for example, Yonge's *Musica Transalpina*, 1588, where the madrigals are ordered according to clef and key). As a result, the unwieldy medieval system of solmization continued to be employed, thus precluding a more modern use of accidentals. The professional singers were doubtless perfectly willing to continue to use this arcane notation since it was less penetrable to amateurs. With the rise of more complex and less conservative secular music, however, the pressure for a freer use of accidentals became greater. Such usage prompted Morley's complaint that 'you shall not find a musicion (how perfect soever hee be) able to *sol fa* it right' (1597, p. 156). The truth of this may be gauged from the table in Playford's *Introduction to the Skill of Musick* (1674) reproduced in Fig. 17. Thus the extreme keys were used 'more by organists, to adapt their playing to the choir, than by composers in writing out works, because of the difficulty which singers have when they see

16   *An Introdu&ion. to*

An exa& Table of the *Names* of the *Notes* in all ufual *Cliffs*, expreffed in the Six feveral Parts of *Mufick*.

TREBLE, G folre ut Cliff *on the fecond Line.*

Sol la mi fa fol la fa fol   fol la fa fol la mi fa fol

la mi fa fol la fa fol la   la fa fol la mi fa fol la

ALTUS, C folfa ut Cliff *on the firft Line.*

Fa fol la fa fol la mi fa   fol la mi fa fol la fa fol

fol la fa fol la mi fa fol   la mi fa fol la fa fol la

MEAN, C folfa ut Cliff *on the fecond Line.*

mi fa fol la fa fol la mi   fa fol la mi fa fol la fa

fa fol la fa fol la mi fa   fol la mi fa fol la fa fol

COUN-

the Skill of Mufick.   **17**

COUNTER-TENOR.

Sol la mi fa fol la fa fol   fol la la fol la mi fa fol

la mi fa fol la fa fol la   la fa fol la mi fa fol la

TENOR.

La fa fol la mi fa fol la   mi fa fol la fa fol la mi

fa fol la mi fa fol la fa   fa fol la fa fol la mi la

BASSE.

Sol la mi fa fol la fa fol   fol la fa fol la mi fa fol

la mi fa fol la fa fol la   fa fol la fui fa fol la ta

Firft learn by Cliffs *to Name your* Notes,
By Rules *and* Spaces *right :*
Then Tune *with* Time, *to ground your* Skill
For Muficks *fweet Delight.*

C   A

Fig. 17 Solmization syllables as given in Playford's *Introduction* . . . (1674 edition)

so many flats or sharps' (Cerone, 1613, 922); 'in deede', says Morley (ibid.) 'such shiftes the Organistes are many times compelled to make for ease of the singers . . .'

While music had a restricted overall compass, transposition into any suitable pitch was feasible; but when, in the fifteenth century, English music began to be sung by choirs of fixed composition, employing a large overall range, the clefs would increasingly indicate not only the direction of trans-position, but its exact extent. This system (i) gave an accurate guide to the intended pitch; (ii) ensured that the absolute pitch of the written note was closely related to its position on the stave (see Ex. 115); (iii) gave the composer a tolerable guide to vocal ranges, since, by avoiding ledger lines and using the correct clefs, he could be sure of keeping within the proper compasses whatever the transposition. For this reason Vicentino (1555, pp. 4, 17) specifically warns against the use of ledger lines and changes of clef. This should not be taken to mean that ledger lines were not used in practice, or that the clef convention was invented to avoid the use of ledger lines. On the contrary, the minimal usage of ledger lines was a corollary of the clef convention: another consequence of the system was that there was more than one manner of indicating the same pitch — hence the existence of different sources at conflicting written pitches, often depending on scribal preference.

The convention of clefs and transpositions outlined was used in English church music of the period c.1500–1625; at the same time, a similar con-vention prevailed on the Continent. Although systematic transpositions of this nature are still found in the work of Schütz, the practice had largely died out by this time. The modal pretence was abandoned in the Baroque period, when the fixed solmization system and the demands of increased written accidentals conspired to allow and require that music be written at the pitch at which it was intended to sound.

VOCAL COLOUR

The existence of a high treble voice in sixteenth-century England, and even the method by which the alto or countertenor voice was produced, requires some consideration, particularly since the question of vocal ranges is clearly related to the problem of timbre. Similarly, the pronunciation of English has some bearing on the question of tone-colour, and indeed on the question of voices and compasses, which might have differed from those of the Continent. Differences in instrumental timbre depend largely on con-struction, and, to a lesser degree, upon technique. The problem of vocal timbre is somewhat dissimilar, for although it may be argued that the construction of the vocal apparatus has little capacity for alteration, there are many possibilities for variant vocal techniques. The term 'natural voice' is frequently used, as is 'trained voice'; but the bewildering variety of vocal timbres, untrained or unnatural, used in various musical fields today, shows that these epithets have little or no specific meaning. The tone of voice is determined by the imposition of acquired technique upon inherent factors. That the latter can be circumvented to a greater or lesser extent by technique is obvious in the gifted mimic. Many singers, however, cannot change their voices in this way; indeed many people, in spite of training, can hardly sing at all.

The observation of family resemblances in vocal timbre, and also of similar racial affinities, underlines the role of inheritance in vocal colour. The Welsh and Italians, for instance, have instantly recognizable voices, whose characteristics have been variously attributed to differences in language, in cultural background, or even the weather. Inherent factors may have their influence on the formation of technique, which is acquired partly by experience, and partly in emulation of teachers, of whom the principal is fashion; yet although it is demonstrable that the compasses of voices can be influenced as much by art as by nature, it is equally true that vocal facility is limited by biological aspects.

The development of languages also testifies to racial or genetic affinities for certain sound formations. Our own language is, so to speak, branded upon us by the conquerors of the past, and a native tongue may be exchanged more or less readily for another; but this does not begin to explain why a daughter language such as French should be so radically different from its parent Latin. Phonology tells us how sound shifts occur, but it does not tell us why. Chaucer's English was recognizably a mixture of Teutonic and French elements, and his pronunciation of many words would have been understood by his continental contemporaries. The radical and swift phonetic changes which took place soon afterwards, resulting in the sound structure of present-day English, is not explicable in conventional terms; to speak of the 'great vowel shift' is merely to describe the phenomenon, which resembles one of René Thom's classic 'catastrophe' models. The possibility of biological influences on phonation must therefore be considered.

Genetic factors in articulation

It may be postulated that genetic factors play some part in determining racial divergences in articulation. However, this area of research is not without its difficulties, the most severe being the question of racial identity: it is difficult to define the English or the British races. Interbreeding has made the survival of racial prototypes difficult to detect, and members of a common stock may be widely scattered. But sometimes, a definite pattern of persistence may be established: we may look, by analogy, at the distribution of various types of British cattle. The relatively small, black, Celtic types (Galloway, Kerry, Angus) still survive, if in a modern form, in a westerly arc around Britain. The Saxons and Jutes brought red cattle;

these can still be found in the Hereford, Devon, Lincoln, Sussex and the Suffolk–Norfolk types which form a circle around England. They have thus broadly remained in the specific area to which they were introduced. Groups of peoples of these districts may have genetical traits in common, particularly in areas which, being isolated, have been less affected by interbreeding.

Within families the role of inheritance can often be identified in the speaking voices of the siblings, especially where they are separated at an early age and grow up apart from their parents. Characteristic inflections and qualities are evident in their speech, even though they may now speak with a

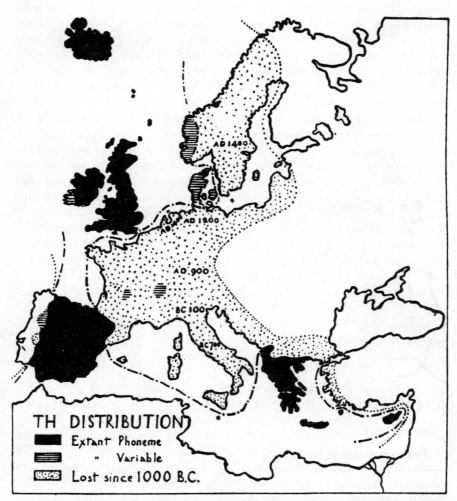

TH DISTRIBUTION
- Extant Phoneme
- " Variable
- Lost since 1000 B.C.

Fig. 18 (a) TH sound map of Europe showing its division into three zones according to present frequency or past possession of the $\eth$ and θ sounds. The dates in the middle zone mark the time of loss.

different regional or social accent. However, the recognition of such family traits, and the separation of endogenous from exogenous factors — as shown in many studies of twins — is relatively simple in comparison with the problem of dealing with racial traits: speakers of one dialect or language may not necessarily form even a loose genetic unit.

The problem was investigated by Darlington (1947) who demonstrated that the distribution of the TH ($\eth$ or θ) sound — a notorious

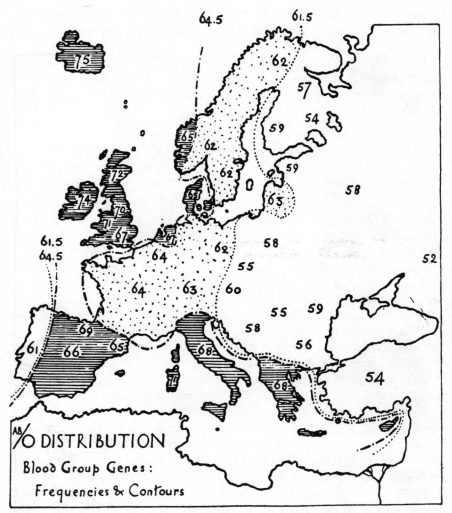

(b) Blood group map of Europe showing the regular gradients and a division into three zones by contour lines at arbitrary values of O-gene frequency in the population.

For references, see Darlington, 1947 pp. 278–9.

difficulty for most continental people learning English — had a strong correlation with the percentage frequency of blood group O, by which at least some genetical similarities can be identified, despite the complex ethnic movements of history. The two maps, given on p. 217, speak for themselves.

It should be mentioned that Brosnahan (1961, q.v.) published a revised comparison which was not quite so dramatic; but since then further data (some given in Brosnahan's appendix) have tended to reaffirm the clines shown in Darlington's maps. This striking suggestion of a biological connection with phonology is a clear indication that racial characteristics may well influence the workings of the vocal organs, and thus the tone-colours of singing.

Further evidence bearing on this problem is to be found in an ornithological phenomenon, investigated by Lack (1943, p. 43). He suggests that certain sounds may well appear more 'natural' to one race than to another:

> . . . even in those species in which the song is highly modifiable, there is an inherited predisposition to learn the correct song. For instance, a nightingale first sang like the other species with which it had been reared, but rapidly changed to the normal song when it heard it in the following year.

Sounds made by varying species or subspecies may impress by their strangeness: the trobador Peire Vidal thought that Germans made a noise like the barking of dogs, while Dio Cassius commented in his *History* that the voices of the Celts were frighteningly deep and loud. Speakers of one dialect or language often regard the tonal character of others as inferior; by the same token, the attitude to the singing timbres of different countries can also differ markedly. 'Galli cantant, Italiae capriant, Germani ululant, Anglici jubilant' (quoted by Ornithoparcus in his *Micrologus* of 1517) was one of many proverbial sayings current in medieval and Renaissance times. Even the way imported words, such as 'envelope' or 'garage', vary according to the adoptive language or dialect has musical parallels. German plainchant manuscript sources, for instance, adhere to a characteristic *A-C-A* formula, while the French favour *A-B-A*, the Italians *A-B flat-A* (cf. Wagner 1911, II; Wulstan 1971a). The animal kingdom shows that such preferences might arise from genetic considerations, rather than those of fashion, or other extrinsic factors: varying song dialects have been observed in different sub-species of the chaffinch (Marler, 1956).

There is enough evidence to demonstrate a general connection between certain aspects of phonation and genetics; but extreme caution is necessary when proceeding to specific cases. When dealing with peoples, the picture of genetic influence is blurred by social dominance and similar extrinsic factors which can influence the determination of 'average' tone quality. The norm is here capable of variation in response to changes in fashion, and is thus more difficult to identify than in a world where change is effected primarily by the paradoxically less capricious mutation of genes.

Nevertheless, although it would be unwise to make direct inferences from such evidence as blood-group counts, it is reasonable to point out the genetic differences which are evident in the formation of the vocal apparatus (Grabert, 1913; Loth, 1931; Luchsinger, 1944). Such differences, together with differences in afferent and efferent brain pathways, are bound to give rise to variations in the facility for pronouncing certain consonants as shown by Darlington — though for our purposes the pronunciation of vowels is more germane, and this topic will therefore be treated in some detail later. For the moment, it is sufficient to emphasize that variations in the vocal apparatus indicate that national divergences will be likely.

This conclusion is reinforced by evidence already put forward, to the effect that the tonal proclivities of racial groups are the cause of variations in pronunciation, and not, as is often maintained, the result. It is hardly sensible therefore to suggest that English singers should ape Italian tone quality, and to blame their lack of success on English vowels; the misguided assumption that features of continental tone-production (whether of the present or past) will necessarily apply to England is difficult to sustain.

It would be equally misguided to assume a direct connection between modern English vocal colour and that of the sixteenth century. To compare the tone quality of even comparatively recent times to that of our own times can be hazardous; the vague notion that the modern 'Handelian' choral society is singing in a tradition directly connected with Baroque style is manifestly wrong. The falsity of such a facile assumption is easily demon-strated — the question of the relative sizes of secular choirs is an obvious point, but changes in fashion concerning the use of voices are equally important. For example, female choral contraltos were virtually unknown in England until their introduction by Mendelssohn; and only in Arne's day had women sopranos displaced boys' voices in the chorus. Even as soloists, castrato and female contraltos were more or less an innovation in Handel's day; hitherto the 'countertenor' (male alto) had been without rivals.

In contrast with this discontinuity, a certain constancy may be observed within the English 'cathedral' tradition. Sheltered from direct contact with operatic (and therefore continental) influence, a distinctly insular tradition may be seen here to extend back at least as far as Purcell. Not only have boys' voices and male altos been a constant feature, but the range of voices has also remained largely unchanged. A comparison of Purcell's alto parts with those of F. J. Read's otherwise unremarkable anthem 'My soul, wait thou still upon God' reveals very similar ranges; however, the higher alto parts of Read's contemporary, Stanford, betray the influence of secular music, with its higher, female alto parts. The tone of both boys' and male alto voices have been the subject of recent change, but here these changes are almost certainly a reversion towards earlier tonal qualities. The influence of this type of vocal timbre is now being felt on secular singing, long dominated by operatic tone-colours.

The preference for boys' and male alto voices seems to have been more widespread in England than elsewhere. At the same time, as already noted, the tenor and contralto voices are not so typically English. Such observations raise questions apparently different from those concerning vowel quality and general timbre. In the latter case the problems are connected with resonance and related anatomical features, whereas the discussion of voice ranges and allied topics appears to have to do·with the size and efficiency of the larynx and respiratory organs. In normal vocal production, laryngeal action can be regarded as primary, and the modificatory processes in respect of resonance as secondary. It is therefore logical to treat these functions sequentially.

LARYNGEAL ACTION

There is a surprising lack of systematic research into the forces which bear upon vocal ranges; a few facts, however, can be adduced. A survey by Gutzmann (1928; cf. Mundinger, 1951) into 3,000 children's voices gave their average compasses as follows:

Ex. 118

Age: 0   1-2 3-5   6   7   8   9   10   11   12-15

[variants in girls' voices denoted in black notes]

These results demonstrate an exclusive use of the chest register. Similar, though less thorough, tests on English children have shown comparable results, which suggest that the employment of higher registers is normally the result of a certain amount of training.

The terms 'head voice' and 'chest voice' have considerable antiquity, and are mentioned by the Arabic theorist al-Farabi in the tenth century AD. Treatises such as those of Mancini (1774) and Tosi (1723) show that the chest voice was regarded as having an upper limit of about *d'* or *e'flat* (pitch differences accounting for a comparatively small margin of error). Modern writers set a similar limit for the normal chest voice of women or children — see, for example, the examination by Nadoleczny (1923) of 600 voices. Nadoleczny's findings also showed that sopranos and contraltos were capable of extending their voices upwards by as much as an octave by employing head-tone.

Although it is commonly believed that tenors are scarcer in England than, say, Italy, it is useful to have statistical support for this notion. Surveys have indicated that in southern Europe there are indeed more tenors than basses; in Sicily the proportion is 5:1. For northern Europe the figures are virtually reversed, tenors being outnumbered 1:4 (Bernstein and Schläper, 1922; Mundinger, 1951). In addition, there is reason to suppose that a low boy's voice will give rise to a tenor voice after the 'break', while a high puerile voice will produce a bass. It is also maintained that the genes producing a high female voice relate to a low voice in the male, and vice versa. (Weiss, 1950, and refs.) Taken together, these observations suggest that a low proportion of tenors is related to a low proportion of (female) contraltos. The English predilection for the male alto voice can be seen as arising from its role as a partial substitute for the rarer tenor voice.

The male alto (henceforth alto) voice uses the head or falsetto register more or less exclusively. The term 'falsetto' unfortunately engenders various notions of falsity and tends to connote an 'unnatural' status — in the past there were frequent suspicions of physical abnormalities, but most people nowadays are aware that altos have the same physical characteristics, and possible ranges, as basses. The stigma of 'unnatural' production, however, remains, due to the implications of the term 'falsetto'. The phrase is first found in the thirteenth century (cf. Villetard, 1907), but the modern use of the word is due to the Italians (cf. eg. Zacconi, 1592 and Mancini, 1774): these and later writers treated the word simply as an equivalent of 'head voice', *voce di testo*, as opposed to chest voice, *voce di petto*.

Modern discussions of singing have considerably obfuscated the question of registers. Many singing manuals have every appearance of being based on scientific fact, but closer inspection almost invariably reveals a series of misinterpretations of experimental data or misapprehensions of the facts. As a result, registers are variously stated to number between one (the concept of registers being thereby denied) and five. The confusion arises partly from different degrees of awareness on the part of singers, and partly from faulty terminology. It is fairly obvious, nonetheless, that some kind of register change is bound to take place somewhere in the range, unless the latter is to be drastically confined. This change may be patent, or virtually imperceptible; here, an analogy with the gear-change mechanism of a car is useful. There are many types of transmission, the crash gear-box, synchro-mesh, automatic and continuously variable systems, offering a series of increasingly smooth changes in which the involvement of the operator is progressively lessened. But the amount of effort required of the driver is irrelevant, as is whether or not the gear-change is noticeable: however gradual or smooth it may be, there must be a gear-change in order to maintain a reasonable ratio of road to engine speeds. Racing the engine too fast or labouring it too slowly in high gear will eventually result in mechanical failure. The same is true of the voice — although the relatively small vocal folds are able to stretch or loosen themselves to produce an astounding variety of pitches, their tensile capacity is not limitless; as with the engine, a gear-change is necessary to prevent impairment of the mechanism.

The terminology of registers is clouded by the use of 'chest register' and 'head register' to denote the 'gear-change' of the voice. Although it is true that there is some localized resonance in these areas, the terms create two misapprehensions. The first is not particularly serious, being the fact that the chest has actually hardly any resonating capacity, producing only forced vibrations; so although the sensation of thoracic resonance is real enough, almost all the amplification of sound takes place, in any case, in the head; the 'chest' resonance is merely produced typically in the lower (pharyngeal) areas, while the 'head' resonance occurs in somewhat higher regions. The second and more unfortunate misapprehension is a failure to recognize that change of resonance location need not take place at the same time as the change in laryngeal function. Although the two tend to be associated, there is a measure of flexibility between laryngeal and resonance registers, and it is precisely this flexibility which is needed to change imperceptibly from one 'register' to another. The transitory area between the main laryngeal registers, in which chest voice is used with head resonance, or head voice with so-called chest resonance, is often felt as a separate 'middle', register.

Leaving aside the question of resonance, the change from chest to falsetto (henceforth, used synonymously with head register) is usually felt as an easing of tension as the voice ascends. This applies as much to the boy's or woman's voice as to the man's, but since the alto is almost exclusively a falsetto voice, and since there is a school which tries to draw a distinction between 'countertenor' and 'alto' voice production, it is essential to be more specific. In 1965, at the Nuffield Institute for Medical Research, Dr G.M. Ardran and I conducted experiments to establish whether there was any difference in laryngeal action between the two 'voices', and, if possible, to discover the mode of action.

Five male volunteers were investigated by radiography. Two were very good singers who might be described as having the 'countertenor' tone, another was a bass producing the classic 'hoot' associated with the phrase 'male alto'; the remainder had a tone quality mid-way between the two extremes. The neck of each volunteer was radiographed in the lateral projection. As a control this was done during quiet breathing: here they were fully relaxed, showing a wide laryngeal airway with the vocal folds turned up into the laryngeal ventricles. Thus only a small amount of air remained in the anterior of the ventricles. These are normal appearances (see Ardran and Emrys-Roberts, 1965, p. 369)

When the note *a* (220 Hz) was sung in the 'chest' register to the vowel 'ah', all the subjects showed the appearances of a vocalized larynx, that is to say there were prominent air-filled ventricles delineating the vocal folds over practically the whole of their length, and there was evidence of the stretching of the vocal folds by the cricothyroid muscles both from the position of the laryngeal cartilages and also from the shape of the airway. When exactly the same note was sung in the falsetto voice, all the subjects showed the same type of change: the air content of the laryngeal ventricles was reduced, indicating that a shorter length (shorter by about a quarter to a third) of vocal fold was free to vibrate. In each instance there was evidence that the cricothyroid muscles were not contracting so vigorously, and there was therefore less stretching of the vocal folds. All the subjects showed a narrowing of the laryngeal vestibule from front to back, which was associated with the backward bowing of the intralaryngeal portion of the epiglottis and its ligament. Other studies have shown that this is associated with the reduction of tension in the false vocal folds, allowing them to bulge medially. This effect can be seen on the radiographs printed in Ardran and Wulstan (1967) which showed (i) the subject producing the note in chest voice, and (ii) the same note sung falsetto. Two sets of pictures contrasted (a) a subject with the so-called countertenor voice, with (b) a bass producing a hooty type of falsetto. The pictures of the falsetto production of (a) and (b) were identical.

The difference between a good and a bad alto rests, therefore, on the difference between the good and bad vocal management of a predominantly head voice technique. Now that the voice has been restored to something approaching its former popularity in England, it is hard to credit that its revival is so recent. The revivication of the voice was due to the artistry, and indeed bravery — for curious reactions preceded its acceptance — of Alfred Deller (cf. Hardwick, 1969). Deller, in common with most of the foremost altos of today, used the falsetto voice almost exclusively; and yet, as with all altos, he could of course sing bass at will. The relationship between pre-and post-pubertal voices in England favours the progression from treble to bass or male alto, rather than the progression from contralto to tenor; coupled with the facility for falsetto found in both men and boys, this has a distinctively genetic appearance.

There is yet another characteristic which the best contemporary altos share, which is the comparatively gradual rate at which their voices 'broke'. Singers whose voices broke more rapidly normally find greater difficulty in producing the typical 'countertenor' tone. This is one of several reasons which make research into the vocal aspects of puberty overdue. As will become apparent later, this question is directly relevant to conditions in sixteenth-century England. Although an extended treatment is not at present possible, the subject of pubertal change nonetheless requires some consideration.

THE 'BREAKING' OF BOYS' VOICES

The causes of the change in boys' voices is not entirely clear. The development of the body is controlled by various hormones which are inhibited at the pubertal period, and the sex difference in pubertal age accounts therefore for certain differences in physique between men and women, such as the longer legs of the man, and his greater vital capacity (ie. lung power). Growth-inhibiting hormones are produced approximately two years earlier by women than by men; castration delays their production still further, one result being the grossly enlarged thoracic regions of castrati caricatured by eighteenth-century artists. The resultant power of tone and breath control of the castrati were astounding, only rarely finding their equal in un-mutilated males.

During the present century the onset of puberty has shifted progressively earlier. The musical effect of this is obvious: the later this change occurs, the better the quality of boy singers, for older boys are larger (particularly in vital capacity) and their intelligence quotient is nearing its limit. So a boy singer of eighteen will have something of the physical and mental capacities of the castrato of Handel's day. Boys of this age were frequently singing soprano at the beginning of this century, whereas now such a boy would be regarded as something of a freak. The boys' choir-desks of many cathedrals and college chapels were often lowered in the course of this century to accommodate progressively younger and shorter choristers. Figure 19, below (taken from Tanner 1962, p. 153 and refs.), shows how the pattern

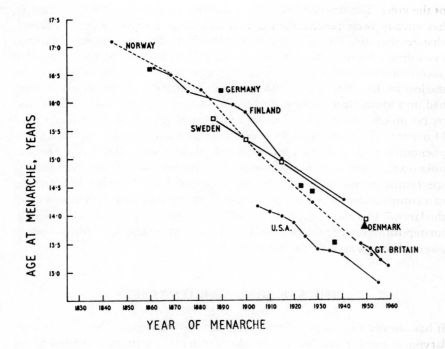

Fig. 19

224

of adolescence has changed in the past hundred years. Although there are genetical differences (both racial and individual) in pubertal patterns, those for Europe are relatively consistent.

Note that this diagram relates to the onset of puberty in the female where the menarche gives an obvious and clear-cut chronology. For the male, the voice-break can be reckoned as occurring approximately two years later; thus the average reading for 1850 would be something like 18 years, and for 1950 approximately 14½ years. This is a far-reaching change, and only now are there signs that the trend is slowing down.

Fortunately, such variations appear to proceed in waves, several of which are evident in history, notably at the end of the Roman Empire. But the causes of such trends remain obscure: Tanner (mentioned above) examines several possible genetic and environmental explanations — the most obvious being nutritional — but is disinclined to point to any as the complete answer. It seems likely that psychological pressures have some bearing; the end of the Roman Empire and the present century have in common an overt attitude to sexuality, and frequent exposure of the young to sexual stimuli may actually hasten the advent of puberty.

Whatever the reasons for the timing of the 'breaking' period, its length is important. Many believe that singing must be stopped during this time, while others insist that regular singing without strain, rather than the disuse of the voice, is essential to the proper development of the changed voice. It has already been noted that the best alto singers report a gradual voice change; they also sang continuously through the breaking period. In many cases they were unaware that their singing voice had changed, for they had unconsciously altered their technique from soprano to alto; remarking only the loss of the top notes, they were subsequently surprised to find that they had, in addition, a bass voice. This curious compensation mechanism seems to be present in almost all voice changes, if to a less dramatic extent. However, although most breaking voices deepen fairly gradually, the phenomenon of a sudden, virtually overnight change is by no means unknown. Since the vocal folds must effectively double in size, such a spectacular breaking of the voice must represent the sudden disintegration of a compensating mechanism, rather than an instantaneous enlargement of the larynx. Current research into this mechanism may reveal that a facility for repositioning the hyoid bone is a crucial factor, and that this control is essential for an easy command of falsetto.

RESONANCE — VOWEL QUALITY

It has already been noted that vocal quality, although dependent upon the laryngeal mechanism, is mainly characterized by differing types of resonance. Changes of resonance, whether resulting from a shift into another laryngeal register, or from a vowel change, or again simply to achieve a different 'tone', are all brought about by movements of organs (principally the tongue and lips). The discussion of the physical basis of tone is therefore most conveniently undertaken by considering vowel quality.

It is generally accepted that there are several well-localized 'formant' regions (ie. frequency bands in which characteristic amplification may take place) which vary for each vowel. Because each note generated by the larynx has a complex harmonic complement, several of these harmonics will be within range of this region whatever the fundamental note, so the amplification characteristics of each vowel can exist more or less independently of the pitch of the note. This phenomenon was demonstrated by Paget (1930) who made models of resonating chambers each answering in frequency to the two main formants of a vowel; their effect when excited by a column of air was surprisingly life-like. There is an assumption that these frequencies are not only fixed for the voice irrespective of the pitch of the generated note, but also for all voices, male and female alike. This is apparently borne out in whispering, where the resonating apparatus is excited into vibration without the use of the larynx. It is usually impossible to tell whether a whispering voice belongs to a man or a woman. But a recording of a man played at twice the speed sounds like a small child, not a woman, and the vowels are still recognizable, if distorted. Vowel recognition is thus due in part to the *relative* frequencies of the formants (the formants for a woman or older child being on average somewhat higher than for a man, those for a small child being considerably higher); but the 'fixed formant' theory is a convenient approximation for simplicity's sake.

Of the five or so recognizable formant regions that exist, the two which have most effect on the perception of vowel differentiation vary independently of each other. Since we recognize that some vowels sound high, others low, it is obvious that one formant rather than the other is responsible for this psychological effect. However, some vowels, appearing to be 'high', are very difficult to sing on a high note, while apparently 'low' vowels are difficult on low notes. This is due to the other formant whose pitch is more nearly related to the places where the voice must resonate in order to amplify itself properly. An illustration of this can be seen in comparing the vowels ī and ā (using the letters to denote Latin, rather than English, vowels). The frequencies of ī are roughly localized about 374Hz + 2400Hz. We say it is a bright, high vowel, but it is more difficult to sing on a high than a low note. In contrast ā has formants centred approximately upon 825Hz + 1200Hz. This vowel, while appearing lower, is easier to sing on a higher note. So, of the two major formants to each vowel, the higher gives its characteristic psychological effect, the lower its main resonance, nearer to the note generated by the larynx.

Vowel characteristics depend on a number of adjustments of the jaw, lips, tongue, and so forth, but the 'cardinal vowels' are governed almost entirely by the position of the tongue. In the 'open' vowels the tongue is low, while in the 'close' vowels it is high. The 'front' vowels depend upon a comparatively forward position of the highest point of the tongue; in 'back' vowels, this high point is farther back. These movements are associated with frequency changes in the two main formants; the degree of fronting or backing influences the higher formant, and the amount of opening or closing is related to the lower formant. The effect of the movements of the tongue on vowel pitch may be ascertained by observing its behaviour during whistling, in which, of course, the pitch changes are effected solely by the modification of the resonating cavities. Since the range available to male and female whistlers is roughly the same, the general acceptability of the 'fixed pitch' theory of vowel formants is underlined.

Standard Latin vowels have been used in the following diagram, for English suffers from the disadvantages of dialect variants, inconsistent spelling and the substitution of diphthongs for long vowels. The 'restored' pronunciation of classical Latin does not have these disadvantages. Rough equivalents would be:

Latin		'Standard' English
ī	as in prīnceps	ee as in spleen
ĭ	as in ĭlle	i as in pin
ē	as in mēnsa	ai as in pain
ĕ	as in rĕgo	e as in pen
ă	as in ămo	a as in man
ā	as in āc	a as in father
ō	as in mōtio	o as in nor
ŏ	as in bŏnus	o as in pot
ŭ	as in ŭxor	u as in pull
ū	as in cūr	oo as in pool
ĕ/ŭ		e as in regard
ŭ/ĕ		u as in punish

The following diagram (p. 228) indicates the approximate frequencies of the Latin pure vowels — data based on Paget (1930), Fletcher (1929), Potter and Peterson (1948). The schematic values (many individual differences occur in different speakers or singers) are projected on to a figure denoting the relative positions of the tongue for each vowel as revealed by X-ray photography (cf. Jones, 1950).

The spical positions of the tongue for each vowel correspond with peaks of amplificatory regions, and with the stylized 'vowel triangle' of the phoneticians. Note that the 'central' vowels of 'rĕgard' and 'pŭnish', so characteristic of English, were virtually absent from Latin, although *bonum* was probably pronounced *bonŭ/ŏ* in classical times. The high formants of the central vowels are lower than the back or front vowel counterparts,

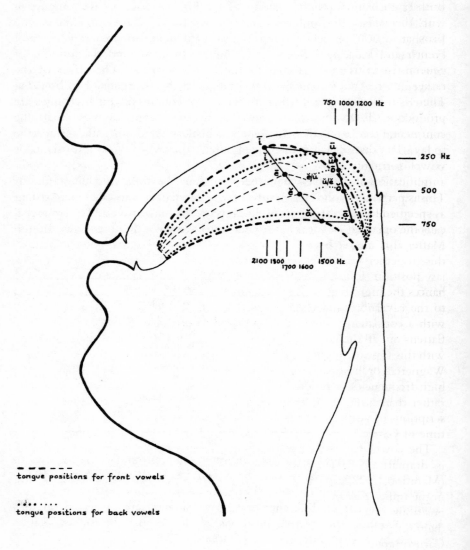

Fig. 20 Schematic frequencies for high and low formants of the cardinal vowels.

and the English vowels generally display lower high formants than their Latin equivalents. Thus the change from Latin to English at the Reformation would have resulted in considerable dulling of the vowel spectrum. Both English and Latin lack the 'front rounded' vowels, ie. those associated with the *umlaut* in German, with corresponding sounds in French (cf. Broshanan, 1961, p. 105). Also absent from English are the nasal vowels of French and Italian. The effect of nasalization and 'front rounding' is a general rise in frequency of the higher formants. English therefore exhibits rather different vowel frequencies than French, German, Latin and Italian. There is thus every reason to suppose that sixteenth-century English vocal production differed from that of the Continent; but both English and continental tone diverged markedly from the type of production prevalent today. The distinguishing factor lies in the treatment of the vowels. The vowel formants shown in the diagram (Fig. 20) demand a dramatic amplification of the higher frequencies of certain vowels (see Dunn, 1950). This is particularly the case if the mouth is opened only a moderate amount, as specified by several sixteenth-century writers: Maffei (1562) for example, calls the opening 'no more than that adopted when reasoning with friends'. Maffei also mentions the contact of the tongue with the lower teeth and this, together with a moderate lateral opening of the mouth and forward jaw position (found in many contemporary representatives of singers) enhances the high frequencies of the vowel formants. This is in stark contrast to the cavernous and chinless gape seen on the operatic stage, associated with a consistently lowered tongue and retracted jaw. This configuration flattens out all the vowels into the characteristic 'plummy' sound associated with this type of singing technique. Overall power, necessary to ride over a Wagnerian orchestra, is achieved in the mid frequency, at the expense of the high frequencies (see Sundberg, 1977). Thus the voice is heavy and dull, rather than brilliant, and distorts the vowels, contrary to the express prescriptions of virtually every writer on singing from von Zabern up until the time of Garcia.

The vowel distortion resulting from the artificial flattening of the tongue is dramatically illustrated by Caruso's recommended mouth positions (Marafioti, 1922, pp. 235–6). These self-styled 'correct' positions are shown in the upper part of Figure 21 and may be compared with the true tongue positions given by Jones (1950), here shown in the lower part of the diagram. These latter are, needless to say, stigmatized as 'incorrect' by Caruso (apud. Marafioti, pp. 233–48).

Marafioti's pictures of Caruso taken in the act of singing each of the five cardinal vowels are peculiarly comical, ranging from an impression of a splenetic *mafioso* to that of a canvassing politician about to engage in statutory baby-kissing. They unwittingly illustrate the 'uncomely gaping of the mouth' disliked by Ornithoparcus and Finck. The Renaissance singer made the vowels with the tongue as in speech; the late nineteenth century,

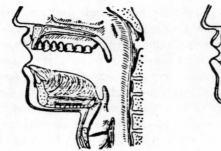
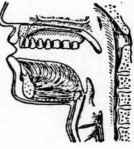

a

e

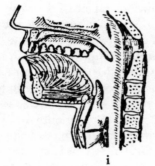
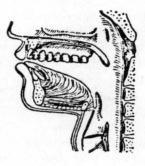

i

o

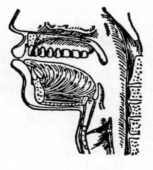

u

(a)

Fig. 21 (a) Caruso's 'correct' vowels (from Marafioti, 1922, images reversed) (b) phonologically true vowels (from Jones, 1950)

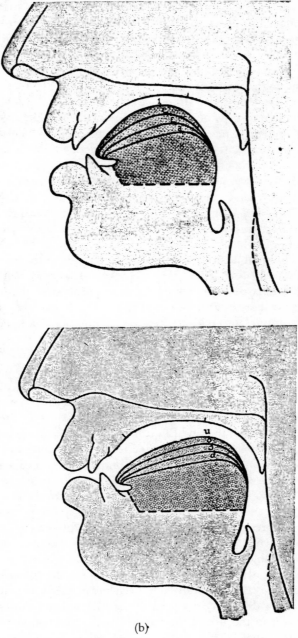

(b)

however, subverted natural methods by attempting to make the vowels with the mouth in order to keep the tongue low and static. It was Garcia (1840) who advocated the new technique which had come from the Parisian Opera a few years earlier and was called the *voix sombrée*. The flattened tongue, withdrawn jaw and low position of the larynx, together with a consequent high breath pressure, fitted in with the Romantic ideal of evenness of loud tone. Its almost exact counterpart is found in the high-pressure diapason stops of the Romantic organ, in which a low frequency harmonic content is made up by high energy sounds. This is in contrast with the classical low-pressure, which generated lower energy sounds having a high-frequency-emphasized harmonic content. The Romantic voice production was not espoused by all, for the old method of production survived with tenacity in certain places, and not only in English cathedral choirs. The agility displayed by Jenny Lind, for example, came from a higher and freer position of the larynx. A notable characteristic of Romantic production is the slowness of the voice in its reaction to pitch changes due to the different position of the hyoid bone and consequent differences in the use of musculature. Zacconi (1592) asked for a 'voice neither forced nor slow' and emphasized the role of throat (ie. glottis) so that rapid passages can be sung with ease, Vicentino (1555) says that a bass 'singing in full voice cannot accommodate' rapid articulation'. Thus the voice required for the divisions in Gibbons' 'Glorious and powerful God' (see p. 190) is necessarily light, and must be able to make use of rapid glottal contractions.

Whereas the Romantic method of tone production evens out the qualities of vowels, and therefore engenders an 'international tone', the Renaissance emphasis on correct vowels necessarily highlights divergent national qualities of each language resulting from the differences in the vowel complements. The loss of the Old English front-rounded vowels in late Middle English (cf. Brook, 1963) would have resulted in changes in vocal timbre, and the subsequent drastic changes in phonology would have had a comparable significance for the singer. The notion that extreme nasal resonance was characteristic of all medieval and Renaissance vocal techniques is belied by several references which dismiss it as a crudity (cf. p. 181); and to take Chaucer's Prioress who 'entuned in her nose ful semely' as proof of an English preference for a nasal timbre is hardly credible, for Chaucer is mocking his subject, and indeed subsequently his glossators.

Nevertheless, the nasal resonance required by the 'mean' voice and its continental equivalents would have been greater than is generally current today. A major difference between the continental and English production lay, however, in the use of the treble voice. Continental singers disliked changing into head voice: Zacconi described the change as 'usually offensive'. The head voice used by the English trebles was doubtless blended, however, so that a marked change of register was not evident. Playford (following Caccini) says (1674, p. 43) that 'Increasing of the Voice in the *Treble* Part, especially in feigned Voices, doth oftentimes become harsh, and unsufferable to the hearing'. Thus the high 'feigned' register was to be sung without stridency; again the agility often required by English trebles (cf. p. 240) dictates a light and flexible tone.

The technique of the Romantic voice not only makes the agility and clarity of the treble voice a physical impossibility, but it rules out the use of the trill, which was coming into fashion at the end of the Tudor period. Ironically, the retracted larynx position engenders the use of vibrato, which is then indistinguishable from the trill. As was noted in the previous chapter, the combination of undifferentiated vowels, loud but dull tone, and wobble, is antipathetic to the performance of polyphonic music. This is manifest both empirically and in the statements of theorists. The latter, taken against the background of the history of vocal physiology, allow a surprisingly accurate picture of Tudor vocal practice to be drawn. Particularly significant is the documentary evidence which may be related to the characteristics and compasses of individual voices, reviewed in the following pages.

DOCUMENTARY EVIDENCE

A description of the five voices, treble, mean, countertenor, (alto), tenor and bass, is given in Charles Butler's *Principles of Musick*. Although published in 1636, his book is retrospective in nature and therefore of considerable importance in relation to earlier music. The bracketed letters refer to his annotations, which are given underneath. The spelling has been modernized.

> Setting is the framing of a Song in Parts: which for the most part (specially in Counterpoint) are four: (a) Bass (b) Tenor (c) Countertenor (d) Mean: of which, in some songs is wanting one or two: and in some, for a voice of a high pitch is added (e) a Treble . . .
>
> All these parts together (though for the deepest Bass-voice and the loftiest Treble-voice) are contained within the compass of 22 notes . . . but ordinarily they do not exceed the number of 19 or 20 . . .
>
> (a) The Bass is so called because it is the basic or foundation of the Song, unto which all other parts be set: and it is to be sung with a deep, full, and pleasing voice.
>
> (b) The Tenor is so called, because it was commonly in Motets the ditty-part or Plainsong: which continued in the same kind of notes, usually breves, much after one plain fashion: upon which the other parts did discant in sundry sorts of Figures, and after

many different ways: or (if you will) because neither ascending
to any high or strained note, nor descending very low, it con-
tinueth in one ordinary tenor of the voice and therefore may be
sung by an indifferent voice.

(c) The Countertenor or Contratenor, is so called, because it
answereth the Tenor, though commonly in higher keys: and
therefore is fittest for a man of a sweet shrill voice. Which part
though it have little melody by itself; (as consisting much of
monotones) yet in Harmony it hath the greatest grace: especially
when it is sung with a right voice which is too rare.

(d) The Mean is so called, because it is a middling or mean high
part, between the Countertenor (the highest part of a man) and
the Treble, (the highest part of a boy or woman:) and therefore
may be sung by a mean voice.

(e) The Treble is so called, because his notes are placed (for the
most part) in the third septenari [octave, ie. the third octave
from Gamut], or the Treble clefs: and it is to be sung with a
high clear sweet voice.

Butler was hardly a reliable etymologist; but one of the many interesting
points about this passage is his use of the term '22 notes' to describe the
overall compass of the voices, using the same terminology as the *Eton
Choirbook*. The top treble note in the third septenari would be written g' (ie.
modern b'' *flat*).

An earlier, but less graphic, description of the voices is in London, BL
Roy. 18.B.XIX, f.8^v (early seventeenth century):

> . . . nature having disposed all voices both of men and children
> into fyve kindes viz: Bases (being the lowest or greatest voyces)
> Tenors, being neither so low or so great, Countertenors, (beinge
> lesse lowe and more higher than Tenors), of which three kyndes
> all mens voyces consist. Then of childrens voices there are two
> kyndes viz: Meane voices (which are higher than mens voyces)
> and Treble voices, (w[hi]ch are the highest kindes of childrens
> voices) . . .

Both of these sources show that five distinct voices were normally recognized.
The same nomenclature, moreoever, is evident in the *Northumberland Household Book* (ed. Percy, 1770), an account of Leckingfield Castle in Yorkshire,
home of Henry Percy, Fifth Earl of Northumberland (the sixteenth-century
manuscript on which Percy based his text is no longer extant):

GENTYLLMEN and CHILDERYN of the CHAPELL.
ITEM Gentyllmen and Childryn of the Chapell xiiij Viz.
Gentillmen of the Chapell viij Viz. ij Bassys — ij Tenors — and
iiij Countertenours — Yoman or Grome of the Vestry j —

Childeryn of the Chapell v Viz. ij Tribills and iij Meanys = xiiij. [pp. 40–41]

Gentillmen of the Chapell — ix Viz. The Maister of the Childre j — Tenors ij — Countertenors iiij — The Pistoler j — and oone for the Organys Childer of the Chapell — vj. [p. 44]

THE ORDURYNG of my Lordes CHAPPELL for the Keapinge of our LADYES MASSE thorowte the WEIKE.

SONDAY
Master of the Childer
  a Countertenor
A Tenoure
A Tenoure
A Basse

MONDAY
Master of the Childer
  a Countertenor
A Countertenoure
A Countertenoure
A Tenoure

TWISDAY
Master of the Chillder
  a Countertenor
A Countertenoure
A Countertenoure
A Tenoure

WEDYNSDAY
Master of the Chillder
  a Countertenor
A Countertenoure
A Tenoure
A Basse

THURSDAIE
Master of the Chillder
  a Countertenor
A Countertenoure
A Countertenoure
A Tenoure

FRYDAY
Master of the Chillder
  a Countertenor
A Countertenoure
A Countertenoure
A Basse

SATTURDAY
Master of the Chillder
  a Countertenor
A Countertenor
A Countertenoure
A Tenoure

FRYDAY
And upon the saide Friday th'ool Chappell and every Day in the weike when my Lorde shall be present at the saide Masse.

THE ORDURYNGE for keapynge Weikly of the ORGAYNS Oon after An Outher As the NAMYS of them hereafter followith WEIKELY.

The Maister of the Chillder yf he be a Player The Fyrst Weke.

A Countertenor that is a player the ijde weke.

A Tenor that is a Player the third weike.

A Basse that is a Player the iiijth weike.

Ande every Man that is a Player to kepe his cours Weikely. [pp. 368–369]

GENTLEMEN of my Lordis CHAPPELL
FURST A Bass / ITEM A Seconde Bass / ITEM The Thirde
Bass / ITEM a Maister of the Childer A Countertenor / ITEM a
Seconde Countertenour / ITEM A Thirde Countertenour /
ITEM A iiijth Countertenor / ITEM A Standing Tenour /
ITEM A Second Standing Tenour / ITEM A iijd Standing
Tenour / ITEM a Fourth Standing Tenor . . .

CHILDRIN of my Lordis CHAPPELL
ITEM The Fyrst Child a Trible / ITEM The ijd Child a Trible /
ITEM The iijd Child a Trible / ITEM The iiijth Child a Second
Trible / ITEM The vth Child a Second Trible / ITEM The vjth
Child a Second Trible.
[pp. 324–5]

THE ORDERYNGE of my LORDES CHAPPELL in the
QUEARE at MATTYNGIS MAS and EVYNSONGE To
stonde in Ordere as Hereafter Followith SYDE for SIDE
DAILYE.

THE DEANE SIDE	THE SECOUNDE SYDE
THE Deane	THE Lady-Masse Priest
THE Subdeane	THE Gospeller
A Basse	A Basse
A Tenor	A Countertenor
A Countertenor	A Countertenor
A Countertenor	A Tenor
A Countertenor	A Countertenor
	A Tenor [p. 367]

There follow a roster for ruling the choir (undertaken by countertenors and
tenors only on p. 370, but by all voices on p. 375); another seating list (p.
371 — differing from p. 367, having four basses) followed by another duty
roster for Lady Mass (this provides for all three men's voices being in
attendance). On p. 373 there appear to be five basses 'setting the choir', but
only four appear (with five countertenors, three tenors) on p. 375 (a *Rector
chori* roster). Payments recorded on pp. 47–8 detail six countertenors, two
tenors and two basses (paid at different rates!) and six boys; on p. 83
(provision of breakfast of bread, beer and fish) there are ten men and six
boys.

It seems from these lists that the Northumberland Chapel began rather
modestly (five boys and eight men) and rose to six boys and fifteen or
sixteen men. The disposition varied only a little, there being three trebles
and two or three means (or 'second trebles'); four to six countertenors; two
to four tenors and two to four basses. These five voices and their des-

criptions correspond with the compasses already identified from the music of the period. The preponderance of countertenors at Leckingfield is also reflected in the music of c. 1500–1625; where a voice is duplicated, it is commonly the alto. Even as late as 1641 Barnard printed four separate books for the countertenors (two for each side of the choir) as against two for the tenors and two for the basses. All the extant collections of partbooks formerly belonging to choirs of cathedral proportions (eg. Durham and Peterhouse, Cambridge) are made up in the same way. The idea which is sometimes put forward that choirs were shuffled about like a pack of cards, and that the pitch and scoring of the music were also subject to day-to-day vagaries is demonstrably false. The evidence shows that sixteenth- and early seventeenth-century choirs were remarkably consistent in constitution.

The character of the five voices identified in the *Northumberland Household Book* and described by Butler and others is revealed partly from the compasses of the music and partly from evidence of the kind discussed below. The individual voices are dealt with in descending order.

TREBLE

The lavish provisions of the Earl of Northumberland's chapel at Leckingfield were looked upon by the jealous eye of Wolsey, with whom Northumberland had an 'ancient grudge' (Cavendish, 1959 p. 243). When the fifth Earl died, it is almost certain that Wolsey took over many or all of the musicians of the chapel upon some pretext or other. In the following letter from the sixth Earl to Thomas Arundel (printed in *Northumberland Household Book*, p. 429), there is reference to something like this taking place, and the Cardinal is now demanding the chapel Mass books, perhaps under the pretence that they were left to him by the late Earl:

Bedfellowe.

After my most harte recomendacion: Thys Monday the iijd off August I resevyed by my Servaunt Letters, from yowe beryng datt the xxth day off July, deleveryd unto hym the sayme day at the Kings town of Newcastell; wherin I do perseayff my Lord Cardenalls pleasour ys to have such Boks as was in the Chappell of my lat lord and fayther, (wos soll Jh[es]u pardon) to the accomplyshement off which at your desyer I am confformable, notwithstanding I trust to be abell ons to set up a Chapell off myne owne. But I pray God he may look better upon me than he doth. But methynk I have lost very moch, ponderyng yt ys no better regardyd; the occasion wheroff he shall perseayff . . .

I shall with all sped send up your Lettrs with the Books unto my Lords Grace, as to say, iiij Anteffonars [antiphoners], such as I thynk wher nat seen a gret wyll; v Gralls [grails or graduals] an ordeorly [ordinal], A manuall; viij Prosessioners [processionals]. And ffor all the ressidew, they are not worth the sending, nor ever was occypyed in my Lords Chapel. And also I shall wryt at this tyme as ye have wylled me.

Yff my lords grace wyll be so good lord unto me as to gyff me lychens [lycence] to put Wyllm Worme within a castell of myn off Anwyk in assurty, unto the tyme he have accomptyed ffor more money recd than unto his colleyg, with such other thyngs reserved as his [grace] shall desyre; but unto such tyme as myne awdytors hayth takyn accompt off him: wher in, good bedfellow, do your best, ffor els he shall put us to send mysselff, as at owr metyng I shall show yow.

And also gyff secuer credens unto this berer, whom I assur yow I have ffonddon a marvellous honest man as ever I ffownd in my lyff. In hast at my monestary off Hul-Park the iij day of August. In the owne hand off

Yours ever assured

H. *Northumberland.*

To my bedfellow
Arundell.

Nemesis, however, was lying in wait. In turn, the king himself was determined to have one of Wolsey's boys. A reluctance to comply called forth more insistent demands:

My lord, if it were not for the personal love that the King's highness doth bear unto your grace, surely he would have out of your chapel, not children only, but also men; for his grace hath plainly shown unto Cornish that your grace's chapel is better than his, and proved the same by this reason, that if any manner of new song should be brought unto both the said chapels to be sung *ex improviso*, then the said song should be better and more surely handled by your chapel than by his grace's.

(*Letters and Papers* II/2, p. 1246, modern spelling)

This letter, dated the 25th of March, 1518 was followed by another on the following day:

The King has spoken to him again about the child of your chapel. He is desirous to have it without the procuring of Cornysche or other.

Wolsey had to relinquish the boy, for a later entry reads (ibid. p. 1252):

Cornysche doth greatly laud and praise the child of your chapel sent hither, not only for his sure and cleanly singing, but also for

his good and crafty descant, and doth in like manner extol Mr.
Pigott [who later also joined the Chapel Royal] for the teaching
of him.

It seems more than probable that this highly valued chorister was a treble.
Cornish was one of the chief composers of the *Eton Choirbook*, and therefore
one of the pioneers of the high treble style; although Wolsey's taste for it
was probably awakened by the work of Richard Davy, *informator choristarum*
of Magdalen College, Oxford, at the time when Wolsey was there, first as
instructor in Grammar, then as Dean of Divinity. Wolsey's overweening
ambition to found his own choir is expressed in a contemporary poem by
Storer, in which the prelate speaks of his desire to make his chapel

> . . . pure devotion's seate,
> Meete for the service of the heav'nly King
> The tongues of the most learned did intreate
> Of his decrees, and skilful priests did sing,
> And singing boyes use their hearts trebling string . . .
>
> (Storer, 1599)

Wolsey's household chapel of ten boys and twelve men (Stow, 1580, p.
934) was clearly a serious rival to the Chapel Royal; the choir at Cardinal
College, Oxford, which had the same choral forces, was probably
equally provocative to the cupidity of the Royal eye. The Chapel Royal
itself, however, had an enviable reputation. Sagudino, secretary to the
Venetian ambassador, commented in 1515 that the voices of the king's
choristers were 'more divine than human'. He added *'non cantavano, ma
giubilvano'*, and went on to comment that the English 'counterbasses
probably have not their equal in the world'. Although the Italian *contrabasso* is merely the equivalent of the English 'bass', this statement may
well refer to the Magnificat on the Eighth Tone by Cornish, which
happens, perhaps uniquely, to include a low *E flat* (sounding pitch) for
the basses and which might have impressed Sagudino. The treble part of
this Magnificat has qualities that may well have caused Sagudino to
describe the singers as 'jubilating' rather than merely singing. Cornish's
Magnificat ends, at the 'Sicut erat', with a series of duets, beginning with
the bass and tenor. The bass is subsequently replaced by the alto, and in
turn the mean takes over from the tenor. As the series of duets ascends
the choir, the complexity of the ornamentation increases, till at length,
when the double strand reaches its apex, the trebles and means join in a
breathtaking display of vocal agility, rounded off by Amen sung by the
full choir. (See Ex. 119).

At the Reformation the high treble style of writing virtually died out, due
to several factors. The more syllabic settings of words (as much due to the
eventual percolation of Franco-Flemish influence as to Reformist ideals),

Ex. 119

coupled with the use of English, rather than Latin, were inimical to the high soaring treble style. The enunciation of consonants and the differentiation of vowels are in any case more difficult at high pitch; this is not helped by the fact that English long-vowels tend to be diphthongs rather than true vowels, nor by the increasing articulation required by a syllabic, rather than melismatic, style of setting.

A further reason for the abandonment of the treble voice was the declining standard of many choirs; this resulted partly from a lack of interest in some quarters, and partly from inflationary difficulties (le Huray, 1967, pp. 39 ff). However, conditions did eventually improve in Jacobean times, and Latin melismatic music also continued to be composed; thus a crucial factor in the eclipse of the treble voice may well have been the increasing rarity of the voice itself.

During the second half of the fifteenth century, boys of Edward IV's Chapel were pensioned off and sent to University at eighteen, but only if their voices had broken: 'And when any of these children comen to xviij years of age, and their voices change, ne cannot be preferred in this chapel . . .' (Myers, 1959, p. 137). But Purcell's voice broke at the age of fourteen, apparently the normal age for his time. At Durham in the 1560's, voices were not breaking much later than fifteen (Thompson, 1929, p. 142) and at Chichester the records (Peckham, 1959) indicate that sixteen was normal in the 1550's, but fourteen and a half to fifteen was average at the turn of the century. The path of this progression lies along the line of the diagram shown on p. 224, taking into account the addition of two years representing the difference between the onset of male and female puberty. In common with its modern counterpart, the Jacobean choir would have had difficulty finding boys as capable as those of the first half of the 'golden age' of the treble style. As already noted, the use of English at the Reformation, and the virtual abandonment of the melismatic style made for technical difficulties. Thus it is significant that the *Gyffard* partbooks (BL Add. 17802–5) which appear to date from the period of the Marian revival of the Latin rite, contains music for trebles, some of it newly composed. But the new Anglican liturgy inspired few pieces for trebles; 'Unto thee, O Lord' ascribed to Gibbons is a rare and comparatively late work for trebles, dating from Jacobean times. Although now extant in the form of an organ score and an isolated alto part, it can be reconstructed with some accuracy (*EECM* 21). Experience in performance, however, confirms that the problems of articulation often verge on the insuperable when the melismatic Latin high treble style is transferred to syllabic textures in English.

The treble and alto voices lie exactly an octave apart, and it is thus obvious that they employed the same falsetto technique. But, partly because the boy's vocal folds are less massy than the man's and therefore more flexible, the change from chest to head register is less noticeable and can thus be used more freely. The rather similar size of the resonating cavities of boys and men (and indeed women) is another reason for slight differences between treble and alto technique, since the resonating chambers of the man are effectively larger in relation to the fundamental frequency. This also brings about greater ease for the man, and difficulty for the boy, in the articulation of consonants and difficult vowels on high notes.

The similar characteristics of the castrato voice and the older boy's unbroken voice have already been pointed out. The castrato and alto tone-qualities were also similar, as will be evident later. Eunuchoid voices can occasionally be observed today; their tone markedly resembles that of both the alto and high boy's voice. This clear, bell-like quality is in accord with the account of the Duke of Würtemburg's visit to Windsor in 1592 which mentions 'exquisite music' in which there was 'a little boy who sang so sweetly amongst it all' (Rye, 1865, p. 17). In 1581 the Englishman, Mulcaster (p. 59) wrote 'musick . . . stands not so much upon straining or fulnesse of the voice so it be delicate and fine in concent'. No 'straining' of the voice is evident in singers portrayed in the sixteenth-century stained glass windows in the Beauchamp Chapel in St Mary's, Warwick — they clearly evince, however, the moderate lateral opening of the mouth and natural jaw position, discussed earlier.

MEAN

During the course of the sixteenth century, the treble voice fell into disuse; as it did so, the mean voice changed its character, due to the raising of its compass to a level approximately midway between the old treble and mean ranges. This range had previously been used only in compositions for high voices alone (eg. Taverner's 'Audivi'). The 'high mean' voice became the norm for Jacobean composers, and its tone may be assumed to have been a blend of old-style treble and mean qualities. The timbre of the old 'low mean' voice, however, would have differed markedly from the treble. In full-choir music the means would sing the second highest part, beneath the brilliant trebles with whom they would hardly compete tonally unless a certain amount of penetrating resonance were employed. The mean compass as given on p. 220 corresponds strikingly with the natural limits of the chest voice discussed previously. The tone of the modern continental boy alto, rather nasal, and using exclusively the chest voice, is clearly a reasonable approximation of the tone quality of the pre-Reformation mean. But because of the use of the English language in later music, the sharpness of tone may well have given place to a somewhat rounder quality as its range rose to meet the treble compass. In passing, it should be mentioned that the persistent misapprehension that 'mean' indicated a man's voice is ruled out by the descriptions quoted on pp. 233–4

COUNTERTENOR (or alto)

It should be clear from the evidence already adduced that the notion that the 'countertenor' is a type of tenor quite distinct from the alto is wholly erroneous. It rests principally upon false etymology: the name of the *contratenor* part of earlier music merely reflected the way in which the composition was put together; the countertenor part was often lower than the tenor. It has already been noted that the sixteenth-century choir employed twice as many altos as tenors; and that the latter are a comparative rarity in England. It is hardly reasonable to suppose, therefore, that there were three times as many tenors as basses in sixteenth-century England, the major proportion being able, as so-called 'countertenors', to sustain parts higher than the Italian operatic tenor of today. This, and other fallacies, are more fully treated in Ardran and Wulstan (1967) and Wulstan (1969). That castrato tone was similar to that of the countertenor or alto is shown by the fact that

Siface (the Italian castrato of some notoriety for whom Purcell wrote the famous 'Farewell') sang for a time in the Chapel Royal. *Coryat's Crudities*, a travelogue published in 1611, tells how the author was astounded to find a singer in Venice 'who had such a peerless and (as I may in a manner say) such a supernatural voice for such a privilege for the sweetness of his voice, as sweetness, that I think there was never a better singer in all the world . . . I always thought that he was a Eunuch . . . Again it was the more worthy of admiration because he was a middle-aged man, as about forty years old' (modern edition, 1905, p. 391). These two passages serve to remove any doubt that countertenor tone could have resembled that of a tenor.

The compass of the countertenor voice rose slightly during the sixteenth century, and by the end of the century the complex arrangement was in use whereby in Full sections the second *Decani* sang the same part as the first *Cantoris*; similarly the first *Decani* and second *Cantoris* countertenors sang the same part. As noted previously, the purpose of this disposition was to support a five-part texture with two independent countertenor parts on either side of the choir, but to dispose what might be the stronger voices on different parts in the Full sections. If anything, the *Cantoris* first countertenor was the principal singer, being allotted most of the solo 'verses' at the turn of the century; and contrary to the practice of the present day, the *Cantoris* countertenor sang higher parts than his *Decani* colleague, a practice which continued until well after the Restoration.

Apart from one or two pieces, the *Eton Choirbook* displays little differentiation in range between one countertenor part and another; indeed in earlier music there is little distinction in the compasses of the countertenor and tenor, which suggests that chest and head registers were used in both voices. However, the difference between the compasses of these voices soon becomes more obvious, suggesting a progressively greater concentration on the falsetto register by the countertenor. The tone would naturally change, and become more 'edgy' (Butler's 'sweet shrill voice'). This development would result in the difference between the falsetto and chest registers being harder to conceal. This circumstance is reflected in the generally rather higher compasses of post-Reformation alto parts, and also in the way composers tended to avoid very low notes in exposed verses. The bottom limit seems to have been low *a'flat* unless some such phrase as 'out of the deep' or 'he hath put down' called for exceptional treatment, in which case the limit could be as much as a fourth lower. Even *a'flat* seems to have caused some difficulty, for various sources of Gibbons' 'This is the record of John' (cf. *EECM* 3 pp. 222–3) show changes from the original *a'flat* to *c'*. Here the problem was probably caused by the difficult vowels with high lower formants on the words *Christ, no* and *Lord*.

In Purcell's time the solo parts are markedly different, some descending as low as *e* or *d*, others hardly going below *c*, and the upper limit of the range also differed accordingly. Thus singers such as Turner and Howell were distinguished as a 'low countertenor' or 'high countertenor' respectively. It seems overwhelmingly probable that by this means falsetto was used exclusively; where a low range is demanded consistently it is possible to develop a powerful low falsetto. Byrd, in his Latin music, occasionally makes a distinction between first and second alto. But the idea of low and high falsetto registers being exploited solo, is most strikingly demonstrated in the work of Tomkins, which shows quite different characteristics in comparison with the earlier technique. Although both low and high notes are often required in verses, they do not normally occure in the same part. For example, in 'Who can tell', there are alternative passages (cf. *EECM* 9, p. 56ff) which show that a command of low and high registers in Verse passages was not necessarily expected. So the change towards the use of two types of solo alto seems to have been taking place at about Butler's time, which might possibly explain why he complains about 'a right voice' being 'too rare'; perhaps he did not approve of the new technique.

The alto was therefore predominantly falsetto, a 'sweet, shrill voice' which was 'edgy' without being raucous. Its tone was not unlike that of the treble or castrato, but was dissimilar from that of the tenor. The change into chest register would have been masked in such a way that the lower notes would appear to be low in the voice, for otherwise there would be no point in setting a lower limit to the range.

TENOR

Butler's remark that the tenor was 'an indifferent voice' is paralleled by Laud's recommendation that in Salisbury there should be 'not more of tenors therein, which is an ordinary voice, than there be of basses and contratenors that do best furnish the choir' (*Historical Manuscript Commission*, Fourth Report, p. 142). The voice so described seems to be what is nowadays termed the 'choirmaster's baritone'. Most 'real' tenors today dislike singing music of the Tudor period, finding their part too low for comfort; the sixteenth-century tenor compass more nearly resembled that of a modern baritone. The lack of development of this voice is attributable to the earlier practice of placing the chant in the tenor. The amorphous range and limited opportunity for expression would lead to less gifted singers being allotted the part; and even when the cantus firmus was not consigned to the tenor, composers tended to perpetuate the limited horizons of the voice.

In the long responsories, such as Tallis' 'Videte miraculum' or Sheppard's 'Verbum caro', the strain of singing both the long-note cantus firmus and the high plainsong is taxing for one group of singers alone. Many establishments had 'singing priests' or 'priest conducts' in addition to clerks, and Wolsey at least (cf. Wilkins, 1737, p. 686) intended the former, in Augustinian manner, to sing the chant, while the latter sang only polyphony. He therefore provided a lavish number of priest-chanters at both Cardinal College (thirteen) and at his private chapel (ten), in addition to the twelve secular clerks singing the polyphonic music together with the boys (sixteen and ten respectively — cf. *Statutes*, 1853, p. 185; Stow, 1580, p. 934).

In a number of four-part pieces written prior to the Reformation, the tenor voice is dispensed with altogether. Davy's St Matthew Passion (*Eton Choirbook*), the 'Western wind' Masses of Taverner, Tye and Sheppard (London, BL., Add. 17802–5) and the four-part carols in the *Fayrfax MS* (Add. 5665) are scored for trebles, means, altos and basses only. In these pieces it is possible that the tenors might have joined with the altos or basses. There are a few cases where the tenor parts are indistinguishable in range from the adjacent voices. In the earlier compositions of the *Eton Choirbook* this results from the as yet imprecise differentiation of voices. In one or two later works, however (usually for men's voices), there appears to be some attempt to introduce intermediate compasses such as were relatively common in madrigalian works. What might be a high tenor part can be seen in the Te Deum for men *à* 5 (Oxford, Ch Ch, 979–83) attributed to Taverner. The top two parts are of normal alto compass, and the plainchant is in the tenor. Between the altos and tenor is a part of similar compass to the alto, but of somewhat lower tessitura. Whether this is to be sung by a low alto or a high tenor is difficult to determine; a mixture of the two voices may perhaps have sung the part. A few pieces call for the baritone voice: two examples are Sheppard's responsories 'Laudem dicite' and 'Spiritus sanctus' for men *à* 5 (Oxford Ch Ch 979–83). Once more, it is the tessitura as much as the range which distinguishes the voice-part from that of a normal bass, though the compasses given by Morley (see p, 212) for old-style men's voices have the Tenor primus and secundus ranges a third apart, the latter range resembling that of a baritone.

In Byrd's Latin music, in common with that of White, there is often a distinction made between first and second tenor; yet Byrd's works for the English rite show no such differentiation. Nor do those of his colleagues. Nevertheless, the tenor voice was to some extent brought out of obscurity by White and later composers. Orlando Gibbons, for example, wrote verses for two tenors in 'We praise Thee, O Father' and in the Second service. Gibbons' pupil Walter Porter subsequently became a pupil of Monteverdi, and it was largely due to him that there was increased interest in the tenor voice; this Italian influence is seen particularly in the work of Restoration composers in which the higher tessitura is more commonly used. In spite of this, the alto voice retained its popularity as a solo voice in church music.

The character of the tenor voice during the period c. 1500–1625 is therefore not as clearly defined as the other voices; it is only later in its history that its distinctive quality emerged.

BASS

The Venetian comment (see p. 239) that English 'counterbasses' had 'not their equals in the world' has sometimes given rise to the notion (apparently confirmed by the appearance of much of the music on paper), that the basses of the period had low voices. But *contrabasso* was a contraction of *contratenore basso*, just as *contralto* was an abridged form of *contratenore alto*; in English *contratenor altus* became 'countertenor', or 'alto', whereas *contratenor bassus* became 'bass'; thus *contrabasso* was simply the ordinary term for the bass voice, as Italian documents attest. It is unlikely that basses sang particularly low parts; as has been noted, the lowest note found in Tudor music, *E flat*, at our pitch, is exceptional for that time. The reason that bass parts would have had higher equivalents today is explained by the necessity for the bass to be properly audible in a complex polyphonic texture. Only in harmonic music, where definition is neither so essential, nor indeed necessarily desirable, is a lower compass and tessitura possible. Thus Morley (1597, p. 166) forbids even the note *A flat* (written *F*) except 'upon an extremity for the ditties sake or in notes taken for Diapasons in the base'. This prohibition is corroborated in the music, for even in the early seventeenth century, *A flat* (modern pitch) was often provided with an alternative.

However, the seventeenth century saw both an expansion of range of the bass voice and a certain amount of differentiation between first and second bass. Written *D* (ie. modern *F*) became comparatively common, even in Verse passages. This reflects the less complex texture, which enabled the bass to be heard on low notes. Extremely low passages for bass are found in the work of Tomkins, particularly in 'Give sentence with me, O God', where *E flat* (modern pitch) is found in solo passages. Evidently a particular singer was in the composer's mind, however, judging by the alterations found in different sources (see *EECM* 9, pp. 169–70). Tomkins was also unusual in demanding a two-octave range from some of his soloists, although normally both high and low notes were provided with alternatives. Nevertheless, top *e′ flat* was becoming comparatively frequent in Verse (and occasionally Full) passages, and *f′* was by no means unknown. Where there were two bass parts, however, it was normal practice for the upper part to be taken by *Cantoris*, the lower by *Decani*; as with the arrangement of alto parts, this is the reverse of the disposition found in modern cathedral choirs. In the early sixteenth century there was also an occasional division between high and low, as in Wilkinson's 'Salve Regina' from the *Eton Choirbook* — again the secundus bassus is higher than the primus, contrary to the modern expectation.

The evidence of the range and tessitura of Tudor music confirms that Butler's 'deep full and pleasing voice' can hardly have been strident and was perhaps akin to the timbre of a light baritone. Plumminess of tone and its associated lack of agility are ruled out by the passages discussed earlier: these demand considerable rapidity of attack which cannot be achieved by a retracted larynx.

VOCAL SCORING

The early sixteenth-century five-part choir consisted typically of trebles, means, countertenors (altos), tenors and basses (henceforward abbreviated as Tr M A T B); in six-part music the normal disposition included two countertenor parts. This division of countertenors also tended to be maintained after the Reformation when the five-part choir generally consisted of means, divided countertenors, tenors and basses (M A A T B).

The size of choirs gives additional evidence as to tone-quality. Leckingfield (two or three trebles, three means, four countertenors, two or four tenors, two or three basses) had two or three voices to a part. The Chapel Royal which accompanied King Charles to Scotland in 1633 was somewhat larger (eight boys, six countertenors, four tenors, six basses), but the modern cathedral convention whereby there are as many boys as men did not persist in Tudor times. Consequently, the voices had to balance by tone rather than by weight of numbers. The division of parts, and the subdivisions found on final chords of many works, show that two or three of each voice was normal in most of the establishments for which the major composers wrote their music.

Indeed, Vicentino (1555) mentions that in churches 'one sings with a full voice with a multitude of singers.' This should not be taken to imply the sound of today's choral society; it merely points up the difference between the forces and timbre of church music as opposed to the solo voices and less sharply-focused tone used in chamber music.

The allocation of voices to each part is normally a simple matter, since after the correct transposition has been effected, the vocal ranges of church music are normally unmistakably characteristic of each voice. It must be stressed once more, however, that although the part-names of the sources frequently resemble the names of voices, they were not necessarily equivalent. Thus, the use of the term *Quatruplex* or *Quatreble* as though it were the name of a voice (cf. Harrison, *Eton Choirbook*) has no more meaning than the possible terms 'quint', 'sext', or 'inferior countertenor'. In the following quotations the references are to the names of parts, or 'sights', rather than to specific voices:

> . . . His proporcions be so hard with so highe a quatrible
> (Cornish: . . . *Truth and Informacion*, 1568)

> . . . He that quadribilithe to hy, his voice is variable

> . . . But he that syngithe a trewe songe mesurithe in the meane

> And he that rechith to hye a trebill, his tewnys is not clere
>
> (BL Roy. D. 11)

Similarly, in the title of Redford's keyboard 'Miserere with a mean' the term merely denotes the middle part, whereas 'Mass *for* a mean' implies the use of a boy's voice at the top. References to men singing 'treble' and 'mean' are therefore to the parts they sing, whereas 'counter', 'tenor' or 'bass' are more likely to describe their voices. It is necessary to underline this point, because of the confusion still evident in modern editions of music of the period.

In the *Eton Choirbook*, as in Butler, the overall compass of the texture was described by referring to its total gamut of notes, eg. '22 notarum'. A range of 22 notes or more would require the use of trebles. A compass of 16 notes would indicate that the composition was for men (or possibly boys) only. Bishop Sherborne (c. 1530) ordained that the men of Chichester should have between them a good range of 15 or 16 notes ('a commune vocum succentu possint naturaliter et libere ascendere ad quindecim vel sexdecim notas': Harrison, 1958, p. 181). The frequent similarity of overall compass of the A A T B and Tr Tr M M ensembles suggests the possibility that music for men's voices was sometimes interchangeable with that for boys' voices. Though Taverner's 'Audivi' is clearly for boys alone, Sheppard's and Tallis' settings, in their present form at least, seem to be for men only. But when transposed upwards they could be sung by boys' voices; it is possible that they were indeed so written originally — the vocal compasses of the Sheppard setting seem more typical of trebles and means, an octave higher than the pitch implied by the source. Certainly the Sarum Rite directed this responsory be sung by boys alone, in common with the verse 'Gloria in excelsis', which was set by all of the composers mentioned. Transposition by a fifth is known to have been effected by clef substitution, and the interchangeability of boys' and men's music appears to be taken for granted in statements such as 'liber pro hominibus tantum vel pueris' (Macray, 1894, p. 209) in documents of the period.

Overall ranges of 17 notes and above call for 'mixed' voices. Where their compass is 17 or 18 notes, it is possible to perform three-part pieces with men only, whereas 17 or 19 notes should include the treble at high pitch, or the mean at low pitch. In Ludford's set of Masses *à* 3 for daily Lady Mass (BL, Roy. App. 45–48: see *CMM* 27) either alternative seems to have been provided for, transposition being effected by clef substitution, if required. Such Masses may well have been in the repertory of the six men of Henry VIII's itinerant chapel provided for in the Eltham Ordinances (1526). Ranges above 19 notes normally involve the use of trebles.

In secular music, as noted earlier, the position is different. Though pieces of large total ranges would not admit of transposition, the evidence suggests that secular vocal pitch was not necessarily regarded as fixed. The significance of Byrd's listing of the 'Songs of highest compass' in his 1588 set (*Psalmes, Sonets & songs*) has already been discussed. The lowermost clefs of these songs are consistently F_4 and G_2. Elsewhere in the madrigalian collections, these clefs appear to be used for the same purpose: in order to indicate that transposition was inadvisable. Facultative transposition was therefore possible in secular works not bearing these clefs (though improbable in the madrigalian works of Byrd, Gibbons, Tomkins, etc. See p. 206). For church music, transposition according to the clefs (as set out on p. 208) is the rule, with the possible exception of (a) three-part music of 18 notes' compass or under, (b) four-part music of 16 notes or under, and (c) sacred, but not properly 'church' music.

Composers naturally displayed preferences for certain combinations of voices, and favoured slightly differing ranges in certain cases; some allusion has already been made to this point, and to some gradual changes in compasses and disposition of the voices during the course of the period. Some of these preferences and evolutionary changes will also be touched upon in the following chapters; but although the transformations brought about by the fortunes of history and fashion are certainly of interest, what is more remarkable is the extraordinary consistency, in spite of these changes, of Tudor vocal colour. In exploiting well-defined vocal peaks, and having careful regard for other matters of tessitura, Tudor composers created a sonority, or rather family of sonorities, *sui generis*. As has been seen in the course of this chapter, these sonorities can be recreated only if the questions of vocal timbre are related to the documentary evidence and considered together with evidence concerning pitch, clefs, and other related questions. The solution to these problems reveals that Tudor church music, for long known to have been remarkable, was indeed unique.

CHAPTER 9

Ad Usum Ecclesiae Anglicanae

> Loe,
> Heere these long usurped Royalties
> From the dead Temples of this bloudy Wretch
> Have I pluck'd off, to grace thy Browes withall
> Wear it, and make much of it.

With these words, Shakespeare's Lord Derby placed the crown on Henry Tudor at Bosworth Field on 22 August, 1485. The new king sought at once to 'make much of it', striving to unite the White and Red Roses in 'faire Conjunction', and to heal the 'Civil wounds' which had resulted from thirty years of internecine strife between the rival Plantagenet factions.

The Welshman had won the day against severe numerical odds and at the cost of incurring considerable financial debts; but these were soon repaid. His skill as an administrator brought increasing wealth and stability to the country, thereby laying a solid foundation for the Tudor Age. The victorious Henry entered London in considerable pomp: at St Paul's a suspended thurible censed him as though 'by an Angell commyng out of the Roof, during which time the Quere sange a solempne Antyme, and after Te Deum Laudamus for Joy of his late Victory . . .' In York, too, Te Deum was 'right melodiously songen with Organ as accustamed' (Leland, 1774 iv, pp. 218 and 191).

Henry himself became rich, and music now flourished at the royal court, although the king's own direct involvement is not particularly evident. Apart from the later presence in England of Welshmen such as Philip ap Rhys, John Tuder and John Lloyd, there is little to hint of any personal association with music. The compositions which date from the closing years of the fifteenth century show, however, that what had hitherto appeared to be a sterile soil for music rapidly brought forth extraordinary fertility.

250

Many of the compositions dating from the 1460's or so are undistin-guished. The music of the *Pepys MS* (Cambridge, Magd. Coll., Pepys Lib. 1236) is often dull, and frequently downright incompetent. Some of its composers seemed unable to master composition in three parts, let alone four, and much of the best music is in the form of duets, or even monodies. One of the 'York' Masses (York, Borthwick Inst. MS) by Cuk (or Cooke) shows, however, a promise of things to come; what is left of his 'Venit dilectus meus' Mass shows the use of a wide-range choir (from bass *a flat* to treble *a flat* three octaves higher). Few other compositions have a compass approaching this; although exceptions are the 'Salve festa dies' in the *Pepys MS* and a Nunc dimittis by Frevylle in the fragments in Oxford Lincoln College MS Latin 124 (see Wathey, 1983). Amongst some fairly pedestrian Masses, the *Ritson MS* (BL Add. 5665) contains Thomas Packe's Nunc Dimittis. This setting with antiphon (for the distribution of light at Candlemas) employs five voices — treble, mean, alto, tenor and bass — and appears to herald the new school of composition whose large-scale sonorities are most obviously manifest in the *Eton Choirbook*. Packe's setting is somewhat clumsy, since the music of 'secundum tuum' serves, willy nilly, for the four subsequent verses; there is, nevertheless, a glimpse of a new breadth of style.

The destruction of choirbooks in the middle of the sixteenth century severely limits our view of this style. Although it is clear that the *Eton Choirbook* had no claim to uniqueness in its time, it is now the sole surviving choirbook containing large-scale polyphony dating from the turn of the century. It preserves the music of twenty-five composers, much of it unknown elsewhere. According to the index, a five-part 'Gaude flore virginali' by John Dunstable was originally in the MS — now imperfect, and lacking something like a quarter of its original contents. It would have been interesting to see this work, though it is unlikely to have been by Dunstable since its range ('21 notarum') is characteristic of later music. Gilbert Banester and Nesbett appear both in the *Pepys MS* and the *Eton Choirbook*. Together with Horwood, Hollingbourne, Lambe, Kellyk and Stratford they represent the rearguard of the fifteenth century. Horwood's 'Salve Regina' seems to be an early work, since it has a tenor and bass which share the same clef and range, and cross continually, after the manner of Dunstable. Greater emancipation of the voices is shown in Horwood's 'Gaude flore virginali' and also his 'Gaude virgo mater Christi'. The latter uses the higher treble range, though here the alto and tenor parts remain largely undifferentiated, as they are in his Magnificat of '23 notarum', the most accomplished of Horwood's works. Nesbett's Magnificat is probably of about the same date, for although it has several florid passages, its style is far removed from the grandeur of later pieces. Little or nothing is known of Nesbett, or indeed any of his contemporaries. William Horwood (also appearing in the *York MS*) seems to have died in 1484, whereas Gilbert

Banester (Master of the Children at the Chapel Royal from 1478 to 1486) died in 1487, and Walter Lambe probably survived until the beginning of the sixteenth century.

Lambe is the most considerable of the older *Eton Choirbook* composers, represented by six antiphons (several more are lost) and a Magnificat. He was born in 1450 or 1451 and became King's Scholar at Eton in 1467, after which he became Clerk, then Master of the Choristers at St George's, Windsor. He appears to have died soon after 1499. Lambe's use of vocal resources is conservative; he never demands a treble *b″ flat* (throughout these chapters pitches refer to modern equivalents determined, as discussed previously, by the clefs), and his middle parts show a somewhat primitive differentiation of tessitura, with rather limited ranges. 'O Maria gratia plena' is, nevertheless, a work of considerable achievement; in the MS it is followed, and indeed overshadowed, by John Browne's 'Stabat mater' *à* 6, which ranks as one of the supreme examples of the antiphon style of the *Eton Choirbook*. Browne is the equal of his more celebrated contemporaries Cornish and Davy, and indeed is often their superior for sheer variety of technique. His four Magnificats (one of seven parts) are lost or severely mutilated, but enough of his compositions remain to demonstrate his mastery of the medium. It is worth looking in some detail at Browne's masterpiece, since it readily exemplifies the techniques of early sixteenth-century scoring.

'Stabat mater' is a long and highly expressive contemplation of the cross. Browne's setting begins quietly with a trio for treble, mean and an alto, apparently *soli*, since the words are shown in red in the MS. These three voices are shortly replaced by a duet consisting of another alto and a tenor, the mean later rejoining the *soli* before the full choir is heard for the first time at 'O quam tristis'. The Full texture in turn dissolves, delayed by a roulade sung by the tenor, which overlaps the revelation, first of a duet for treble and mean, and then of a trio for alto, tenor and bass: the full choir then interpolating the brief question 'In tanto supplicio?'

Ex. 120

After this splendidly rhetorical cadence, a sequence of passages for various combinations follows. As before, each of these sections is punctuated by choral passages, some narrative, some contemplative, and some expressing the venom of the rabble shouting *crucifige*, which marks the apex of the piece. There follows a dramatic change of metre and tone colour. Four men's voices underline the suffering of the sorrowing mother in a superb imitative section whose musical ideas are deliberately developed separately from the words when an undulating triplet figure is briefly introduced. Words and music unite, however, at the word *commemorans*, and at *in maestitiam*, after which a melisma in which triplet imitation is again heard introduces a plangent duet for treble and mean, followed by further sections for a variety of duets and trios, interspersed with choral episodes. Often, as at the climax at *dulciflue*, or at *in nobis*, the choir is spurred on by the upward scalewise progress of the tenors. At *per quem dando* the focus once more dissolves and settles on to a series of solistic entries, during which the choir enters unexpectedly on the word *Amen*, and the doleful vigil of Jesus' mother is brought to an exultant and purposeful end.

This kaleidoscope of sound, a series of arching musical vaults viewed from constantly changing perspectives, can hardly be represented in a mere diagram, but at least the variety of vocal permutations employed by Browne may usefully be illustrated by such means:

Fig. 22 Vocal scoring of Browne's 'Stabat mater' in schematic form. Full choir sections shown in black.

This method of ringing the changes among every possible combination of voices is consistent throughout the *Eton Choirbook*, and indeed remained a characteristic of the antiphon style up to the Reformation and beyond; but Browne's handling of the technique in 'Stabat mater' is nonetheless incomparable in its inventiveness.

His antiphon 'Stabat juxta Christi crucem' is for men only (*à* 6), as are his elaborate 'O regina mundi clara' and a 'Salve regina'. 'O Maria salvatoris mater' is for eight voices; the now imperfect 'Stabat virgo mater christi' uses the extreme *b″flat* for trebles; but the 'Stabat mater' is probably his masterpiece, and one of the highest achievements of the *Eton Choirbook*. For poignancy it is equalled only by Browne's own 'Jesu mercy' in the *Fayrfax MS*, and for sheer weight of sound it is only approached by Wilkinson's nine-part 'Salve regina'.

Banester, Davy, Cornish and Browne all contributed Passion carols to the *Fayrfax MS*. The four-part texture used by Browne and Cornish in these carols is unusual in church music, but was employed by Davy in his setting of the St Matthew Passion. Richard Davy was at Magdalen College,

Oxford, for a short while between 1490 and 1492, where he composed his long 'O Domine coeli terraeque'; according to the Eton copyist, the work was written in one day ('hanc antiphonam composuit Ricardus Davy uno die Collegio Magdalene Oxoniis'). Davy made full use of the Magdalen trebles, often using them in pairs (or 'gimels'). Although the extreme treble notes are often overdone in pieces such as 'Salve regina', Davy's use of the voices is otherwise conservative. Nothing remains of his Masses, which were bound together with antiphons, a Magnificat *à* 5 and other Canticles in books once in the possession of Magdalen College (Harrison, 1958, p. 457). Apart from the now fragmentary setting of the Passion, his most considerable remaining work, both in size and in its inspirational level, is 'In honore summae matris'. Davy's extensive use of duets is characteristic; also typical is the way in which he antedates Tye's liking for unexpected changes of harmony — something not far removed from the 'interrupted cadence' of later styles — notably at the word *castitate* in this piece.

Robert Wilkinson was at Eton between 1496 and 1515, becoming Master of the Choristers there in 1500. His 'Salve regina' and the round 'Jesus autem transiens' (a canonic setting of the Apostles' Creed) appear in the *Eton Choirbook* apparently in his own handwriting. These compositions are highly symbolic: 'Salve regina' is written with illuminated initial letters to each of the nine voice parts identifying the nine choirs of angels (*seraphyn, cherubyn* and so forth), and a rhyme is added at the foot of the righthand page. 'Jesus autem transiens' is in thirteen parts, representing Our Lord and his twelve Apostles, each of whom (including Mathias, who replaced Judas Iscariot) is represented by a successive petition of the Creed. The *ut supra* indicates that the round should be repeated, probably thirteen times, and ending with the last voice singing the antiphon 'Jesus autem transiens' (Jesus then going through their midst). The total range is thirteen notes; this love of symbolism, often found in medieval and Renaissance compositions, frequently achieves the status of a secret cypher.

The statutes of Eton College specified the various Masses and Offices which were to be said or sung each day. In addition, the choir was to sing an antiphon each evening before the image of the Virgin. In Lent, the 'Salve regina' was ordained; otherwise (and also on feast days falling within Lent) some other Marian antiphon was to be sung 'in the best manner which they know'. The choir sang from a lectern on which the choirbook (the *Eton Choirbook* measured about 60 × 43cm, with staves of 2cm wide — the *Caius Choirbook* was even larger) was placed in view of the whole choir. In Wilkinson's 'Salve regina' for example, the nine parts are disposed over the two pages of the open book. The boys' parts appear at the top left (*Quatruplex* and *Triplex*) and right (*Medius*). Doubtless the eyesight of the boys, coupled with the fact that they would have rehearsed the piece for longer than the men, dictated that their parts should be at the top of the page, but some choirs may have adopted the procedure of having the boys standing on benches behind the men.

The contents of the *Eton Choirbook* were limited to Marian votive antiphons (such antiphons were not intended to frame the psalms of the Offices, but were composed as separate invocations to the Virgin), together with settings of Magnificats and the Davy Passion; all of this music would presumably have been sung in the same location in the chapel. Another book (or rather, a set of partbooks) would have contained the Masses, and other music would have been distributed in further sets of books. King's College, Eton's sister foundation at Cambridge, had a large library of Masses, antiphons and other music (Harrison, 1958, p. 432) which was presumably similar to the library at Eton. Such are the losses of the sources, that the only large-scale early Mass surviving is by William Pasche in the *Caius Choirbook* (Cambridge, Caius College MS).

Wilkinson's use of cantus firmi is old-fashioned and elaborate. William Cornish 'Junior' (to distinguish him from another of the same name, perhaps his father) was more forward-looking; his surviving works show a more limited

Fig. 23 Choir at Mass (from *Secundus liber tres missas . . .*, printed Attaignant, 1532) Although a continental scene, the choir lectern *in medio chori* is clearly shown. The choir stalls are mostly occupied by lay people.

use of cantus firmus in his antiphons, of which only four are now extant in a performable state. Cornish's 'Ave Maria' and 'Gaude virgo' are four-part music for men, while the 'Salve regina' and 'Stabat mater' are for full choir, *à* 5. The latter work occasionally uses very high notes for trebles (*c'''*), means (*g''*) and tenors (*a'flat*) for dramatic effect, although the compasses in 'Salve regina' are more conventional. The Masses mentioned in the King's College Inventory are lost, but a splendid Magnificat (already quoted on p. 240 survives in the *Caius Choirbook*, which uses the full range of the voices, including a low bass *E flat*.

Cornish's music admirably sums up the early sixteenth-century style. There is a love of virtuosity, of cross rhythms and of long arching melismata, but there is also an integrity of design and climax of which he and Browne are the outstanding exponents. Edmund Turges and Henry Prentyce alone show a comparable development of vocal technique, as is shown in their Magnificats found in the *Caius Choirbook*. This latter MS was written for the collegiate church of St Stephen's, Westminster, and, in common with the slightly earlier *Lambeth Choirbook*, dates from the first quarter of the sixteenth century. The Magnificat by Prentyce is his only surviving composition, but Turges is represented in the *Eton Choirbook* by two settings of 'Gaude flore virginali' (one of them for men). The latter also wrote three no longer extant Magnificats, secular songs found in the *Fayrfax MS*, and a Kyrie and Gloria in the *Ritson MS* (where his name is misspelt 'Sturges'). His Magnificat in the *Caius Choirbook* shows an extravagant liking for ornament and cross-rhythm, traits which are particularly evident in the section 'Quia fecit':

Ex. 121

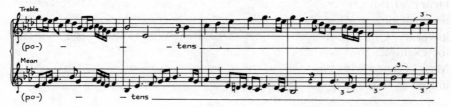

In the Gloria there is a fairly close connection with Cornish's setting, since an elaborate A T B 'sicut erat' is followed by a similarly florid 'et in saecula'. However, the correspondence between the two settings is generally only superficial, Turges' 'Amen' being considerably more extensive, yet achieving little of the brilliance and grandeur of Cornish.

The other major composers found in the *Caius* and *Lambeth Choirbooks* are Fayrfax and Ludford, whose works occupy the greater part of these MSS. Fayrfax was born in 1464 and died in 1521, while Ludford was apparently younger, probably dying in 1556. Both were a good deal more conservative in their vocal demands than composers such as Davy, Wilkinson, Cornish and Turges. Fayrfax, the only major contributor to the *Eton Choirbook* not mentioned hitherto, has several connections with Cambridge, where he gained the degrees of Bachelor, and later Doctor of Music. The Mass and Magnificat entitled 'Regali' were presumably composed for King's College. By 1502 he was organist of St Alban's Abbey, for which he wrote the 'Albanus' Mass: at that date he was paid by Queen Elizabeth of York for an antiphon in honour of the Virgin and St Elizabeth — presumably his magnificent 'Aeterne laudis lilium':

Ex. 122

For his doctorate at Cambridge (he was later honoured also by Oxford) he wrote the Mass 'O quam glorifica' (1504). By the time of the funeral of Henry VII and the coronation of Henry VIII in 1509, Fayrfax's stature was such that he headed the lists of Gentlemen of the Chapel Royal at these ceremonies; and several of his secular works are found in the *Fayrfax MS* and *King Henry VIII's MS*. 'Lauda vivi Alpha et O' ends with a prayer for Henry VIII. It exemplifies one or two traits found in the later Taverner; the resonant phrase 'nosque tuos pios famulos' is echoed musically an octave lower by 'O peccatrix et adjustrix'. This kind of repetitive device is found, for example, in Taverner's 'O Christe Jesu, pastor bone'; and Fayrfax's Mass 'Tecum principium' has a sequential passage of the type much used, indeed over-used, by Taverner:

Ex. 123

This sequential device was much used by Redford in his organ music, where the insistent use of elaborate rhythms is also found. Although generally eschewed by the sedate Fayrfax, the 'O quam glorifica' Mass contains often pointless complexities; these — doubtless due to the Mass being an 'exercise' for the D. Mus. — far exceed the metrical demands made by Cornish and Turges.

Twice Fayrfax links Mass and Magnificat with the same cantus firmus, or by other material. The 'Regali' and 'O bone Jesu' Masses have complementary Magnificats, and the fragmentary antiphons 'Gaude flore virginali' and 'O bone Jesu' also have similar connections.

The 'Regali' Magnificat exemplifies the typical descending figure used in the opening notes of almost every other contemporary Magnificat (but absent in 'O bone Jesu', since it is presumably derived from the antiphon). Here it occurs together with a rising motive, also a cliché in Magnificat settings:

Ex. 124

The 'Albanus' Mass uses an extensive cantus firmus pattern; it is employed forwards and backwards, upside down, and upsidedown backwards. Similar devices were also used, with the same cantus firmus, in the fragmentary 'O Maria [or *Albanus*] Deo grata'.

The connection between the 'O bone Jesu' pieces, however, concerns the borrowing of a section of the antiphon to form the head motive of each of the movements of the Mass, together with the 'Amen' of the antiphon, which is adapted to form the end of the Gloria, Credo and Agnus. The tradition of linking Mass and antiphon appears to begin with Fayrfax, and continues through to Tallis, Sheppard and Tye, all of whom use the same technique — though the latter composers' models, eg. 'Cantate' and 'Euge bone' respectively, are no longer extant. Fayrfax thus appears to have been an influential composer, a bridge between the older composers of the *Eton Choirbook* and those of Taverner's generation. His ingenuity with cantus firmus is matched only by the Mass 'O quam suavis' attributed to John Lloyd. Not only is the tenor of this Mass written in cypher, but even the composer's name is encoded (if the identification by Thurston Dart from the phrase 'Hoc fecit iohannes maris' — *maris* being taken as 'flood' = Flud = Lloyd, is accepted).

Ludford's festal Masses have affinities with those of Fayrfax; those which survive are 'Benedicta' and 'Videte miraculum' *à* 6, 'Christi Virgo' and 'Lapidaverunt' *à* 5. 'Inclina' is imperfect, 'Regnum mundi' and 'Leroy' are fragmentary, and others are lost. A complementary Magnificat 'Benedicta' is extant, and five antiphons exist in varying states of imperfect preservation. The Mass 'Lapidaverunt Stephanum' was clearly written for St Stephen's, Westminster, where he was attached. Ludford is nearly as conservative as his more illustrious contemporary, though his music is occasionally more florid than that of Fayrfax, as in his Mass 'Videte miraculum'. He often sets the complete Creed, which was unusual in the first half of the sixteenth century.

The circumstances surrounding the partial setting of the Creed are curious. A Mass by Dunstable has a 'telescoped' setting of the Creed, in which the words of more than one petition are heard simultaneously, as in a medieval ballade setting. A continental manuscript probably failed to fill in the words of the second part, and an imitator seems to have followed this omission slavishly, thus giving rise to a tradition of Credo omissions from Dufay onwards, and reimported into England in the earliest surviving Masses after Dunstable's time. The 'missing' sections occur between 'Cujus regni non erit finis' and 'Amen', although the text is sometimes resumed earlier, particularly at 'Et expecto' — where a longer omission often commences at 'sedet ad dexteram'. Occasionally a section near the beginning (eg. 'Deum de Deo' until 'vero') is also dropped.

Ludford's Masses generally use the Creed text without any such mutilation, as for example his set of Lady Masses for each day of the week. These Masses exist in four presentation books bearing the arms of Henry VIII and Catherine of Aragon; they cannot be much earlier than 1509, the date of his coronation and marriage, and no later than 1533, the year of their divorce: the Masses therefore probably date from the period 1520–30. From the musical point of view they are on the dull side, but liturgically the Masses are more noteworthy, since many of the variable parts of the Mass, the Propers, are set alongside the invariable Ordinaries. There are three voice parts (the ranges and clefs are for various combinations of voices) and a fourth book has 'squares' and other measured monodies for the *alternatim* parts of the Kyrie, Gloria, Sequence and Credo, and for the whole of the Offertories and Communions. Since only incipits for the words are provided, except in the Kyries, it seems clear that these 'squares' are mostly cantus firmi upon which the organist would improvise. The Kyrie, Alleluia and Sequence were treated *alternatim*; the Offertory and Communion were played by the organ alone, whereas the Sanctus and Agnus were treated entirely vocally. The Masses for Wednesday and Friday include a wholly vocal Gloria and Credo (on which days the Kyrie was perhaps sung with organs *alternatim*), but on other days the organ and voices were heard in alternation. The Office and Grail (the English words for Introit and

Gradual) were seasonal, and were sung to plainchant, as was the Tract — sung instead of the Alleluia on Sundays, Mondays, Wednesdays and Fridays in Lent, and at certain other times.

Ludford's Lady Masses thus offer a unique glimpse into liturgical practice of the period. It is widely known that Felix namque (for the Lady Mass 'Salve') and other Offertories were commonly played by the organ alone; and *alternatim* organ hymns, Masses and so forth are common enough; but the elaborate interplay of vocal and organ polyphony for the weekday Masses (cf. the 'ordering' of the Northumberland Chapel on pp. 234–6) shown in Ludford's cycle is notable. Normally, the organ provided polyphony when the choir was not present: in Ludford's cycle it enriches the weekday services, doubtless those of St Stephen's, Westminster.

Polyphony, both vocal and instrumental, was frequently improvised. The 'squares' of Ludford's Lady Masses are presumably the bass parts of some lost partmusic which in turn became the cantus firmus for improvised polyphony. Similarly, the 'faburden', an improvised bass to a chant, also became used as a cantus firmus; and it was employed in place of the chant itself, in Magnificats, hymns, and the like. The technique of faburden is set out in a sixteenth-century MS:

Ex. 125

It is notable that the earliest liturgical (as opposed to paraliturgical) organa surviving in medieval treatises represent improvised versions of the Te Deum and psalms. Together with hymns these forms continued to be improvised, particularly in procession, until the Reformation. In procession, written-out polyphony would have been perilously difficult to perform. The Te Deum which welcomed Wolsey to St Paul's 'which was solemnlie songen with the King's trumpets and shalmes' was probably of this improvised type of polyphony.

The Salisbury or Sarum Use began as a local usage associated with Saint Osmund, but it had already acquired considerable authority by the beginning of the thirteenth century, when Bishop Poore settled many of its details, both in regard to its ceremonies and its plainchant. Thereafter, it overtook almost all of the other rites which had hitherto maintained their independence, with the exception of those of York and Hereford. In 1542, on the eve of the Reformation, the Convocation of Canterbury ordained that the Breviary of the Sarum Use be adopted throughout its province. Thus, the *Breviarum ad Usum Insignis Ecclesiae Sarum* became *ad Usum Ecclesiae Anglicanae* (this latter title being given to several Sarum Primers, which were devotional books designed for the laity). The chants for the Breviary were found in the *Antiphonale* or Antiphoner containing most of the music for the Offices; those for the Mass were found in the *Gradale* or Gradual. Many other Service books, such as the Processional and Hymnal, were also required to serve the complex ceremonials and plainchants of the Sarum Use.

Wolsey's private chapel and his Cardinal College at Oxford were provided with a large number of 'priest conducts' to sing the plainchants. His statutes of 1519 for the Augustinian canons (cf. Wilkins, 1737, III, p. 686) prohibited their use of polyphony, the less austere role of polyphonists being assigned to lay clerks. This division between chanters and polyphonists seems to have been carried over to his secular chapels — a particularly useful provision in view of the enormous amount of singing which had to be done on any feast day of even minor status.

The polyphony used on Ferias, ordinary Sundays, feasts and 'semidouble' feasts was not extensive and often did not make use of trebles. On 'semi-doubles', for example, only the ninth respond at Matins was allowed to be sung polyphonically, whereas on 'greater doubles' the third, sixth and ninth responds might be set. On 'greater doubles' almost all of the major chants (but normally

Fig. 24 Cardinal College, much as it was in Wolsey's time. (from Loggan, *Oxonia Illustrata*, 1675)

excluding psalms, respond verses and the like) of Matins, Lauds, Prime, Mass, Compline and Evensong (Vespers) could be sung polyphonically. Some idea of the task of Wolsey's choir may be gauged by imagining the members of Cardinal College assembled for Matins and first Mass of Christmas Day (the 'Missa in gallicantu' or 'Mass at cockcrow') in 1527, two years after its foundation. The Cardinal himself (or perhaps his aide, Bishop Longland) officiating at Mass would be assisted by a large number of auxiliaries — the Dean (John Higden, lately President of Magdalen) would be in his stall on the right just inside the choir screen, the Precentor opposite him on the left. The Chancellor and the Treasurer, the Subdean and Succentor came next in order, followed by the other canons in the highest stalls: at the east end the Gospeller (the senior deacon) sat on *Decani* and the Pistler (the subdeacon) opposite. In the second form, in front and lower down, sat the thirteen priest-conducts and the twelve clerk-conducts. In front, on the first form, were the sixteen choristers and probationers, together with the thurifers and taperers, boys whose voices had broken and whose duties now included (besides the waiting in Hall which all the boys had to undertake) the carrying of the thuribles and candles in the ceremonies. Some of these would also be junior scholars of the college.

The choir was in the charge of the *informator choristarum*, John Taverner, whom (by paying a salary lower only than that of the principal canons and professors of the House) Wolsey had persuaded to leave Tattershall two years earlier. Taverner would be at the end of an exacting day, having begun at 5 a.m. with Mary Matins sung by the boys, then an hour later the full choir sang Matins and Prime, followed by Lady Mass. At seven in the morning, the 'Salve regina' was sung, together with the 'Ave Maria' punctuated by bells, and 'Sancte Deus': Taverner set both of the latter antiphons polyphonically. Requiem Mass followed, then at 9 a.m. the choir sang the Mass of the Day. At 3 p.m. the boys sang the Mary Evensong, followed by the full choir singing the main Evensong, doubtless including a Magnificat by Taverner. After this, Compline was sung, and then three polyphonic antiphons, probably 'Gloria tibi trinitas' (of which there is no trace, but which presumably provided the model for his Mass of the same name), 'Mater Christi' and 'O Wilhelme, pastor bone' in honour, respectively, of the Trinity, the Virgin, and William of York, and ending with a prayer for Wolsey himself.

After this wearing day, Taverner (probably looking quite as glum as some miniature portraits suggest) and the choir contemplated yet another long ceremonial as midnight approached. As the bells chimed, the last of the scholars took their places and said Pater noster and Ave Maria to themselves (*privatim*). The whole college waited for Dean Higden to sing 'Domine labia mea' ('O Lord open thou my lips'), to which all responded, continuing with the Versicles and Responses, ending with Alleluia. The Precentor and three other rulers, wearing magnificent copes and bearing their staves of office, took their places on the choir step, and sang the first two words of the antiphon 'Christus natus', which the choir, facing them, repeated. Then the rulers sang the verses of the Invitatory psalm 'Venite', between which the choir interpolated alternately the whole antiphon (after the odd-numbered verses) or the words 'venite adoremus' (after the even-numbered verses). After the Gloria, the opening two words, 'Christus natus', were followed by the entire antiphon sung by rulers and joined by the choir at 'venite' at which point the choir turned inwards.

The two *Decani* rulers then began the hymn 'Christe redemptor', joined, in the second line, by the whole *Decani* side; the second verse (not played on the organ, since the feast was solemn, and probably not sung to polyphony because of the length of the Service) was sung by the whole of *Cantoris* and so on, by sides.

The three nocturns of Matins then commenced. Every nocturn consisted of three psalms, each framed by antiphons, a Versicle and Response, and of three lessons each followed by a responsory, the last often sung polyphonically. As with 'Christus natus', only the first word or so of the first antiphon 'Dominus' was intoned by the Dean (subsequent antiphons were begun by a different singer in descending order of seniority), after which the two rulers of that side began the psalm (the first being 'Quare fremuerunt gentes'). *Decani* continued 'et populi meditati sunt inania' after a pause, closely followed by *Cantoris* singing the next verse, pausing at the half verse, then continuing the verse (closely followed by the third *Decani* verse); and so on throughout the psalm until the end of the Gloria, after which the antiphon began again, now introduced by two *Decani* rulers, ('Dominus . . .') and this time continued by the whole choir '. . . dixit ad me; filius meus es tu ego hodie genuite'. The first words of the second antiphon ('Tamquam sponsus') were immediately intoned by the Succentor, after which the psalm was begun by two *Cantoris* rulers and continued by the whole *Cantoris* side. In this fashion the three psalms of the nocturn, and indeed those of all three nocturns, were sung.

After the third psalm, two surpliced boys, standing on the choir step between the rulers, sang a melisma to 'Tamquam sponsus' to which the Response 'Dominus procedens . . .' was said inaudibly (*secretim*), as was the Pater noster by the officiant and the Dean: the latter resumed the chant, however, at the words 'Et ne nos inducas in temptationem' to which all replied 'sed libera nos a malo'. Meanwhile the most junior clerk had ascended into the pulpitum in the choir-screen, where he requested a blessing from the officiant, and the blessing was duly intoned by the officiant from his stall, to which all responded with 'Amen'. Formerly, particularly at Christmas, the movement to the pulpitum had been marked by a *conductus*, or carol, often ending with 'Jube Domine', but this custom seems to have died out before the sixteenth century.

The junior clerk (on other days it was a chorister) intoned the lesson, ending with the formula 'Haec dicit Dominus convertimini ad me, et salvi eritis'. While he went to the presbytery to ask a blessing of the Cardinal and then returned to his place, there followed a responsory. Usually this, the first respond, was chanted; but at Christmas five boys moved to the altar, removing the black cloaks which they normally wore over their surplices. The word 'Hodie' was intoned from the choir step by two *Cantoris* clerks of the second form (since the responds were begun — in the opposite way to the antiphons — in ascending order of seniority); and the choir continued the chanted respond while the two beginners returned to their stalls. At the verse 'Gloria in excelsis' the boys sang in polyphony from the altar, in imitation of the angels singing 'Peace on earth, to men of goodwill'. A setting of this verse is found in the *Pepys MS* and later settings by Tallis, Sheppard and Taverner also survive, the latter doubtless written for Cardinal College:

Ex. 126

After the verse the boys resumed their places and the next junior reader ascended the pulpitum; meanwhile the second half of the respond was chanted again. The second lesson and responsory followed (during which the altar and choir were censed by the Dean and the Gospeller); then the third lesson and responsory followed, completing the first nocturn of Matins.

The second nocturn (three psalms with their antiphons intoned by beginners in descending rank, followed by lessons and responds intoned in ascending rank) continued after the same fashion; and the third nocturn ensued. After Wolsey himself, seated on his throne, had read a homily by the Venerable Bede, the ninth respond, 'Verbum caro' was chanted.

While the last section of this respond was being sung, the Gospeller would ascend the pulpitum to announce (after 'Dominus tecum: *Et cum spiritu tuo*') the beginning of the Gospel according to St Matthew. The Response 'Gloria tibi Domine' having been sung, he recited the genealogy of Christ, Wolsey intoned the Te Deum from his throne, and then moved to take part in the censing during its singing — accompanied by the ringing of the tower bells. At Cardinal College, the Te Deum may have been sung to faburden or possibly performed *alternatim* to an organ setting such as Blitheman's. Towards the end of the Te Deum, at 'per singulos dies', the bells began to be 'rung down', producing a clashing sound until the end of the hymn.

As the bells ceased, marking the end of Matins, Mass commenced at once. The four rulers intoned the Office (ie. the Introit) immediately after the Te Deum had ended: meanwhile, the celebrant and his servers retired to vest themselves in chasubles and dalmatics for the Mass; since Matins and Mass were sung together no preparatory prayers intervened. The Mass Office continued after the word 'Dominus' with the choir joining in with the rest of the antiphon 'dixit ad me filius meus es tu ego hodie genuite'. The rulers began the psalm 'Quare tremuerunt', with the choir joining in at the half-verse 'et populi . . .'. The choir repeated the antiphon 'Dominus dixit . . .' and the rulers and choir sang 'Gloria patri', followed again by the antiphon.

At the Gloria of the Office the taperers led the procession from the vestry, followed by the subdeacons (of which the senior was the Pistler or Epistle reader), the deacons (of which the principal was the Gospeller), and finally the celebrant. At the altar step the celebrant, flanked by the Gospeller on the right and the Pistler on the left, said the Pater noster *secretim*, audibly ending 'Et ne nos inducas in temptationem', to which his assistants replied 'Sed libera nos a malo'. After a Versicle and Response the celebrant said his confession, absolved by the assistants, to which the celebrant replied 'Amen': the assistants' confession followed in like manner, after which a general absolution was pronounced by the celebrant. After further Versicles and Responses, the celebrant said a silent prayer, rising to kiss his assistants and moving to the top of the altar steps. All took up their stations, the celebrant in the centre, the Gospeller one step down on the right, the Pistler two steps down on the left. The taperers put down their candles on the altar step. Bowing and joining his hands (in this he was imitated by the Gospeller and the deacons behind him), the celebrant said the prayer 'Aufer a nobis' and then stood upright (the Pistler adjusting his chasuble), kissed the altar cloth and said 'In nomine Patris . . .' with the sign of the cross.

The Office having ended, one of the taperers brought the bread, wine and water, the other bringing the basin and towel. The Gospeller took incense and, saying 'Benedicite' to the celebrant, had the incense blessed by him. The Gospeller placed the incense in the thurible, after which he took it from the thurifer and gave it to the celebrant, who censed the altar, and then was himself censed by the Gospeller. The celebrant kissed the Epistle book, after which the priests took their seats at the sedilia. Meanwhile, the troped Kyrie 'Deus creator' had been commenced by the four rulers, the choir joining in at 'tu theos ymon', probably alternating *Decani* and *Cantoris*, ending the last petition Full.

When the Kyrie was finished, the celebrant moved to mid-altar, the Pistler and Gospeller now taking up different positions. The precentor followed him to give him the note for the Gloria; having intoned this, he and his assistants moved back to the sedilia and said the text *privatim*. The choir, bowing (they also bowed at 'adoramus', 'suspice', and 'Jesu'), continued the Gloria. The variable parts of the Mass (the troped Kyrie, the Office, Grail, Offertory and Communion), although allowed to be sung to polyphony were usually chanted in a long Service; but the Gloria and other Ordinaries of the Mass would have been sung to partmusic — possibly that of Taverner's 'Gloria tibi trinitas', which has pride of place in a set of partbooks (now the *Forrest-Heyther* partbooks) copied at Cardinal College:

Ex. 127

At 'In gloria dei patris', the choir crossed themselves; then, at the end of the Gloria, the celebrant turned to the altar and, crossing himself, sang the Collect for the day, preceded by the Versicle and Response: Dominus vobiscum *Et cum spiritu tuo*. Before the choir sang 'Amen' to the Collect and sat down, two clerks of the second form ascended to the pulpitum and sang the troped Lesson peculiar to Christmas Day, 'Laudes deo dicamus', in which Isaiah's prophecies are explained. Settings for this exist by Johnson (for mean and alto, possibly used at Cardinal College) and Sheppard (for two altos): in both the singers perform sometimes in two parts, but elsewhere they chant alternate sections, representing the words of the prophet and its interpretation. Toward the end of the 'Laudes' the Pistler was escorted down the choir to the pulpitum, where he took over to intone the Epistle. This ended, clerks of the second form intoned the Grail (Gradual) 'Tecum principium', which was taken up by the choir. The three clerks sang the verse 'Dixit dominus' until the final word of the verse, at which they were joined by the choir. Meanwhile three coped clergy from the highest form, having ascended into the pulpitum, began Alleluia; their first phrase was repeated by the choir, who added a long melisma called the neuma. The soloists intoned 'Dominus dixit', taken up by the choir at the last word 'genuite', after which the clergy began the Alleluia again but without the neuma being sung: instead the soloists returned to the choir, bowed and went to the vestry to remove their copes, after which they returned to their places. To the sound of bells the rulers, meanwhile, began the Sequence 'Nato canunt omnia', taken up by the duty side (*Decani*) and alternating thereafter with *Cantoris* until the last verse, sung Full.

This elaborate ritual continued through the Gospel, Creed, Offertory, Sursum Corda and Sanctus, most of which was chanted; for only the Creed and Sanctus would have been polyphonic. If, as is possible, the setting was Taverner's 'Gloria tibi trinitas', the Benedictus section of the Sanctus would have begun with the famous prototype of what was to set the fashion for the instrumental In Nomine:

Ex. 128

The Pater noster and the polyphonic Agnus Dei followed, after which the Communion was chanted. The complex ceremonial of the Mass came to an end only when the Cardinal chanted the Postcommunion; then after the usual Versicle and Response the Gospeller sang the 'Ite missa est' for the day to which all replied 'Deo gratias'.

Ex. 129

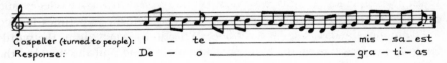

After a prayer, the Cardinal and his assistants and servers bowed to the altar and recessed to the vestry; the college thereupon retired to bed for the few hours which intervened before the 'Missa in aurora'. This brief survey of the college day gives some impression of the task confronting the choir: the pressures upon its time also demonstrate that the chants could hardly have been sung languidly, as is sometimes maintained; hence the provision that chanting was faster on major feast days.

Prior to his appointment to Cardinal College, Taverner was a clerk at Tattershall in Lincolnshire. The 'O Michael' Mass (which betrays a certain lack of polish and contains many imperfections) probably dates from these earlier years, together with the more mature Mass 'Corona Spinea'. His

Oxford works are doubtless the 'Mater Christi', 'Gloria tibi' and 'Sancti Wilhelmi Devotio' Masses. This latter is entitled 'Small Devotion' in the source, but it is based on what survives as the antiphon 'O Christe Jesu, pastor bone'. This text, however, is clearly a clumsy adaption of 'O Wilhelme pastor bone', the name and the prayer for the founder being expunged when Wolsey was disgraced. The original words, as Harrison pointed out, are an antiphon to St William (a predecessor of Wolsey in the See of York), 'Small Devotion' being a scribal misreading of 'S. Will Devotio' (Harrison, 1958, p. 341).

Taverner's 'Mean' Mass (ie. for a choir without trebles) is a ferial Mass, on a smaller scale than those already mentioned, as is his 'Plainsong' (ie. homophonic) Mass; both of these probably date from his return to Lincolnshire. His other church music, dating from various periods, includes Kyries, Propers, votive antiphons, three Magnificats and settings of various responds, together with the St Nicholas prose 'Sospitati dedit'. The Te Deum ascribed to him is more likely to be by Sheppard or some similar composer. An instrumental piece 'Quemadmodum' and one or two fragmentary songs are all that survive of Taverner's secular music.

The brilliance of Cardinal College was short-lived; its sky darkened first in 1528, when tremors of reformism were felt. Many of its canons had been attracted from Cambridge (though Wolsey had failed to secure Cranmer, Walter Haddon and Mathew Parker) and were of a humanistic and reformist persuasion. Illegal books were discovered at the college, and Taverner himself was involved in the incident. Though ending in tragedy for some of his colleagues, Taverner escaped the stake, being, as the Dean said 'unlearned, and not to be regarded'. This local storm raged and died down within the year, but in 1529, Wolsey's failure to bring about the king's divorce from Catherine of Aragon had more serious consequences, for Wolsey's downfall brought down everything connected with him, including his college.

The higher the tree, the harder it falls. Wolsey, by setting himself up as the greatest person next to the king, had aroused widespread enmity. In life, few besides Skelton had dared to rail against him, but at his death many songs and ballads were sung, gleefully celebrating the demise of the once proud prelate. A weariness of body and spirit overcame him, and he died in bed in Leicester, sparing himself what undoubtedly would have been a more public death in London. With his disgrace, the great college which he cherished was run down. Its vestments, plate, music and other articles were confiscated by the king. The quantity of vestments was probably enormous — Magdalen, for instance, boasted more than a hundred chasubles and a hundred and fifty copes. Taverner returned to Lincolnshire, fully expecting that the college would be destroyed. It narrowly escaped this fate however, being instead refounded by Henry VIII as Christ Church, the college chapel becoming the cathedral of the new diocese of Oxford.

The statute under which Wolsey was impeached was that of *praemunire*, of setting his authority over that of the crown. Ironically, by making himself the focus of papal authority in England, and while flaunting the power of a legate *a latere* and the pomp of the Cardinal, he served Henry's purpose well — his doings ensured that the Act of Royal Supremacy would be regarded by most of the clergy and laity alike as preferable to what they had seen as an odious abuse of ecclesiastical power.

Henry had already begun the dissolution of the monasteries: this rapacious work was continued with increasing zeal by Thomas Cromwell and his henchmen, one of whom was Taverner, now living in Boston. Rood lofts were burned, and images of the Saints were smashed. Many ancient foundations were soon in ruins and their musicians dispossessed. Thomas Tallis was a victim of the dissolution of Waltham Abbey in 1540. Yet while this aspect of the Reformation was under way, earlier events at Cardinal College were echoed in Windsor, where John Merbecke was imprisoned in 1534, for 'the copiying out of a worke, made by the greate Clerke Master Jhon Calvin, . . .'. This, together with his own 'greate work' (a concordance in English) was confiscated and destroyed. In July of that year Merbecke was tried for heresy and condemned to be burned at the stake, a penalty which his three co-defendants shortly suffered — Merbecke alone escaping through the intervention of Gardiner. The zealous Merbecke nonetheless gave up composition, working for the reformist cause. Of his few surviving works, the Mass 'Per arma justitia' has some fine passages; the antiphons 'Ave Dei patris' and 'Domine Jesu Christe' show several signs of modernity, notably in their close-knit imitation.

Osbert Parsley's 'Conserva me' is also worthy of note, as are his Lamentations. Unfortunately, the latter are constructed with the plainchant as a cantus firmus in the top part and, since Parsley was unable entirely to free the polyphony from the restrictions of the chant, there are several dull passages as a result. The irreverent triple time figure at *falsa et stulta* is amusing, however and the homophony at *sibilaverunt* is a felicitous touch, emphasizing the hissing of the mocking enemy.

Parsley and Merbecke are overshadowed, however, by Hugh Aston, whom Wolsey had first approached for the post at Cardinal College eventually filled by Taverner. Aston's Masses (see also p. 111) 'Videte manus meas' and 'Te Deum' (founded on his antiphon 'Te matrem dei laudamus') are powerful works prefiguring the vigour of Sheppard's style, but his antiphons 'Gaude virgo mater Christi' and 'Ave Maria' appear to be his most mature works. These compositions evince signs of modernity in their technique and bridge the gap between the votive antiphons of the *Eton Choirbook* and those of the Marian period by composers such as William Mundy. The spirit of change was in the wind, however, and texts increasingly emphasized the worship of Jesus rather than the veneration of Mary and the Saints.

Votive antiphons to Mary are nonetheless abundant in the *Peterhouse* partbooks, the last great manuscript set of the pre-Reformation years, where Jesus antiphons are also prominent. According to Nick Sandon (1977), these books (Cambridge, Peterhouse 471–4 *olim* 40, 41, 31 and 32) were copied between 1539 and 1541, at about the same time as the later compositions found in the *Forrest-Heyther* partbooks. The Peterhouse set contains music by Ludford, Merbecke, Aston, Taverner and Tallis. These composers are featured alongside earlier pieces by Richard Pygott, William Pasche and Fayrfax and among lesser composers of the later generation such as Avery Burton, Thomas Appleby, Richard Bramston, Thomas Wright and others. Perhaps the most impressive works by a lesser composer are the Compline antiphons to the Nunc Dimittis, 'O rex gloriose' by John Mason, together with other compositions by the same composer for men's voices. Unfortunately, the Peterhouse set lacks the tenor book, although this part can often be restored without too much difficulty. More seriously, however, the treble book is also missing for several of Taverner's works in this collection, including the 'Sub tuum praesidium' (apparently a 'plague' antiphon) 'Sancte Deus' and 'Ave Maria', all presumably composed for Cardinal College, with which the MS clearly had some connection. Taverner's 'Sancte Deus' and 'Ave Maria' are copied into the MS as though they were a continuous piece. Since it was only in 1532 that the new Statutes specified this order (Wolsey's order put the 'Ave Maria' first), the source from which they derive could not have been earlier. The Oxford connection is, however, even stronger in regard to Appleby, Mason and several other composers who figure in the books. Since the aforementioned were connected with Magdalen College around 1540, it seems that a considerable part of this repertory represents that of Magdalen immediately prior to the appointment of John Sheppard as *informator*.

Of the considerable number of works of the later layer of these partbooks, the most notable are a Magnificat by Appleby, the 'Mean' Mass by Taverner and one of a similar nature by Tye. Unlike the Mass 'O bone Jesu' by Fayrfax, and indeed most of the Masses in the *Peterhouse* partbooks, those by Tye and Taverner are not apparently derived from a pre-existing antiphon or cantus firmus. The imitation technique of these works is also more thorough-going and up to date, as is evident in the Magnificat settings of Appleby and Darke, where the traditional faburden cantus firmus and several other conventions hitherto observed in Magnificat settings are abandoned.

In common with many works in the *Peterhouse* partbooks, Alwood's Mass 'Praise him praiseworthy' in the *Forrest-Heyther* partbooks also marks a movement towards greater clarity of texture, allied with a more systematic use of imitation, and moving away from the dense, more luxuriant style of Fayrfax and Ludford. This change is manifest in Aston, Merbecke and Taverner's later works. The sparer lines are particularly evident in the music of Tye and of his son-in-law Robert White, and especially notable in the later works of Tallis and in the music of John Sheppard. These four were the most considerable composers active during the closing years of Henry's reign.

The senior, Thomas Tallis, was probably born in about 1505 since he called himself 'verie aged' in 1577. He was organist of Dover Priory in 1531, and in 1536 was at St Mary-at-Hill near Billingsgate, after which he moved to Waltham. His large-scale antiphons 'Ave Dei patris', 'Ave rosa sine spina', 'Salve intemerata' and 'Sancte Deus' probably date from these years, together with the Mass 'Salve intemerata', and the respond 'In pace'.

At the dissolution of Waltham Abbey in 1540, Tallis moved to Canterbury (for which the *Peterhouse MSS* may have been compiled) and, at about the same time, became a Gentleman of the Chapel Royal. Several of Sheppard's works probably also date from about this time, particularly after 1543, when he was *informator* at Magdalen. He may well have written the 'Cantate' Mass, one of the finest of all sixteenth-century Masses, for Magdalen, since it appears in the *Forrest-Heyther* partbooks. The long antiphon 'Gaude virgo christifera' probably dates from this time, together with a large-scale Magnificat (much of it lost), and various other works, including a few office responds.

'Gaude virgo' unfortunately survives in an imperfectly preserved source, although the missing treble can be supplied without too much difficulty. The third word in the source is *christipera*, which could either be a mistake for *christipara* (bearing Christ in the womb) or *christiphera* (Christ-carrying). Since Sheppard was not above misaccenting his texts, *christipára* is possible; but the rhythm of his setting favours *christífera*. Tallis' 'Gaude gloriosa', a similarly large-scale antiphon, appears to date from roughly the same time.

Tallis and Sheppard's works demonstrate the rise and eventual culmination of office polyphony. Earlier, several composers had set the respond 'Dum transisset' for Easter, and many of them used the same stock figure for the beginning (see Hofman, 1973), a tradition not unlike that of the common opening found in Magnificat settings. Taverner's setting appears to have initiated the vogue, but another version (copied by Baldwin as a second setting purporting to be by Taverner) is unlikely to be authentic. The sections of the respond text are joined together in such a way that the insertion of the verses is impossible, as in Tallis' 'In jejunio'. The work in question is thus of later date, composed at the time when the so-called 'respond-motet' had come into vogue after the demise of the Sarum Rite.

It is clear from the surviving sources that although polyphony was allowed for the hymns and responds of the Office Hours, few of these were normally sung polyphonically. The main exceptions were 'Gloria in excelsis' (ie. 'Hodie nobis'), 'Audivi', 'In pace', 'Gloria laus', and 'Dum transisset'. The first three are set in such a way that polyphony replaced the soloists' chant, but the newer-style responds such as 'Dum transisset' treated the polyphonists as though they were the choir. The different styles of settings are exemplified in Sheppard's 'In manus tuas' settings, one of which is on the old patterns, while the other two, marked 'corus', are in the newer style:

Plainchant originally sung:

Soli	Chorus	Soli	Chorus
In manus tuas	Domine: Commendo spiritum meum	Redemisti . . .	Commendo spiritum meum

Sheppard's 1st setting:

Polyphony	Chant	Polyphony	Chant

Sheppard's 'Corus' settings:

Chant	Polyphony	Chant	Polyphony? or chorus Chant

Apart from 'Gloria in Excelsis', 'In pace' and 'Audivi', Sheppard's responds generally follow the 'corus' pattern. In the responds for Evensong (or 'Vespers', an equivalent but a much shorter Service than Matins), and for the last respond of each nocturn at Matins, a Gloria Patri was sung. Sheppard's 'Reges Tharsis', for example, had the following pattern:

Soli (Chant)	Polyphony
Reges Tharsis (incipit only)	Et insulae . . . Reges Arabum . . . Domino deo . . .
Et adorabunt . . .	Reges Arabum . . . Domino deo . . .
Gloria patri . . .	Domino deo . . .

As may be seen, the polyphony became shorter after each chanted verse, resulting in a musical form which resembled a modified rondo. The vigour which Sheppard imparted to responds such as 'Reges Tharsis' or 'Verbum caro' (in which the trebles end on a high three-part chord of B flat) is only partly due to the presence of treble voices — the hymn 'Jesu salvator saeculi, redemtis', without trebles, is equally powerful, as are the settings for men of 'Spiritus sanctus' and 'Laudem dicite'. The sublimity of the Compline responds 'In pace' and 'In manus tuas', however, are captured again in the long respond, with prose, for Candlemas — 'Gaude, gaude, gaude, maria virgo'. Tallis' compositions in these genres are less notable; his 'In pace' compares unfavourably with Sheppard's, and the settings of 'Te lucis ante terminum' are merely workaday music. Nonetheless, Sheppard was not above writing dull music, as for example some of the rambling and often crude passages of 'Media vita'. This work, which nonetheless has fine moments, was probably composed at Magdalen as a pair to the 'O rex gloriose' by his predecessor Mason (both pieces being Lenten antiphons to Nunc Dimittis). Yet banal works are rare amongst Sheppard's large volume of compositions. The Paschal Kyrie with its Gradual 'Haec dies', or 'Filiae Hierusalem' are much more typical; and nothing can compare with the etherial quality of his two 'Libera nos' settings.

Compline was an important Office at Magdalen, as its many polyphonic settings show; the college statutes prescribed that 'Libera nos' with the Compline versicles beginning 'Benedicamus patrem' should be recited on rising, and before lying down to sleep. Sheppard's settings of 'Libera nos' may have been composed for solemn occasions such as the obit of the founder, William of Wayneflete. The delicate filigree of the six upper voices, woven about the long note cantus firmus in the bass (the second setting being on a faburden), evokes a votive fervour unequalled in any other sixteenth-century work. Had Sheppard written nothing else, the 'Libera nos' settings would remain objects of wonderment:

Ex. 130

Different but no less fervent emotional heights were later scaled by Tallis, writing in the newer style which produced his 'Absterge domine', 'O nata lux' and 'In jejunio'. Because much of Sheppard's considerable surviving output (next to Byrd, he was by far the most prolific Tudor composer) embraced only the mid-century style, critics have pointed to his lack of works in the Elizabethan manner, and judged Tallis to be the more versatile composer. Yet Sheppard was not alive to give witness to his prowess in the new style: he can hardly be judged *in absentia*. When like is compared with like, there is little doubt that Sheppard is an Olympian figure of mid sixteenth-century polyphony. That much of his music has lain so long in need of restitution (due to the greater part of it languishing in imperfect sources) was unfortunate; but the availability of all his music in modern editions will enable him to take his rightful place as one of the brightest stars in an already brilliant age. Certainly the 'Cantate' Mass, probably written somewhat later than Taverner's 'Gloria tibi trinitias', is a commanding monument to his genius. As with Taverner's Mass, a cantus firmus is used (though not as insistently, nor is it clear what kind of cantus firmus is involved), and other material from what must be presumed to be a lost work is employed. Of the many remarkable passages in the Mass it is difficult to single out one above all; but the following excerpt gives something of its essence:

Ex. 131

(Sheppard, 'Cantate' Mass : Benedictus)

Sheppard's other Masses are not on the same grandiose scale. The 'Frences Mass' was clearly written in response to some variety of challenge from abroad; it has much in common with similar 'Mean' Masses of Tye and Taverner, melodically and rhythmically, including the exaggerated episodes of triple time. The high clefs of the source of this Mass are clearly wrong — downward transposition would result in wholly untypical voice-ranges. The clefs appear to be a clumsy attempt by the scribe to adapt a Mass for M A T B (normal transposition) for men: the same scribe's adaption of Taverner's 'Dum transisset' from five to four voices is far more successful.

Unlike Taverner's and Tallis' similar Masses, Sheppard's 'Plainsong' Mass sets the text for *alternatim* singing, and includes the Kyrie. None of these 'Plainsong' Masses have much to commend them, apart from a ferial brevity. The same must be said for the Mass 'Be not afraid' for men's voices, which is a disappointing work, and its crudity, when compared with the polish of the four-part Magnificat for men, does not show Sheppard in his best light — set against the 'Cantate' Mass it seems an inexplicable aberration.

Sheppard's other Mass, the 'Western wind', is on a higher level. It is entirely based on a secular cantus firmus which is heard repeatedly throughout, as in similar Masses by Taverner and Tye. Tye's is the least accomplished, whereas Taverner's suffers, in common with many of his other Masses, from a sixteenth-century mannerism which later beset Giovanni Gabrieli and Henry Purcell. Here, the insertion of triple time passages becomes a mere quirk, and is often wearisome; the 'dona nobis pacem' section which brings this Mass to a curiously unsatisfactory close is particularly unfortunate. Sheppard's slavish imitation of this device in each movement, with attendant mis-accentuations, is equally maladroit.

The song on which the composers based their settings is found in a variant version in BL Roy. App. 58. As was noted earlier, the songs found in this source are often courtly transformations of popular tunes: the version used by Taverner may well have been another transformation — it has the extra line characteristic of a carol adaption, perhaps by Taverner himself. The likelihood is that the three Masses were written after Taverner had left Oxford, and while Tye and Sheppard were at the Chapel Royal. The cantus firmus may have been chosen to demonstrate that English composers were as capable of writing a Mass enshrining a secular song as their continental colleagues. Or an obscure theological point may have been at issue, it is certainly odd that the only English cantus firmus Masses on a secular song should be associated with a mildly salacious text:

> Westron wynde when wyll thou blow
> The smalle rayne down can rayne
> Cryst yf my love were in my armys
> And I yn my bed agayne.

So runs the text of Roy. App. 58, and despite the fact that the words of the version used in these Masses clearly differed, the use of the tune would doubtless have struck an English congregation as somewhat incongruous. Perhaps this was the intention — to show up the oddity of the continental practice of using secular cantus firmus.

Tye's other Masses include a 'Mean' Mass (one of the better settings in this genre) and the highly original 'Euge bone', where again a lost antiphon presumably supplied the model. This pairing of antiphon and Mass (often mistakenly dubbed a 'parody' Mass) is probably the last of a long line of such pairings. The remarkable achievement of this work is the compromise between the expansive style of the festal Mass and the pithiness of the smaller scale Mass. There are telling uses of homophony at the beginning of the Sanctus, and at the penultimate Agnus Dei (for some reason he adds an extra petition to this movement), and Tye does not find it necessary to make the latter movements as long as the Creed: his contrasted use of expansive treble gimels and chordal passages compare favourably with Taverner's tendency towards verbosity:

Ex. 132

Paul Doe (*EECM*, 24) has suggested that the 'Euge bone' Mass was composed for Edward VI, since some of its material is related to his setting of the prayer 'Quaesumus omnipotens' including the phrase 'famulos tuos', which would be appropriate to the members of the Protectorate.

Tye had many associations with the royal family. As the future Edward VI's tutor he was represented in a play dating from 1605 — in which the young prince is admonished by Tye and subjected to a beating by proxy (the brunt of which was borne by another youth). Still active in Elizabeth's reign, Tye sometimes played organ music for the Queen 'which contained much music, but little delight to the ear; she would send the verger to tell him he played out of tune: whereupon he sent word that her ears were out of tune'. This, if we are to trust Anthony à Wood, was the 'peevish and humoursome man' of his later days.

Besides his three surviving Masses, Tye's 'Peccavimus' *à* 7 is his most considerable piece, and stands out as one of the best of the late votive antiphons. His 'Ad te clamamus' is probably not a partial setting of the 'Salve regina', but an anthem in which the opening petition was deliberately omitted, and thus dates from the last years of Henry's reign, when the exaggerated veneration of Mary, which had gathered impetus in the Middle Ages, was curtailed. It is notable that his other (fragmentary) votive antiphons are in honour of Christ — 'Ave caput Christi', 'Te Deum' and 'Sub tuam protectionem'. His two large-scale Magnificats, alas, are also fragmentary.

Tye's son-in-law Robert White probably composed mostly after the Reformation, although 'Tota pulchra es', 'Regina coeli', together with his

Magnificat and one or two psalms, may have been composed before Edward's accession. Sheppard, Tallis, Tye and White were to carry the flame of composition across the uncertain terrain of Edwardian years, over the turbulent waters of Mary's reign of terror, and into the haven of the Elizabethan compromise. Ironically, it was the immoderate King Henry who had kept the church together in a spirit of moderation, and fostered the gradual reform of its liturgy and music. Thus composition flourished, and Tallis, Sheppard and Tye wrote much of their best music; but the death of the old king left a political and spiritual vacuum which was to be filled with winds from abroad, and which all but extinguished the music of the church during Edward's unhappy reign.

CHAPTER 10

A Playn and Distincte Note

The forces which came together to cause the Reformation of the English church are complex and widely misunderstood. The most common mis-apprehension is that Henry seceded from Rome merely because of his amatory intrigues. Although the question of divorce certainly precipitated matters, the root cause of the conflict was part political and part religious. According to the fashions of the time, Henry's love-life was not particularly scandalous, and was irrelevant to the question of divorce; after all, his equally amorous sister, Queen Margaret of Scotland, had her marriage dissolved in 1527 — on grounds which seemed flimsy even to Henry. The need to produce a legitimate male heir was a more serious matter: the memory of the Wars of the Roses was still fresh, and Henry, determined not to weaken the Tudor succession which his father had so carefully established, thus sought divorce. Nonetheless, it was the fact that Catherine of Aragon was related to the Holy Roman Emperor, and that Spanish and other interests were not well served by the proposed divorce, that lead to the expected annullment being witheld by the Pope. That a foreign prince, whether temporal or spiritual, should have dominion over the succession to the English throne was a wholly unacceptable intrusion upon Tudor sovereignty; Henry's secession was thus primarily a political event. *heir*

Far from being a Protestant, Henry had been given the title *fidei defensor* by the Pope, and would have no truck with what he considered to be a heretical doctrine. Yet the power of church over state was, nevertheless, something which had to be curtailed, a process already begun by the dissolution of the monasteries. Following the failure of Wolsey to secure the divorce in 1529, Henry summoned the Reformation parliament, which passed various bills to weaken papal authority, culminating in the Act of Supremacy of 1534. In spite of the pious intransigence of Thomas More and

John Fisher which cost them their lives, the majority of the clergy had been sickened by the abuse, particularly by Wolsey, of ecclesiastical power. Thus, the reform of the Breviary in 1536 (which deleted references to the Pope) was welcomed, as was the Act of Ten Articles concerning the observance of the Mass.

At the same time, however, in response to a request in 1534 for an authorized English version of the Bible, Coverdale's Bible was ordered to be set up in every church. This was a momentous event: there had been a long battle for a vernacular version of the scriptures, bitterly resisted by the dogmatists who feared the undermining of their authority. Wolsey had written to the Pope warning of the dangers of a vernacular Bible: the mysteries of religion, he said, must be kept in the hands of the priesthood. Even Luther (though speaking of the vanity of authorship) was moved to echo Callimachus in saying that 'a multitude of books is a great evil'.

The fourteenth-century Wycliffite version of the Bible was a hopelessly literal rendering of the Latin, on which Purvey and others greatly improved; all were declared heretical. In the early years of the sixteenth century, Tyndale worked upon a substantial revision, writing a tract in 1538 upon the translation of scripture. This was roundly contemned by Thomas More, whose negative attitudes as Chancellor had by now earned him the name of Thomas the Cancellor. More's *The Confutacion of Tyndales aunswere* . . . (1538) took Tyndale to task for many footling matters, one of which was the misuse of 'no' for 'nay' (at that time the latter was the correct denial where an affirmative was expected) in the famous passage in the first chapter of St John — 'Arte thou a prophete?' And he aunswered; 'no'. Unfortunately More himself mixed up the two words, and the criticism thus rebounded upon himself.

Coverdale's Bible was considerably indebted to Tyndale's work. Although it was authorized in 1536, it was only in 1543 that it was appointed to be used in the Services, after Te Deum and Magnificat. Meanwhile, the Act of Six Articles of 1539 asserted Catholic doctrine in England and promised the stake for heretics. This was in reaction to the spectre of Lutheranism, with which Henry had had some dealings in 1538: these were born of political expedience, but abandoned soon after, Henry contenting himself with the abolition of superfluous feasts and a purge against idolatry. By 1542, many of the old monastic houses dissolved by Henry VIII had been refounded as new cathedrals; but only in 1544 did the first major liturgical reform come to pass. Primers in English had been much used by the laity and clergy for private devotion, although not for use in public services. The first public vernacular liturgical book appeared in 1544, when Cranmer's English Litany, the fruit of much labour, was published. The King desired that the people should be instructed in its uses so that it might be 'sung with such reverence and devotion, as appertaineth' since formerly they 'used to come very slackly to the procession'. (Cox, 1846, p. 494) The Procession, or Litany, was particularly appropriate for times of war: the struggles with Scotland and France caused Henry to ordain its use throughout the realm. In the Litany Cranmer set it 'as nere as may be, for every sillable a note; so that it may be song distinctly and devoutly'. But as le Huray has pointed out (1967, p. 6), this letter to Henry (*State Papers of Henry VIII*, I, pp. 760–1) concerned only monody: the interpretation that Cranmer was referring to polyphony, or that his private views amounted to an edict, is wholly false.

In 1547 the pace of change accelerated. Henry's death in January was quickly followed by injunctions in August, made in the name of Edward VI who was only a minor. A weak and vacillating Cranmer could not stem the tide of the extremists. By 1548 many Services were in English, and the observation of special ceremonies for Candlemas, Ash Wednesday, Palm Sunday and Good Friday was outlawed. In 1549 the Act of Uniformity promulgated the new English Prayer Book.

Fig. 25 Extract from Merbecke, *booke of Common praier noted*, 1550. Four types of note values, including the 'strene' and dotted note, are used.

Fortunately, Cranmer had been working on a revised Breviary (which owed much to the Spaniard Cardinal Quiñones' Breviary) as well as an

English translation of the Mass and Offices; so his versions were available to the 'certain bishops and notable learned men of this realm' (cf. Procter and Frere, 1902, p. 46) who sat with Cranmer to draw up the new rites. The work of this committee is obscure, since the 1666 Fire of London destroyed the records of Convocation; but it is fairly clear that the splendid prose of the Collects, and many other fine passages to be found in the Prayer Book, were due to Cranmer. The new Services, in Cranmer's mind, were nothing more than simplified English versions of the old rites. The rebels of the west country claimed that the English Service was 'like a Christmasse play': in reply, Edward asserted that the new Service was 'none other but the olde. The selfe same wordes in Englishe which were in Latine, saving a fewe things taken out.' (cf. Fox, 1580, p. 1305–6)

Cranmer's Matins was a curtailed version of the old Matins and Lauds, while Evensong consisted of the Offices of Evensong (Vespers) and Compline run together. The Mass ('the Supper of the Lorde and the Holy Communion commonly called the Masse') was much simplified, by omitting the Grail (Gradual) and Alleluia, providing a selection of offertory sentences in place of the old Offertory, and making similar provisions for the Communion. Other alterations included the restoration of the *epiklesis* and the forbidding of the elevation (a medieval invention), both of which were important reversions towards the liturgy of the early church, as was the communion in both kinds (the wine had been withheld from the laity in the Middle Ages). Extra-biblical texts were rigorously pruned to a minimum throughout the Mass and Offices of the new rites.

Cranmer's Prayer Book was thus a triumph of compromise, preserving the essentials of the Mass, Offices and other Services within one book, while excluding many of the medieval accretions which had made the liturgy both cumbersome and overgrown with extra-biblical dogmata. He picked a careful path between conservatism of the one extreme and the fanatical reformist zeal of the other: he allowed vestments and liturgical practices to be 'used or left as every man's devocion serveth without blame.' Although one or two of his translations are paler than his Latin originals, and though some of his revisions were ill-advised, the majestic language of Cranmer's First Prayer Book, and its careful refinement of the liturgy are models which, alas, have not been heeded by the liturgical reformists of the present day. The new vernacular Services of our own times — be they Anglican or Roman — contrast sharply with Cranmer's, being both muddle-headed liturgically and platitudinous stylistically. The majesty and mystery with which Cranmer imbued his Services, to help uplift the people toward the eternal have been banished; the misguided efforts to bring God down to earth in contemporary dress have simply made him disappear into the crowd.

The influences of moderation were as unheeded in the sixteenth century as they are now. The extremists (notably Bishops Holgate and Ridley) were carried by the tide of despotism and anarchy which now flowed apace under the villainous 'Protector' Northumberland. Bells and organs were melted down and the riches of churches were pillaged. The universities also suffered. The damage done by Henry's dissolution was meagre in comparison with the appalling destruction and plunder of the Protectorate: the Edward VI schools founded in his name were financed by blood money. Countless chantries had already been dissolved; Newark, Tattershall, Ottery St Mary and many other famous choirs had been disbanded. The remainder (including the Royal Peculiars of Fotheringay and St Stephen's, Westminster) were quickly suppressed in 1547, under the Chantries Act.

The desolation of the churches was matched by the ravaging of the liturgy. Martin Bucer, who had been installed at Cambridge in the Chair of Divinity and could hardly speak a word of English, was critical of Cranmer's Prayer Book. So was his opposite number at Oxford, Peter Martyr (an Italian). Calvin (the 'Geneva Pope') added to the clamour. Thus, a second Prayer Book was foisted upon the country in 1552 by the bigots, in which the Mass was dismembered and all kinds of absurdities were perpetrated. The chopping-up of the Mass (now 'the Lordes Supper or Holye Communion') may have been done in order to rid it of 'Romishness' and medieval superstition. Ironically, however, the mumbo-jumbo of repetition so carefully excised by Cranmer was restored in different ways (in exhortations, confessions and recitals of command-ments); and the decidedly un-Romish *epiklesis* which he had restored for sound theological reasons was abandoned, thus unwittingly moving the mutilated Mass back in a Romeward direction. The sickening looting of the churches and their organs by brigands, together with the Calvinistic revisions of the Prayer Book, gave musicians no cause to love the Edwardian Reformation. Only fanatical Protestants like Merbecke would have derived some satisfaction from the events of 1552, when Zwinglian doctrines were enforced by the Forty-Two Articles; and it is to be doubted that Merbecke's enthusiasm would have been unalloyed when he found that his *booke of Common praier noted* (1550) was outdated and useless within two years of its publication.

The reaction to Protestantism was fierce and equally fanatical. When the puppet king died in 1553, Queen Mary immediately executed Northumberland, who tried to declare himself a papist after all. Two years later, poor Cranmer and Latimer were burnt at the stake together with some three hundred others, including Hooper and Ridley who, in com-mon with what were seen as rats leaving a sinking ship, were the real villains of the drama. They are commemorated alike by a memorial in St Giles, Oxford, some distance from the Broad, the actual site of their martyrdom; until recently, the door through which Cranmer and the others were led to the stake remained in the wall of St Mary Magdalen's

❧ The burnyng of the Archbiſhop of Caunterbury Doctor Thomas
Cranmer, in the Towneditch at Oxforde, with his hand firſt thruſt into the fire, wherewith
he ſubſcribed befote.

Fig. 26 The Death of Cranmer (from Fox, *Actes & Monuments*, (1570)

church. In this place, thanks to the nineteenth-century Oxford Movement, remains a more fitting memorial to Cranmer: here the Mass and other Services are celebrated in a manner which unites the doctrines and ceremonies of the ancient Catholic church with the commonsense separation of dogma and sincerely held belief. This unity of diversity was the achievement of the Anglican Church of Elizabeth.

In the 1550s, however, the liturgical football was being kicked about with scant regard for the damage it might do. Musically, the effect was disastrous. The experimental versions of Services, along with those of the First Prayer Book, were set by various composers, but the life expectancy of these texts was short: they were likely to be useless and superseded within a year or so. Under these circumstances, it is hardly surprising that little worthwhile music survives from Edwardian times. Cranmer's 1544 Litany was monodic, although four-part arrangements of it appeared soon afterwards. Various other settings of early texts are evident in the *Wanley MSS* (Oxford Bodleian Mus Sch e. 420–2 — tenor part missing) which contain, besides music for the 1549 Prayer Book, several pieces whose texts are derived either from Primers, or from the versions which Cranmer and others had prepared before the form of the first Prayer Book was finally fixed. These partbooks also contain English adaptations of Masses by Taverner and others. Because they are as highly melismatic as their originals, these adaptations presumably date from before the Lincoln Injunctions of 1548, which specifically mentioned 'a playn and distincte note, for every syllable one.' (le Huray, 1967, p. 9) Tye's somewhat crude Nunc Dimittis, beginning 'Lord, let thy servant now depart in peace' (le Huray, 1965) is clearly prior to 1545 when the 'King's' Primer was printed. This publication superseded two earlier Primers: 'Marshall's' of 1535 and 'Hilsey's' of 1539. Since Tye's text appears to derive from the versions given in these earlier Primers, the setting is unlikely to be later than 1545, when they were suppressed. Some of the Wanley Communion settings probably date from 1547 when a draft translation was in use: the 'King's' Primer version of the Apostles Creed is used in place of the Nicene Creed, since apparently the latter was not available in English. Sheppard's Second service has the same peculiarity, but this is not necessarily evidence of an early date, since composers often took their words from earlier settings (as with the telescoped or omitted Creed sections in Henrician masses), rather than seeking their text in the Service books. On the contrary, Sheppard's Second service is manifestly a later work than his First, yet its text nevertheless corresponds with that of the First Prayer Book. Sheppard's isolated settings of the Te Deum, Magnificat and Nunc Dimittis probably date from the brief period when these English versions of Canticles were used in the Breviary Matins, Evensong and Compline. Unfortunately, these works survive only in a single partbook (BL Add. 29289) which also includes three separate settings of the Creed, a Kyrie and the Offertory 'Lay not up for yourselves'.

Another single partbook (BL Add. 15166) includes forty-one metrical psalms by Sheppard set to texts found in Sternhold's *Certayne Psalmes* of 1549. These may have been composed in the expectation that metrical psalms would be used in the new Services. It was not to be, however, for despite their increasing popularity as devotional music, metrical psalms remained outside the liturgy, with the exception of Psalm 128, which appears to have been used regularly. This psalm was appointed for the Solemnization of Matrimony; but although Tye's setting of it follows the prose text, the Wanley setting (specifically marked 'Weddings') is of the metrical version. Philip van Wilder also composed a metrical setting of the same psalm which clearly had a wide currency at the time; indeed, it seems to have remained in use at the Chapel Royal in the seventeenth century, where the metrical text was sung as a 'Full anthem' at the Queen's Churching in 1605 (Rimbault, 1872, p. 169).

Tye's 'O God be merciful' was probably also written for weddings, this, Psalm 67, being an alternative to Psalm 128 in the 1549 Prayer Book. The earliest version of this anthem is in the *Lumley* partbooks (BL Roy App. 74–76) which, like the *Wanley* partbooks, contain texts predating the establishment of the First Prayer Book; a second, lengthier, version is found in a large number of sources. Two peculiarities stand out in Tye's setting of this psalm. First, there is a resemblance (or rather, a frequent correspondence) with Sheppard's setting; secondly, there is much bodily repetition — a whole contrapuntal phrase being more or less exactly repeated, as though being sung by the opposite side of the choir. This litany-like repetition is hard to explain. It is found in several of Tye's anthems, in Sheppard's version of 'O God be merciful' and in his 'Our Father'. The settings of the Lord's Prayer found in the *Wanley* partbooks were for use in connection with the Litany, so it is not unlikely that this repetitious habit arose from this direction. Archbishop Holgate's 1552 injunctions to York Minster contain a reference to 'reports or repeatings' which might conceivably refer to this practice, though 'reports' might be taken simply as a condemnation of the repetition associated with syllabic polyphony.

The style of English church music of this period is curiously stilted probably because of the barrage of injunctions which sought more or less to ban music of any sort, or at least anything but the plainest of the plain. It is indeed strange to find that van Wilder's setting of 'Blessed art thou' is far more assured than contemporary settings by indigenous composers. In spite of Henry's importation of foreign musicians (the chief of whom were Philip van Wilder, a Fleming, with Ambrose Lupo and Dionisio Memo who were Italians), the all-pervasive imitation of Franco-Flemish polyphony was slow to graft itself on to English style. Although pieces by van Ghizeghem and other continental composers are found in *King Henry VIII's MS*, the English composers took hardly at all to the chanson style, either setting their vernacular texts homophonically, as in 'Blow thy horn, hunter' or taking over the texture of the Marian antiphon into carol compositions such as Cornish's 'Woefully arrayed' (*Fayrfax MS*). Sometimes the two styles are mixed, syllabic declamation coming alongside elaborate melismas; only occasionally does the chanson style as found in 'Quid petis, O fili' by Pygott (*King Henry VIII's MS*) obtrude for any length of time. This style is still remarkably rare even in the partsongs of the mid-century found in the *Mulliner Book*. 'O happy dames' by Sheppard moves like a chanson, as does Tallis' 'When shall my sorrowful sighing slack'; but the latter's 'Like as the doleful dove' is more typical.

The courtly carol, both sacred and secular, appears to have continued its vogue throughout Henry's reign. Richard Kele's *Christmas carolles newely Inprynted* appeared in 1550 (without music), twenty years after the printing of *XX Songes* (1530, the music of which is now virtually lost). The carol structure of the macaronic 'Nolo mortem . . . Father behold' attributed to Morley (but ascribed by Philip Brett to the mid sixteenth century) is obvious, as is the form of Sheppard's fragmentary 'Of all strange news'. Other carols have been identified by John Milsom (1981): Robert Johnson's 'Benedicam Domino', Sheppard's 'Vain, vain' and William Mundy's 'Prepare you', together with others, even more fragmentary, by Merbecke ('A maid immaculate', surviving only in the section 'A Virgin and mother') and Sheppard ('Stephen first after Christ' and 'What comfort at thy death', which may or may not come from the same carol).

The influence of the carol upon the early anthem is particularly manifest in a Lumley anthem identified by Judith Blezzard (1971) as being based upon 'Blow thy horn, hunter'. A repetition of the end of the verse, prior to the return of the refrain, has already been noted as being characteristic of the carol; this feature is found as late as Byrd's 'Lullaby' of 1588, and seems to have solidified into the wholesale repetition of the second section in the mid-century partsong. Together with the alternation of homophony and polyphony characteristic of many carols and partsongs, this repetition is a notable feature in the early anthem. Tallis' 'If ye love me' and Sheppard's equally fine 'I give you a new commandment' both begin homophonically, break into polyphony, and have a repeated second section.

Ex. 133

Tallis' superb 'Hear the voice and prayer', on the other hand, begins contrapuntally, later giving place to harmony; it too has a repeated second section:-

Ex. 134

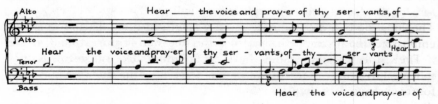

It is notable that these works are for men's voices. The four-part texture (as opposed to the three voices of many Henrician carols) suggests that boys' voices may have been omitted because of lack of rehearsal time for the music of the new rites. Several of the liturgical settings of the *Wanley* and *Lumley* partbooks are for men's voices. Even more notable, however, is the difficulty which perfectly competent composers such as Tallis apparently found when setting texts for the new English church. The word 'toward' in 'Hear the voice and prayer' is set clumsily, as are several passages in his antiphon-style 'Blessed are all they'. Tye is an even worse offender: the words 'be it' are set to one note in the early version of 'O God be merciful' and the underlay of *The Actes of the Apostles* is remarkable for its perversity:

Ex. 135

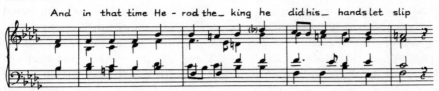

The infelicities of underlay seem to stem partly from the rigid desire to keep to a syllabic underlay (which was coincident, but not a requirement, in the earlier carol) and partly as a consequence of the failure to deal satisfactorily with the very short syllables of English, absent in Latin. In melismatic settings the problem of the super-short syllables may be disguised; in syllabic settings they have a habit of obtruding unpleasantly. Even in the majestic 'Rejoice in the Lord' of the *Mulliner Book* (anonymous, though often wrongly attributed to Redford, and possibly by William Mundy) the problem confronts the composer at the first note:

Ex. 136

The long note (Purcell uses a short note in his setting) unfortunately emphasizes the peculiarity inherent in the first vowel of *Rejoice*.

Tye's *Actes of the Apostles* was printed in 1553 with a fulsome dedication to King Edward; the work is an excruciating rendition into verse of the first fourteen chapters of the Acts of the Apostles. The music merely emphasizes the inferior quality of the words. It is unfortunate that modern adaptations of Tye's *Actes* have proliferated a sub-species of anthem whose dubious merit lies solely in its simplicity. 'O come ye servants of the Lord' and similar substitutions of more recent times do nothing to further the cause of Edwardian church music.

Although some other English pieces by Tye have similar qualities, there is much that rises above the level of the *Actes*. His Magnificat and Nunc Dimittis (apparently written to complete Parsley's Morning Service) is on a much higher plane, as are his anthems 'Christ rising again' and 'To Father,

Son and Holy Ghost'. The former sets the text of the 1552 Easter Anthems (the 1549 Prayer Book included Alleluia, omitted by Tye and the 1552 Prayer Book), while the latter appears to be a gloss on the 'Laudes deo' (the troped Lesson of the Christmas Mass at Cockcrow) and is indeed entitled 'Lawdes Deo' in BL Add. 31390. The piece seems originally to have been instrumental, to which an English text and an Amen were later added, present in one surviving source only. Several other anthems also appear to be adaptations. 'From the depth' belongs to the 'Ut re mi' genre, while 'Deliver us', 'I will exalt' and 'I have loved' seem to form a sequence of instrumental pieces connected with the Office for the Dead. 'I lift my heart to thee', alternatively entitled 'Amavit', also seems originally to have been an instrumental work.

More than one anthem ascribed to Tye is of dubious attribution. In the case of 'O God be merciful' the early version may be by Tye, upon which Sheppard improved, answered by Tye's later version. Or perhaps the 'Sheppard' anthem is yet another version by Tye. 'O Lord God of hosts' and 'Haste thee, O God' are also attributed alternatively to Sheppard and Tye, but here the style points fairly decisively towards Sheppard's authorship.

Little of Tye's English music is for men's voices, which perhaps takes it out of the mainstream of London Edwardian music, for the *Wanley* and *Lumley* partbook sources, together with the collection *Certaine notes. . . .*, have a great deal of music for men's voices. Although *Certaine notes. . . .* was not printed by Day until 1565, its compositions are mostly Edwardian, and many of them are by Caustun, whose musical talents are so meagre that a friendship with the publisher must be assumed. The most remarkable work bearing his name is none other than Taverner's 'In Nomine', now set to English words:

Ex. 137

The only other printed music for the new rites (apart from Cranmer's Litany) was Merbecke's *booke of Common praier noted* (1550) which prunes the Sarum plainsongs to a slavish note-per-syllable pattern. An earlier adaptation (BL Add. 34191) is less procrustean, and follows the Sarum chants more closely. Both adaptations were probably intended to be sung in a manner midway between that of plainchant and the measured declamatory style found in some of the 'Plainsong' Masses of the last years of the Sarum Rite. Merbecke uses the black breve as the standard note value, calling it a semibreve, together with a 'strene' (the old liquescent cephalicus, which had come to mean a doubled note) and a diamond 'prycke', half the value of his 'semibreve'. The use of dotted–notes furthers the impression that a rhythm not unlike that of the *vers mesurés* is envisaged. This was not new in England (cf. p. 22)) but the rhythms were particularly associated with Calvinist tunes, so Merbecke may have been deliberately making his adaptations of the chants 'protestant'.

The polyphonic settings of Wanley ofen follow these *vers mesurés* rhythms and are frequently based upon chants or faburdens (particularly the Te Deum and Magnificat settings). In the Communion, the 1549 Kyrie is set, followed by the Gloria, Creed, Sanctus and Agnus, and a selection of Offertory and post-Communion settings is included in the contents of Wanley. As to the offices, the Te Deum and Benedictus for Matins and the Magnificat and Nunc Dimittis for Evensong are set, together with a selection of 'Antems' which, although not mentioned in the Prayer Books appear to have been allowed, if not encouraged; only in later times did the Prayer Book include the rubric 'In Quires and places where they sing, here followeth the anthem.' The Burial Service and the Litany is also provided for by Wanley, together with a Venite for Matins, the 'Easter anthems' and one or two other items of a similar nature. Conspicuously absent are the Versicles and Responses for Matins and Evensong, the Introits for Communion, or indeed virtually any other psalms, except those which figure as anthems. To this latter there is one exception, 'O clap your hands', of which mention will be made later.

The considerable contents of Wanley are all anonymous. Adaptations of Taverner Masses ('Mater Christi', 'Sancti Wilhelmi' and the 'Mean' Mass) can be traced, as can the authorship of Caustun, Johnson, Mundy, Okeland, Sheppard, Stone, Tallis and Whytbroke in anthems and other music. In general, however, the music is as faceless as it is anonymous, though an honourable exception is the following unattributed anthem:

Ex. 138

(*Wanley* MSS – Bodl Mus Sch e 420-2 no. 26)

Only the anthems by Sheppard and Tallis reach the same level, and even these composers apparently found it difficult to achieve a consistently high standard in their English works. William Mundy, the composer of 'O Lord the maker of all thing' (a Primer translation of the Compline hymn 'Christe qui lux') and of several fine anthems, also contrived to set three extremely dull Services for men (apparently written for the men of St Mary-at-Hill after the choir school had been suppressed in 1548). Sheppard's First service is little better, and the same must be said of Tallis' First service (often erroneously known as the 'Dorian'). All of these settings, however, make use of sectional antiphony between *Decani* and *Cantoris*; and Sheppard's Service actually contains some momentary eight-part writing as the two sides dovetail between phrases. The pattern of beginning in homophony and later breaking into counterpoint, is handed from the anthem to the Service, though of course the antiphony between sides is a legacy of the Sarum psalmody. The choir is divided into four parts throughout, which seems to be a characteristic of most Edwardian music, as for example the four-part Services of Robert Johnson, Robert Parsons and William Mundy. The five-part Services of Tallis, Sheppard, Parsons and Mundy probably date from early Elizabethan years.

The most curious aspect of Edwardian church music is the lack of provision for psalmody. For the Venite at Matins, Merbecke merely gives the first verse (set to a highly simplified version of the Sarum eighth tone) and the rubric 'And so forth wyth the rest of the Psalmes, as they be appointed'. The same rubric is found at Evensong. The Canticles are very fully written out, but the Introits for the Communion Service are again dealt with summarily. Where written-out polyphony was concerned, no problem arises, but even the monodic chanting of the psalms poses difficulties. The 'pointing' of the Prayer Books was rudimentary, indicating only the position of the half-verse; neither the Prayer Books nor Merbecke make any reference to the 'flex' which, in the Sarum chant, accommodated tripartite verses; nor do they solve numerous other difficulties connected with the pointing. Choirs which attempted to chant the psalms in English would have been confronted with formidable problems. For this reason, monodic psalmody would have been as troublesome to write out and perform polyphonic as it was monodic versions of the psalms; an example of the latter (founded on the Sarum fifth tone, third ending) is found in the *Wanley MSS*:

Ex. 139

O clap your hands together all ye people   O sing un-to God with the voice of thanks-giving

This stilted rhythm and dull harmony has little merit, and may have been the kind of music which inspired Sheppard to compile his forty-one metrical psalms. Metrical psalms, as already noted, rarely achieved any liturgical status, so Tallis' several settings of the Prayer Book texts were more useful in the Services. These 'special psalms' for various days, preceded by the Preces and Responses, date from the Elizabethan period, and broke new ground. Later settings, by Byrd, Gibbons and others, gradually dispensed with the chant, which Tallis had always included in the tenor part.

This style of setting persisted, both with and without the chant in the tenor part, until the Civil War. It was only afterward, in the publications of Lowe (1661) and Clifford (1663) that a freer style of declamation was hinted at, more akin to the Italian *falso-bordone* manner of chanting. The writing out of the music in a shortened form was an obvious step, and with it the 'Anglican chant' was at the half-way stage. The gradual standardization of the number of notes in the chant occurred in the eighteenth century, but it was not until the nineteenth century that a more elaborate 'pointing' — a system whereby words and music could be accurately fitted together — was invented. Unfortunately, the nineteenth-century method induced a tendency to gabble to the reciting note as though imitating the rhythm of a runaway horse, contrasted by a sharp reining-in for an exaggeratedly slow mediation at the half-verse fence. Its legacy is the hideous 'Anglican bump', a musical tumulus which the present century has endeavoured to flatten, albeit with inconsistent success.

The Anglican chant, which at its best (though it has to be said it has its correspondingly worse moments) is a striking feature of English church music, was thus born from the seed of confusion implanted by the Edwardian Prayer Books. Even more, the Anglican cathedral and collegiate Evensong, and to a lesser extent Matins, remain as a joint testimony to Cranmer's liturgical genius and to the often comparable genius of composers in complementing his Prayer Book.

In spite of the clerks being forbidden to wear the tonsure, and of other restrictions, the ideal of worship as the *opus dei* continued much as before, and the tradition of sung Offices has persisted in college chapels and cathedral choirs. The misunderstanding of this aspect of the liturgy is to be regretted, for there is a great deal of difference between a ritual of great beauty offered on behalf of the people, and paltriness and incompetence being excused in the name of a mythical common denominator. These things Cranmer understood when he specified the role of the 'Clarkes'. The Protestant party, however, attempted to denude the Services of all their dignity. It was an unfortunate, but probably necessary historical accident that the bloody intervention of Queen Mary should swing the pendulum in the other direction; equilibrium was not to be restored until the time of Elizabeth.

CHAPTER 11

The Lighte of Candelles

When Mary came to the throne in July 1553 the country lurched from the bigotry of the Protestant party to the fanaticism of a Roman reconversion. The Bucers and the Peter Martyrs fled to the Continent, but Cranmer, Latimer, and others chose to face death and scorn the stake. An earlier Protestant sermon by Latimer was ironically prophetic:

> . . . Awaye wyth Bibles and up wyth beades; awaye wyth the lyg[h]te of the Gospel & up wyth the lighte of cand[e]lles . . .
> 'Sermon on the Ploughers' (1548)

To him the matter was as simple as this; but it was the likes of poor Latimer who were the cause of the revulsion felt by many English people toward what was regarded as a foreign religion. Musicians were doubtless glad of a return to the Sarum Rites, which promised a good deal more splendour and stability than the mean and constantly changing Edwardian Services.

Parliament repealed the Act of Uniformity and even cancelled the divorce between Catherine and Henry, Mary's mother and father, thus establishing her legitimacy. It demurred, however, at the queen's demand for the restitution of papal authority and of the sequestrated church lands. Parliament also refused to invoke penalties against those who failed to attend Mass. The beginning of Mary's reign was thus relatively peaceful, and there was little conflict between the queen and her subjects.

Within a year, however, matters were different. The idea of a woman monarch ruling alone was not to Tudor taste, but to confer kingship by marriage upon a low-born Englishman or a high-born foreigner was equally odious, whatever the exigencies of the succession. Thus, her alliance with Philip of Spain, against the virtually unanimous advice of her ministers, was not a popular move. Parliament was aghast; her subjects were enraged.

Fig. 27 A Sarum missal printed in Mary's reign (John Day, 1557)

Having rid themselves of one pack of foreigners, another threatened to take its place. Sir Thomas Wyatt in particular took a dim view of this prospect, and lent his undoubted military acumen to a rebellion which more nearly succeeded than any other since the Wars of the Roses; had Mary taken Gardiner's advice and fled from London, Wyatt would have won the day. But it was not to be: instead of breaching the walls of London in triumph, he was consigned to the Tower, from which he was taken to the block, his actions already having brought the innocent Lady Jane Grey to a similar fate. She had been queen briefly on Edward's death, only to be toppled immediately by the rival claims in favour of Mary. If these deaths were politically necessary, those of three hundred common folk, Kentish followers of Wyatt, were not. As a result, the populace was now openly hostile; and at the same time the heart of the queen hardened. In March, a month after Wyatt's abortive coup, Mary was married by proxy to the remarkably ill-favoured Philip. In July the ceremony was conducted in person in Winchester.

On November 24th, the most cherished of Mary's plans came to fruition. In Edward's days, Cardinal Pole had been exiled from England for treason; subsequently he narrowly missed being Pope, and was even a candidate for Mary's hand. She forced Parliament to annul the charge against Pole, and to accept the supremacy of the papacy. It still stood firm, however, on the question of church lands. Both houses met on the 29th, and the realm was formally absolved from schism by Reginald Pole.

During the first year or so of Mary's reign, church musicians would have had an enormous task to restore the lapsed Sarum Rite. It seems not improbable that the *Gyffard* partbooks (BL Add. 17802–5), which date from Mary's reign, reflect the transitional arrangements of the Chapel Royal in the first years of its new monarch. The partbooks seem to be fair copies of a repertory of Masses, Magnificats, antiphons, a Passion, psalms, hymns and responds, many of which are by Tallis and Sheppard, the two principal composers of the Chapel. It is remarkable, however, that a considerable quantity of the music is for men, which may reflect the initial difficulty of instructing a virtually untrained set of boys in the Sarum liturgy and its polyphony. Much of the music is for Easter, probably that of 1554. Taverner's 'Dum transisset' is arranged for four voices, although his 'Audivi' appears in its original version for boys as demanded by the Sarum Rite. This is not the case with Sheppard's 'Audivi' where the voice ranges seem to indicate a setting for boys transposed down an octave. Tallis' setting may possibly have been freshly composed for men; it seems not to be an Henrician work, in contrast with Sheppard's.

A curiosity of the MSS is that they are more or less liturgically ordered, but in addition (as pointed out by Bray, 1969), the composers are often assembled in order of seniority. Thus Robert Cooper, Barber and Robert Johnson (a Scotsman, born in about 1490) come before Taverner, van Wilder, Tye, Tallis, Sheppard and Blitheman. Thomas Wright's 'Nesciens mater' is one of the gems of the collection, together with Richard Bramston's 'Recordare domine'. Other minor composers who contributed distinguished work to the collection are Knight ('Sancta Maria') and Hoskins ('Speciosa facta es'). The anonymous 'O bone Jesu' appears to be continental, but could conceivably be by van Wilder. After a Te Deum setting (anonymous, for men) there are Mass Propers and Ordinaries, after which the contents consist mostly of Office polyphony from All Saints to Easter, followed by Jesus Mass Propers, further Masses, Magnificats and antiphons. Amongst the preponderant music for Easter are settings for men of the processional psalms 'Laudate pueri' by Sheppard, and 'In exitu' composed jointly by him together with sections by 'Mundy' and 'Byrd' (both of whose Christian names are difficult to assign at present).

At least some of this music may date from All Saints' Day (November 1st) in 1553 until about the same time the following year, during which the choir of the Chapel Royal built up its repertory prior to restoring the former splendour of the high treble style. In November of 1554, Stow (1580) records that a sermon was preached, before which was sung 'Ne timeas Maria', and after, 'Te Deum' and 'Salve festa dies' (Bray, 1981). Sarah Cobbold has pointed to the thematic connection between 'Ne timeas Maria' (from the respond 'Dixit Angelus') and Sheppard's Mass 'Be not afraid'; the possibility that the Mass was composed for the same occasion is strengthened by the fact that the latter is evidently a hurried and un-accomplished composition for men's voices. Sheppard's Easter 'Salve festa dies' of the *Gyffard* partbooks could have been used on this occasion (the part set by Sheppard is the same for all seasons). Also, if the possibility is allowed that the Te Deum appearing under the name Taverner is actually Sheppard's (it seems considerably more characteristic of the composer than his less grandiose six-part setting), this work may have completed a trilogy of pieces for men's voices composed by Sheppard for this occasion, in-cluding what is presumably the lost work 'Ne timeas' on which the Mass was based. Be that as it may, there are two settings for men of 'Audivi' (November 1st) in the *Gyffard* books, so it is at least likely that the boys were not yet ready to take up their accustomed prerogative. Tallis' 'Hodie . . . Gloria in excelsis' (the opening is set in polyphony) for men points in the same direction. Unlike his 'Audivi', this seems to be a trans-posed version of an earlier work, but it seems likely that the settings by Taverner of these responds languished for some time unperformed, to be superseded by the settings of Sheppard and Cooper. The 'Frences' Mass of Sheppard seems also to have been an arrangement of a much older work (see p. 274).

The 'absolution' of the nation by Cardinal Pole may well have occasioned Tallis' 'Suscipe quaeso', as Jeremy Noble (apud Doe, 1968) has pointed out. It is set for the same voices (M M A A T B B) as the 'Puer Natus' Mass of Tallis which would have been doubly appropriate at Christmas 1554, since Queen Mary was confident (wrongly, it turned out) that she was carrying an heir to the throne (Doe, 1968).

Philip's magnificent *Capilla flamenca*, whose seven boys, four altos, six tenors and four basses included Philippe de Monte, was accompanied by the brothers Cabezon, and many other distinguished musicians. They joined

Fig. 28 A continental woodcut (sixteenth century) showing a choir round a lectern. Note the stave of the *rector chori*.

forces with the English Chapel Royal (and St Paul's choir) to celebrate Mass on December 2nd, and probably on Christmas Day. The curious disposition of voices in the 'Puer natus' Mass probably reflects that of the *Capilla*; the caballistic cantus firmus treatment, and density of the imitation, may well have been a manifesto by Tallis to show the foreigners the mettle of his English pasture. Similarly, the 'double' imitation of 'Suscipe quaeso' may have had a similar function.

In 1555 religious events took a turn for the worse, for this was the year of the burning of Cranmer and the other Oxford Martyrs. Persecution continued with a vengeance until Mary's death in 1558, but musicians probably put these matters to the back of their minds. Most of the hymn and respond settings of Sheppard and Tallis probably date from the Marian years. As conditions improved, music for means and trebles became more prevalent, and several 'duplicate' settings may be ascribed to the development and revision of the Chapel Royal repertory of office polyphony, to which

Redford, Parsons and Mundy contributed, and especially Tallis and
Sheppard, in a cycle of polyphonic responds and hymns. The culmination
of the respond style is found in the Candlemas compositions 'Gaude, gaude,
gaude' by Sheppard, and 'Videte miraculum' by Tallis. The latter redresses
some of the balance of inspiration which was hitherto in Sheppard's favour.
In 'Videte miraculum' the musical emphasis on the word 'Maria' does
palpable homage to the monarch. Tallis' 'Gaude gloriosa', which also has
many Marian references in the text, may have been revived at this period,
although it may well have been written specifically in honour of Queen
Mary, since the doggerel text may be interpreted as a reference to the
restoration of the 'true' church:

> Gaude Virgo Maria, quam dignam laude celebrat ecclesia,
> quae Christi doctrinis illustrata te matrem glorificat.

The pauses printed in *Tudor Church Music* in between the sections for
reduced voices and the Full sections are erroneous. As John Milsom has
pointed out, these pauses should be confined to the ends of the Full sections,
as indicated in the sources.

'Gaude gloriosa' is a fine work, though it is somewhat overshadowed by
Sheppard's 'Gaude virgo christiphera' with which it has much in common.
Both of these votive antiphons seem to have been the inspiration for
Mundy's 'Vox patris coelestis'. The same composer's 'Maria virgo
sanctissima' is an outstanding large-scale work, but the even longer yet
carefully sustained 'Vox patris' stands as one of the finest compositions,
perhaps the finest, of the genre. Although Mundy's 'Videte miraculum' is
dull in comparison with Tallis' setting, 'Vox patris', with its surer sense of
architecture, and its incomparably more singable lines, is greatly superior to
'Gaude gloriosa'. In the latter, Tallis spends his climax too soon at the treble
and mean gimel section 'Gaude virgo'; Mundy leaves his gimel 'Veni ad me'
until immediately prior to the last Full section. Not only are Mundy's vocal
lines more grateful to sing, but this section, and the whole work, has a
stronger sense of climax:

Ex. 140

This was the apogee of the grandiose Marian antiphon: its days were now numbered. The musical structure, whereby Full sections alternated with sections for reduced voices of various combinations, had served not only the antiphon, but also the Mass and Magnificat. It was briefly adapted to the more concise style of the times by Robert White and others, and even made brief appearances in English settings, many of which bear the *in medio chori* rubric. Tallis' 'Blessed are they' is written in this style, but is doubtless an adaptation of a Latin original (cf. Milsom, 1982) — indeed it is entitled 'Beati immaculati' in one source. The original was doubtless a good deal more syllabic than, for example, his 'Ave Dei patris'; but in the vernacular version the declamation becomes somewhat relentless.

Several psalms by White (perhaps early Elizabethan) are also in the antiphon style, and Sheppard's 'O sing unto the Lord' (also ascribed to Tallis) may have had a Latin original 'Cantate domino' (unconnected, however, with the Mass of the same name). These antiphon-style psalm settings are of a comparatively rare type: they were replaced by the more modern straightforward imitative psalm settings which enjoyed a considerable vogue. It is not improbable that the new fashion was initiated by Robert Johnson who brought this French mode via the 'ould alliance' of his native Scotland. His settings of 'Deus misereatur', and two of 'Domine in virtute', contrast sharply with the old-fashioned luxuriance of his 'Ave Dei patris' and 'Gaude Maria virgo' (a five-part work arranged in the *Gyffard* partbooks in four voices — see Kerman, 1962).

Sheppard's 'Deus misereatur', whose sectional character appears to have been designed to accommodate the antiphon 'Mandatum' with which the psalm was sung on Maundy Thursday (it was also sung on Good Friday with a different antiphon) seems to be liturgical, in common with the four-part processional psalms found in the *Gyffard* partbooks. 'Beati omnes', 'Judica me' and 'Confitebor' (the Canticle of Isaiah is a non-Vulgate version) are clearly paraliturgical in character and may be Elizabethan in date. 'Voce mea', represented by a single voice part underlaid with English words, is doubtless a remnant of another of Sheppard's psalms. In these works, the concision of the style does not allow his music to develop its customary breadth, and the syllabism often makes the treble parts difficult to sing. His psalms, nevertheless, are given pride of place in Baldwin's manuscripts (Oxford Ch Ch 979–83), which incidentally preserve (save for the tenor part) the majority of Sheppard's music. Baldwin's connection with Sheppard appears to have been close since, unlike the other composers, Sheppard is referred to merely as 'Mr. S.'.

Another of Baldwin's MSS (BL RM 24. d. 2) contains tantalizing snippets of antiphons by Sheppard and indeed many works by other composers, which no longer exist elsewhere. Similarly, Oxford Ch Ch 45 also contains *disjecta membra* of a wide variety of works, including parts of Sheppard's great six-part Magnificat. The Full passages of this work now survive merely in the form of an isolated alto partbook (Bodleian Mus Sch e 423) whose contents serve to emphasize how much magnificent polyphony from this period has been lost.

Sheppard's six-part Magnificat continues the old antiphon-style layout, as do the settings of Tye, White, Parsons, Mundy and others. The points of similarity in their settings, too, carry on the tradition of copying formulas in Magnificats. Unfortunately, in common with most of these works, Sheppard's six-part setting is imperfectly preserved. A later Magnificat for men's voices by Sheppard, however, survives intact: this appears to have echoes of the earlier large-scale work:

Ex. 141

The problem of the chronology of Sheppard's music is exacerbated by the almost complete lack of knowledge of his career. Although Tallis' junior, he is likely to have been born in 1515 or so, since his supplication in 1554 for the Oxford D.Mus. had the usual formula 'studiosus musices quatenus viginti annos'. From 1543 to 1548 he was *informator choristarum* at Magdalen College, in succession to Appelby who had resigned his post after only one year (returning to Lincoln and thus affording an intriguing parallel with Taverner).

In 1553 Sheppard joined the Chapel Royal as Gentleman (Stowe 571 f.36v, and Exch. Rolls 434, 5–10). In the latter MS there is a reference to the supply of livery, which may have been in connection with the coronation of Queen Mary in 1553. Being a member of the 'Queen's Chapel', as some MSS describe him, did not necessarily mean losing his connections with Magdalen; but there are several problems connected with the college records at this date which may have confused Sheppard with at least one other member of the college with a similar name; certainly Sheppard was not a Fellow, as is sometimes stated.

The Chapel Royal records (Exch. Rolls 434, 5–10) show Sheppard to have presented a roll of songs to the queen on New Year's Day 1557, and to have been a member of the choir at the coronation of Elizabeth in January 1559. He must have died soon after, since his name does not appear amongst the deaths or resignations recorded in the Chapel Royal *Cheque Books*, which are extant from September 1560 onwards.

Sheppard's outstanding achievements are many and varied. Besides the masterly 'Cantate' Mass and several other earlier works, the forceful quality of his responds and hymns is incomparable. The striking sense of urgency and power is immediately obvious to the listener. It is true that his sonorous effects are often achieved by means which, examined in close-up, are unconventional, perhaps angular; but his writing is always supremely vocal, and the overall effect is almost invariably carefully judged. The bold brushwork of his lines does not follow a painstakingly pencilled sketch — his canvas is impressionistic, shocked with vibrant colour. Thus, full harmony is achieved in the four- part Magnificat at the occasional expense of counterpoint, for, in common with Bach, he was not above allowing a leading note to fall (see Ex. 141). His virtuosity over a cantus firmus is remarkable, for example in the delicate filigree of six high voices in the two settings of 'Libera nos', woven with consummate mastery over the darker ground-pattern of the cantus firmus moving in slow notes in the bass. In splendid contrast, the cantus firmus of 'Verbum caro' is the platform for a series of virtuoso gestures which culminate in a blaze of sound as the trebles trumpet forth in celebration of the Incarnation. If these effects are sometimes achieved at the expense of convention, it is because he considered the listener more important than the pundit. Preparations of suspensions on discords, upward-resolving suspensions, and other striking peculiarities are perfectly explicable in sound, if not reconcilable with Palestrina's technique. His unconventionality does, however, pose problems for the editor attempting to distinguish between error and individuality, and for the restorer trying to follow his footsteps to replace the missing parts which fate has laid aside. Sheppard's office polyphony probably formed, as we have seen, a Chapel Royal repertory to which several composers also contributed, notably Tallis: the younger participants in this collegiate effort were Mundy and Parsons, who survived well into Elizabethan times.

Parsons apparently wrote very little English music. His Latin output is more considerable: the six-part Latin Magnificat is a striking work, as are 'Credo quod redemptor', 'Libera me' and 'Peccantem me' which evidently influenced Byrd. His 'Domine quis habitabit' is apparently connected with White's third setting, since it seems (one part being missing) to be on the same lines, for three pairs of voices. 'Retribue servo tuo' on the other hand, is set in the old 'antiphonal' style, though it has several vigorous moments of almost Baroque ornamentation, a characteristic even more marked within the antiphon 'O bone Jesu'. Parsons' sole surviving hymn setting is the Whitsun 'Jam Christus astra', which is heavily influenced by Sheppard's style.

The achievements of William Mundy are considerable; indeed, the lines which Robert Dow included in his partbooks (Oxford Ch Ch 984–8) punningly compared his moon to Byrd's sun: 'Dies lunae [his name was sometimes spelt 'Moondaye' or 'Monday'] Ut lucem solis sequitur lux proximae lunae Sic tu post Birdum Munde secunde venis.' As already mentioned, 'Vox patris coelestis' must be accounted as one of the supreme achievements of the age. The early 'square' masses, and his Magnificats and other pieces in the *Gyffard* partbooks, are the least interesting of his works, and there are several others which fail to rise above a humdrum level. However, the powerful 'Sive vigilem' and the striking 'Beatus et sanctus' are worthy of note, as are one or two of the hymns which he seems to have contributed to the Chapel Royal cycle — 'A solis ortus' being one of the most impressive. Mundy's psalms are set in a variety of ways; 'Eructavit cor meum' is in the old antiphon style, whereas 'Noli aemulare' and 'Domine quis habitabit' are similar in technique to Sheppard's psalms. The superb 'Adolescentulus sum' is presumably of late date, since its style is Elizabethan. Continental influence is manifest in Mundy's choice of texts: as Henry Chadwick showed (apud Harrison in *EECM* 2) the text of his 'Miserere' is based upon a humanist version which had been printed, parallel with the Vulgate, in 1556.

Robert White also composed a considerable number of psalm settings. Unlike Mundy, virtually all of White's music has been published; yet it has still not seen the recognition which it deserves. In 1926 the editors of *Tudor Church Music* wrote as follows: 'There is a comfortable belief that time and change try reputations by some infallible touchstone; that the worthiest will survive; and that the iniquity of oblivion does not scatter its poppy quite so blindly after all. This belief is sharply challenged by the case of Robert White. Even when the renown of the English polyphonic school was at its lowest ebb, Byrd and Tallis retained some parcels of honour. White, whose music, for skill, invention and sincerity, is worthy to stand by theirs, and whose contemporary reputation was high . . . has been even as a name neglected.'

Today, more than half a century later, White's name is certainly not neglected, but whether the quality of his music has yet properly been appreciated is an open question. Nevertheless, it has to be admitted that there are, so to speak, two Robert Whites. One was addicted to intricate counterpoint whose intellectual content far outstripped the emotional. Here the lofty ingenuity of the composer floats too far above our heads. The other Robert White reconciles this technical prowess with a warmer, more approachable manner of expression. The works imbued with this latter personality display such originality that White must lay claim to being one of the brightest lights in the brilliant firmament shared by Tallis, Sheppard and Mundy.

The biographical details of White's life are somewhat sketchy. The first event of any certainty was his taking of the Bachelor of Music degree at Cambridge, awarded to him on December 13th, 1560. The Grace book records that he had pursued his musical studies for ten years; although this sort of phrase was somewhat formulistic, it is reasonable to assume that White was something like twenty-five when he took his degree. This means that at his death in 1574 he would have been forty or so. His career included appointments at Ely, Chester and finally Westminster Abbey. His duties in these places over a comparatively short life, perhaps coupled with a rather severe attitude to composition, may have precluded his leaving a large volume of works to posterity. He appears, however, to have had considerable holdings of land — perhaps the management of this occupied some of the time which otherwise might have been devoted to composition. But his comparatively small output may, at least in part, be attributed to the 'iniquity of oblivion'. Almost certainly he wrote more, perhaps a great deal more, Anglican church music: Burney, the opinionated author of *A General History of Music* (1776): apparently owned a MS of the sixteenth century described as 'Mr. Robert Whyte, his Bitts, of three Parte Songes, in Partition [that is to say, in score] with Ditties, 11, without Ditties 16.' The latter, explains Burney, were 'short fugues or intonations in most of the ecclesiastical modes'. These keyboard pieces have more or less vanished without trace; and although some In Nomines for concerted instruments survive, nothing is known of any secular vocal music.

Of the music which has come down to us, White's Magnificat is probably one of his earlier essays in composition. It bears the stamp of Taverner's influence in the way the contrapuntal lines are organized, in its use of cantus firmus, and in the vocal characteristics of each line. Although the mature White is not yet evident in this work, we can see something of his *persona* in its youthful freshness. The treble part (save for a few sections found excerpted in Oxford Ch Ch 45) is unfortunately lacking, which although not catastrophic, is serious enough in the 'Esurientes', which appears to call for a treble gimel. White's contrapuntal ingenuity is nowhere more evident than when he works to a cantus firmus. In 'Regina coeli', for men's voices, the tenor sings the plainchant in long notes, acting as a musical mainmast to which the sails of polyphony are attached, an unusual procedure in a votive antiphon. 'Tota pulchra es' exhibits the same peculiarity.

These cantus firmus antiphons may have been composed between 1554–1562 for Trinity College, Cambridge. In the latter year White succeeded Christopher Tye at Ely, and subsequently married Tye's daughter Ellen. The two men are linked also by the individuality of their music; their works are pervaded alike by certain idiosyncratic qualities. White's somewhat technical attitude to composition is observable in the way he took up the difficult challenge of using the same text twice or several times, for example, the Compline hymn 'Christe, qui lux es et dies', which he set four or more times. Clearly he was much attracted to its text, and in his varied treatments he shows great ingenuity. All the settings are *alternatim* and all include the chant as cantus firmus: the first, in note–against–note style, was later imitated by Byrd; the second has the chant in long notes in the treble. The third setting — the finest of them all — also has a treble cantus firmus; here the cerebral and emotional qualities meet on equal terms:

Ex. 142

In the fourth setting of this hymn, the level of inspiration is slightly lower; nonetheless it is still a striking work, particularly in its final bars. Although all of these five-part settings are vocal (a further, purely instrumental setting *à* 4 exists), they do not appear to have been conceived for liturgical use. They enjoyed a considerable vogue as instrumental pieces, in which form they were imitated by Byrd.

White's main preoccupation, however, was his psalm settings. In common with Mundy, his earlier essays in this genre are in the old-fashioned antiphon style of which 'Portio mea' and 'Justus es' are perhaps the most impressive; although 'Exaudiat te' and one of the versions of 'Domine quis habitabit' have memorable passages. White turned three times to the latter text, the final setting for three pairs of voices (though one is missing in the source) being incomparably the finest. There is a good deal of word painting which culminates in 'non movebitur', where an appropriately obstinate figure seems to move on almost reluctantly to the resonant Amen. White returned to the same psalm in English for one of his not particularly inspired English works composed for the Elizabethan rite.

In one of his MSS of 'Christe qui lux' (see Fig. 29) Dow wrote a Latin motto:

> Maxima musarum nostrarum gloria White
> Tu peris, aeternum sed tua musa manet
> (White thou glorious leader of our art;
> Thou hast died, but thy muse lives on in eternity)

White's death was tragically early: he, and, indeed his whole family, fell victim to the plague. His Lamentations may be regarded as something of a swan song, for they are amongst his most accomplished music, and it is not impossible that they were amongst his latest works. The earlier setting of the Lamentations, for six voices, is greatly inferior. The five-part version reworks some of the earlier material with a surer hand. In common with Tallis' Lamentations, the work is non-liturgical since it deviates from the Sarum liturgy, but White's handling of the text differs markedly from that of Tallis. White employs trebles (Tallis used means),

Fig. 29 Dow's tribute to White (Ch Ch 985 f.19)

but yet achieves an intentionally less dramatic texture, emphasizing more the resigned and hopeless tone in the words of the prophet. There is nevertheless a unique intensity in this music, which strikes a somewhat more continental note than that of most of his contemporaries. The Lamentations *à* 5 of White and Tallis are in reality pairs of settings, each of which end with the petition 'Jerusalem, convertere ad dominum deum tuum'. It is noteworthy that these composers, together with Byrd, appear to have avoided duplication, for they rarely set the same portion of the text as each other. Their use of certain archaic formulae, particularly at the cadences, also unites these three composers.

At the end of his copy of White's Lamentations *à* 5, Dow wrote the following couplet:

> Non ita moesta sonant plangentis verba prophetae
> Quam sonant authoris musica maesta mei
> (No sadder are the plangent words of the prophet,
> than the gloom of this composer's music is to me)

Some of its flavour may be savoured in the following extract, which consists of the setting of one word, the Hebrew letter *Teth*. In the original acrostic poem, each verse began with a different letter of the Hebrew alphabet: the Latin plainchant preserved this literary conceit by setting the letter to a melisma before each verse. This practice was echoed in polyphonic sections, allowing the composer the luxury of abstract composition. Such passages are the musical equivalent of an illuminated initial letter:

Ex. 143

It is interesting to note that one of the pavans of the *Dublin Virginal Book* (Ward, 1983, no. 21) is founded upon a similar passage, the letter *Lamed*.

White's Lamentations follow Parsley's in their use of treble voices. Tallis', for means, appear to have been influenced by the Lamentations of Alfonso Ferrabosco II, who was an intermediary in bringing the style of Lassus to the attention of the English. Up until the end of Mary's reign, Tallis' style is best suited to the expansive antiphon texture: he is not so successful, as we have seen, in the less prolix respond and hymn. 'Videte miraculum', however, displays the expressive and more up-to-date technique which Tallis was later to develop, and which was denied by death to Sheppard. It was not until the Elizabethan period, when Latin polyphony was no longer part of the English rite, that Tallis seems to have felt thoroughly at ease in the new style. Even in the manifesto which he published jointly with Byrd, the *Cantiones quae ab argumento sacrae vocantur* of 1575, there is a good deal which is tentative or old-fashioned; but 'Absterge domine', 'In jejunio', 'Salvator mundi' and the hymn 'O nata lux' (none of which are liturgical) show how far Tallis has moved from 'Candidi facti sunt', 'Honor virtus' and 'Te lucis', all of which are liturgical in origin.

In the Lamentations, Tallis writes some of his most concentrated polyphony. As with White's settings there is an opportunity for 'pure' music in the settings of the introductory Hebrew letters. Tallis chooses to use M A A T B voices in low tessitura: as a result, his sonorities are traduced if the work is sung at the written pitch by incorrect voices. Almost every page of the long first Lamentations setting is memorable, but the section beginning 'plorans ploravit' is perhaps especially notable — its wonderfully sombre end, melting into the plaintive call to Jerusalem, which is eventually made to sound like low, distant organ chords, has a peculiarly portentous quality:

Ex. 144

'Daleth' in the shorter second setting of the Lamentations has a similar cadence, vilified by Morley, but shared by many works of Tallis. The letter *He*, incidentally, was mistakenly written *Heth* in several sources. The focal point of this setting is, again, the transition prior to the peroration. Once more, Tallis' favourite cadence (Doe, 1968) is used to telling effect in 'Parvuli ejus ducti sunt captivi ante faciem tribulantis', followed by 'Jerusalem convertere', set in a different manner from the first (indeed the two settings are in different keys): here the rise and fall of the appeal to Jerusalem is achieved by different means:

Ex. 145

Tallis' psalm settings ('Domine quis habitabit' and 'Laudate dominum') are not particularly distinguished essays in the fashionable genre. Equally un–satisfactory is a curious paired setting of the Latin Magnificat and Nunc Dimittis, which was presumably designed for Walter Haddon's Latin version of Evensong in the Elizabethan Prayer Book (Doe, 1968, p. 38). The use of trebles with a syllabic underlay makes for a certain awkwardness not found in the non-liturgical setting of 'In manus tuas' for similar forces. 'O sacrum convivium', without trebles, became popular in Elizabethan times, both in Latin and English, though it is not perhaps on the level of some of the other pieces printed in the *Cantiones . . . sacrae* of 1575.

Tallis' masterpiece is unquestionably 'Spem in alium'. This phenomenal composition for forty voices can only be described in a series of superlatives. Its conception appears to have originated as a challenge to a somewhat dull forty-part piece by Striggio, and it has been suggested that the composition was written for the ill-fated Duke of Norfolk and performed during his brief freedom in 1571 (Stevens, 1982). Tallis' technical achievement lies in the fact that no voice appears to be marking time by merely filling-in with conventional formulas until its turn to shine comes round again. On the contrary, it is possible for each singer to imagine that he has been given the most telling part of the texture. Tallis treats the eight choirs (each disposed in the Tr M A T B fashion which was by this time a rarity) now separately, now in succession, sometimes polychorally, and sometimes as a massive forty-part texture; but nowhere is there the slightest evidence of technical restraint or faltering of inspiration. The expansive treatment of the text allows the voices to achieve the breadth denied them in the paired Magnificat and Nunc Dimittis. It is invidious to single out any particular moment in the work for comment, but the section beginning with a dramatic rest before all forty voices sing 'respice' ('ponder' — involving a musical pun), after which four of the choirs sing in pairs, is perhaps particularly notable:

Ex. 146

The work ends after another 'respice' after the same manner, and a long conclusion for all forty voices.

Together with the miniature 'O nata lux' (scored for Tr M A T B), the Lamentations, with several compositions in the 1575 *Cantiones*, 'Spem in alium' is a magnificent testimony to the fruitful autumn of Tallis' life, which set the seed for the spring blossoming of his close friend and follower, William Byrd.

Unlike Tallis, Byrd became a member of the recusant sect. Although Latin polyphony was neither forbidden by Elizabeth, nor interpreted as a token of illegal rites, it was necessary that Tallis and Byrd's 1575 collection should be called *Cantiones quae ab argumento sacrae vocantur*, a title which mendaciously implies that the choice of sacred words is coincidental. Much of Byrd's Latin music can be interpreted as music which might be sung for enjoyment, or as Latin anthems which were permitted where Latin was understood; yet the greater portion exemplifies Byrd's passionate espousal of the Roman faith, which was by now doubly illegal in that its ties with the Sarum Rite were broken, and it had become a foreign and indeed traitorous observance.

Byrd's earliest efforts, such as the vocal 'Christe qui lux' setting, the Lamentations, or 'Laudate pueri,' are works of considerable merit, but nevertheless show him in a state of flux. 'Laudate pueri' is nothing but an adaptation of an instrumental fantazia. 'Christe qui lux' attempts to outdo White, by shifting the cantus firmus through successive voices and keys; but the interest of the scheme is abrogated by the staidness of the harmony in comparison with White's. Byrd also closely modelled one of his instrumental versions of the hymn on another of White's settings. The Lamentations take something from Tallis, including the archaic cadences, but the intensity which Tallis so effortlessly maintains is more sporadic in Byrd. 'Emendemus', however, gives a foretaste of the expressive range which maturity was to encompass.

Parsons' music appears to have influenced several of Byrd's pieces: 'Peccantem me' and 'Libera me' have antecedents in works of the same title by the older composer. Unquestionably, however, Alfonso Ferrabosco II's music provided a last on which Byrd was to fashion much of his early music. Lassus and other continental composers were much taken with the revival of classical Latin prosody, and often affected settings in the 'Roman Sapphic' and other metres. 'Ecce jam noctis' and 'Siderum rector' both follow the classical pattern of longs and shorts transmitted through Ferrabosco:

Ex. 147

Byrd and Ferrabosco appear to have been friendly since they vied with each other in producing canons on the 'Miserere' plainchant. Byrd's debt to Ferrabosco probably ceased when the latter fled to Italy as a consequence of suspicion of his activities as a spy. Byrd also engaged in 'friendly aemulation' (to use Peacham's phrase) with de Monte, whom perhaps he had met when the chapel of Philip II of Spain came to England. In 1583 he sent an eight-part setting of part of the psalm 'Super flumina', to which Byrd replied with 'Quomodo cantabimus'. As Kerman has shown, however (1981), the correspondence was a covert assertion of the recusant position. Edmund Campion had recently been executed for treason or martyred for his beliefs, depending on the view taken of his activities. Byrd's own wife had been cited for recusancy in 1577, and he himself was cited in 1587. The tolerance which Elizabeth had shown towards the adherents of Roman Catholicism began to evaporate after Pius V had given them a choice of loyalty to faith or queen, but not both; and it became clear that the Jesuit evangelists coming in from abroad were not above attempting to undermine the political stability of the country, or determining upon its actual conquest. These were therefore trying times for the recusants, who could not escape being tarred with the same brush as the fifth columnists: and in the people's memory the horror of Bloody Mary's excesses was still fresh.

Many of Byrd's Latin works from this period, including the 'Super flumina' — 'Quomodo' correspondence, have a *double entendre*. In the latter, the verses are, as Kerman says, 'pointedly rearranged' in an allusion to the 'Babylonish captivity' in which the recusant families imagined themselves to be held. Increasingly, Byrd's music becomes a vehicle for political manifesto: this facet of his character may be seen at large in his two collections of *Cantiones sacrae* (1589 and 1591). The inter-relationships of the recusant families, their manuscripts and their connections with Byrd, have been studied by Brett (1964) and Hofman (1973). A thorough examination of Byrd's Latin music has been undertaken by Kerman (1981) in a manner which is often informative. Kerman's insistence on designating liturgical items as 'motets' is unfortunate, however, as is his failure to recognize the vocal forces involved in much of Byrd's music. 'Defecit in dolore', for example, the masterly and extended work for men's voices which headed his *Cantiones* of 1589, is treated as though it were for the same combination of voices as 'O quam gloriosum'. This is particularly misleading, since the sombre key and voices used in 'Defecit in dolore' provide a sharp contrast with 'O quam gloriosum' whose vocal ranges (when the transposition dictated by the clef has been allowed for) are quite different, as was recognized by Fellowes in his complete edition of Byrd's works.

Fellowes did not grasp, however, that 'Infelix ego' (1591) is for the old-style choir of trebles, means, two altos, tenor and bass. Indeed, the work is a recrudescence of the old antiphon style in which the scoring is varied between full and reduced forces. Although the texture is archaizing in one sense, the feeling of the work is decidedly modern; indeed, the text appears to have been borrowed from Lassus. It is a long work, in three separate sections (for some reason, modern critics describe these sections as *partes*, with all the attendant problems of macaronic syntax): such divisions of Byrd's published works possibly reflect a deference on the part of the composer to offer lengthy compositions to a public which might demur at such apparent prolixity. At this period Byrd was fond of large-scale works, in which he rarely failed to sustain both musical interest and emotional tension. 'Infelix ego' is a case in point: throughout the length of this astonishing technical essay interest never flags, and climax follows climax without, however, allowing the possibility of bathos. The third section, after several earlier emotional peaks, builds up an atmosphere of exquisite contrapuntal intensity which dissipates soon after the first appearance of the word *miserere*; but a further final crisis is again reached on the same word, this time in homophony, in which the sudden change of harmonic direction is as striking as it is brilliantly timed.

Ex. 148

'Tristitia et anxietas' (1589) is another lengthy masterpiece; together with 'Defecit in dolore' it demonstrates Byrd's capacity to keep the listener on tenterhooks for long periods, and to drain the last drop of emotion from the music, its performers and audience. 'Ad dominum cum tribularer' (surviving in a wordless manuscript) exhibits the same incomparable qualities.

It is thus difficult to sustain Kerman's view that this is an early work. Byrd's nine-part 'Domine quis habitabit' is nearly as pedestrian as Tallis' setting of the same text, and lacks the imaginative treatment of White's third version. Ferrabosco's 'Ad dominum' is ingenious, making much use of the minor second to engender a plaintive effect; but the massive eight-part texture of Byrd's 'Ad dominum' is more demanding than the forces required by Ferrabosco, and displays a sustained plangency achieved by a truly remarkable technical prowess. As with Tallis' 'Spem in alium' there is no hint of 'filling in'; each voice continuously appears to have a fundamental contribution to make, and yet the basses are able to make their point with relative ease amongst this closely-argued discussion. In common with 'Defecit in dolore' and 'Tristitia et anxietas' the first section ends as though nothing further can be said, only to continue with an even more intense peroration. Kerman's perception of this piece is curiously hampered by preconception. To call the opening point 'dull' and to upbraid Byrd for repeating it in the same key betrays a preference for sight over sound: the care with which Byrd does not pre-empt the harmonic or contrapuntal climaxes is obvious to the listener, as is the carefully controlled ululation of the opening of the second section 'Heu mihi' whose luxuriant working-out deftly points up the coming phrase 'prolongatus est.'

Kerman's attitude to the mirage of sixteenth-century 'modality' must also be treated with considerable caution — having noted the 'aberrant key signatures' of some of the 1575 *Cantiones* he warns against relying on them for 'determining a composition's mode'. The aberration is not Byrd's, but that of misguided modal theory. The issue is further confused by a discussion of clefs and ranges in relation to a so-called *Klang* and *Tonartsystem*. The significance of the clefs, as we have seen, is hardly one of Teutonic abstract organization, but a reflection of English colouristic preference: Byrd's choice of clefs and tonal ranges depend on the key he has in mind, and the attendant vocal tessituras which he exploits in a given key. Although it is anachronistic to speak of 'F major', it is equally incorrect to speak of 'Ionian': as in his keyboard music, Byrd is thinking in the tonal system of the period discussed in earlier chapters, not in some trumped-up modal system invented by Glareanus in the book (1547) 'which he tooke in hand onely for the explanation of those modes' (Morley 1597, p. 147).

Apart from these issues, however, Kerman is often illuminating; in particular, the significance of Byrd's texts is finely studied. After the 'political' works found in manuscript and the two *Cantiones* collections of 1589 and 1591, Byrd turned to liturgical composition for the clandestine recusant rites. That he was able to publish his massive cycle of polyphony without penalty is a remarkable testimony to the regard in which he was held; but it is notable that the Masses (1592–5, see Clulow, 1966) and *Gradualia* (1605–7) were Byrd's last publications of Latin music. Altogether, over 200 Latin works are known. A considerable portion of these are found in his *Gradualia*, a compendium of Mass Propers for the church's year according to the Roman rite, and without parallel outside Isaak's *Choralis Constantinus*. The organization of this massive collection has been studied by Jackman (1963), who showed the intricate manner in which the sections were intended to be rearranged for liturgical use — a Gloria borrowed here, or an Alleluia inserted elsewhere. Unfortunately, Byrd's zeal often outstripped his imagination. In particular, the three-part music is frequently dull; the Mass, the 'Turbarum voces' (St John Passion) and Propers are often insipid. The larger Masses (which Brett has shown to have antecedents in Taverner's 'mean' Mass) do not reveal much of Byrd's fervour until the

Agnus Dei, which in both the four-and five-part Masses takes on a sudden intensity. Similarly, although there is much of interest amongst the Mass Propers, few of the feasts are provided with uniformly fine music. The Mass for All Saints' Day is a striking exception, however; the Introit 'Gaudeamus' is a vigorous work, while the Gradual and Alleluia 'Timete dominum' is in serene contrast. The Offertory 'Justorum animae' is a concentrated work of especially affective style, and is one of Byrd's most intensely expressive compositions. The Communion 'Beati mundo corde' achieves what might seem to be the impossible task of following the intensity of 'Justorum animae'; its beatific affirmation of faith is a fitting culmination to the All Saints' Mass.

The *Gradualia* often include exuberant pieces, but it is obvious that Byrd's propensity in his Latin music, no less than in the rest of his output, was towards introspective music. The justly famous 'Ne irascaris' (whose second section 'Civitas sancti tui' achieved wide circulation in the English version 'Bow thine ear') is the quintessential Byrd, but the vigour of 'Haec dies' (1591) or of 'Laudibus in sanctis' is less typical. The latter, which opens the 1591 collection, is Byrd's most sustained essay in a jubilant mood: the text is a metrical version of Psalm 150, each of whose three sections is splendidly climactic, as for example the 'laude dei' of the end of the second section. The long third section is full of playful allusion to the words — the tripping 'agili laudet', the dancing triple-time of 'laeta chorea pede', the gently tinkling rhythms of 'cymbala dulcesona' (appearing also in cunning augmentation) — a series of miniatures leading up to the Halleluia which, if sung too loudly, pre-empts the climax which should follow at 'tempus in omne deo', bringing the work to a clarion-like flourish in which the word *deo* is trumpeted abroad.

Byrd was born in 1543 or 1544 (since his will of 1622 refers to 'the 80th yeare of myne age'). As we have seen, however, his *Gradualia* appear to have been valetudinarian: the English Services seem to have claimed his attention thereafter. His admirer, Morley (1597, p. 115), mentioned the 'vertuous contention' of Ferrabosco and Byrd, setting canons on the 'Miserere'; contrasting this contention 'without envie' with the 'backbiting' of others. It is remarkable that Morley's own Latin output is heavily indebted to continental models, including Ferrabosco, and there is grave suspicion that he deliberately put his name to the work of others. 'Gaude Maria virgo' has been shown by Pike (1969) to have been by Peter Philips, while 'Laboravi in gemitu' has recently been identified as continental. Bearing in mind the derivative elements in his solo songs and his failure to acknowledge the sources of his *Consort Lessons*, the 'backbiting' to which Morley refers may have been well deserved. At all events, it is perhaps wise to suspend judgement on Morley's Latin works until their canon is firmly established. 'Domine dominus noster' and 'Domine, non est exaltatum' were probably written, as the source suggests, at the age of nineteen. They are undistinguished, and contrast sharply with 'De profundis' and the works printed in his treatise of 1597, whose accomplishments are of a different order. Apart from Byrd and Alfonso Ferrabosco II, few composers set Latin texts after the Armada, with the exception of the emigrants Philips and Deering, who composed a good deal of Latin music, some of which may have been sung in English recusant circles. English composers, notably Lupo, Kirbye, Weelkes and Nathaniel Giles wrote a certain amount; the latter's 'Tibi soli' (surviving in a wordless source) and 'Vestigia mea' have the appearance of being fine works. Richard Nicolson, an Oxford musician, composed a magnificent and unusual setting of 'Cantate domino'. The recusant Martin Peerson and other Caroline composers also contributed to the repertory.

Strangely, however, the interest in Latin music was greater in the time of the Commonwealth, when its texts were no longer remotely associated with the liturgy. By then the achievement of Sheppard, Tallis and White, Parsons and Mundy, had receded into history, as had the anguish of the Marian period which nurtured them; and even Byrd's enormous Latin output was largely forgotten after his death. Only in their music for the new Anglican rites were the names of these composers to be consistently remembered in the cathedral repertory.

CHAPTER 12

The Chauncels as in Tymes Past

Elizabeth came to the throne of a country beset by daunting economic, political and religious problems. These difficulties were to some extent related, which emphasized the momentous decision which she had to take as to whether to continue the connection with the papacy (whose influence, however, she would doubtless seek to pollard, as her father had done) or to follow the path upon which Cranmer had embarked before Mary had diverted him to his pyroligneous fate. Ideally, she would have gone back to her father's Reformation, but it soon became clear that the choice lay between stark alternatives: a more radical defiance of papal authority or of utter subjection to it. In choosing the former, she carried Parliament with her, at least in the Lower House. The Lords were more reluctant. By April 1559, however, the Elizabethan Settlement was accomplished — at no small cost, it is true, for the new Prayer Book was the wretched 1552 book in new guise. The rubrics of the 1559 Prayer Book nevertheless still harked back to the practices of 1549, and were thus adjudged 'Popish' by the party which was to become the new Puritan sect. Those, on the other hand, who refused to take the Oath of Supremacy to Elizabeth, became the new recusants.

The balance was tipped in favour of a break with Rome by the signing of the treaty of Cateau-Cambrésis, thereby ending a disastrous war upon which Mary had embarked, exposing the country to military derision, political enfeeblement and financial ruin. Elizabeth was thus confronted with a task similar to that undertaken by her grandfather. To her abiding credit she proved herself equal to it; and if her good husbandry was achieved at the cost of being unable to provide adequately for such luxuries as church music (with the exception of her own Chapel Royal), she nevertheless restored confidence in what had been a debased currency, and gave meaning to the word 'sterling'.

In the many problems of her reign, whether of rebellion or war, vagabondage or unemployment, she showed herself an unusually able strategist. Close-fisted she may have been, but she allowed Hawkins access to enough funds to build the ships which so brilliantly out-manoeuvred the Spanish Armada. And by making apprenticeship statutory, unemployment was checked and the mobility of labour stabilized. The power of the guilds had already increased under her father (thus making for a clear distinction between amateur and professional musicians, for example); this, and a new emphasis on 'courtly' manners and speech, began to draw up the lines of new class distinctions.

Elizabeth saw to it that the new Anglican church avoided the worst excesses of Geneva. The preface to her Prayer Book stated that 'the chauncels shall remain, as they have done in tymes past'. Musically, there was an ambivalence: in spite of a directive at Norwich (Watkins Shaw, apud le Huray 1967, p. 38) discouraging the use of partmusic on ferial occasions, Osbert Parsley's memorial there shows every evidence of harmony between chapter and choir:

Osberto Parsley

Musicae Scientissimo
Ei quondam Consociati
Musici posuerunt Anno 1585.

Here lies the Man whose Name in spight of Death
Renowned lives by Blast of Golden Fame,
Whose Harmony survives his vital Breath,
Whose Skill no Pride did spot, whose Life no Blame.

Whose low Estate was blest with quiet Mind
As our sweet Gords with Discords mixed be.
Whose Life in Seventy and Four Years entwin'd,
As falleth mellow'd Apples from the Tree,
Whose Deeds were Rules, whose Words were Verity:
Who here a Singing-man did spend his Days,
Full Fifty Years, in our Church Melody;
His Memory shines bright whom thus we praise.

In general, however, the 'low church' party seems to have had the upper hand in the early years of the Elizabethan Settlement, a hand which seems to lean heavily on the unduly restrained church music of the time. Repeated attempts were made to curtail the effective practice of church music. An edict in connection with Winchester Cathedral in 1571 ran thus: '*Item*, that in the choir no more shall be used in song that shall drown any word or syllable, or draw out in length or shorten any word or syllable . . . also the often reports and repeating of notes with words or sentences . . . shall not be used'. (cf. le Huray, 1967, p. 38)

Tallis' music of this period illustrates the constraints evidently felt by composers of the time. His 'O Lord, give thy holy spirit' is Elizabethan in technique, but is no more expansive than his Edwardian pieces; the five-part Te Deum, however, gives some hint of things to come. His settings of the Preces, Responses and psalms are workmanlike, with occasional flashes of the Tallis of the Latin music; but he seems to have been disinclined to contribute much to English Service music, preferring to express himself in the medium of Latin 'sacred' (as opposed to liturgical) music.

Sheppard, however, set a Second service, which is considerably more vigorous than his First. The earlier Service is for two M A T B choirs, whereas the Second has a five-part (M A A T B) disposition, reverting to four parts in the *Decani* and *Cantoris* sections. Sheppard, together with Mundy and Parsons, who composed similar Services, appears to have been influential in establishing conventions of scoring and form in this type of music. Each Canticle or movement tends to begin with a homophonic full texture, shortly afterward breaking into counterpoint, sung by alternate sides of the choir. The conventions of the early anthem and of psalmody were thus transferred to Service music. The linking of the beginnings of the various movements by 'head motive' harks back, on the other hand, to the tradition of Masses modelled upon votive anti-phons; and it is also intriguing to note that the peculiar tonal scheme of the plainchant Te Deum was carried over into Sheppard's setting; indeed, the tonal design of many later settings was influenced by this feature (Aplin, 1979). The roots of Tudor polyphony were thus far from dead.

Several anthems for the high treble voices were adapted for use in places such as Ludlow (Smith, 1968). More remarkably, Anglican Service music for the trebles was newly composed at about this time. Mundy's Evening service 'In medio chori', together with a Morning service (apparently unrelated) are striking examples of the genre, and Sheppard's Magnificat and Nunc Dimittis 'for trebles' is one of his most assured compositions, giving a glimpse of this composer recapturing the exuberance of his respond settings. Athough surviving only in the form of an organ score, something of Sheppard's original texture may be made out, as for example in the Nunc Dimittis (Ex. 149).

Of Sheppard's younger contemporaries, Parsons wrote comparatively little English church music before being tragically drowned in the river Trent at Newark in 1570. A Magnificat and Nunc Dimittis of Mundy's was written as a completion 'to Mr. Parson's service in five parts'. Mundy composed a considerable number of Services (including the dismal settings for men's voices), complemented by a similarly wide range of anthems. Some of the anthems are merely ascribed to 'Mundy', and may not be by him; many, particularly some of those for men's voices, are as crude and uninviting as the Services for the same forces. 'O Lord, the maker of all thing', however, is justly popular; 'O Lord, I bow the knees of my heart' deserves to be better known.

Ex. 149

(Reconstructed from organ score, Tenbury 791)

Mundy's Verse anthems are of particular interest in that they represent some of the earliest essays in the genre. Even earlier, however, is the setting of a metrical prayer in the *Wanley* partbooks quoted by le Huray (1967, p. 218): although no longer surviving, an instrumental accompaniment must have supported the solo line, the latter being repeated wholesale as part of the chorus texture. A less basic technique is employed in Farrant's 'When as we sat in Babylon', a setting of a metrical version of Psalm 137. Although in its extant form the accompaniment is for organ, it is conceivable that viols were originally involved (cf. Reeve, 1971). The chorus repeats a modified version of the final bars of the Verse, in the manner of the carol repetition discussed earlier. Exactly the same technique is employed in Mundy's Verse anthems, 'Ah helpless wretch' and 'The secret sins' (which although ascribed to Gibbons in some sources is clearly, as le Huray points out, Mundy's 'lost' anthem of the same name). Both of these anthems, though surviving with organ accompaniments, have every appearance of having been scored originally for concerted instruments.

'Ah, helpless wretch' is to a text from *Seven sobs of a sorrowfull soule for sinne* printed in 1583 by William Hunnis, who succeeded Richard Edwards as Master of the Choristers at the Chapel Royal. Hunnis seems to have been peculiarly afflicted by an urge to compose doggerel, even to the extent of providing a verse disposition:

317

MY LAST WILL AND TESTAMENT
To God my soule I do bequeathe, because it is his owne,
My body to be layd in grave, where to my frends best known;
Executors I wyll none make, thereby great stryffe may grow,
Because the goodes that I shall leave wyll not pay all I owe.

The alliterative text of 'The secret sins' is manifestly out of the same stable, and it is evident that these early Verse anthems have strong connections with the concerted songs of the choirboy plays with which Edwards, Hunnis and Farrant were connected. These plays were much in fashion in the early Elizabethan years, in which the audience might 'mewe at passionate speeches, blare at merrie, finde fault with the musike, whew at the children's Action, whistle at the songs: and above all, curse the sharers' [clothiers who had sworn the uniqueness of their models to clients who then saw the same thing on stage]. (Dekker, 1609)

Although Parsons, Edwardes and Nathaniel Patrick wrote concerted songs associated with these plays, no corresponding Verse anthems by these composers survive; but Farrant and Byrd (particularly the latter) were prolific in both genres. One of Byrd's presumably earliest anthems of this kind is 'Alack when I look back', which employs a tune and text from Hunnis' 1583 collection. Here, the early Verse anthem pattern is evident, consisting of an accompanied solo verse whose final bars are repeated chorally, in a carol-like echo; only in the last verse is there a more extended chorus. This refrain pattern is transmitted back, in turn, to several of Byrd's concerted songs; some of these have a solo repeat, but others are provided with chorus parts and thus lie wholly within the mould of the Verse anthem. Sheppard's 'Of all strange news', a late example of an antiphon-style carol in English, may have been influential in the development of the Verse anthem; equally, however, the loss of the contrast between chanted and polyphonic sections which had been a lively feature of the Latin responds and Magnificats, was made good by the alternation of Verse and chorus.

The influence of psalmody on the early technique of Verse anthems and Services has already been noted. The use of 'reports and repeatings' in this kind of music was frequently attacked by the cliché-ridden writers of the time, one of whom (Browne, 1582) observed that 'Their tossing to and fro of psalmes and sentences is like tenisse plaie.'

Mathew Parker's *Psalter* (c. 1567), has directions for 'The Rectors', 'The Quiere' and 'The Meane', apparently singing in alternation. A similar pattern is adopted by Byrd in his 'Third psalm to the Second preces'. Discounting 'Lift up your heads', which is merely an adaptation of his 'Attollite portas' (1597), Byrd's psalms show a transitional stage in the development of psalmody. Tallis was content to set the psalm-tone in the tenor, and to proceed, alternating *Decani* and *Cantoris*, in a *falso-bordone* style; but although in the Preces and Responses the proper chant is retained in the tenor, only one of the special psalms uses a plainchant.

The First preces and responses of Matins and Evensong were sung by priest ('O Lord, open thou our lips') and choir ('and our mouth shall show forth thy praise'). Unlike the corresponding part of the Sarum Rite, however, the choral responses were polyphonic; and the choral 'Glory be . . . Praise ye the Lord' followed immediately after 'O Lord make haste to help us'. In turn, the special psalms followed, also set polyphonically.

Byrd's 'Psalms to the First preces' are clearly later than those attached to the 'Second preces'. Furthermore, the third psalm of the latter is accompanied by the organ. After an organ introduction, a mean sings the first verse 'Teach me, O Lord' in triple time, followed by the second verse in choral *falso-*

Fig. 30 Gibbons' Preces (from Barnard, . . . *Selected Church Musick,* 1641)

bordone, in which the chant of the *tonus peregrinus* is heard in the uppermost part. This procedure extends throughout the whole psalm. 'When Israel came out of Egypt' adopts a different technique: apart from a solo intonation it employs choral antiphony after the manner of Tallis; but here, however, Byrd makes no reference to the psalm-tone. 'Hear my prayer' is similar, save that there is no solo intonation — the same pattern is followed in 'O clap your hands' for the First preces. The assemblage of psalms is possibly due to Barnard, who printed a large selection of them in his publication dated 1641; the sequence of Byrd's psalms veers between works of manifestly differing styles and dates, of which 'Save me, O God' (for the 'First preces') is doubtless the latest. Here the setting is in triple time throughout, and was obviously paired with the Magnificat and Nunc Dimittis of the Third service, for the latter makes use of the same time signature and of similar melodic material. 'Save me, O God' alternates unaccompanied Verse sections for four upper voices, and four or five lower voices, thus affording an interesting, if slight, recrudescence of the votive antiphon texture of earlier times: the Full chorus appears only at the Gloria.

Byrd's Services reflect the general development of the form during the Elizabethan and Jacobean period. His First service (the numberings, often by Barnard, are convenient, but are not to be relied upon as a chronology) is a Short service. This type of Service normally proceeds in four-part antiphony throughout, and is relentlessly syllabic. Byrd's setting of the Venite is of this kind, but the Te Deum begins and ends in five parts, as does the subsequent Benedictus; and various styles appear side by side. Similarly, the Kyrie (ie. the Responses to the Commandments) is Full throughout, while the Creed alternates five- or six-part Full sections with sections for high and low reduced voices. An alternative four-part version appearing in some sources is clearly an adaptation; indeed, Communion settings rarely contained anything but Kyrie and Creed. The Sanctus setting attributed to Byrd is also spurious.

The Evening canticles of the Short service appear to be later in date, since their scoring is more consistent (M A A T B, with some M A T B sections). It is possible that the earlier parts of the Service date from Byrd's period at Lincoln, where he was organist from 1563, whereas the later parts may well date from his appointment to the Chapel Royal, where he succeeded Parsons on the latter's untimely death in 1570. In common with many musicians, he held the two appointments in plurality; at least at first; but in December 1572 he relinquished his Lincoln post for good.

The Second service exists in two versions, the earlier being represented by the *Tenbury Organ Book*, the other by an Ely source. In its revised form it is a mature work, embodying accompanied Verse passages; that it is related to the Verse psalm 'Teach me O Lord' is evident from the section 'as he promised', which makes use of the *tonus peregrinus*. In common with the Full services, a 'head motive' binds the Magnificat and Nunc Dimittis together:

Ex. 150

The Third service, in triple time, is a Full service for alternating five-voice choirs. As in the Second service, only the Evening canticles are set. In the Great service, however, the Morning canticles (including Venite) are included, as are the Kyrie responses and Creed. The massive texture, often including ten-part writing, is in complete contrast to the 'Short service' style. Although not entirely syllabic, the length of the settings derives not from the use of melisma, but from the repetitions involved in a thorough-going imitative texture. Byrd's Great service is a splendid contribution to the Anglican liturgy, and a reminder that in spite of his firm adherence to Roman Catholicism, he was a loyal member of the Chapel Royal under Elizabeth and James; as the queen said of the Earl of Worcester, he was a 'stiff papist and a good subject'. There is no doubt that 'O Lord, save thy Servant Elizabeth our Queen' was a sincere tribute; and other English Full anthems (notably 'Prevent us O Lord', 'Sing joyfully', 'Arise O Lord', 'Unto the hills' and 'Turn our captivity' — several of which he published in madrigalian collections) are equally fine. 'Exalt thyself' (see James, 1981) is a landmark in the history of the Full anthem, since it makes use of the ternary form taken up by Gibbons in his closely related 'Hosanna to the Son of David', and by Weelkes in his macaronic 'Gloria in excelsis'.

The latter, however, is also related to the carol, a form which has a prominent place in Byrd's work, and which seems to have had a particular popularity in recusant circles. Besides 'This day Christ was born' (1611) he also printed 'An earthly tree' and 'From Virgin's womb' (both in 1589); the latter both exist in alternative, less elaborate MS adaptations, apparently for church use. In their original versions, in common with 'O God, that guides' (1611), strophically set consort song verses are followed by a musically unrelated chorus.

Ex. 151

These fine works are matched by the setting of 'Christ rising' printed in 1589, showing, as with 'Have mercy' (1611), the perfect marriage of the concerted song with the Verse anthem. In 'Christ rising' the old pre-echo with which the Verse section is linked to the chorus is now treated with greater freedom. This feature is dispensed with altogether in the first part of the anthem; in 'Christ is risen again' the Verse and chorus are integrated in a masterly fashion which helps to mark Byrd as one of the most consistent innovators of Verse techniques.

The Verse service is technically a Service in which accompanied soloistic passages are essential to the texture; several Full services have Verse indications or organ accompaniments which are dispensable, and thus do not fall within the genre. The earliest Verse service proper was possibly by Farrant, whose priority in the field of the Verse anthem has already been discussed. Although his Verse service (existing now only as an organ score and bass chorus part) does not have the musical interest of Byrd's Second service, its pioneering quality must nevertheless be recognized. The Verses appear to have been for mean throughout. Of Farrant's other music, 'Hide not thou thy face' and 'Call to remembrance' remained in use for the Maundy services at the Chapel Royal for a long time (Rimbault 1872, pp. 178–9, 182). 'Lord, for thy tender mercies' sake', sometimes attributed to him, is surely by John Hilton. Farrant's Full services have some merit, but on the whole his music is disappointing. His involvement with choirboy plays and the founding of the Blackfriars theatre probably left him little time in which to develop as a church composer. It is not inconceivable that he tired of some of these duties, since he resigned his post at St George's, Windsor, in 1569, to return to his old position as Gentleman of the Chapel royal; there he remained until his death in 1580 or 1581.

At St George's, Farrant was succeeded by Nathaniel Giles, formerly a chorister at Magdalen College, Oxford. Giles also followed Hunnis as Master of the Children of the Chapel Royal, whilst retaining his post at Windsor, in 1597. In common with Farrant, an involvement in choirboy plays is reflected in Giles' Services and anthems: his considerable quantity of Verse anthems includes many solos for means. Although his music is of variable — indeed frequently vapid—quality, Giles at times raises himself to the front rank, and incidentally shows himself to be no stranger to chromaticism:

Ex. 152

His development of the Verse anthem is often highly individual. In some examples the Verse and Full passages alternate without any repetition, but in others there are developments and recapitulations which contribute a good deal to the interest of his style. Giles arrived in Windsor in 1585, the year of Tallis' death.

The death of Thomas Tallis marked the end of an era, a sentiment eloquently voiced in Byrd's Elegy (see p. 27, which concludes 'Tallis is dead, and music dies'. He was buried at Greenwich, where a memorial was engraved celebrating his long service throughout four monarchies, and his lovable temperament. The inscription, long since perished, was recorded by Stow (apud Strype, 1720):

> Enterred here doth ly a worthy wyght,
>> Who for long tyme in musick bore the bell:
> His name to shew, was Thomas Tallys hyght,
>> In honest vertuous lyff he dyd excell.

> He serv'd long tyme in chappel with grete prayse
>> Fower sovereygnes reygnes (a thing not often seen);
> I meane Kyng Henry and Prynce Edward's dayes,
>> Quene Mary, and Elizabeth oure Quene.

> He mary'd was, though children he had none,
>   And lyv'd in love full thre and thirty yeres
> Wyth loyal spowse, whose name yclypt was Jone,
>   Who here entomb'd him company now beares.
>
> As he dyd lyve, so also did he dy,
>   In myld and quyet sort (O happy man!)
> To God ful oft for mercy did he cry,
>   Wherefore he lyves, let deth do what he can.

Edmund Hooper, who was born in Devon in 1553 or so, also came to London at about the same time as Nathaniel Giles. He was a member of Westminster Abbey Choir in 1582, becoming Master of the Choristers in 1588. Subsequently he also became an organist of the Chapel Royal (Gibbons was at that time junior organist) having been appointed in 1604 as Gentleman of the Chapel. Hooper's work follows much the same lines as Giles': several Services in the various types are of considerable interest, although he does not extend his technique beyond that of Byrd. The same must be said of his Full and Verse anthems, many of which have instrumental accompaniments. Of these, 'Hearken ye nations' and 'O God of Gods' are occasional pieces for royal events, and perhaps acted as models for similar pieces by Gibbons: the latter composer, however, usually managed to avoid setting doggerel of quite such a low level. The quality of his texts, together with the possibility of several misattributions, has clouded the question of Hooper's true stature, but his music nonetheless compares favourably with that of Thomas Morley.

  With the exception of the dramatic 'Out of the deep', Morley's anthems are generally somewhat uninteresting. The Preces, Responses and psalms are extremely dull, and the Burial sentences ascribed to him appear to be highly derivative. The 'Three minnoms service' has many similarities with Byrd's Third service, which was also alternatively entitled the 'Three minnoms' service: it seems, as in his Latin music, that Morley's magpie instincts are at work again. The Short service is unpretentious, but the Verse service ranges through the Morning canticles, Communion and Evensong in a curious mixture of styles, beginning as a Full service and concluding with an elaborate Verse setting of the Evening canticles. This rag-bag of types, and several curious resemblances to Byrd's First service and to the Services of other composers, notably Hooper, give cause to suspect that Morley's patchwork technique was more formidable than his originality of invention.

  As a theorist, Morley is most valuable when he records his personal views; the parts of his treatise derived from continental authors are less interesting, and in spite of his pedantry in technical matters, the musical examples which he prints are often far from being technically irreproachable. More informative are his anecdotal descriptions of the state of music in his times; his complaint concerning the low state to which music had fallen rings true (1597, p. 179). Others indeed put the point more strongly. An anonymous Jacobean writer says:

The first occasion for the decay of music in Cathedral Churches and other places where musick and singing was used and had in yearly alowance began about the nynthe yeare of Queene Elizabeth . . . A poore singingmans maintenance in a Church of a new erection [ie. of the new foundation] doth not answere the wages and entertainment that any of men giveth to his horskeeper. (BL Roy. 18. B. XIX).

Fig. 31 Interior of St Paul's. (from Hollar's *View of London*, 1647)

In a similar vein, Boswell (1572) wrote that 'singinge men, and Choristers might goe a begging, together with their Maister the player on the Organes.'

This state of affairs was partly due to Elizabeth's frugality, and partly due to the effects of raging inflation. In an effort to provide more realistic wages for the clerks, choirs were often brought down to half-strength, with obvious consequences for the music. Small wonder, then, that discipline was lax, and in some places the singing men sang so out of time as to resemble 'not a Consort but a Peale' (Earle, 1628); and of some choristers 'scarce 4 of them can sing a note; the sufficiency of voice and skill in Cathedral Churches is utterly decayed' (BL Roy. 18. B. XIX). This is in sharp distinction to the romantic description of the music at St Paul's by Sanliens (cf. p. 42):

[Gossip]	'Harken, I do heare a sweet musick: I never heard the like.'
[Host]	'See whether wee may get to the quier, and wee shall heare the fearest voyces of all the cathedrall churches in England.'
[Gossip]	'I beleeve you: who should have them, if the Londonners had them not?'
[Host]	'I thinke that the Queenes singyng men are there, for I doo heare her baase.'
[Gossip]	'That may be: for, to tell the trueth, I never heard better singyng.'
[Host]	'Hearken, there is a good versicle.'
[Gossip]	'I promise you that I would heare them more willingly singe, then eate or drinke.'

Conditions at the Chapel Royal may have been tolerable, but elsewhere the practice of church music seems to have been at such a low ebb that involvement in secular music was the only way to earn a sufficient income from music. In provincial cathedrals such as Chichester, discipline was unbelievably slack and morale was low. The accounts of the management of the choir (cf. Brown, 1969) give the impression that the cathedral services had considerably less dignity than would be expected of an ill-run circus. To be part of this understaffed shambles might well drive a saintly man to drink, and it is evident that Thomas Weelkes was no saint; his indolent and drunken behaviour eventually cost him his post there, and possibly had earlier lost him a regular place in the Chapel Royal. This Falstaff in his character, however, may well have been as much the effect, rather than a cause, of his tribulations.

In the halcyon days of youthful ambition, Weelkes composed his consistently best music, as may be found in his earliest madrigal collections. Later, the higher levels continue to be reached, but less often. The same thing is probably true of the other forms of composition in which he wrote, which display as many troughs of inspirational level as crests. Yet, although his madrigals no doubt represent the essential Weelkes, it is his Anglican Service music which chiefly commands attention, for it is here that his most individual contribution is to be found.

Weelkes' Services exemplify the varieties established by earlier composers, but with some interesting variations. His Short service (no. 7 in David Brown's numbering) is neither more nor less distinguished than other examples of the period. It would have been hard to contribute much that would be markedly different from the musical rhetoric of his colleagues, when restricted to a note-against-note homophony. The 'Eighth' service, however, is for five parts, and allows a more expansive texture and scope for individuality. Though it survives only in organ score, Verse sections are evident in the Service, and it is also clear that five-part antiphony was intended throughout much of the texture. Since two complete five-part choirs are effectively demanded, it is unlikely that the work was written for Chichester, whose choir had more limited resources. Byrd's five-part Third service is considerably less grandiose in scale, and does not break loose from the severity of the homophonic Short service style — indeed, few comparable settings approach the originality and breadth of Weelkes' 'Eighth' service, whose texture is as varied as that of a Verse service. Although it survives only in organ score, the indications of the partwriting in the 'Eighth' service are unusually full, allowing reconstruction to be undertaken with reasonable confidence. A regular feature of Weelkes' Services is the use of quotation from an anthem; the appearance of these contrafact sections in the Services suggest that anthem and Service were composed for use at the same time. However, the quotations are too short to aid greatly the piecing together of Weelkes' lost originals: in the 'Eighth' service, for example, only the Amen of the Magnificat can be derived from his anthem 'O how aimiable'. The following extract gives some idea of the elaborate style of this work:

Ex. 153

In the 'Ninth' service, described as being 'for seven voices', the texture is even more elaborate, for the bass and mean are consistently doubled, the five-part choir M A A T B becoming M M A A T B B; but reckoning on the doubling of the two alto parts and the tenor, there is the possibility of ten voices being used simultaneously, so this work is really in Great service style. The tenor part is missing from the MSS, as is one of the alto parts; the amount of reconstruction varies, depending on whether the two tenors and four altos appear to be independent. Only the Amen of the Magnificat appears to be for ten voices, although elsewhere ('he hath put down') there is a passage in reduced scoring where the two extant parts were clearly joined by three others, an alto and two tenors. Besides the alternation of *Decani* and *Cantoris*, there is a good deal of reduced scoring and part antiphony which, as is characteristic of the Great service, was often sung Verse, by *soli*. The mean and the bass, however, are each divided (though not necessarily singing together) throughout.

The problem of reconstruction is simplified by the close-knit imitation, characteristic of Weelkes' music in general; and there are also quotations from 'O Lord, grant the King a long life' at 'and the rich he hath sent empty away' and at the Amen of the Nunc Dimittis. Of the many fine passages in the Service, including the ten-part Amen of the Magnificat, the section 'For mine eyes have seen' in the Nunc Dimittis is particularly striking, the more so since it leads on, with a sure sense of climax, to the section 'and to be the glory'. If this were not enough, Weelkes still manages to restrain the texture from its final burgeoning. 'Glory be to the father' begins in antiphonal style, followed by a Full section: it is here that Weelkes' technical prowess is evident, for 'as it was in the beginning' gradually ascends to a brilliantly highlighted top G — appearing for the first time in the whole Service.

Ex. 154

A change of rhythmic emphasis, and a telling use of a *D flat*, brings the work to a spacious close.

There can be little doubt that this Service was composed for the Chapel Royal — the quotations from 'O Lord grant the King a long life' and its scale leave little doubt that the meagre choirs of Winchester (where Weelkes spent some of his early years) or Chichester were not the resources for which Weelkes wrote his grandiose, indeed regal, work.

Weelkes' anthems contain some outstanding contributions to the literature. 'Laboravi', apparently written under the influence of the setting circulated under the name of Morley, was possibly an 'exercise' for his Oxford B.Mus. This represents Weelkes' only Latin work, for although 'Gloria in excelsis deo' has a Latin refrain, the remainder of the latter is in English. The use of the refrain–verse–refrain pattern clearly harks back to the carol, of which 'Gloria in excelsis' is a late example. Apart from its ternary form (which Weelkes also used in the well-known anthems 'Alleluia I heard a voice' and 'Hosanna') this carol is also remarkable for its madrigalian key change — particularly appropriate to the words 'Crave thy God to tune thy heart':

Ex. 155

A selection of Weelkes' anthems is printed in *MB* XXIII; as with his Services, many of them are incomplete. 'O Lord arise', 'When David heard', 'O Jonathan' and 'O Lord, grant the King' are all fine examples of the Full anthem, but the level is not always uniformly high. The Verse anthems also display various levels of achievement; 'Give the King thy judgements', 'In thee O Lord' and 'Plead thou my cause' are good examples; and 'Give ear, O Lord' (to a text from Hunnis) is one of his best essays in this field, and perhaps ranks amongst the finest of the period. (Ex. 156).

Several madrigalian traits stand out in Weelkes' anthems: occasionally, as in 'Hosanna to the Son of David', they impart a slightly laboured quality — Gibbons' setting of the same text, while not as overtly dramatic, is more controlled. His four published books of madrigals, which occupied Weelkes during the ten years or so spanning the turn of the century, show him to have run the whole gamut of the techniques of the period.

He ranges from the expressiveness of 'O care thou wilt despatch me' and 'Thule, the period of cosmography', through the more conventional imagery of 'As Vesta was' and 'Like two proud armies', to the light touch of the cries of London and 'The ape, the monkey and baboon'. It is these collections where Weelkes is found at his most consistent, and there is no

Ex. 156

doubt that although his church music is more uneven, he was one of the greatest of the English madrigalists. The Services which have been singled out, nevertheless, as having a particular significance in the music of the period, have some of this madrigalian freedom which marks them out from the run of contemporary Service music.

Of Weelkes' senior contemporaries, John Bull, John Mundy (who also composed several madrigalian works), Elway Bevin, Nathaniel Patrick and John Holmes are worthy of mention. Bull's limited output of church music includes the Verse anthem 'Almighty God, who by the leading of a star' together with lesser gems such as 'In the departure of the Lord'. Bull composed no Service music, but Bevin, Patrick, Holmes and the two John Farrants provide useful Canticle settings. Mundy's reputation was sufficient to be included in a roll of honour in one of Baldwin's MSS: 'I will begine with White, Shepper, Tye, and Tallis, Parsons, Gyles, Mundie, th'oulde one of the queenes pallis; Mundie yonge, th'oulde man's sonne, and likewyse others moe; There names would be to longe, therefore I let them goe.'

Notwithstanding this tribute, Mundy's 'Sing joyfully unto God' is the only anthem to have achieved wide currency in the present century.

Michael East was also primarily a madrigalist, and indeed was himself a publisher in this field. Apart from 'When Israel came out of Egypt', which he printed in one of his madrigalian collections, his church music has not fared well. His Verse service, although the voice parts are extant, lacks its organ accompaniment. East, somewhat younger than Weelkes, was roughly the same age as Adrian Batten who composed a large amount of church music, some of which is of considerable merit: the same may be said of the Ely composer John Amner. These composers of the Jacobean age were more prone to modernisms, due to the influence of the madrigal, than their seniors.

Sir Thomas Leighton's *Teares or Lamentacions of a Sorrowful Soule* was published in 1614. Leighton wrote its texts a year previously while imprisoned (wrongly, if we are to believe him) for debt. On his release he secured the 'best composers of the age' to set some of his words. This was no mean boast, and what is more remarkable is the very high quality of the settings, for commissioned works can often turn out to be disappointing. Leighton persuaded composers such as Coprario and Bull to compose for forces unusual to them, and elicited masterpieces from almost every composer, including exquisite gems from Byrd and Gibbons.

The collection seems to have initiated a vogue for somewhat pietistic texts, which are also evident in Myriell's unpublished collection of 1616 entitled *Tristitiae Remedium* (BL Add. 29372–7) and the related source Oxford Ch Ch 56–60 (bass missing). Many of the items in these collections are sacred madrigals — indeed, Wilbye's 'O God the rock' is merely a reworking of 'Draw on sweet night'. The works of Peerson, Ward and Ravenscroft appearing in these collections are often of considerable interest. Ward's 'Down caitiff wretch' (whose second part 'Prayer is an endless chain of purest love' is displaced by Myriell) is remarkable; and yet, though anthems of this kind are clearly from a madrigalist, Ward's church music proper shows him able to take on a different mantle:

Ex. 157

Apart from the Baroque flourish of passages such as these, Ward's church music is more staid than his contributions to the collections already mentioned. The items in these anthologies are often so festooned with madrigalisms (eg. Robert Jones' 'Lament, lament') that it is difficult to reconcile their music with sacred words. This is not so, however, in works such as Peerson's 'O let me at thy footstool fall' or Ford's 'Miserere my maker' (set to the same text as the song quoted on p. 34) whose chromaticisms, though arresting, do not obtrude to the level of mere mannerisms. The madrigalian character of these sources (cf. Monson, 1982) reflect the fact that lack of reward had forced many Jacobean church musicians to write domestic music.

At Court, meanwhile, there was a marked rise in the composition of occasional pieces by composers such as Allison, Bennet, Hooper, Gibbons and Tomkins. The Gunpowder plot of 1605, for example, inspired a rash of thanksgiving anthems. In the provinces, the state of church music was at a low ebb, although the music of William Smith of Durham is an honourable exception. His other music is mostly forgotten, but his Preces and Responses are virtually the only set, apart from Byrd's and Tomkins', which remain evergreen amongst the somewhat sparse and dull foliage of the settings by Tallis, Morley, Gibbons and others.

It was in their Services and anthems that Byrd, Weelkes, Tomkins and Gibbons continued to uphold the standards established in earlier years. Tomkins lived on into another age, so his special position will be considered separately. Of the rest, who all died within a year or two of each other, Gibbons is the presiding genius of Jacobean church music.

Both Oxford and Cambridge lay claim to having nurtured Orlando Gibbons, for although he was born in the former city in 1583, the family moved to Cambridge about five years later. There he was a chorister at King's College, Cambridge from 1596, taking the degree of B.Mus. in 1606. By this time, however, he had become organist of the Chapel Royal, having been appointed in 1604 when only twenty-one years of age. A contemporary report of his playing speaks of him as having 'the best hand in England'; another writer, on hearing him perform, said 'the organ was touched by the best Finger of that Age.'

In 1622 Gibbons became a Doctor of Music at Oxford, in the company of his friend William Heyther, in whose name the Professorship of Music was founded. The Statutes required an exercise in eight parts for this degree, and since Heyther was no composer, the formalities were satisfied by Gibbons himself writing 'Dr. Heyther's Commencemt Song' — the anthem 'O clap your hands'. In the next year Gibbons was appointed organist at Westminster Abbey; but soon after, in 1625, he died suddenly while attending King Charles, as a Gentleman of the Chapel Royal. The king was at Canterbury awaiting the arrival of his new wife, Henrietta Maria, from France; it was there, on the fifth of June that Gibbons was apparently seized by a fatal attack of apoplexy.

Although Gibbons died at a comparatively early age, this circumstance can hardly account for his small output — a couple of Services, between two and three dozen anthems, a book of madrigals, a moderate amount of keyboard and concerted music and a few other miscellaneous pieces. In comparison with Purcell, who died rather younger, or with the enormous output of Byrd, these few works look meagre indeed. It may be that Gibbons spent a great deal of time as a performer that he was a perfectionist in this and in his compositions, or that he was simply a slow worker. All of these reasons may account for the comparatively slender legacy with which we are left. But because of this it is particularly precious, and it is important to try to recover some partially lost works: something like a dozen of his anthems exist either as organ scores alone, or with several parts missing. The ravages of time may often be made good, as in several similar works by Weelkes, with a fair degree of confidence; and since this represents such a sizable proportion of Gibbons' output, the task is well worthwhile.

Yet, even the works which have apparently been preserved entire for us are not what they seem. There is evidence that many of the Verse anthems now existing with organ accompaniment were originally designed for concerted instruments. The Second service may have had this type of accompaniment, for one of the sources has a wordless part which may well have come from an earlier instrumental version; similar traces are found in the anthem 'Behold, I bring you glad tidings.' Elsewhere, for example in 'Almighty God, who by thy Son', repeated notes in what is now the organ part seem much more characteristic of another instrument; nor does the complex counterpoint, involving several uncharacteristic stretches, in 'O God the King of Glory' seem particularly suited to the organ. Yet the curious fact is that, apart from one anthem ('See, see, the word is incarnate'), the consort accompaniments are preserved solely in one manuscript, and one of intriguing pedigree at that.

Oxford Ch Ch 21 is singular in more than one regard: it is in score format, which at that time was an extreme rarity, and, additionally, it has an enigmatic connection with Orlando Gibbons. The manuscript was long thought to be his autograph, but it is clearly in a later hand, plausibly ascribed to his son, Christopher. Whether or not this be the case, the versions of this MS seem to be authentic and dubious by turns. 'See, see, the word is incarnate' exists in a similar version in an independent source (Myriell's *Tristitiae remedium*) but not elsewhere. Some of the anthems in Oxford Ch Ch 21 have headings concerning the authorship of the words, or the circumstances of composition, which surely derive from the composer. The anthem 'Blessed are all they that fear the Lord' is described as a 'wedding Anthem first made for my Lord of Summersett' (he married the notorious Lady Essex in 1613); but against this obviously personal information, the version of this anthem found in the score ends in a manner which is spectacularly different from that found in the other MSS; it has a Baroque flourish which seems to be somewhat in advance of English taste in 1613. Looking closely at the Christ Church source, other oddities are apparent. A pair of consecutives appear in 'This is the record of John', which Gibbons is hardly likely to have written; 'We praise thee, O father' lacks the introduction found in the organ sources, and in 'Glorious and powerful God' one of the 'points' appears upside down (the effect is rather like hearing the word 'cuckoo' with its notes sung backwards) whereas the organ score sources have this passage in an evidently correct form (cp. the peculiarities of the opening of 'Sing unto the Lord' — see *EECM* 3). For these and many other reasons Gibbons is unlikely to have written many of these versions as they stand. On the other hand 'Glorious and powerful God' is here in five parts, while all the other versions of this immensely popular anthem are clearly four-part arrangements of the original; and there are many unique anthems, including two occasional pieces composed for the King, and at least one (the rather miserable and etiolated 'O Lord, in thee is all my trust') seems to be an early work. The testimony of the manuscript is thus peculiarly contradictory.

A plausible solution to this contradiction is that Christopher compiled what may have been intended as part of a 'complete edition' of his father's work. Some of it ('See, see, the word', 'This is the record of John', the royal anthems and some of the other occasional anthems) was drawn from reasonably accurate instrumental sources to hand, even if Orlando (or Christopher) touched up the ending to 'Blessed are all they.' But although the remaining Verse anthems were written with instrumental accompaniments, the original versions were perhaps lost, and so had to be reconstituted from the sources in current circulation. The errors and additions to 'We praise thee O Father', 'Sing unto the Lord' and 'Glorious and powerful God' are most easily explained in this way. It is possible to go further, and assert that probably most, if not all, of his Verse anthems were originally designed for concerted accompaniment; therefore, some of the versions of the manuscript have a status comparable with modern reconstructions of Gibbons' works.

Our attitude towards a composer's work is markedly different from that of Gibbons' contemporaries. Nowadays most performers at least pay lip-service, whatever happens in practice, to the idea that a composer's work is sacrosanct. The Elizabethans, however, felt free to emend or arrange a work, sometimes drastically. This attitude, coupled with the hazards associated with the manuscript transmission of music, at once makes the task of restoring the composer's intentions often difficult, but also offers the consolation that modern reconstructions are sometimes as true to the composer's intentions as many early versions.

Gibbons' Full anthems survive intact, apart from 'I am the resurrection' whose first alto and tenor parts are missing. In spite of this, it is evident that the anthem is one of Gibbons' most polished works:

Ex. 158

The same high standard is reached, and perhaps exceeded, in the two highly-charged miniatures which Gibbons contributed to Leighton's 1614 Collection, 'O Lord, how do my woes' and 'O Lord, I lift my heart to thee' (printed in Wulstan 1971b: the versions in *EECM* 11 — particularly of the latter, which omits the repeat — are not always reliable in matters of detail). The six-part 'O Lord, in thy wrath' is in a class of its own; together with the serene 'Almighty and everlasting God' it has deservedly retained its place for half a century in the cathedral repertory since Fellowes brought this music once more to light. The same is true of 'Hosanna to the son of David'. Although closely modelled on Byrd's 'Exalt thyself' — formally (both evince an A B A structure) and, to some extent, melodically — Gibbons nevertheless creates a far more exciting texture, and exhibits a stronger sense of design. The master stroke is that the Verse opening is recaptured, before the Full forces have concluded their section, towards the end of the work. Far from being lost in the texture, this more distant 'Hosanna' captures the ear and the imagination in a telling fashion, and points up the striking ending of the work. The large scale 'O clap your hands' written as Heyther's D. Mus. exercise, is in eight parts throughout; but the first section treats the choir as an eight-part entity, while the second section, 'God is gone up', makes full use of the alternation between *Decani* and *Cantoris*. This vigorous anthem is one of Gibbons' most extended essays, and must also be accounted as one of the masterpieces of the period.

'Lift up your heads', the dismal 'O Lord in thee is all my trust', 'Deliver us, O Lord' and 'Out of the deep' (if indeed this is by him, and not by Byrd) are all either early works or pieces over which Gibbons did not lavish his customary care. 'O Lord increase our (my) faith' is not by Gibbons, though so ascribed by Tudway: in common with 'Why art thou so heavy', it is by the somewhat later composer Henry Loosemore.

Turning to the Verse anthems, Gibbons' mastery of the form is unquestionable. 'See, see, the word is incarnate' (the words, according to Oxford Ch Ch 21, were 'made by Doctor Goodman, Dean of Rochester') is an appropriate setting of a fine text. The 'Baroque' ending at 'and heaven laid open to all sinners' is striking, as are several other passages, particularly the carefully contrived climax at 'the powers of hell are shaken'. This anthem, together with the justly well-known 'This is the record of John' shows the uncanny ability of Gibbons to enfold a declamatory voice part within a fully worked-out contrapuntal texture, uniting the *prima* with the *seconda prattica*.

'Sing unto the Lord' is equally fine, with its unusual opening duet for two basses, and the effective word painting at the words 'when I go down into the pit'. The work is also a good example of the variety of technique employed by Gibbons in the Verse anthem, sometimes having no repetition between the Verse and Full sections, sometimes dovetailing the sections. 'We praise thee, O Father' is another fine example: here the unusual feature is the mellifluous duet for tenors at 'for he is the very Paschal Lamb'. 'Blessed are all they' (1613), 'Glorious and powerful God', 'If ye be risen', 'Lord, grant grace', and 'O God the king of glory' must all be mentioned as being in the front rank. 'Behold thou hast made my days' (1618) is not so successful. According to Oxford Ch Ch 21, which is the sole source of these circumstantial headings, 'This Anthem was made at the entratie of Doctor Maxcie, Deane of Winsor the same day sennight before his death'. Perhaps pressure of time caused the composer to adapt some of his 'lachrymae' pavans to do duty for the section 'O spare me a little' which verges on the comical, due to the peculiarly inapposite verbal repetitions.

The occasional anthems are often successful, particularly 'Great King of Gods' written in 1617 'for the King's being in Scotland'. This fine piece is a companion to the concerted madrigal 'Do not repine, fair Sun' which was also occasioned by James' return to his native Scotland, which he had not seen since becoming King of England in 1603. Much expense and labour surrounded the visit: the chapel of Holyrood was refurbished, a new Dallam organ was installed in a case by Inigo Jones, and the Edinburgh students presented laudatory addresses in Greek and Latin Verse. 'Do not repin, fair Sun' plays upon the return of Scotland's son, and makes reference to the place where the sun rose (for James was born in Edinburgh), only to be outshone by regal majesty (Brett, 1981).

James, 'the wisest fool in Christendom', was also honoured in 'O all true faithful hearts' (1619 — 'A thanksgiving for the King's happy recovery from a great dangerous sickness'). The later 'Thou God of wisdom' (fragmentary, but able to be completed) is less successful, but 'Grant, O holy Trinity' (apparently for King Charles on Trinity Sunday, which fell on the 12th of June in 1625 — the year of Gibbons' death) shows that Gibbons' lapses were merely temporary.

In the latter anthem, the Verses require reconstruction, as in 'Almighty God, who by thy son', which apparently (cf. *EECM* 3) begins without an organ introduction. The justification for this unusual procedure is not only the exigencies of the counterpoint: Full anthems had no written-out introduction, and the Nunc Dimittis of Gibbons' Second service begins vocally, with no organ introduction — since an 'Offertory' voluntary was often played before the anthem (cf. Rimbault, 1872, p. 169 and le Huray, 1967, p. 165), it seems likely that an organ piece of this nature provided the necessary note for the opening voices.

Of the fragmentary Verse anthems, 'So God loved the world' is not so successful as 'Almighty God, which hast given', although 'Lord we beseech thee' is one of Gibbons' finest essays in the medium. 'Praise the Lord, O my soul', for trebles, is also a work of high quality, standing beside 'O clap your hands' with which it shares a common motive ('O sing praises'): this borrowing incidentally dispels the doubt, expressed by one writer, that 'Praise the Lord' is not by Gibbons. 'Unto thee, O Lord', however, although printed in *EECM* 21, seems unlikely to be by the same composer.

The apparently late anthems 'Thou God of wisdom', 'So God loved the world' and 'Teach us by his example' (surviving only in a single voice part) all seem to be based upon texts by George Wither, who was an uneven poet of somewhat tempestuous character. Wither spent some of his life in and out of prison for offending various authorities: his work, although sometimes sublime, was often unbelievably trite. In 1622 he published a book of metrical psalms with very amateurishly arranged tunes. It seems more than likely that Gibbons saw this volume, and proposed collaboration in a further volume which became the *Hymns and Songs of the Church* of 1623. Since only the tune and bass were printed, the 'Hymns', were presumably designed for extempore accompaniment or for the possible addition of vocal parts. Some of the tunes are of a high quality, but others bear the marks of having been ineffectively tampered with by an amateur. Wither's book was issued with music in at least twelve different formats, some of which have fundamental differences, others misprints; in at least one case it looks as though the printers dropped the type on the floor between one impression and another, and put it back incorrectly. It seems from this that Gibbons probably did not see the final prints until it was too late — Wither having made several alterations and additions to Gibbons' music. For example, Song 14 seems to be an indifferent arrangement of phrases found in some of the other tunes. Song 34 appears to be altered and lengthened as Song 9, and longer still as Song 44. Only one of these (possibly Song 9) is likely to be the original. Song 46 is used as Song 47 (in a different metre) in some editions, and Song 41 is so horrible that Gibbons cannot possibly have had a hand in it; however, Song 67 (which appears earlier in Prys' Welsh *Llyfr Psalmau* of 1621) was possibly arranged by him. Wither's collaboration has all the appearance of an enthusiastic and meddlesome amateur, whose mercurial changes of mind can hardly have been followed by Gibbons.

The Service music of Gibbons is significant, though comparatively small in quantity. The disarming quality of the First service in four parts conceals the technical assurance which marks this work as one of the finest Full services of the whole period. His settings of the Preces are frankly dull, though the associated psalms, such as 'I will magnify thee' for the Second preces, are finely wrought. 'The eyes of all' has some Verse passages, and 'Awake up my glory' has a more elaborate Verse treatment. Although the organ part for the latter has not survived, the loss is not wholly irreparable. Similarly, although the organ part for one or two sections of the Second service is no longer extant, the problems of reconstruction are not too severe.

There can be little doubt that the Second service is one of Gibbons' finest works: it stands out as being the most accomplished of all Verse services, and is a major landmark in the history of English church music. Although the Venite is not set, there is an elaborate Te Deum and Jubilate (Gibbons was one of the few composers to set this alternative to the Benedictus prescribed in the later Prayer Books), together with the usual Evening canticles. The surviving organ part for the Morning service (in common with that for 'Glorious and powerful God') clearly relates to a shortened arrangement of the original. That the longer version is Gibbons' own is made clear by the Gloria of the Jubilate (the same as that of the Magnificat and Nunc Dimittis), quite apart from the lack of balance and breadth evident in the truncated version. In this Service, the quintessential Gibbons is always evident, from the dramatic duets and double duets at 'he hath shewed strength' or 'he hath put down' to the serene 'he remembering his mercy':

Ex. 159

The Second service represents Gibbons at his incomparable best. Nowadays, it is difficult to see why his Verse anthems and Services were long reckoned to be inferior to his Full anthems. The editors of *Tudor Church Music*, for example, saw fit to conclude that 'his merits were somewhat overestimated by his contempories' and to find 'crudities' in 'pioneer work' such as 'O God the king of glory'. Since they described the indifferent 'Lift up your heads' as a work of 'bold assurance', we may place less confidence in these and other considerably more unfortunate judgements, than in Tudway who wrote, at the turn of the eighteenth century, that Gibbons' works were 'the most perfect pieces of Church music which have appeared since the time of Tallis and Byrd.' In particular, their assertion that the Verse anthems were inferior to the Full does not stand up to close scrutiny, for while there are good and bad examples of both types, the quality of many of his Verse pieces is extraordinarily high. If one characteristic were to be singled out, it is perhaps the reconciliation of a Baroque declamatory style with a thorough-going Renaissance contrapuntal texture. 'This is the record', 'We praise thee O Father', 'Sing unto the Lord' and almost all his other Verse settings have in their solo passages the declamatory quality of recitative without its musical limitations. Gibbons set the standard for later generations, through his pupils Walter Porter and Christopher Gibbons which, in spite of the puny efforts of men like Child in the intervening years, was carried forward by Blow and Purcell. Both of the latter composers had a habit of using a canonic Gloria to their Services, a device which dates back to Gibbons' First service. In the combination of declamation and expressive counterpoint found in many of Purcell's and Blow's works, it is not difficult to see the influence of Gibbons; and there is little doubt that Purcell's extraordinary Fantazias also owe much to the same composer.

A year before Byrd's death in 1623 Peacham wrote in *The Compleat Gentleman*:

> For Motets and Musick of piety and devotion . . . William Byrd, whom in that Kind, I know not whether any may equal, I am sure none excell, even in the judgement of France and Italy who are very sparing in the commendation of strangers, in regard of that conceipt they hold of themselves. His *Cantiones Sacrae* as also his *Gradualia* are meer Angelicall and Divine; and being of himself naturally disposed to Gravity and Piety, his rein is not so much for leight Madrigals or Canzonets; yet his Verginella and some others in his first Set, cannot be mended by the best Italian of them all.

An amusing remark in one of Dow's partbooks (Oxford Ch Ch 984–88) quotes Cicero as saying that the British have no plunder to offer except slaves, and none of these is skilled in letters or music: 'Byrd' says Dow in a Latin rejoinder, 'is the man who absolves the English from this reproach'. Gibbons (with which *Parthenia* claimed a parallel with Lassus) and Byrd, together with Dowland and many others, consciously took up the challenge of the supposed superiority of continental music. And although English music may have been slow to follow the latest fashions, notably the vogue for recitative which it splendidly ignored, its technical achievements by no means lagged behind the Continent, save on a purely superficial level. Yet

339

the greatness of the age had reached its apogee. As Byrd said in the preface to his *Gradualia* of 1605, 'The swan, they say, sings the sweeter when death approaches.'

The age of the silver swan was coming to a close. The death of Byrd (in 1623), of whom Morley said was 'never without reverence to be named of the musicians', was followed by Gibbons' sudden collapse and death in 1625. King James had died earlier that year: King Charles and Queen Henrietta were married by proxy, after which the new queen came to Canterbury. There, before the marriage festivities could begin, Gibbons was, as his epitaph says, 'deprived of life by a lamentable rush of blood [apoplexy] and the cruel hand of fate; and was translated into the celestial choir on Whitsunday, 1625.' The epitaph spoke of his 'fingers rivalling the harmony of the spheres', of his upright and agreeable personality, his musicianship, and the grief of his wife. His temperament paralleled that of Byrd: they were both (as Gibbons' portrait suggests) 'naturally disposed to Gravity and Piety'.

With the accession of the ill-fated Charles to the throne, and the death of Gibbons, the Golden Age of English church music came to an end. Echoes of this age were still resonant, however, in Worcester, where Tomkins continued to compose in the old style and, in the twilight after the sun of the Tudor age had set, recalled in his music the glow of its many achievements.

CHAPTER 13

Distracted Tymes

Although he was born in c. 1572, Thomas Tomkins was intellectually a child of the reign of Henry VIII. One of the most important manuscripts dating from Henrician times, and which includes most of the surviving liturgical organ music of the period, was one of his treasured possessions. Several of its pieces are annotated in such a way as to show that Tomkins frequently performed them, and doubtless came under their tutelage. Sometimes he is content to comment 'an excellent verse' or 'a good old indeede'; elsewhere he warns himself 'the cliffe changes' or 'a crotchet rest.' Later in the manuscript (BL Add. 29996) there are scores, in his own handwriting, of the music of other composers from whom he learned much, such as Ferrabosco and Byrd, together with pieces by his contemporaries Gibbons, Farmer, Morley and his friend Nicholas Carleton. The latter's 'Verse' for two players inspired Tomkins to write his own 'Fancy, for two to play', and some of the experiments in chromaticism found, for example, in Tomkins' music for viols, may well have been influenced by Carleton's chromatic keyboard pieces.

Tomkins' many compositions — madrigals and psalm tunes, keyboard music and English church music — entitle him to an honoured position in several chapters of this book; it is a curious fact that he has a significant connection with many of the topics covered in the preceding pages. His autograph manuscripts, for example, shed valuable light on the question of virginalist ornaments; and the fact that these MSS are ordered into keys is of more than passing interest. Tomkins had strong views about key, as is evident in a remark in one of his MSS (Paris Cons Rés 1122): there is an instruction to the effect that certain compositions were to be recopied and, 'being in the key of gamut to be suited and sorted together. And whatsoever Fancies or selected Voluntaries of worthe to be placed in their owne native keyes not mingling or mangling them together with others of contrarey keys: But put them in theyre Right places.'

This is a valuable confirmation that composers, especially English composers, thought in 'keys' rather than in modes. It would be interesting to know Tomkins' judgement of modern critics who attempt to ascribe Tallis' 'Videte miraculum' to the 'Phrygian mode' and to resort to the suppression of accidentals by way of argument. His use of the false relation, if not excessive, is certainly not bashful: 'Almighty God, the fountain of all wisdom' would have called forth Morley's pedantic obloquy; and doubtless one of his verses (*MB* V no. 30) which uses the 'English cadence' relentlessly as its point, would have been described as 'out of the capcase of some old organist.'

It may be argued that 'Almighty God, the fountain of all wisdom' is one of Cranmer's most moving Collects, certainly it is his most original; but it was not until Tomkins that it was set to music of an answering fervour. The hand of Cranmer is writ large on many of Tomkins' pages; more than any other composer, he was keenly responsive to the Prayer Book Collects, which he frequently set. Nor did any other composer provide more splendid Preces, Responses and psalms; and his Third or 'Great' service is one of the finest of its kind.

In connection with Morley, it is interesting to note that Tomkins was the owner and avid annotator of a copy of the *Plaine and Easie Introduction to Practicall Musicke* of 1597. Several emendations occur in his hand, and there is an intriguing list of additional musicians appended to the column of 'Practicioners' whom Morley listed at the end of his work. The canons which Tomkins added to the relevant section of Morley's book are perhaps the most valuable of the annotations, however, and show that Tomkins was a considerably better 'practitioner' than Morley. By a happy coincidence, Tomkins' copy of the work was given to the library of Magdalen College, Oxford, where Thomas took his B.Mus; it is fortunate also that the modern reproduction published in 1971 by the Gregg Press is of this copy.

Tomkins' work expresses the spirit of the age, of 'friendly aemulation', rather better than Morley's. The opening motive of Byrd's Second service is quoted in Tomkins' Fifth, and 'Hear my prayer' which uses a point derived from Gibbons' 'Behold, thou hast made my days'. An In Nomine for viols also makes use of a bass by Gibbons; and there are many other borrowings. But Tomkins pays Byrd and Gibbons back handsomely, along with Giles, Ward, Dowland and many others, in the dedications to his *Songs of 3.4.5. and 6 parts*, printed in 1622.

This set of books was published long after the madrigalian vogue had passed, a circumstance reflected in the title — *Songs* rather than 'madrigals'. The three-part songs show a remarkable variety achieved within a technically difficult texture, while the four-part songs are even more varied. Here Dowland is doubly honoured in 'O let me live for true love', for his name appears as its dedicatee, and his 'lachrymae' trademark is gently mocked in this delightful song: its second part is dedicated to John Daniel, whom Tomkins perhaps considered second only to Dowland. The stock character of the town crier is the subject of 'Oyez, has any found a lad?' dedicated to Coprario; transalpine echoes are found both here and in 'Weep no more' and 'Yet again' (the latter two songs being dedicated to two of Tomkins' brothers). Denis Stevens, in his indispensible book on the composer (1957) has drawn attention to the *sospiri* crotchet rests at the word 'sighs', to the 'Gesualdo–like chordal juxtapositions at "laughs and weeps"', and to many other Italianate features of the collection.

The musical puns in which Tomkins indulges while portraying his friends and relations, ineluctably call to mind the spirit in which a much later English composer characterized his 'friends pictured within'. The equivalent of Elgar's Nimrod is there too, for 'When David heard' is dedicated to Thomas Myriell, for whose *Tristitiae Remedium* of 1616 this outstanding lament was first written:

Ex. 160

This grief-laden style is paralleled in many other works of Tomkins. It is remarkable that he achieves his plangent effects, not by exaggerated chromatic shifts, but by the skilful juxtaposition of sharp and flat notes. This technique is evident in 'Absalom my son', in 'When David heard'; and at the words 'dying', and 'thine eyes have slain' in 'Phyllis, yet see him dying', where the augmented triad unites the extreme inflections of the scale. Although the latter madrigal is dedicated to his neighbour Carleton, the chord is also a tribute to Gibbons, who used it at the words 'O death come close mine eyes' in 'The silver swan'. Phineas Fletcher (the poet of 'Drop, drop slow tears'), and the musicians William Heyther and John Ward are also honoured in fine songs; and though the three last items of the collection have the appearance of being afterthoughts Stevens rightly comments upon the concluding 'Turn unto the Lord', by saying that it is a 'noble ending to a book of songs whose excellence cannot be over-rated.'

Quite apart from its musical worth, 'When David heard' is an important piece of evidence confirming the significance of the clefs in determining the pitch level of the music of this period. In the *Songs* of 1622 the piece is printed a fifth higher than in *Musica Deo Sacra* (1668), but with different clefs (see p. 211). Taken together with the statement in the Tenbury copy of *Musica Deo Sacra* and Thomas Tomkins' letter preserved in the Bodleian Library, here is proof that music in 'normal' clefs was sung at organ pitch, a minor third higher than today's standard, and that Tomkins' use of a particular set of 'high cliffs' as Morley called them, demand downward transposition. It is moreover fortunate that Tomkins' correspondence about the old Worcester organ should be preserved, for without it it is doubtful that the problem of the duality of organ and choir pitch would have been satisfactorily resolved. 'When David heard' also provides a hint concerning the participation of other instruments in vocal music. Charles Butler (1636, p. 5) mentions hearing this example of Tomkins' 'exquisite invention, wit and art' in the Music School at Oxford, where it was performed by 'sweet well-governed voices, with consonant instruments'.

Although Tomkins was not an undergraduate at Magdalen College (he became a member merely in order to supplicate for the degree of B.Mus) he was friendly with Arthur Philips, who succeeded Nicolson both at Magdalen as organist and in the University as Heyther Professor of Music. BL Add. 29996 contains a 'Ground' for keyboard dedicated to Arthur Philips. Heyther himself was honoured by Tomkins in the 1622 *Songs*: the text 'Music divine' was particularly appropriate for the man in whose name the Chair in Music had been founded, and upon whom the University had conferred the D.Mus. in the same year. Heyther's choice of Richard Nicolson to be the first holder of the post might appear curious, but the latter's madrigals show that he was no mean composer, and his concerted songs — particularly the 'Cuckoo song' and the equally felicitous 'In a merry May morn' are outstanding examples of the genre. It is particularly to be regretted that Nicolson composed so little church music, for 'O pray for the peace of Jerusalem' is a masterpiece, as is 'Cantate domino'; and the exquisite concerted anthem 'When Jesus sat at meat', composed for St Mary Magdalen's day, has an especial place in Oxford music. If the series of songs in BL Add. 17797 is by Nicolson, they show him to have been both a gifted composer and one intrigued by technical problems. Various hymn-tunes from Sternhold and Hopkins' *The Whole Booke of Psalmes* are taken bodily as the voice part, while the instruments bring these dull tunes on to an altogether different plane by weaving a sensuous web of polyphony upon the In Nomine cantus firmus. Quite apart from the technical achievement of reconciling two cantus firmi at once, the music, moreover, shows no sign of technical restraint, and flows with unencumbered freedom.

Peerson composed similar concerted settings of Sternhold and Hopkins' tunes, and Dowland's 1597 'Lamentation' for Henry Noel are in effect a set of elaborate chorale-like arrangements of these melodies. The singing of psalms was much practised by the Puritan party of the Church of England, and it has to be remembered that the raising of the standard of musical literacy in England was due to the Puritans' insistence on singing psalms 'in stede of unseemlay Ballades' (Hake, apud Daman, 1579). Although Henry VIII, Queen Mary and Queen Elizabeth were at least tolerable musicians, their ordinary subjects, as was seen earlier, were far from being a nation of singers and viol players of popular supposition. The fashion for psalm singing (especially strong in the Reformed Church of Scotland) had a beneficent effect both on musical standards and upon the economics of music publishing: a large number of psalters was issued in the late sixteenth and early seventeenth century, some of the most interesting being Tailour's *Sacred Hymns . . .* (1615) 'set to be sung in Five parts, as also to the Viole and Lute and Orpharion.' Tailour's settings were extremely florid (see Frost, 1953), while most other collections (eg. those of Daman, 1579; East, 1592 and Allison, 1599) were content to present note-against-note harmonizations of the 'church tunes'. Tomkins contributed two psalm tunes to an anonymous book entitled *The CL Psalms of David* (1615); they were reprinted in Ravenscroft's collection of 1621. Five further hymns are found in *Musica Deo Sacra*, the monumental collection of Tomkins' church music published, probably by his son Nathaniel, in 1668 after Thomas' death.

Although appearing well outside the Tudor period, *Musica Deo Sacra*, in common with Barnard's publication dated 1641, is a retrospective collection. Unlike Barnard, however, *Musica Deo Sacra* includes an organ part. As Morehen has pointed out (1972) Barnard's failure to include an organ part was prompted, at least in part, by technical difficulties connected with the type-setting methods of the time. There is every sign of these difficulties in the 1668 set.

It seems probable that Thomas had carefully preserved his church music with a view to publication, a prospect which dimmed as the years of Cromwell came to pass. On his father's death in 1656, Nathaniel may have felt it incumbent upon him to bring Thomas' hopes to fruition. This act of filial piety preserved the greater part of Tomkins' church music. The collection is not without its flaws, however, for apart from simple mistakes, the underlay of the words to the music is far from satisfactory in an alarming number of cases. Whether this was the printer's fault, or Nathaniel's, is not clear; it is highly unlikely that the blame can be laid at Thomas' door, for he was a meticulous, not to say pernickety, copyist, leaving directions (Stevens, 1957, p. 132) to recopy a book of keyboard pieces 'that the player may venture upon them with comfort.'

The hand of Nathaniel may have been responsible for the curious adaption of 'See, see, the shepherd's queen' (from the *Songs* of 1622) as 'Holy, holy, holy'. The false accentuation of *holý* is intolerable to modern ears: the grossness of the underlay can barely be excused on the grounds of changes in pronunciation. It is true that certain words in the Tudor period were accented differently from modern English, and musical settings often preserved archaic extra syllables in words such as *almes, tempta-ti-on* and *thro-row-out*, while *spirit* was almost uniformly set as a monosyllable, and *highest* often was. Some words, such as *unto*, varied their pronunciation according to the accentual complexion of the surrounding syllables, whereas words such as *July* and *holy* were probably pronounced with level stress. Thus Morley's 'April is in my mistress' face' sets *Júly* as though accented on the first syllable: this underlay is uncomfortable only because of the subsequent shift of the accent to *Julý*. But by the mid seventeenth century it is unlikely that the pronunciation *holý* would have been acceptable: it is difficult, therefore to credit Thomas with so evident a barbarism — the ill-fitting adaption of 'See see, the shepherd's queen' must therefore be debited to an over-enthusiastic Nathaniel.

Musica Deo Sacra was advertised in the *London Gazette* as being 'in ten books whereof one is the organ part.' Since there are only four separate partbooks (the *Decani* and *Cantoris* parts being printed on opposite pages in the same books) this number was questioned by Stevens (1957, p. 72). The advertisement however, should surely have read 'ten books *and one which* is the organ part.' A set of ten voice parts would be the normal minimum requirement for a standard choir, since the two contratenor parts were usually bound in separate books: the fact that Nathaniel had printed them under one cover was a device intended as an economy (to his own, rather than the purchaser's advantage); this accounts for the 'ten', the same number as comprised Barnard's earlier set of books. The extra boys' copies would have been done out in manuscript; though at Worcester, Barnard's books — if these are the twelve 'old' books mentioned (see Stevens, p. 73) in an inventory beside the 'Eight new books' (*Musica Deo Sacra*) — may have included the luxury of two extra *medius* parts.

Musica Deo Sacra clearly ranges through Tomkins' whole working life, and includes five Services, the First and Second of which are of the Short service type: they differ, nevertheless, in their technique, for the second is more varied than the first and is palpably a more mature work. The gem of the set, however, is the Third or Great service, which, while not as lengthy as Byrd's, is as concentrated in inspiration as Weelkes' 'Ninth' service, whose technique it sometimes resembles.

In this Service, another shortcoming of the four printed books is evident: the Verse rubrics give inadequate directions as to the precise disposition of voices; the instructions require amplification if a modern performance is to do justice to Tomkins' doubtless complex intentions in the matter of antiphony.

The Fourth and Fifth services are Verse settings, with a florid organ part. In common with the Full services, the tradition of 'head motives' is kept up, thus enclosing the late flowering of Tomkins' art within the walls of the Tudor garden. The opening motive of the Fourth service is taken from Byrd's Second, though Tomkins' over-extended treatment is not as successful as Byrd's more restrained model. The Fifth service is more consistent, despite some passages (particularly in the Morning canticles) having a seemingly mechanical quality. The abundance of dramatic bass verses is notable; it seems likely (as in the case of several striking bass verses in the anthems) that Tomkins composed these for a favourite singer. However, there are also fine verses for other voices, for example the double mean verse at 'as he promised' in the Magnificat and 'To be a light' in the Nunc Dimittis.

The quality of Tomkins' inspiration falls sharply in the Sixth and Seventh services, which Nathaniel, rightly, did not include in *Musica Deo Sacra*. Reconstructions of these Services which have been made by Peter James and David Evans, show that for the most part, they do not rise above a workmanlike level. The same can hardly be said of the 'Psalmody' (ie. the Preces, Responses and psalms), which are of a consistently high standard. The disarming simplicity which hides the technical mastery of 'Lord who shall dwell in thy tabernacle' (apart from a slight awkwardness with the word *tabernacle*) is an apt demonstration of *ars artis celandae*.

Many fine anthems are included in *Musica Deo Sacra*, and although it is true that the level of inspiration is occasionally low, it is generally a matter for wonderment that Tomkins is able to say something new in such a large number of works. In the Full anthems there are masterpieces alike in the three-part anthems (especially the seven penitential psalms), those for four parts (some of which are for men's voices), and especially amongst the five-part anthems which include such gems as 'Almighty God, the fountain of all wisdom' and 'When David heard'. In larger-scale textures Tomkins is less consistently successful, though 'O sing unto the Lord' and the massive twelve-part 'O Praise the Lord, all ye heathen' deserve mention. A solitary Latin anthem, 'Domine, tu eruisti' (Rose, 1971) may have been intended for Peterhouse, Cambridge, where Latin was in use in the 1630s.

'Behold, I bring you glad tidings' is an elaborate Christmas Verse anthem with a ten-part chorus to the words 'Glory be to God in the highest'. In common with 'O praise the Lord', this anthem was presumably written for the ample resources of the Chapel Royal. The Coronation of James I called forth the Full anthem 'Be strong and of a good courage', but a much finer work, which does not appear in *Musica Deo Sacra*, was inspired by the deeply-felt loss of Prince Henry in 1612. 'Know you not' must have been one of the 'several anthems to the organs and other wind instruments' performed on the occasion of the funeral on December 7. Peter James, who published a reconstruction of this anthem (1971), points to its 'remarkable use of chromaticism and abrupt modulations'(see Ex. 161).

The consort parts to this anthem (the end of which is quoted on the final page of this chapter) have not survived, but those for several other Verse anthems are extant. 'Above the stars my saviour dwells', with its ardent ending 'Come Lord Jesu, come away', is less colourful in the printed

Ex. 161

arrangement with organ accompaniment than in its concerted version.
'Thou art my king O God' (whose bass verse was rearranged by Edmund
Hooper for two basses) also survives with instrumental accompaniment, in
common with the fine 'Rejoice, rejoice', an anthem for the Annunciation.
An unusual feature of this work is that the chorus section precedes the first
Verse section, which includes a remarkable piece of word painting at 'when
the angel Gabriel, with an humble reverence, gave the salutation'. This
humility is depicted by a monotone voice part against a genuflecting instrumental tenor:

Ex. 162

This remarkable anthem was not, however, printed in *Musica Deo Sacra*. In
common with several other similar works, it exists in imperfect sources;
fortunately, however, only a certain amount of restoration is necessary to
render them performable. As with many of Tomkins' works in this state,
such as 'The Lord bless us' (on the text of Moses' priestly blessing) and
'Jesus came when the doors were shut' (St Thomas Didymus), convincing
reconstructions have been completed by Peter James.

Several other Verse anthems, notably 'Out of the deep' and 'Hear my prayer', instrumental were probably originally written for instrumental accompaniment which no longer survives. The former belongs to a class of about half a dozen Verse anthems involving, as in 'Know you not', the high treble voice. Few ascend above *a''flat*, however, although 'Know you not' and 'O that the salvation' involve top *b''flat*. It is interesting to note that, in the organization of choirs of the Tudor period, the *primus* or *Decani* singers took the lower part if there were a differentiation: thus the treble parts are assigned to the *secundus medius*, while several low bass parts are given to the *primus bassus* (often extending, as in 'Give sentence with me' — at the words 'afar off' — to low *E flat*). The reversal of this disposition, whereby *Decani* takes the upper part, seems to date from some time after the Restoration, for in Purcell and others the convention of *Cantoris* taking the higher part is still evident.

Tomkins' alto ranges are often particularly low, even in Verses (cf. 'Hear me when I call'); nonetheless, high notes are also called for — including top *d''flat*. In instances of this kind, however, Tomkins normally writes an alternative, as for example in 'Who can tell', whose passages involving the high *c''* are provided with alternative, lower, phrases. Similarly, high bass notes extending to *f* (as in the two-octave range of 'Sing unto God') are provided with alternative passages.

The anthems for trebles clearly emanate from the Chapel Royal where Gibbons, Tomkins, Weelkes, John Holmes, Barnard and others appear to have been involved in a brief revival of interest in the voice. The most curious fruit of this period is Gibbons' 'This is the record of John' whose alto solo is found transposed up an octave for treble in the Peterhouse version. Tomkins' debt to Gibbons is evident in several works. His 'Almighty God who hast given' uses material from 'Almighty God which hast given' by Gibbons; 'Hear my prayer' leans heavily upon his senior's 'Behold, thou hast made my days', even down to imitating the slightly ridiculous 'O spare me a little, me a little' which Gibbons hastily arranged from one of his 'lachrymae' pavans; but for all that it is a fine work and by no means inferior to its model.

Several more borrowings from other composers are apparent, notably in 'O pray for the peace of Jerusalem', based on Nicolson's Full anthem of the same name. Frequently, when Tomkins uses the thematic material of other composers, he cannot resist the temptation to amplify, often to an extent which gives the impression of gratuitous prolixity; but at his best the control of the medium is nicely judged. 'Behold, I bring you glad tidings', for example, far from owing anything directly to Gibbons' setting of the same words, is a superior work. The dancing 'tripla' rhythm in the organ part at 'tidings of great joy' is a felicitous touch, comparable with the dramatic *tirata* at '*raise* my duller eyen' in 'Above the stars'. Tomkins' habit of using rising scalewise passages is sometimes irritating; it is curious that many of these figures in the organ part of *Musica Deo Sacra* do not occur in other organ sources, and vice versa. It seems that they were of an improvisatory nature, and were often not a germinal part of his conception. Similarly, sporadic ornament strokes occur from time to time: but the rarity of the signs does not necessarily preclude the more heavily ornamented style familiar in purely keyboard music.

The declamatory style — 'Behold, the hour cometh' is a fine example — is well developed by Tomkins. 'Leave O my soul' is also highly dramatic. The end of 'My beloved spake' is particularly well judged; the words 'and come away' appear to recede on a distant echo:

Ex. 163

The sudden squall of rapid organ passage-work at the word 'tempest' in 'The Lord, even the most mighty God', followed by an appropriate motive at 'shall be stirred up', is one of a multiplicity of examples of Tomkins' imaginative ideas. Although he is often hampered by simpering or plain doggerel texts, he frequently manages to gloss over these limitations. The unfortunate metrical version of Psalm 23 'My shepherd is the living Lord' is perhaps not entirely mitigated by the musical invention, but elsewhere Tomkins often succeeds in concealing the embarrassing jingle of his doggerel texts.

The formal patterns espoused in Tomkins' Verse anthems offer a bewildering display of structural virtuosity. The techniques he employs are a long way from the stereotyped forms of the early Verse anthem. Although 'I will lift up mine eyes' begins with an archaistic chanted Incipit it is otherwise far from archaic in style; in some anthems repetition is excluded, in others it is pervasive, and there is an astonishing array of patterns which fall in between these extremes.

Although Tomkins' Verse anthems are his most memorable contribution to English church music, the significance of his Full anthems and Service music should not be forgotten. His Funeral sentences, including the chromatic 'I am the resurrection' (which to some extent recalls 'When David heard'), are the only significant settings of these texts before Purcell.

Tudway's judgement was peculiarly acuitous when he referred to Tomkins' 'very elaborate and artful pieces, and the most deserving to be recorded and held in everlasting remembrance' (cf. Stevens, 1957, p. 94).

Musica Deo Sacra was published close upon a century after Tomkins' birth. In common with Henry VII he was born in Wales; as has been noted, much of his music reflects earlier developments. His aberrant brother of the same name was expelled from the choir of St David's and went away to sea to become part of history, perishing in the last stand of the *Revenge*, against hopeless odds, in 1591. No less than fifty-three Spanish ships fought for fifteen hours; only at the last were the 150 English overwhelmed by 5,000 Spaniards. By the time of this heroic tragedy the Tomkins family had moved to Gloucester (cf. Evans, 1984). John, who was Thomas' illustrious half-brother, became organist of King's College, Cambridge, and was subsequently organist at St Paul's and the Chapel Royal; he is commemorated both in Phineas Fletcher's verse and in a moving elegy by William Lawes beginning 'Music, the master of thy art is dead'. Thomas' other relatives were often no less distinguished; another Thomas (the son of his half-brother John) achieved high academic distinction, and his half-brothers Giles and Robert became Court musicians.

Thomas' career began at St David's, where he was probably in the cathedral choir which, as elsewhere, had dwindled pitifully in Elizabethan years. After moving to Gloucester, Thomas, at no small sacrifice to his father, was sent to London in order to study music with his 'ancient, and much reverenced master, William Byrd' as the dedication of one of the *Songs* has it. He was appointed at Worcester in 1596, succeeding Nathaniel Patrick (although the unsatisfactory John Fido had acted as stand-in for a few months). In 1601 Morley accorded him the distinction of including 'The fauns and satyrs tripping' in *the Triumphes of Oriana*. In 1607 he took his Oxford B.Mus., and from then on composed a good deal of music, some of which may be ascribed with certainty to these years during which he was an 'extraordinary' member of the Chapel Royal while remaining organist of Worcester. Only in 1621, on the death of Hooper, did Tomkins become an organist at the Chapel Royal, Gibbons being at that date the senior organist.

About this time his *Songs* were published; some of his instrumental music perhaps also comes from this period. Tomkins imitated Gibbons in writing a sequence of Fantazias *à* 3 (fourteen of them, plus two In Nomines), and there are fantazias for five and six instruments (four for the latter), and nine pavans for five instruments. An Ut re mi and an alman are his only four-part instrumental works. Many of these compositions are remarkable for their imagination and vitality, none more so than the three-part essay in canonic chromaticism quoted by Stevens:

Ex. 164

Tomkins' keyboard music belongs principally to the later years of his life. Some of the 'Miserere' settings and the Felix namque Offertory (here he harked back to forms he had found in the Henrician manuscript of keyboard music in his possession) may well be early pieces, but others are dated between 1648 and 1652. There are In Nomine settings dating from 1647 to 1652 and numerous other works of this kind — fancies, voluntaries and so forth. There is an 'Ut re mi . . . For a beginner', though there are several other pieces which would hardly be suitable for a tyro organist or virginalist. Yet Tomkins never sinks into the Lisztian virtuosity of Bull: indeed he is often laconically critical of his older contemporary. Byrd's 'Quadran galliard' is described in one of his MSS as 'Excellent for the matter', while Bull's 'Quadran pavan' is merely 'Excellent for the hand'. In the 'Substantial Verse: maintaining the point', Tomkins' desire to achieve almost symphonic proportions is evident. Another notable characteristic is his avoidance of the clichés of earlier keyboard music: his 'grounds' and 'The perpetual round' are far removed from the often jocular essays of Byrd and Bull, being more serious workings of thematic material of the kind favoured by Purcell and Bach. His pavans and galliards, too, are far from conventional. The Pavan and Galliard in a minor (*MB* V, nos 47 & 48) are exquisitely turned:

Ex. 165

As with the *Songs*, the keyboard music abounds with references to Tomkins' personal life. 'A Toy . . . made at Poole court' is a reference to his friend John Toy, whose *Worcester Elegy and Eulogy* (1638) contains the following lines:

> To Master Thomas Tomkins, Bachelor of Musicke.
> And thou great Master of melodious skill,
> This holy harmony didst helpe to fill;
> When in this dismall Cadence, no sound else

Was heard but Mournefull groanes and mortall bels.
Thy hand an Organ was of ample good
To act in tune, and cheere our mourning mood.
According to thy Tenor, thou didst lend
Us Meanes, our low and base state to mend.
T'accomplish now this song of courtesie,
In triple time our thanks shall trebbles be.
These lines are Briefe, but know, thy Restlesse song
Of fame, shall stand in notes both large and long.

Toy also delivered the funeral oration upon Alice, Tomkins' dearly beloved wife — a truly moving tribute. Her death was a particularly severe blow to Tomkins, the more so since his hand and eye were failing, and events elsewhere were plunging him into deeper despair. His autograph keyboard manuscript is an eloquent testimony to these things: his handwriting is less steady, and the titles of the works reflect the wider tragedy into which the country was embroiled. The 'Pavan; Earl Strafford' is dated 1647, some six years after Strafford had been executed by the king, weakening to the demands of the Puritan Parliamentarians. Lord Canterbury, too, is

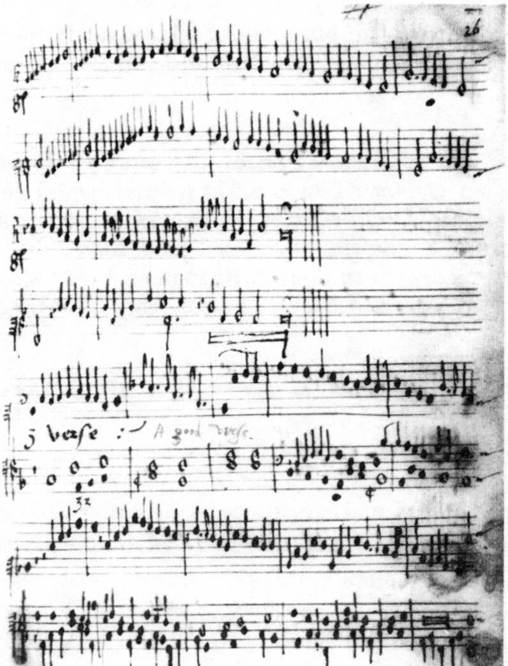

Fig. 32 MS comments in Tomkins' handwriting ('a good verse') (in BL Add. 29996 f.26)

commemorated in a pavan dated 1647. More eloquent still is 'A sad paven: for these distracted Tymes' dated February 14, 1649. The weak King Charles had exchanged his corruptible worldly crown for an incorruptible life after death.

The rapine destruction of the Parliamentarians hit Royalist Worcester and the loyal Tomkins especially hard. The cathedral organ which he had seen built was smashed, and the choir was silenced. The old composer repined, and went to live at Martin Hussingtree, with his newly-wedded son Nathaniel; such happiness as he might there have enjoyed must have been heavily tinged with the thought that his church music would perhaps be heard no longer. The seeds of the evil which brought about the fanatic puritanism had been sown in the Reformist years of Edward's reign and in the bloody years of Mary's. Elizabeth had succeeded in uniting her church in the path of moderation, but the bigotry of Jesuit and Puritan was still fertile. Its bitter harvest is still reaped from time to time. Cromwell's fervour is echoed, with differing accents, on either side of a contemporary religious divide. The parties, as with Cromwell, mistake self-righteousness for righteousness. The words of one of their countrymen were prophetic: 'We have just enough religion to make us hate, but not enough to make us love one another.' And so the tolerant days of Elizabeth and James were over, and 'civil wounds' which Henry VII had stopped, flowed again.

After two years at Martin Hussingtree, Thomas Tomkins died in 1656, being buried there in the churchyard on June 9th.

> Of ðis Mꝺꝺᵉ is ðat paſſionatᵉ Lamentation of ðe good muſical King, for ðe deaꝼ of his *Abſalom :* Compoſed in 5. Parts by Mr 7*b.Tomkins,* now-Organiſt of his Majeſti'sChappel.De melodious harmoni werᵉof, wen I heard in ðe *Muſik-ſkꝺꝺꝇ,* weiðer I ſꝺꝺldᵉ morᵉ admirᵉ ðe ſweetᵉ wel governed voices (wiꝼ conſonant Inſtruments) of ðe Singers; or ðe exqiſit Invention, wiꝼ, and Art of ðeCompoſer, it was hard to determin.

Fig. 33 Comment on Tomkins in Butler, *Principles of Musick*, 1636. The orthography is Butler's phonetic system.

Tomkins death brought to a close the late autumn of Tudor music, whose high summer had ended in 1625, the year in which the death of Orlando Gibbons had followed close upon that of Byrd. Tomkins' achievement was to set the seal upon the madrigal, keyboard and instrumental music, and upon the Anglican Service and anthem, themselves born out of the fertile anguish of earlier years. Much Tudor music has been lost to us, due to a lack of respect for old-fashioned manuscripts, to wanton destruction by misguided zealots, or merely because of the insouciant ravages of time; in spite of this, a large quantity nevertheless survives. Wren's *si monumentum re-*

quiris, circumspice would be an appropriate epitaph for this music if interpreted in spirit, rather than to the letter; for it is not enough to look about the silent vaults of the printed page; the glory of Tudor music is its sound. When the depredations wrought by fortune have been made good, and misunderstandings due to the effluxion of time have been resolved, then the true colours of this music, restored and burnished, may be heard again, expressing the inexpressible across the centuries. That Tudor music seems so near to us today is a testimony to its lasting greatness; it is thus fitting that this epilogue to a man and his age should be brought to a close with music:

Ex. 166

REFERENCES

The references which follow refer, generally speaking, to books and articles which have been specifically mentioned in the text: works by standard authors and those given a full reference in the text are not normally entered here. As already mentioned, references to musical editions are generally for identification purposes. In addition to those references given in the text, the main series which should be consulted for various composers are:

Chapters 5 & 6

MB: also edition of *FWVB* (ed. Fuller Maitland & Barclay Squire, 1899, R 1963). The foregoing, and other editions of the virginalist sources, are often inaccurate as to the ornaments, however. The edition of *Nevell* by Hilda Andrews (1926, R 1969) is substantially accurate.

Chapters 9–12

MB (*Eton Choirbook* in rather short note-values and without transposition); *EECM* (some volumes similarly); *CMM* (untransposed, bar-less, early vols); *TCM* (long note-values and untransposed): the new *Byrd Edition* returns to the long note-values and is inconsistent in transposition; the older Fellowes edition of the *Complete Works of William Byrd* on the other hand, is unreliable in different ways. The treatment of underlay varies widely throughout these various editions.

Abbott, D. & Segerman, E. (1974)
  'Strings in the 16th and 17th Centuries', *Galpin Society Journal*, XXVII, pp. 48–73.
Agricola, Martin (1532)
  Musica figuralis deudsch, Wittenburg (Facs. 1969) ⁵1545.
Agricola, J. F. (1757)
  Anleitung zur Singkunst, Berlin. (Facs. 1966)
Allen, W. S. (1965).
  Vox Latina, Cambridge.
Andrews, Hilda (1926, ed.)
  Byrd, *My Ladye Nevells Booke of Virginal Music*, R 1969, New York.
Andrews, H. K. (1962)
  'Transposition of Byrd's vocal polyphony', *Music and Letters*, XLIII, pp. 25–37.

Anglo, Sydney (1969)
  Spectacle, pageantry, and early Tudor policy, Oxford.
Aplin, John (1979)
  'The Survival of Plainsong in Anglican Music . . .', *Journal of the American Musicological Society*, XXXII, pp. 247–75.
Ardran, G. & Emrys-Roberts, E. (1965)
  'Tomography of the larynx', *Clinical Radiology*, XVI, pp. 369–76.
Ardran, G. & Wulstan, D. (1967)
  'The Alto or Countertenor Voice', *Music and Letters*, XLVIII, pp. 17–22.
Ascham, Roger (1570)
  The Scholemaster, London.
Baines, Anthony (1957, ³1967)
  Woodwind Instruments and their History, London.
Ballard, C. F. & Bond, E. K. (1960)
  'Clinical observations on the correlation between variations of jaw form and variations of oro-facial behaviour, including those for articulation', *Speech Pathology and Therapy*, III, pp. 55–63.
Barnard, John (1641)
  First Book of Selected Church Musick, London. (Facs. 1972).
Barnfield, Richard *et al* (1599)
  The Passionate Pilgrim, London, 1599. (Facs. 1883).
Bathe, William (c. 1587)
  A Briefe Introduction to the skill of song, London. (Facs. 1982).
Beck, Sydney (1959, ed.)
  Morley, *The First Book of Consort Lessons*, New York.
Beer, R. (1952)
  'Ornaments in old Keyboard Music', *Music Review*, XIII, pp. 3–13.
Bernstein, F. & Schläper, P. (1922)
  'Über die Tonlage der menschlichen Singstimme', *Sitzungsberichte der preussischen Akademie der Wissenschaften, (Physik. –Math. ICI)*.
Beze, Th. de & Marot, Clement (1551, ²1554)
  Octante trois pseaumes . . ., Geneva.
Blakemore, Colin (1977)
  Mechanics of the Mind, Cambridge.
Blezzard, Judith (1971)
  'The Lumley Books', *Musical Times*, CXII, pp. 128–30.
Blezzard, Judith (1981)
  'A New Source of Tudor Secular Music', *Musical Times*, CXXII, pp. 532–5.
Boswell, J. (1572)
  Works of Armorie, London.
Bray, Roger (1969)
  'British Museum Add. MSS. 17802–5 (The Gyffard Part-Books): An Index and Commentary', *RMA Research Chronicle*, VII, pp. 31–50.
Bray, Roger (1971)
  'The Interpretation of Musica Ficta in English Music c.1490-c.1580', *Proceedings of the Royal Musical Association*, XCVII, pp. 57–80.

Bray, Roger (1978)
'16th-century musica ficta: the importance of the scribe', *Journal of the Plainsong & Mediaeval Music Society*, 1.
Bray, Roger (1981, ed.)
John Sheppard, *Collected Works 2: Hymns*, Oxford.
Brett, Philip (1961, ed.)
Gibbons, *Do not repine, fair Sun*, London.
Brett, Philip (1962)
'The English Consort Song, 1570–1625', *Proceedings of the Royal Musical Association*, LXXXVIII, pp. 73–88.
Brett, Philip (1964)
'Edward Paston . . . a Norfolk Gentleman and his Musical Collection', Translations of the Cambridge Bibliographical Society, IV, Cambridge.
Brett, Philip (1981)
'English Music for the Scottish Progress of 1617', *Source Materials and the Interpretation of Music* (ed. Bent), London, pp.209–226.
Britton, J. (1847, ed.)
John Aubrey, *The natural history of Wiltshire*, London.
Brook, G. L. (1963)
English Dialects, London.
Brosnahan, L. F. (1961)
The Sounds of Language, London.
Brown, David (1969)
Thomas Weelkes, London.
Brown, David (1973, ed.)
Thomas Weelkes, 'Evening Service No. 5 'In medio chori' . . ., Sevenoaks.
Brown, David (1974)
Wilbye, London.
Browne, Robert (1582)
A Treatise of Reformation without Tarying for Anie, Middelburg (R 1903).
Burmeister, Joachim (1601)
Musica autoschedastikē, Rostoch.
Butler, Charles (1636)
The Principles of Musik, London. (Facs. 1970).
Calendar of State Papers . . . Venetian
Ed. Rawdon Brown *et al* (1864) London.
Cambridge Songs
Ed. Karl Breul (1915), Cambridge. (R 1975).
Cavendish, G.
The Life and Death of Cardinal Wolsey, ed. Sylvester, Early English Text Society, 1959, London.
Cerone, D. P. (1613)
El Melopeo y Maestro, Naples. (Facs. 1969).
Clark, J. Bunker (1974)
Transposition in Seventeenth-century English Organ Accompaniments and the Transposing Organ, Detroit.
Clark, Kenneth (1969)
Civilization, London.

Clifford, J. (1663, ²1664)
The Divine Services and Anthems, London.

Clulow, Peter (1966)
'Publication Dates for Byrd's Latin Masses', *Music and Letters*, XLVII, pp. 1–9.

Clutton, Cecil (1956)
'The Virginalists' Ornaments', (letter) *Galpin Society Journal*, IX, pp. 99–100.

Clutton, Cecil & Niland, Austin (1963)
The British Organ, London.

CMM = *Corpus Mensurabilis Musicae* (series, 1947–)
American Institute of Musicology.

Cole, Elisabeth (1953)
'Seven problems of the Fitzwilliam Virginal Book', *Proceedings of the Royal Musical Association*, LXXIX, pp. 51–64).

Cornish, William (1568)
A Treatise between Truth and Informacion, apud Skelton (1568).

Cox, J. E. (1846)
Miscellaneous writings and Letters of Thomas Cranmer, (Parker Society), Cambridge.

Cressy, David (1980)
Literacy and the social order. Reading and writing in Tudor and Stuart England, Cambridge.

Daman, William (1579)
The Psalmes of David in English Meter, London.

Dannreuther, Edward (1893–5)
Musical Ornamentation, 2 vols., London.

Darlington, Cyril E. (1947)
'The genetic component of language', *Heredity*, I, pp. 269–286.

Dart, Thurston (1964) 'A Note on the Music' [in the Evesham Abbey Bible]
English Historical Review, LXXIX, pp. 777–8

Dart, Thurston (1956)
'The Printed Fantasies of Orlando Gibbons', *Music and Letters*, XXXVII, pp. 342–9.

Dart, Thurston (1957, ed.)
Clement Matchett's Virginal Book, London.

Dart, Thurston (1958)
'The Repertory of the Royal Wind Music', *Galpin Society Journal*, XI, pp. 70–77.

Dart, Thurston (1961, ed.)
Parthenia Inviolata, New York.

Dart, Thurston (1961) 'Ornament Signs in Jacobean Music for Lute and Viol' *Galpin Society Journal* XIV

Day, John (1562)
The Whole Booke of Psalmes . . ., London.

Dekker, Thomas (1609)
The Gul's horne-book, London.

Diruta, Girolamo (1593)

Il transilvano. . . , Venice.
Doe, Paul (1968) ²1976 *Tallis*, London.
Doe, Paul (1960)
'Latin Polyphony under Henry VIII', *Proceeding of the Royal Musical Association*, XCV, pp. 81–96.
Doni, G. B. (1635)
Compendio del trattato de' generi e de' modi della musica, Rome.
Donington, Robert (1982)
Baroque Music: Style and Performance, London.
Dunn, H. K. (1950)
'The calculation of vowel resonances, and an electrical vocal tract', *Journal of the Acoustical Society of America*, XXII, pp. 740–753.
Duckles, Vincent (1957)
'Florid Embellishment in English Song of the Late 16th and Early 17th Centuries', *Annales Musicologiques*, V, pp. 329–45.
Dugdale, W. (1818, with additions by H. Ellis)
The History of St Paul's, London.
Earle, John (1628, 1629, 1633)
Micro-Cosmographie, London (R 1868).
Edwards, Warwick (1971)
'The Performance of Ensemble Music in Elizabethan England', *Proceedings of the Royal Musical Association*, XCVII, pp. 113–23.
E.E.C.M. = *Early English Church Music* (1962–)
Various editors, London.
Ellis, A. J. (1880)
'The History of Musical Pitch', *Journal of the Royal Society Arts*, R 1880–1 with addendum.
ELS = *The English Lute-Song* (series 1920–)
begun as *The English School of Lutenist Song Writers*.
EMS = *The English Madrigal School* (series 1913–)
revised and continued as *The English Madrigalists*.
Evans, D. R. A. (1984)
'A Short History of the Music and Musicians of St David's Cathedral, 1230–1883', *Welsh Music*, VII, 8, pp. 50–66.
Fantini, Girolamo (1638)
Modo per imparare a sonara di tromba, Rome (Facs. 1934).
Farmer, J. (1591)
Divers and Sundry Waies of Two Parts in one, to the number of Fortie, uppon One Playn Song, London.
Fellowes, E. H. (1921)
The English Madrigal Composers (²1948, R 1975), London.
Fellowes, E. H. (1936, ²1948)
William Byrd, London.
Ferguson, Howard (1962)
'Repeats and final bars in the Fitzwilliam Virginal Book', *Music and Letters*, XLIII, pp. 345–50.
Finck, Hermann (1556)
Practica musica . . ., Wittemberg (²1556, Facs. 1969)

Fletcher, H. (1929)
  Speech and Hearing, London.
Ford, Robert (1982)
  'Bevins, Father and Son', *Music Review*, XLIII, pp. 104–8
Fox, John (1570, 1580 etc.)
  Actes & Monuments, London.
Frere, W. H. (1898, ed.)
  The Use of Sarum, Cambridge.
Frescobaldi, Girolamo (1608)
  Il primo libro . . ., Antwerp.
Frescobaldi, Girolamo (1615)
  Toccate & partite, Rome.
Frost, Maurice (1953)
  English and Scottish Psalm & Hymn Tunes, London *c.1543–1677,*
  Oxford.
Galliard, J. E. (1742, ²1743)
  Observations on the Florid Song . . ., London (²Facs. 1926).
Galpin, F. W. (1910)
  Old English Instruments of Music, London (4th ed. rev. Dart, 1965).
Ganassi, S. di (1543)
  Lettione Seconda, Venice. (Facs. 1924).
Garcia, Manuel (1840)
  École de Garcia: Traité complet de l'art du chant, Paris.
Geminiani, Francesco (1751)
  The Art of Playing on the Violin, London, (Facs. 1952).
Gibbons, (1612)
  see *EMS*, V.
Glarean, Heinrich [Henricus Glareanus] (1547)
  Dodecachordon, Basle, (Facs. 1969).
Glyn, Margaret (1925, ed.)
  O. Gibbons: Complete Keyboard Works, London.
Gombrich, E. H. (1960)
  Art and Illusion, London.
Grabert, W. (1913)
  'Anthropologische Untersuchungen . . .', *Zeitschrift für Morphologie
  und Anthropologie* XVI, pp. 65–94.
Grove V : *Grove's Dictionary of Music and Musicians*
  Fifth edition, edited by Eric Blom (1954), London.
Gutzmann, H., jnr. (1928)
  Physiologie der Stimme und Sprache, Bern.
Hardwick, M. & M. (1968)
  Alfred Deller. A Singularity of Voice, London.
Harley, John (1970)
  'Ornaments in English keyboard Music of the seventeenth and early
  eighteenth Centuries', *Music Review*, XXXI, pp. 177–200.
Harrison, F.L1. (1958, ²1963, R 1980)
  Music in Medieval Britain, London.

Harwood, Ian (1981)
  'A case of double standards?', *Early Music*, IX, pp. 470–81.
Hendrie, Gerald (1963)
  'The Keyboard Music of Orlando Gibbons (1583–1625)', *Proceedings of the Royal Musical Association*, LXXIX, pp. 1–15.
Hickman, Roger (1983)
  'The censored publications of *The Art of Playing the Violin . . .*', *Early Music*, XI, pp. 73–76.
Historical Manuscripts Commission
  Fourth Report, London, 1875.
Hobbs, Michael (1982, ed.)
  Orlando Gibbons, *Six Fantasias for viols in six parts*, London.
Hofman, May [Mrs Ballerio] (1973)
  The Survival of Latin Music by English Composers 1485–1610, DPhil thesis, Oxford University.
Holborne, Anthony (1597)
  The Cittharne Schoole, London, R 1973.
Holman, Peter (1981, ed.)
  The Royal Wind Music, Vol. II, London.
Hopkins & Rimbault)1855, ³1877)
  The Organ:its History and Construction . . . London, R 1972.
Hunter, Desmond (1983)
  Virginalist Embellishment MA Thesis, University College, Cork.
Jackman, J. (1963)
  'Liturgical Aspects of Byrd's *Gradualia*', *Musical Quarterly*, XLIX, pp. 17–37.
James, Peter (1971, ed.)
  apud Wulstan (1971b). Cf. pp. 116–134, 156 and 159.
James, Peter (1981, ed.)
  Byrd, 'Exalt thyself O God', Oxford.
Jones, Daniel (³1950)
  The Pronunciation of English, Cambridge.
Karpeles, Maud (1974, ed.)
  Cecil Sharp's Collection of English Folk Songs, London.
Kennedy, Peter *et al* (1975)
  Folksongs of Britain and Ireland, London.
Kerman, Joseph (1962)
  The Elizabethan Madrigal, New York.
Kerman, Joseph (1981)
  The Masses and Motets of William Byrd, London.
Lack, David (1943, ⁴1965)
  The Life of the Robin, London.
Legg, L. G. W. (1936, ed.)
  Hammond, (1635), *A Relation of a Short Survey of the Western Counties*, Camden Society, Misc. XVI.
Leland, J. (1774)
  De rebus Britannicis Collectanea (ed. T. Hearne; 6 vols.), London.
Letters and Papers, Foreign and Domestic, of Henry VIII (1864–1920) Vols. I–VII.

Le Huray, Peter (1962, ed.)
Weelkes, 'Evening Service "for trebles"', London.
Le Huray, Peter (1965, ed.)
The Treasury of English Church Music, Vol. II, London.
Le Huray, Peter (1967)
Music and the Reformation in England 1549–1660, London; ²1978, Cambridge.
Le Huray, Peter (1981)
'English Keyboard Fingering', *Source Materials and the Interpretation of Music*, ed. Bent, London, pp. 227–257.
Loth, E. (1931)
Anthropologie des parties molles, Paris.
Lowe, Edward (1661)
A Short Direction for the Performance of Cathedrall Service, Oxford.
Luchsinger, R. (1944)
Erbbiologische Untersuchungen . . . des Kehlkopfes, Archiv Julius Klaus Stiftung *Soz. u. Rass.*, XIX, pp. 393–441.
Lumsden, David (1954, ed.)
An Anthology of Lute Music (see also 1968 ed.) London.
Mace, Thomas (1676)
Musick's Monument, London. (Facs. 1958).
Macray, W. D. (1894)
A Register of the Members of St Mary Magdalen College, Oxford, I, London.
Maffei, G. C. (1562)
Delle lettere del Signor Gio. Camillo Maffei . . ., Naples.
Mancini, G. (1774)
Pensieri . . . sopra il Canto Figurato, Vienna.
Marafioti, P. M. (1922)
Caruso's method of voice production, New York, R 1981.
Marler, P. (1956)
'The voice of the chaffinch and its function as a language', *The Ibis*, XCVIII, pp. 231–61.
Mendel, Arthur (1948)
'Pitch in the 16th and Early 17th Centuries', *Musical Quarterly*, XXXIV, *passim*.
Mendel, Arthur (1949)
'Devices for Transposition in the Organ before 1600', *Acta Musicologica*, XXI, pp. 22–40.
Mendel, Arthur (1978)
'Pitch in Western Music since 1500: a Re-examination', *Acta Musicologica*, L, pp. 1–93.
Merbecke, John (1550)
The booke of Common praier noted, London.
Mersenne, Martin (1636)
Harmonie Universelle, Paris. (Facs. 1965).
Milsom, John (1981)
'Songs, Carols and *Contrafacta* in the Early History of the Tudor Anthem', *Proceedings of the Royal Musical Association*, 107, CVII, pp. 34–45.

Milsom, John (1982)
'A New Tallis Contrafactum', *Musical Times* CXIII pp. 429–31
Milton, John (1637)
A Maske presented at Ludlow Castle . . ., London.
Monson, Craig (1982)
Voices and Viols in England, 1600–1650. The Sources and their Music, Ann Arbor.
Morehen, John (1972, ed.)
John Barnard, *First Book of Selected Church Music* (Facs. [Farnborough]).
Morley, Thomas (1597)
A Plaine and Easie Introduction to Practicall Musicke, London. (Facs. 1971, Farnborough).
Morris, Desmond (1977)
Manwatching, London.
Moryson, Fynes (1617)
An Itinerary, London. (Facs. 1971).
Mulcaster, Richard (1581)
Positions . . ., London.
Mundinger, F. (1951)
'Zum Vererbungsproblem der menschlichen Singstimme', *Folia Phonatrica*, 3.
Murphy, G. (1939)
'Callen O Custure Me', *Éigse*, I, pp. 125–129.
MB = Musica Britannica (series 1951–)
Myers, A. R. (1959, ed.)
The Household of Edward IV, Manchester.
Myriell, Thomas (1616, unpublished: BL Add. 29372–7)
Tristitiae Remedium.
Nabokov, Vladimir (1964, ²1965)
Notes on Prosody, London.
Nadoleczny, M. (1923)
Untersuchungen über den Kunstgesang, Berlin.
Neighbour, Oliver (1978)
The Consort and Keyboard Music of William Byrd, London.
New Grove, The (ed. Stanley Sadie), 1980.
Nordstrom, L. E. (1976)
'The English Lute Duet and Consort lesson', *Lute Society Journal*, XVIII, pp. 5–22.
'Ornithoparcus' (1517)
Micrologus [= Musice active micrologous], Leipzig, trans. Dowland (1609), London.
Ornsby, G. (ed. 1869)
The Correspondence of John Cosin, D. D. Surtees Society, LII.
Ortiz, D. (1553)
Trattado de glosas, Rome.
Osborn, J. M. (1961, ed.)
The Autobiography of Thomas Whythorne, Oxford.
Paget, Sir Richard (1930)

Human Speech, London.

Peacham, Henry (1612)
Minerva Britanna, London. (Facs. 1971).

Peacham, Henry (1622)
The compleat gentleman, London. (Facs. 1968)

Peckham, W. D. (1959)
The Acts of the Dean and Chapter of the Cathedral Church of Chichester, 1545–1642, Sussex Record Society, LVIII.

Pike, Lionel (1969) '"Gaude Maria virgo": Morley or Philips?' *Music and Letters*, pp. 127–35.

Playford, John (1655, ⁷1674)
Introduction to the Skill of Musick. (Facs. 1966)

Plummer, Charles (1887, ed.)
Elizabethan Oxford . . ., Oxford.

Potter, R. K. & Peterson, G. E. (1948)
'The representation of vowels and their movements', *Journal of the Acoustical Society of America*, XX, pp. 528–535.

Praetorius, Michael 1618, (3 vols: references to II unless stated).
Syntagma Musicum, Wolfenbüttel. (Facs. 1958.)

Price, D. C. (1980)
Patrons and Musicians of the English Renaissance, Cambridge.

Procter, F & Frere, w. h.)²1902)
A New History of the Book of Common Prayer, London.

Prynne, Michael (1954) see
Grove's Dictionary of Music and Musicians, 5th edition, Vol. V. s.v. 'lute'.

Puttenham, George (1589)
The arte of English poesie, London. (Facs. 1968)

Quantz, J. J. (1752)
Versuch einer Anweisung die Flöte traversiere zu spielen, Berlin. (³Facs. 1953)

Rapson, Penelope (1981)
A technique for identifying textual errors and its application to the sources of Thomas Tallis, Oxford DPhil.

Ravenscroft, Thomas (1614)
A Briefe Discourse . . ., London. (Facs. 1971).

Reeve, Robert (1971, ed.)
apud Wulstan (1971b). Cf. pp. 41–48, 155 and 157.

Rimbault, E. F. (1872)
The old Cheque Book . . . of the Chapel Royal, Camden Society, N. S. III.

Robbins, R. H. (1959)
Historical Poems of the XIVth and XVth Centuries, New York.

Robinson, Thomas (1603)
The Schoole of Musicke, London.

Rose, Benard (1971, ed.)
apud Wulstan (1971 b). cf. pp. 106–115.

Rosseter, (1601)
see *ELS* series 1, VIII, IX

Rye, W. B. (1865)
  England as seen by Foreigners, London.
Sainliens, Claude de [Claudius Hollybande] (1573)
  The French Schoolemaister, London.
Samber, J. B. (1707)
  Continuatio ad Manductionem Organicam, Salzburg.
Sandon, Nick (1977)
  'The Henrician Partbooks at Peterhouse, Cambridge' *Proceedings of the Royal Musical Association*, CIII, pp. 106–40.
Sandon, Nick (1981)
  'Another Mass by Hugh Aston?', *Early Music*, IX, pp. 184–191.
Santa María, Tomás de (1565)
  Libro llamado arte de tañer fantasia. Valladdid. (Facs. 1972.)
Schlick, A. (1511)
  Spiegel der Orgelmacher und Organisten, Mainz.
Simpson, Christopher (1659, ²1667)
  The Division Viol . . . (Facs. of 1667, ed. London 1955).
Skelton, John (1568) *et al*
  Pithy, Pleasant and Profitable Works, London, 1568.
Smart, Peter (1642)
  A Catalogue of Superstitious Innovations, London.
Smart, Peter (1628)
  The Vanitie and Downefall of Superstitious . . . Ceremonies, Edinburgh.
Smith, Alan (1968)
  'Elizabethan Church Music at Ludlow', *Music and Letters*, XLIX, pp. 108–121.
Statutes of the Colleges of Oxford, printed by desire of H.M. Commissioners (1853), London.
Steele, John (1958)
  English Organs and Organ Music, Diss., Cambridge University.
Sternfeld, Frederick (1963, ²1967)
  Music in Shakespearean Tragedy, London.
Sternfeld, Frederick (1971)
  'Shakespeare and Music', apud *A New Companion to Shakespeare Studies*, ed. Muir and Schoenbaum, Cambridge.
Stevens, Denis (1950)
  'A Part-Book in the Public Record Office', *Music Survey*, II.
Stevens, Denis (1952)
  The Mulliner Book: a Commentary, London.
Steven, Denis (1955)
  'Tudor Part-Songs', *Musical Times*, XCVI, pp. 360–2.
Stevens, Denis (1982)
  A songe of fortie partes . . .' *Early Music*, X, pp. 171–81.
Stevens, Denis (1957, ²1967)
  Thomas Tomkins, London.
Stevens, John (1961)
  Music & Poetry in the Early Tudor Court, London, ²1979, Cambridge.
Storer, T. (1599)

The Life and Death of Thomas Wolsey, London.
Stow, J. (1580)
Chronicles of England, London.
Stow, J. (1618)
Survay of London. London.
Stow, J. (1720 ed. Strype)
Survey of London, London.
Sundberg, J. (1977)
'The acoustics of the Singing voice', *Scientific American.*, CCXXXVIII/3, pp. 82–9.
Tanner, James M. (²1962)
Growth at Adolescence, Oxford.
Thomas, W. R. & Rhodes, j. j. k.)1971)
'Schlick, Praetorius and the History of Organ Pitch', *Organ Yearbook*, II, pp. 58–76.
Thompson, A. H. (1929)
The Statutes of the Cathedral Church of Durham . . ., Surtees Society, CXLIII.
Thompson, John (1961)
The Founding of English Metre, London.
Tinctoris, J. (1476)
Liber de natura et proprietate tonorum, Naples.
Tomkins, Thomas (1688)
Musica Deo Sacra.
Tosi, P. F. (1723)
Opinioni de' cantori antichi e moderni . . ., Bologna. (Facs. 1966)
TCM = *Tudor Church Music* (series, 1923–9, appendix, 1948)
Vicentino, Nicola (1555, ²1557)
L'antica musica ridotta alla moderna prattica, Rome. (¹Facs. 1959)
Villetard, H. (1907)
Office de Pierre de Corbeil, Paris.
Von Zabern, Conrad (1474)
De Modo bene cantandi choralem cantum, Mainz.
Wagner, Peter (1895–21)
Einführung in die gregorianische Melodien, Leipzig.
Walther, J. G. (1732)
Musicalisches Lexicon, Leipzig. (Facs. 1953).
Ward, John (1957, ²1964, ³1983)
The Dublin Virginal Manuscript.
Ward, John (1960)
'The Lute Misic of Royal Appendix 58' *Journal of the American Musicology Society*, XIII, pp. 177–225.
Warlock, Peter [Philip Heseltine] (1927, ed.)
John Dowland, *Lachrimae . . .*
Wathey, Andrew (1983)
'Newly Discovered Fifteenth-Century English Polyphony at Oxford', *Music and Letters*,, LXIV, pp. 58–66.
Webbe, William (1586)

A Discourse of English Poetrie, London.
Weelkes (1598)
 see *EMS*, X.
Weiss, D. A. (1950)
 'The pubertal change of the human voice', *Folia phoniatrica*, II, pp.
 126–59.
Whythorne, Thomas (1571)
 Songes for Three, Fower and Five Voyces, London.
Whythorne, Thomas (1590)
 Duos, or Songs for Two Voices, London.
Wilbye, (1609)
 see *EMS*, VII.
Wilkins, D. (1737)
 Concilia Magnae Britanniae, London.
Wilson, John (1959, ed.)
 Roger North on Music, London.
Wood, Anthony à (modern ed. Bliss, 1813–20) London.
 Athenae Oxonienses.
Woodfield, Ian (1984)
 The Early History of the Viol, Cambridge.
Woodfill, Walter, (1953)
 Musicians in English Society, Princeton.
Wulstan, David (1967)
 'The Problem of Pitch in sixteenth-century English vocal Polyphony',
 Proceedings of the Royal Musical Association, XCIII, pp. 79–112.
Wulstan, David (1969)
 Letter in *Music and Letters*, L, p. 426.
Wulstan, David, (1971a)
 'The Origin of the Modes', *Studies in Eastern Chant*, II, pp. 5–20.
Wulstan, David (1971b, ed.)
 An Anthology of English Church Music, London.
Wulstan, David (1978, ed.)
 John Sheppard: *Collected Works*, 2: *Responds and Varia*, Oxford.
Wulstan, David (1979a, ed.)
 'Magnificat & Nunc Dimittis (The Ninth Service)', Oxford.
Wulstan, David (1979b)
 'Vocal colour in English sixteenth-century polyphony' *Journal of the
 Plainsong and Mediaeval Music Society*, II, pp. 19–60.
Wulstan, David (1983)
 Septem discrimina vocum, Cork.
Zacconi, L. (1592)
 Prattica di Musica, Venice. (Facs. 1982).
Zarlino, G. (1571)
 Dimostrationi Harmoniche, Venice. (Facs. 1966)
Zarlino, G. (1588)
 Sopplimenti Musicali, Venice (Facs. 1966).

Index

Italic page numbers refer to music examples

Index